Landscaping the Human Garden

Landscaping the Human Garden

Twentieth-Century Population Management in a Comparative Framework

---

Edited by AMIR WEINER

Stanford University Press / Stanford, California

2003

Stanford University Press
Stanford, California

Published with the assistance of the Center for Russian and East European Studies at Stanford University.

Printed in the United States of America
on acid-free, archival-quality paper.

Library of Congress Cataloging-in-Publication Data

Landscaping the human garden : twentieth-century population management in a comparative framework / edited by Amir Weiner.

p. cm.

"This volume grew out of a workshop held at the Stanford Humanities Center, Stanford University, on 28–29 March 1997."

Includes bibliographical references and index.

ISBN 0-8047-4622-2 (cloth : alk. paper)—
ISBN 0-8047-4630-3 (pbk. : alk. paper)

1. Political atrocities—Congresses. 2. Political persecution—Congresses. 3. State-sponsored terrorism—Congresses. 4. Genocide—Congresses. I. Weiner, Amir
HV6322 .L363 2003
303.6—dc21 2002010784

Original Printing 2003
Last figure below indicates year of this printing:
12 11 10 09 08 07 06 05 04 03

Designed by Eleanor Mennick
Typeset by Heather Boone in 10.5/12.5 Bembo

In memory of Eyal Sela

Contents

Contributors

OMER BARTOV is the John P. Birkelund Distinguished Professor of European History at Brown University. His books include *The Eastern Front 1941–1945: German Troops and the Barbarisation of Warfare* (1985, 2d ed., 2001); *Hitler's Army: Soldiers, Nazis, and War in the Third Reich* (1991); *Murder in Our Midst: The Holocaust, Industrial Killing, and Representation* (1996); and *Mirrors of Destruction: War, Genocide, and Modern Identity* (2000). He has also edited the volumes *The Holocaust: Origins, Implementation, Aftermath* (2000); *In God's Name: Genocide and Religion in the Twentieth Century* (2001, with Phyllis Mack); and *Crimes of War: Guilt and Denial in the Twentieth Century* (2002, with Atina Grossmann and Mary Nolan). His new monograph, *Germany's War and the Holocaust: Disputed Histories*, will be published in 2003.

GORDON H. CHANG is a professor of history at Stanford University and specializes in the history of United States–East Asia relations and in Asian American history. He is the author of *Friends and Enemies: The United States, China, and the Soviet Union, 1948–1972* (1990), and he edited *Morning Glory, Evening Shadow: Yamato Ichihashi and His Wartime Writing, 1942–1945* (1997) and *Asian Americans and Politics: Perspectives, Experiences, Prospects* (2001).

ISTVÁN DEÁK is Seth Low Professor Emeritus at Columbia University. His publications include *Weimar Germany's Left-Wing Intellectuals: A Political History of the "Weltbühne" and Its Circle* (1968); *The Lawful Revolution: Louis Kossuth and the Hungarians, 1848–1849* (1979); *Beyond Nationalism: A Social and Political History of the Habsburg Officer Corps, 1848–1918* (1990); and *Essays on Hitler's Europe* (2001). His current research project is on collaboration, resistance, and retribution in World War II Europe.

ELISABETH DOMANSKY has taught at the Department of History, Indiana University, from 1994 to 1999. Her publications include coediting and contributing to *Der lange Schatten des Krieges: deutsche Lebens-Geschichten nach 1945* (2000); and *Eine Offene Geschichte: Über kommunikativen Tradierung der nationalsozialistischen Vergangenheit* (1999).

PETER HOLQUIST is an associate professor in the History Department of Cornell University. He is author of *Making War, Forging Revolution: Russia's Continuum of Crisis, 1914–1921* (2002); "To Count, to Extract, to Exterminate: Population Statistics and Population Politics in Late Imperial and Soviet Russia," in Ronald Suny and Terry Martin, eds., *A State of Nations: Empire and Nation-Making in the Age of Lenin and Stalin* (2001); and "La Question de la violence," in Claudio Sergio Ingerflom, ed., *Le siècle des communismes* (2000). He is now working on a coauthored book with David Hoffmann, *Sculpting the Masses: The Modern Social State in Russia, 1914–1941* and a new project on international law in late imperial Russia.

CLAUDIA KOONZ teaches courses related to genocide and Nazi Germany at Duke University. She is the author of *Mothers in the Fatherland: Women, the Family and Nazi Politics* (1987) and the forthcoming book *The Nazi Conscience.*

NORMAN M. NAIMARK is Robert and Florence McDonnell Professor of East European Studies at Stanford University. He is director of Stanford's programs in International Relations and International Policy Studies. Naimark is the author of, among other studies, *The Russians in Germany: A History of the Soviet Zone of Occupation, 1945–1949* (1995) and *Fires of Hatred: Ethnic Cleansing in Twentieth-Century Europe* (2001). He is presently working on a study of Soviet policies toward postwar Europe.

DANIEL ORLOVSKY is a Professor of History and George A. Bouhe Research Fellow in Russian Studies, Clements Department of History, Southern Methodist University. He is the author of *The Limits of Reform: The Ministry of Internal Affairs in Imperial Russia, 1802–1881* (1981), and various studies on imperial Russian bureaucracy, the February Revolution and Provisional Government, and the social history of white-collar workers in the revolutionary and Soviet periods. He is currently working on the "hidden class," or employees and professionals in the Soviet era.

MARY LOUISE ROBERTS is a professor of European Women's History at the University of Wisconsin, Madison. Her publications include *Civilization Without Sexes: Reconstructing Gender in Postwar France* (1994); and *Disruptive Acts: The New Woman in Fin de Siècle France* (forthcoming).

AMIR WEINER is an associate professor of history at Stanford University. He is the author of *Making Sense of War: The Second World War and the Fate of the Bolshevik Revolution* (2001) and several articles on the Soviet war experience. He is currently working on a book about the history of the Soviet western frontier, 1939 to the present.

YAEL ZERUBAVEL is the founding director of the Bildner Center for the Study of Jewish Life and the chair of the Department of Jewish Studies at Rutgers University. She is the author of *Recovered Roots: Collective Memory and the Making of Israeli National Tradition* (1995), which won the 1996 Salo Baron Prize of the American Academy for Jewish Research, and numerous articles on the relations between history and memory, Hebrew literature and culture, war and trauma, and Jewish immigrant experience. She is currently working on two books: *Desert Images: Visions of the Counter-Place in Israeli Culture* and *The Elusive Native: Jewish Identity and the Burden of Memory*.

Acknowledgments

THIS VOLUME grew out of a workshop held at the Stanford Humanities Center, Stanford University, on March 28–29, 1997, and from an ongoing dialogue among the participants. I would like to express heartfelt thanks to the following Stanford University groups for making this project possible: the Institute for International Studies; the Office of the Dean, School of Humanities and Sciences; the German Studies Program; the Center for Russian and East European Studies; the Taube Center for Jewish Studies; and the Department of History.

I would also like to express special thanks to Eric Weitz, who read the manuscript for the Press and offered invaluable comments for each of the papers and for the volume as a whole; to Reginald Zelnik, for his excellent comments on the last draft of the Introduction; and to Steven Zipperstein, Yuri Slezkine, Peter Kenez, Shulamit Magnus, Reginald Zelnik, David Hoffman, Joel Beinin, Andrew Jenks, Steven Barnes, and Stuart Finkel, all of whom enriched the deliberations and greatly contributed to the project.

Portions of Chapter 1 also appear in "State Violence as Technique: The Logic of Violence in Soviet Totalitarianism" by Peter Holquist in *Cultivating the Masses* by David Hoffman and Peter Holquist, © 2003 by Cornell University and reprinted by permission of the publisher, Cornell University Press. Chapter 6 was originally published in *The American Historical Review* 103/3 (June 1998): 771–816. A greatly expanded version is available in Omer Bartov, *Mirrors of Destruction: War, Genocide, and Modern Identity* (New York: Oxford University Press, 2000), chap. 3. Some material in Chapter 10 has been adapted and reprinted by permission of the publisher from "Soviet Deportation of the Chechens-Ingush and the Crimean Tatars," in *Fires of Hatred: Ethnic Cleansing in Twentieth-Century Europe*, by Norman M. Naimark, Cambridge, Mass.: Harvard University Press, © 2001, by the President and Fellows of Harvard College.

This volume is dedicated to the memory of my boyhood friend Eyal Sela, killed in action November 6, 2001.

Landscaping the Human Garden

AMIR WEINER

Introduction: Landscaping the Human Garden

> A map of the world that does not include Utopia is not worth even glancing at, for it leaves out the one country at which Humanity is always landing. And when Humanity lands there, it looks out, and, seeing a better country, sets sail.
>
> —Oscar Wilde, *The Soul of Man Under Socialism*

> For when the bough that has been cut off is grafted in, a new wound is made in the tree, to admit of its reception, that life may be given to the branch that was perishing for lack of the life that is furnished by the root. But when the newly received branch has become identified with the stock in which it is received, the result is both vigor and fruit; but if they do not become identified with, the engrafted bough withers, but the life of the tree continues unimpaired. For there is further a mode of grafting such a kind, that without cutting away any branch that is within, the branch that is foreign to the tree is inserted, not indeed without a wound, but with the slightest possible wound inflicted on the tree.
>
> —Saint Augustine, *Treatise on the Correction of the Donatists*

IF RECORDED history has been any indication, humans seem to have been more dissatisfied than content with their inner and social state. A strong sense of imperfection and the urge to correct it have marked the social and political condition in its various incarnations. Political evolutions and revolutions have gone hand in hand with religious mediations and excommunications and, all too often, with the destruction of the spiritually deprived or biologically unfit. In pagan Sparta, puny and deformed babies were thrown off a precipice on Mountain Taíyetos—appropriately named "the place of rejection"—a fate considered better for both the child and the state.[1]

The aspiration for improvement and the perfection of human nature and society can thus be traced back well before the dawn of the modern era. But only when the horizons opened by the advent of this era and the principles underlining the scientific revolution of the sixteenth to seventeenth centuries began to inform the political, economic, and cultural domains, together with the inevitable disappointments, did the unique confluence of ideologies, social scientific paradigms, and institutions with the desire to transform existing order and nature take place, all under the growing power of the state. The refusal of the modern state to accept restrictions on its aspirations and practices intensified sharply at the outset of the twentieth century, although it varied according to capacity and ideological convictions. Yet this very refusal was rooted in the modern secular state's assumption of responsibility for the spiritual, social, and physical well-being of its subjects. With the diminishing power of divine doctrines and their institutional incarnations, such as the Catholic Church in the premodern era, which had often restrained the state's violent schemes, the modern state was restrained by and accountable to no one in its drive to remold society and individuals.[2]

The key to this sea change lay in the discovery of the masses as both a source for legitimacy of the sociopolitical order and as a raw material by which to mold a purer, healthier, and more aesthetic society. The transition from a fixed and fatalistic sociopolitical order of the so-called "Great Chain of Being" to the era of mass population politics gave birth to significantly more ambitious state policies and institutions. No longer were self-improvement and perfection the pursuit of the selected few, mainly religious orders, with broad segments of the population such as Jews or slaves left out of the transformative concerns. In the modern state, each and every individual counted, and loyalties once confined to the familial and local domains were now transferred to impersonal modes of association and abstract ideologies. It was not accidental that the longing for a total revolution was born in the wake of the attempts of various European thinkers to overcome the dehumanizing spirit of modern society and their dissatisfaction with the limited scope and impact of a political upheaval such as the French Revolution.[3]

Along, too, came the confidence that the same knowledge and tools mastered by the new state and its agencies to tame the unpredictable forces of nature were also applicable to human nature and society. The modern state aspired for and gathered ever more knowledge about its subjects and terrain with the stated goal of transformation, and it exuded abundant confidence in its ability to do so. Around the turn of the nineteenth century, European states entered what David Landes calls "the first statistical era," when officials realized that numbers were too important a matter to be left to chance and consequently created a systematic and regularized program for the preparation and preservation of data for the use by other agencies of the state. It was only a matter of time until the "new conceptions of the role of the state and the character of economic change made it desirable to go beyond the collation and arithmetical transformation of simple raw numbers and to create aggregative and analytical indicators of a much more highly processed character." Not only was the capacity of the modern state to effect change increased significantly, but population politics were no longer simply a means to an end; instead, they were transformed into sweeping new visions of states and societies. The populace was made "legible," in James Scott's words, through relentless measuring and standardization, through mapping, census taking, passportization, and mental and physical cataloging. With the urge to know more about the population, social reality was now quantified and the notion of society came into being.[4] To be sure, over the course of time and many fatal schemes, the modern state would eventually accept limits on its aspirations and the exercise of its power. In the meantime, attempts to sculpt a "New Man" and society through the abolition of the market and private property, intensive indoctrination, manipulation of the gene pool, mass deportations, ethnic cleansing, and elimination of social classes and genocide, to cite some of the major tools, became political currency. Until then, however, the confidence in the transformative powers of the state and its moral grounding continued to expand.[5]

The discovery of society gave birth to new mass politics that sought to overcome traditional divisions, mainly of class and political parties. In some cases, such as the Russian czarist government, the pressure of total war forced the state to encourage and deal with new mediating bodies that often sought social and political transformation. In many others, however, the unprecedented expansion of the body politic before and especially during the Great War, and the captivating vision of a homogenous and harmonious socio-national body, entailed the rejection of mediating bodies between state and society. Within the extensive literature celebrating—undoubtedly with some justification—parliamentarism, professionalism, and individualism as the epitome of modernity, Hannah Arendt, Jacob Talmon, and George Mosse's essays on illiberal modernity were often glossed over by critics. The state's focus on the organization of "everyone and everything," to use Arendt's apt phrase, and the simultaneous popular rejection of liberal democracy throughout the European interwar landscape bred a new form of corporatism, that, as Daniel Orlovsky argues in his contribution to this volume, paved the way to an all-intrusive state whose legacy lingers until the present day. By then, the new sites of national politics, as Stephen Kotkin has recently noted, transferred from the royal palaces, houses of parliament, or backrooms to army barracks, public squares, factories, sport stadiums, and the female bodies as the natural habitat of the various authoritarian regimes that populated Europe and actively sought the transformation of their subjects.[6]

It seemed as if no daily function, however mundane, was beyond mobilization. This merits a word of caution. True, the "Gardening state," to use

Zygmunt Bauman's metaphor, blossomed throughout Europe in the wake of the Great War. The European political landscape was marked by planned economies, elaborate surveillance systems, and thoroughly politicized eugenics research. Yet the intrusions on public and private lives coexisted, albeit tenuously and reluctantly, with the acceptance of autonomous spheres, whose violation was considered either too costly, futile, or unethical, and often all three. The discourse on individual rights, the cultivation of institutional buffers between citizen and state, and the acceptance of the insurmountable complexity of the economy effectively tamed the aspiration for unhindered perfection throughout Europe and the Americas.[7] And yet it was this ethos of constant mobilization that turned a subway line in Moscow, to cite one example, from a means of transferring people from point A to point B to a "majestic school in the formation of the new man," in the words of one contemporary. It was an elaborated exercise in cultivating the proper public conduct among the newly arrived city dwellers and exposing them to the marvels of the new science and history.[8]

Not surprisingly, whether on the road to, in the midst of, or in its aftermath, total war looms over the present studies. Indeed, total wars and their consequences have been both the embryo and outlet for governmental transformative schemes across the ideological spectrum. Writing in the United States in the midst of the Second World War and drawing on his personal experience in revolutionary and civil war Russia and later in the American Great Depression, the sociologist Pitirim Sorokin concluded that the totalitarian trend—the ultimate expression of transformational politics—owed more to circumstances than to ideological planning and convictions. "The main uniform effect of calamities upon the political and social structure of society," argued Sorokin, "is the expansion of governmental regulation, regimentation, and control of social relationships and a decrease in the regulation and management of social relationships by individuals and private groups." Such an increase of totalitarianism, continued Sorokin, manifests itself first in those fields of social relationships in which the calamity creates the gravest emergency, such as during famine, when governmental regimentation embraces all food relationships from domestic production, to distribution, consumption, export, import, rationing, pricing, and so on. If the calamity is complex, and involves famine, pestilence, revolution, and war, then the increase of dictatorship and regimentation becomes fairly encyclopedic, extending to practically all fields of social relationships.

Like other prominent contemporary observers of the European upheaval in the wake of the Great War, most notably Freud, Sorokin did not hold men and ideas accountable. Whoever and whatever they were, they merely responded in a universal fashion to certain conditions. No matter who is at the helm, the expansion of governmental regimentation is inevitable "as the rise of temperature in influenza or pneumonia." "Totalitarianism is not created by Pharoahs, monarchs, and dictators; the Lenins, Stalins, Mussolinis, and other *Fuhrers* are merely the instruments of deeper underlying forces that decree an increase of totalitarianism during signal calamities," wrote Sorokin, concluding with an optimistic note that this phenomenon is always destined to decrease once the crisis conditions are gone. The leaders can affect this change or be ousted.[9]

Undoubtedly, circumstances such as the brutal experiences of total wars, famines, revolutions, and civil wars exerted a substantial impact on the evolution of totalitarian regimes. Each calamity ordained policies and strengthened the hand of institutions that developed their own vested interest in a permanent and ever-expanding population management, if only because of the self-serving motives of increasing their budget, manpower, economic clout, or all three. Yet, as the various contributors to this volume concur, neither circumstances nor institutional interests explain the different reactions to the same experiences, why certain institutions, such as state surveillance, political police, and planned economies, were created in the first place, and most intriguingly, why so many of the emergency regimentation policies and institutions persisted well after the conditions that precipitated them dissipated. The roots of transformative politics and their endurance in peacetime compel us to look beyond the immediate crucible of war.

The nineteenth century witnessed the emergence of body and hygiene metaphors as a scientific vocation supported by powerful national societies and political lobbies, and often endorsed by the state as a national issue. Triggered often by a sense of national decline following setbacks in the domestic and international fronts, eugenics appeared as a remedy for every social and political malaise, nothing short of a modern salvation.[10] It was in this spirit that the leading figure in the Soviet eugenics movement declared it in 1922 to be the religion of the future, on equal standing with socialism. "The ideals of socialism are bound up with our earthly life," wrote Nikolai Kol'tsov.

> But the dream of creating a perfect order in the relations between people is also a religious idea, for which people will go to their deaths. Eugenics has before it a high ideal which also gives meaning to life and is worthy of sacrifices: the creation, through conscious work by many generations, of a human being of a higher type, a powerful ruler of nature and the creator of life. Eugenics is the religion of the future and it awaits its prophets.[11]

Alas, Kol'tsov was already behind the times, as Michael Burleigh succinctly comments. The new religion already had legions of prophets and implementers.[12] Eugenics, as another reviewer has correctly observed recently, was not so much a clear set of scientific principles as it was a "modern" way of talking about social problems in biological terms, referring to society as an organic body that had to be guided by biological laws, and allaying social fears and moral panics with scientific authority. Political, cultural, and professional elite of different ideological convictions sought to promote their agendas under the umbrella of the new cult.[13]

The year 1912 saw the first International Congress for Eugenics.[14] Fueled by a declining birth rate, anxieties of being surrounded and overwhelmed by nonwhite races, rising waves of immigration, and unprecedented demographic losses in the first global war, the obsession with the perfection of the populace led to the systematic appropriation of the private sphere by the state for the alleged improvement of its international standing. Positive eugenics and its destructive twin, euthanasia, enjoyed an almost universal endorsement during the first half of the twentieth century. The belief in the ability to improve human society by manipulation of its gene pool, extermination of the unfit, or the tight management of the sociocultural environment was enthusiastically celebrated as the ultimate sign of progress on both sides of the Atlantic, often in places that are not immediately associated with these policies, such as Latin America.[15]

Sterilization of the mentally ill—often a code for the socially weak—was advocated by the democratic Left, liberals, communists, and fascists alike, and mutually inspired and supported through the exchange of information. The state of California, a pathfinder in the implementation of prewar eugenic sterilization, was cited approvingly by left-wing German professionals; Nazi sterilization legislation was profiled and propagated in public exhibitions, churches, and high schools in the United States in 1934 and was praised by both Scandinavian and German Socialist medical experts.[16] Between 1935 and 1975, none other than the Swedish welfare state forced the sterilization of nearly sixty-three thousand people, mostly women, often because they were considered racially or socially inferior. Driven by the same logic, about forty-five hundred mental patients were forced to undergo lobotomies under officially encouraged eugenics programs that started in Sweden in the 1920s. It should have come as no surprise that the enthusiasm for the forced sterilization was rationalized in part as compensation for the rising costs of pronatalist policies and the need to guarantee a healthier future generation. In the memorable words of one of the chief advocates of the sterilization campaign, "we must not be so taken up with the idea of freedom and civil rights for each and every person in this generation, that we forget the just demands of the next." Tellingly, the absolute majority of operations were conducted after the Second World War, despite the exposure of Nazi practices and their legacies.[17] Despite the increasing racial undertone of the European experiment with eugenics before the Second World War, one could not ignore that its appeal cut across not only ideological divisions but also ethnic and religious divisions, with Jewish scientists highly visible in the Weimar eugenics movement.[18]

Gender became a political arena where the battle over the nature of the nation was ferociously fought as well. Abortion, as Mary Louise Roberts asserts in her discussion of post–Great War France, was considered a "searing affront to the dead," just as pronatalism was seen as the cure for the perceived bionational decay. Long held as either symbols of the nation or the main beneficiaries of social revolutions, women now found themselves as literal instruments in the regeneration of the nation, if only in a reversed fashion. The cult of the family in its communist, fascist, and liberal variations espoused fertility and motherhood as the highest form of patriotism and the source of social stability. But, as Elisabeth Domansky argues regarding the German home and battlefronts during the Great War, the little autonomy the family had before the war was completely lost, as the family turned into a militarized-biologized domain—as were all other institutions, class included—vulnerable to a state that did its utmost to dominate the most intimate spheres of reproduction. In a war that was consciously fought as a Darwinist struggle of survival of the fittest, the female body became a battlefront, not only metaphorically.

Ironically, if not surprisingly, pronatalist policies across the board failed to achieve their main goal: increasing the size of indigenous European populations. The overwhelming financial crisis during the interwar period debilitated both the state's incentives for promoting higher rates of reproduction and the citizens' own willingness to compound their already dim economic existence by raising additional children. This very failure, however, only increased the sense of crisis and anxiety, and in turn, the search for other venues to improve the biological stock.[19] Here, Claudia Koonz's contribution offers an intriguing redirection of Bauman's gardening metaphor. Focusing on the "desirable" plants and the gardener's zealous apprentices, instead of only the weeds and the gardener, she demonstrates the gendered racial "blueprint" that inspired the design of the Nazi garden and supplied the core imagery that popularized it by projecting an "Aryan" identity powerful enough to inspire pride yet vulnerable enough to make the threat of racial dangers credible.

The aesthetic urges were not confined to the manipulation of the individual's genes. Rather, they went hand in hand with relentless efforts to maximize mass mobilization and organization. The cross-ideological resentment of the balkanization of the body social in the wake of the ongoing industrial revolution, the commercialization of life and commodification of the individual, and the political upheavals that rocked Europe well into the twentieth century were a fertile ground for a new kind of redemptive collectivism, aptly named Romantic Anti-Capitalism.[20] Driven by mutually supporting anxiety and assuredness, scientific messianism rooted in the Enlightenment ethos was transferred into the political programs of protest movements that now crossed the threshold into political power.[21] The aesthetic vision of an unshakable, well-coordinated social harmony captured the political imagination well before the outbreak of World War I. Reflecting on the nature and rising specter of socialism at the close of the nineteenth century, Georg Simmel placed the new ideology and movement firmly within the modern tendency to organize "all of society symmetrically and equally structured according to general principles," combining control and coordination with aesthetic urges and desire for harmony. Rejecting the popular view that reduced socialist utopia exclusively to the needs of the stomach, and consequently to an ethical dimension, Simmel pointed instead to the conflict between socialistic and individualistic tendencies as the origin of socialist aesthetics:

> That society as a whole should become a work of art in which every single element attains its meaning by virtue of its contribution to the whole; that a unified plan should rationally determine all of production, instead of the present rhapsodic haphazardness by which the efforts of individuals benefit or harm society; that the wasteful competition of individuals against individuals should be replaced by the absolute harmony of work—all these ideas of socialism no doubt meet aesthetic interests.[22]

Simmel prophetically concluded that "this general trait of socialistic plans attests to the deep power of attraction in the idea of an harmonic, internally balanced organization of human activity overcoming all resistance of irrational individuality. This interest, a purely formal aesthetic one, independent of all material consequences, has probably always been important in determining the social forms of life."[23]

Whatever its ideological coloring, social engineering possessed a tremendous capacity for violence. The mobilization of the legal and medical professions for the goal of organizing society shifted the political discourse to new realms. The pretense of scientific criteria and measures to study and work on the population meant that the state would employ the most advanced and radical tools, without which the transformation and management of the population could not have taken place.[24] And it was perfectly logical that the most radical forms of mass extermination were preceded by the smaller-scale destruction of groups categorized as incompatible and irredeemable both medically and legally, then supplemented by military-industrial methods of operation.[25] Hence, the presence of professionals in the midst of most social-engineering enterprises became another trademark of the modern era. As Gordon Chang claims in his treatment of the internment of Japanese Americans during World War II, there was nothing unique in the fact that liberal professionals were in charge of designing educational and social programs for the molding of these American citizens into "proper" Americans. With much less violence and an undeniable range of unprecedented benefits, multiple agents of the new welfare state aggressively sought the management of everyday life of the citizenry. By the war's end, these professionals populated state bureaucracies operating well within a cross-ideological ethos of rational and impartial management of society.[26] This trend intensified despite the shadow cast by the recent past when professionals sworn to biosocial transformation joined forces, voluntarily or forcibly, with revolutionary regimes such as those of the Soviets and the Nazis, resulting in the removal of political and ethical inhibitions, and taking social-engineering enterprises to unprecedented extremes. Whereas the totalitarian shadow effectively tamed the radicalizing tendencies of social engineering across the Atlantic and discredited the ideologies that took it to such violent extremes (and with regard to the Soviet model, only gradually and partially), the drive to expand the management of the population not only did not diminish but continued to grow.

The fusion of scientific and utopian visions created a stable menu of categories and practices and a dynamic mode of applying them. The expanding welfare state and the cleansing state were opposite ends of the inclusionary-exclusionary axis, which became the trademark of transformative modern politics.[27] Soon to follow was the mass uprooting of large segments of the population from their homes and daily lives. Beginning in the second half of the nineteenth century, the remapping of Europe and its periphery, from the Caucasus in the early 1860s to the Balkans on the eve of the Great War, evolved around so-called voluntary resettlement, population exchanges, or the unmixing of peoples, a rather polished, ex post facto legitimization of ethnoreligious cleansing. The forced removal of ethnic "weeds" was an integral part of the remaking of the body national all across the ideological spectrum.[28] By no means a novelty, the mass deportations at the turn of the century nevertheless featured new developments that set them apart from earlier eras when the state's reluctance to lose large numbers of its indigenous subjects or allow political and religious aliens into the domain, and the simultaneous inability of the refugees to sustain themselves for a long time, worked to keep the numbers relatively low. As one authority on the modern refugees problem asserts, the sheer size of the waves of forcibly displaced people (some sixty million in the course of World War II) was greater than ever before, prompting contemporary scholars to declare the thirty years prior to 1944 as "the era of refugees." In addition, refugees (in itself a modern term, previously reserved to expelled French Protestants) existed outside of the web of national community and civil society. Finally, the duration of displacement was dramatically extended, regenerating itself in camps and concentration areas.[29]

István Deák's assessment of the authoritarian East Central European states as practically failures in each of their social-engineering schemes except for ethnic cleansing is a telling one. Where transformative aspirations in other realms failed miserably due to bureaucratic inefficiencies, the cleansing of minorities, mainly Jews and, in the postwar years, Germans, was carried out successfully due to a large degree of widespread popular support. Pursuing this line, Norman Naimark's chapter on ethnic cleansing in the Soviet Caucasus and the Crimea, Poland, and Bohemia is a case in point. First, mass deportations were not limited to wartime or to authoritarian regimes. Not only was this policy endorsed by communists and liberals alike, but, tellingly, both American and British leaders who gave their blessing to the massive population transfer in the latter case were concerned mainly with its potential economic impact and lack of orderly conduct. The uprooting of millions of people had already become an integral part of the political game, with everyone pointing to the successful Turkish-Greek precedent in the early 1920s as the proper example. Moral concerns were nowhere to be found. Furthermore, Naimark's essay points to an intriguing differentiation in ethnic cleansing carried out by nation-states and multiethnic polities. Either for the simple reason that the sites of deportation were still within the empire or union's boundaries, or the avowed commitment to the leveling of the deported groups with the rest of the population, and sometimes returning those groups to society, multiethnic structures continued to engage deportees in their new locations well after their physical removal.

A central theme in several essays concerns common threads that ran through totalitarian enterprises, as well as the particular features that set them apart from each other. For one, the colonial experience undoubtedly left deep imprints on European policies and ideologies by providing a sense of limitless possibilities and the power to pursue them and by introducing the racial factor into the gardening enterprise.

> The conquest of the earth, which closely means the taking it away from those who have a different complexion or slightly flatter noses than ourselves, is not a pretty thing when you look into it too much. What redeems it is the idea only. An idea at the back of it; not a sentimental pretense but an idea; and an unselfish belief in the idea—something you can set up, and bow down before, and offer a sacrifice to

reflects the narrator of Joseph Conrad's *Heart of Darkness*.[30] By the time Conrad wrote these words, this "idea" had already made inroads on the European continent. It was not by chance that the articulators of racial policies in interwar and wartime Europe launched their careers as anthropologists studying "race mixing" in the colonies, nor was it only symbolic that during the liquidation of the Warsaw Ghetto uprising in April 1943, SS foreign troops, such as the Ukrainian and Baltic police units and the Trawniki men, were referred to as *Askari*, the Swahili term for African soldiers and policemen in the service of German and the successive British powers during the colonial era.[31] Still, nontotalitarian "gardening states" reserved their most violent schemes for their colonial domains, while displaying considerably more restraint at home.[32]

It was, however, the profound sense of messianic eschatology that helped remove all (or almost all) inhibitions on methods of perfecting the body social and created systems of concentration camps, mass deportations, and killings. Indeed, both Soviets and Nazis went out of their way to underline this difference. Unlike the philistines who constantly lament brutality and the loss of lives, and who preach reconciliation, the ultimate goal of the promoters of the social-engineering project—a genuine moral-political unity of society—could be reached only through an irreconcilable and violent struggle, declared Soviet ideologues.[33] Another theoretician explained while looking at the bright prospect of communism after victory in World War II:

> Communist revolution is necessary not only to overthrow the rule of the exploiting classes and to liberate the working masses, but also for the cleansing of people from the filth of the old world. The history of the Great October Socialist Revolution and the socialist construction in the USSR shows how systematically, step by step, this vital cleansing process is taking place, how in the course of desperate class struggles between the exploiters and exploited a new man is born—a man of the communist society, with a totally new worldview and a new moral-political makeup.[34]

From Germany, roared Adolf Hitler, the cleansing of the Jewish filth is the actual fulfillment of Christian millenarianism:

> Christ has been the greatest precursor in the struggle against the Jewish world enemy. Christ had not been the apostle of peace that the Church had afterward made of him, but rather was the greatest fighting personality that had ever lived. For millennia the teaching of Christ had been fundamental in the fight against the Jew as the enemy of humanity. The task that Christ had started, he [Hitler] would fulfill.[35]

Second, the campaign to eradicate internal enemies within the totalitarian state actually intensified *after* all residues of real political opposition had been crushed, whether the Communists in Nazi Germany or in the Soviet case, following the declaration that Socialism had now been built.[36] Terror becomes total, Hannah Arendt noted, when it becomes independent of all opposition.[37]

To be sure, although Nazi and Soviet aesthetics may have been similar, they were not identical. Unlike the Nazis, the Soviets did not gloss over residues of the old world in the souls and minds of their subjects. The belief in the malleability of human nature precipitated unlimited and random terror. It was this boundless ambition and sweeping mandate—as distinguished from the Nazi genocidal yet far more selective terror—that accounted for the significantly larger number of employees in the service of the political police and not, as has been recently argued, the lesser popularity of the Soviet regime. All had to be engaged in the purification campaign, either as purgers or purged and often as both. Not only did Soviet citizens usually attach their signatures to the denunciations of their fellow citizens, but large parts of the periodic cleansing operations took place in public, with active participation of the population. Throughout the post-Stalin years, millions of Soviet citizens were actively engaged in communal policing in almost every housing and working unit, as well as in patrolling the streets.[38] It was practically inconceivable to expect in the Soviet Union anything like Heinrich Himmler's speech in Posen in October 1943, in which the architect of the "Final Solution" emphasized the historical necessity of the extermination of Jewish vermin, together with the acknowledgment of the survival of inhibitions among the perpetrators ("And then they come 80 million worthy Germans, and each has his decent Jew. Of course the others are vermin, but this one is an A-1 Jew"), the need to accommodate these inhibitions, and, above all, the need to maintain integrity and decency in their bourgeois sense ("We had the moral right, we had the duty to our people, to destroy this people. . . . But we have not the right to enrich ourselves with so much as a fur, a watch, a mark or a cigarette or anything else").[39] These were not merely generalizations. Himmler was well aware of complaints by none other than SS officers against the unmitigated murder of women and infants and the excessive brutalities in the course of the deportation of Jews. "The troops have been trained by their officers," argued an army officer following the massacre of some ninety Jewish children ranging in age from a few months to four years old in the Ukrainian village of Bila Tserkva on August 22, 1941,

> to have a decent soldierly attitude and to avoid violence and roughness towards a defenseless population. . . . In the case in question, however, measures against women and children were undertaken which in no way differ from atrocities carried out by the enemy about which the troops are continually being informed. It is unavoidable that these events will be reported back home where they will be compared to the Lemberg (L'viv) [Soviet] atrocities.[40]

The best way to prevent such excesses and the impression of being blindly raging sadists, wrote one such officer in Berlin, would be adherence to form ("This does not exclude that, when time comes, with all due form, one can occasionally give a Jew a kick in the rear, but even then it should be done with decency") and compassion for certain categories ("Among the [beaten] Jews there were Jewesses with small children in their arms. This sight was both degrading and shameful").[41] Nazism, as understood by the architect of the "Final Solution" and his lieutenants, was rooted in action. Students of the

Wehrmacht (regular army)—the single largest institution in Nazi Germany and an active participant in atrocities—have shown that as long as soldiers carried out orders, even if reluctantly, they had no reason to fear disciplinary action for expressing their personal disgust. In some cases, they were even given a choice to avoid active participation in massacres.[42] In the Soviet polity, entertaining much milder thoughts, let alone expressing them, marked people as internal enemies. Many thousands of Communists and non-Communists lost their freedom, and often their lives, after being charged with entertaining deviationist thoughts and failing to rid themselves of residues of the "old world." "We have no ready-made pure people, purged of all sins," reflected Viacheslav Mikhailovich Molotov, Stalin's second in command, explaining the rationale of Soviet terror. And, as he made clear both while in and out of office, this was an intolerable state of affairs.

The endowment of theological and later ideological and political adversaries with biological-hygienic characteristics was deeply rooted in European history. Most important, its appearance as mainstream rhetoric dated back to backlash against heresy in the Middle Ages, which meant not a fight between the church and outsiders or between believers and unbelievers but rather a struggle among Christians. In explanations of its nature, heresy was consistently compared with poison and incurable disease. Heresy, contended church theologians, is generated by polluted air, infecting a man by penetrating the viscera, and equated with cancer, an incurable disease that called for the amputation of the infected member. When William the Monk scolded Henry of Lausanne, "You are a leper, scarred by heresy, excluded from communion by the judgment of the priest according to the law, bare-headed, with ragged clothing, your body covered by an infected and filthy garment," his words did not sound much different from mid-twentieth-century totalitarian excisional rhetoric in which groups and individuals perceived to be hostile were continuously referred to as vermin, pollution, or filth, and were subjected to ongoing "purification."[43]

The drive against modern secular heretics assumed critical urgency largely due to their alleged elusiveness, argues Omer Bartov in his chapter. The elusive internal enemy could mask himself with the help of blood mixing or a Westernized facade that forced the Nazi regime to continually strip generations of contagious, false layers in its boundless quest for "purity." That enemy could also be a spy and a saboteur with a party card in his pocket or one whose mind was still imbued with prejudices of the old capitalist society, forcing the Soviet state to dig deep into his social and political past in order to eradicate "this weed which in some manner grew up between the stones of our bright and well-constructed building."[44] In the Nazi world, as in other genocidal enterprises, concludes Bartov, the elusive enemy was simultaneously ubiquitous, indestructible, and protean, begotten from and breeding a powerful sense of victimhood by the perpetrators, giving themselves a moral blank check in the defense of their threatened world.

The Nazi-Soviet comparison has turned into a cottage industry in recent years and by no means always an enlightening one. Such a comparison is inevitable and merited on the grounds of the mutual commitment to social engineering through violent means; the ensuing demographic, psychological, and ethical implications; and, not least, the fact that both systems constantly scrutinized one another. Unfortunately, the comparison is often reduced to body counting, with Communists around the globe beating the Nazis to the punch by killing nearly 100 million people versus 25 million by the Nazis.[45] For one, this is an ahistorical and demeaning argument. The Third Reich's four-year extermination machine was stopped only by military defeat. It has also not been convincingly demonstrated that the 1932–33 famine, the worst calamity in Soviet history, was a premeditated genocide by the Stalinist regime, rather than the catastrophic outcome of incompetent, arrogant, and callous authorities. The key question, however, remains why the all-powerful Communist regimes that had the capacity to launch genocidal campaigns did not resort to operating death camps. When Stalin's successors opened the gates of the Gulag, nearly three million inmates returned home. When the Allies liberated the Nazi death camps, they found there tens of thousands of human skeletons awaiting their inevitable execution.

This end point is also the starting point of contributions in this volume that deal with Soviet and Nazi excisional practices. Peter Holquist and Amir Weiner focus on the nature and implications of sociological and biological categorization of those targeted as obstacles on the way to Soviet and Nazi-style harmony.[46] Holquist situates Bolshevik state violence within the aesthetic enterprise that predated the establishment of the Bolsheviks in power and was the ethos within which Bolshevik ideology emerged and functioned. Violence was a technique—one may argue a most favored one—for cleansing the politicosocial body human weeds and sculpting an ideal-type, machinelike, harmonious society. Although these aspects were common to the Nazi and Soviet totalitarian projects, Holquist draws attention to several distinctive features of Soviet excisional practices, most important the individualized hermeneutics for each subject, which meant the creation of voluminous archives cataloging individuals, an inconceivable practice in the Nazi cleansing operation that sought the total physical destruction of an entire "race" by industrial means. One has only to recall the testimony of Margarete Buber-Neumann, a German Communist who survived both Soviet and Nazi concentration camps. Having lost her husband in the Great Terror, exiled to Kazakhstan, and then handed over to the Gestapo in the wake of the Molotov-Ribbentrop Pact, Buber also lost all traces of belief in Soviet Communism. Still, when comparing the two penal systems, she pointedly noted that in the Nazi camps "You had lost all human rights—all, all without exception. You were just a living being with a number to distinguish you from the other unfortunates around you."[47] Buber, we may add, was a political prisoner, and not one of the millions of Jews or Soviet POWs herded and slaughtered as an undifferentiated mass.

Indeed, as Weiner argues, Marxist regimes struggled with whether to assign primacy to either the "objective" category of class origin or the "subjective" criteria of conduct and experience. In polities founded on the Marxist premise of the primacy of acculturation, but simultaneously engaged in the constant eradication of social strata presumed to be illegitimate, the tension between nurture and nature was a constant.[48] It intensified as the Soviet polity advanced along the road to Socialism and Communism and radicalized its purification policies both qualitatively and quantitatively. Following the Second World War, social and ethnic categories and practices were totalized in a marked shift: enemy groups previously considered to be differentiated, reformable, and redeemable were now viewed as undifferentiated, unreformable, and irredeemable collectives. This totalization of the Marxist sociological paradigm challenged the commitment to the primacy of nurture over nature in the ongoing social-engineering project, not unlike the earlier-quoted dilemma posed by Saint Augustine fifteen hundred years before. It also invited a comparison inside and outside the Soviet Union with contemporary biological-racial paradigms, most notably, that of Nazi Germany, one that the Soviets were well aware of yet wanted to avoid at all costs.

The Soviets, contend Holquist and Weiner, persistently rejected the primacy of the biological over the sociological. Soviet contemporaries were extremely anxious to avoid any tendency to degenerate into a "zoological" ethos. The principle of human heredity and its potential practices, whether exterminatory euthanasia or positive eugenics, were officially repudiated in the Soviet Union from the early 1930s on. Throughout the 1930s, Soviet leaders, most notably Stalin himself, reacted vehemently against any suggestion that their sociologically based model of the human subject could be equated with any biologically based, genetically coded enterprise, whether it was the racial Nazi polity or contemporary eugenics and euthanasia policies, enjoying widespread acceptance during that decade. When the totalization of categories and practices in the wake of the war drove home the inevitable comparison with the Nazi racial-biological code, the Soviets went out of their way to emphasize that their destruction of internal enemies was not genocidal and that unlike the death camps in the capitalist world, their own penal system remained true to its corrective mandate. "In contrast to the capitalist countries, where concentration camps are sites of torture and death, the correctional labor camps of the Soviet state are a distinctive school for the re-education of a worldview bequeathed to us by the capitalist society," claimed a 1944 brochure of the Cultural-Educational Department of the Gulag (the very existence and title of such a department is telling).[49]

This was no empty rhetoric. The class-based Soviet theory and practices of social engineering seemed to present an ominous obstacle to the application of uniform social targeting. Classes, strata, and layers were neither faceless nor homogeneous. Rather, they were variegated and arranged in a hierarchical order based on the services their members had rendered to the Communist drive. Responsibility and accountability were assessed on the individual's merit, even though this principle was often compromised in the course of exercising the structuring acts. Hence, extermination drives such as the 1919 anti-Cossack campaign were brought to a halt before completion for no other reason than the fear of degenerating into a racial-genocidal campaign. Moreover, individuals targeted in the course of purges maintained the right to appeal and often did so successfully, and after the initial deadly phases of deportations, throughout the 1930s and 1940s children were either spared the fate of their parents or won earlier rehabilitation, just as Jews continued to populate party and state institutions at the height of the official anti-Semitic campaign. Ruthless and murderous as any, Soviet power was not anchored in racial-genocidal ideology and institutions and did not amount to the Nazi negation of humanity. Therefore, even the total deportations during and after the war were explained by the alleged conduct of the condemned nations and not by their race or ethnicity.

How and when did the gardening ethos wane? Or, is it better to ask, did it ever wither away? Mark Mazower's reminder that liberal democracy as we conventionally recognize it today, with the individual and his rights as the core of the sociopolitical order, has been institutionalized only from the mid-1950s on, when the impact of the wartime trauma, the fear of all-consuming purges, and the rise of consumerism compelled European regimes and parties to accept some limits on their transformative powers.[50] Moving eastward, the renunciation of mass terror in the Soviet Union, the abandonment of collectivization and acceptance of a modus vivendi with the church in East Central Europe, along with the abandonment of integral socialism by the German Social Democratic Party, were key markers of this shift. The various origins of the scaling down of state ambitions—self-imposed limitations by the victors of the Second World War, Stalin's successors' fear of another endless cycle of terror in the Soviet Union, and the rise of effective civil societies in liberal democracies—pointed to a common reluctance to accept without challenge the costs of radically transformative drives. This was not, however, an inconsequential closure. The paradoxical embrace of the welfare state by liberal democracies drew on this phenomenon, albeit on different scales and degrees of coercion, curtailing radical social engineering on the one hand, and preserving, on the other, a large role for the state and for softer gardening policies. Moreover, with the exception of the above-mentioned continuation of forced sterilization of the mentally ill in the Scandinavian welfare states, well after the end of the war until the mid-1970s the sites of radical social engineering moved out of Europe and the Americas to China and Cambodia, where collectivization of agriculture, violent cultural revolution, and genocide were powerful reminders of the deep roots and appeal of the urge for transformation.

Here Yael Zerubavel's contribution to this volume adds an important, although often glossed over, explanation. The powerful myths that drove social-engineering campaigns in various societies proved rather vulnerable to the growing, visible gap between declaration and deed. When such a gap appeared unbridgeable, popular belief and commitment began to crumble and forced a reevaluation of ideological creeds. Cynicism and humor, in this light, were more than artistic expressions of disenchanted cultural elite or fringes. Zionist leaders and ideologues could reasonably claim success in their drive to transform the Diaspora Jew into a farmer-warrior. Israelis seemed to have internalized military service in a spiritual army long before actual service in the real army begins, and nursery school children fantasize army life (including wishing each other on the occasion of their birthday that they be a tank) to a point where military service does not signify breaking with the past or being introduced to new values.[51] Such an upbringing was supported by foundational myths of heroic sacrifice, defeats and triumphs that sought to inculcate the worldview of the founding fathers as well as routinize a state of permanent mobilization. But, as Israeli society matured and the pioneering age of larger-than-life heroes and constant demands for sacrifice for the collective good turned into a distant past, so did the corrosive impact of irony take its toll. And so, side by side with the wearing down of foundational myths, the image of the war widow, the hitherto sacred embodiment of stoic sacrifice, became fair game, the subject of self-mockery and rebellious defiance against further demands and expectations by state and society.

Even with the evident decline of mobilizational politics, the revulsion of forced eugenic policies, and the rejection of ethnic cleansing as a legitimate policy, the urge to landscape the human garden is bound to be part of our present and future. Today, the main impulse behind human cloning and related undertakings in the laboratories of liberal democracies seems to be the desire to alleviate suffering. And yet, could anyone guarantee that the impetus to genetically perfect human beings will remain checked when the institutions and principles in question have remained the same? Wilde, perhaps, had it right. Utopia is the one country at which Humanity always lands and for which it continues to search.

PETER HOLQUIST 1

State Violence as Technique

The Logic of Violence in Soviet Totalitarianism

> Proletarian compulsion in all its forms, beginning with execution by shooting and ending with the compulsory labor obligation, is—however paradoxical this might sound—*the means for producing a Communist humanity from the human material of the capitalist epoch.*[1]
>
> —Nikolai Bukharin, *Economics of the Transition Period* (1920) [italicized portion underlined by Lenin, with his marginal notation: "Precisely!"]

> "Not only strength, but beauty," demanded the builders. . . . But as great as it was, a second purpose lay behind this great undertaking. This was the reforging of the men and women. . . . Success was to be measured in human terms as well as in terms of engineering.[2]
>
> —*Belomor* (1934)

WITH THE OUTPOURING of materials from the Soviet archives, there has been a tidal wave of literature on Soviet "repression."[3] Yet scholars continue to treat such violence as an unintended consequence of the Soviet project, as some unforeseen malfunctioning rather than the product of its working out. Other than the "Stalin as evil genius" thesis, there now exist two main schools on Soviet "Terror" among historians: it was either the product of tensions, be they social or political;[4] or it was the instrumental attempt to suppress opponents, real or imagined.[5] Regardless of differences, most approaches based on new archival materials share one common feature: they treat Soviet applications of violence as purely repressive, however manic or irrational. Indeed, violence is described as manic and irrational precisely because it so inexactly corresponds to its supposed repressive function.[6] As a result, actual instances of applied violence are treated as a rupture or deviation from a supposedly more normal Soviet policy.

Some scholars of Nazi Germany have cast a comparative glance at Soviet applications of violence but have tended to treat it as qualitatively different than Nazi violence. (However, those Germanists such as Dan Diner are quite right to condemn some Soviet historians' facile comparisons to the Holocaust, such as Robert Conquest's Belsen analogy.)[7] Despite its clear instrumentality and massive extent, Soviet state violence is deemed incomparable to the Nazi use of violence for two reasons.[8] First, Soviet terror is presented as an arbitrary and irrational product of Russian backwardness—an Asiatic argument, if you will. This proposition operates upon the assumption that it was Russian backwardness rather than its embrace of modernity that led to state terror. Second, Soviet violence is presented as more acceptable because, unlike Nazi violence, it was practiced in the name of a progressive and universal ideology. The first argument is simply based on an unfamiliarity with the nature and application of Soviet state violence. The second blatantly disregards how the Soviet project set about realizing its universal aspirations and does not take seriously the image that the Soviets set about to make universal.

Soviet applications of state violence upon the politicosocial body were meticulously targeted and assiduously planned. To be sure, Soviet power simultaneously strove to cultivate society and each individual in it. But state violence was inextricably related to this desire to operate upon society as artifact. Dekulakization (the policy pursued in 1929–32 to "eliminate the kulaks as a class") and the Great Terror (a term frequently given to the Soviet state's massive employment of violence in 1937–38) were not inevitable products of either Marxism or even Bolshevism; but the Bolshevik aspiration to cultivate a socialist society, and as, part of that, to cultivate each individual, envisioned violence. Although its intensity varied, the use of violence in this way was not limited to the 1930s but dates back to the founding of the regime.[9] That is, Soviet state violence was not simply repressive. It was employed as a tool for fashioning an idealized image of a better, purer society. After Victor Shklovsky's seminal 1915–16 essay on formalist art, Soviet policies might best be described as "state violence as technique."[10] In the Soviet Union, as throughout Europe, technique—"the effective management of resources, both natural and human"—had become "a value and an aesthetic goal, not merely as a means to an end."[11]

One can portray Soviet state violence in light of Claude Lefort's thoughts on the nature of totalitarianism, specifically his observations on the place and consequences of "the image of the body in totalitarianism."[12] Of course, "totalitarianism" has been one of the key prisms for understanding the Soviet experience, so prevalent, in fact, that one leading historian, Stephen Kotkin, has called for it to pass into "a well-earned retirement."[13] As Kotkin suggests, totalitarianism in the Soviet field operated with its own historically situated agenda, particularly to bracket Nazi Germany and Stalinist Russia as anomalous regimes.[14] Sovietologists, however, demonstrated a marked preference for one particular current of totalitarian thought: the more static variant that viewed itself preeminently as a social science (notably, the Friedrich-Brzezinski model, with its checklist of six key totalitarian attributes). By and large, the Soviet field eschewed a different totalitarian tradition, a more philosophical-historical one, elaborated, among others, by Hannah Arendt and Jacob Talmon.[15] Notably, this latter strand was more concerned with the origins, rather than with the operation, of twentieth-century totalitarian regimes, and as a consequence it read Nazi Germany and Stalinist Russia into the general current of European history. Moreover, this more historicized strand of totalitarianism emphasized the phenomenon as an ethos rather than as a structure and attempted to explain how individuals came to embrace such movements.

I would like to read Lefort's treatment of totalitarianism in light of the latter tradition. Totalitarianism as ideology, Lefort claims, operates in particular ways. First, rather than distinguishing power from society, totalitarianism conflates them. It seeks to encompass power and society as part of one system, to homogenize social space. Totalitarianism in fact understands power specifically "as *social power*," as "society itself *qua* conscious, acting power." (Elisabeth Domansky's contribution to this volume likewise insists on the emergence not just of a totalitarian state but of a totalitarian society.) Lefort thus insists that totalitarianism is not simply about structures but the ethos animating those structures. Consequently, one cannot distinguish between a "body social" and "body political"; one must speak instead of one politicosocial body. Second, totalitarianism seeks to homogenize this politicosocial space in an attempt both to represent and to realize the "People-as-One." It not only denies, but seeks to eliminate, all forms of heterogeneity and division. Third (and here Lefort prefigured many current studies of Nazi policy), the campaign against enemies is seen as a form of prophylaxis, a drive to ensure the integrity of the politicosocial body by eliminating tumors and parasites.[16] And finally, Lefort suggests that totalitarianism's image of the body is combined with that of the machine, operating with both medical-prophylactic and technical-productionist imagery.

On this last point, Lefort understands the body narrowly in medical terms. This scientific-medical understanding of the body also predominates in current historical treatments of other (and particularly Nazi) interwar prophylactic projects as well. Although scholars have yet to examine them systematically in these terms, Soviet applications of violence likewise were intended as prophylactic measures for securing the health of a pristine socialist polity. From radically different perspectives, Alexander Solzhenitsyn and Viacheslav Molotov nevertheless both describe Soviet state violence as prophylactic interventions: Solzhenitsyn termed it "social prophylaxis" whereas Molotov defined the 1937 operations as "a prophylactic cleansing."[17] This chapter argues for viewing Soviet policies in these terms.

But to understand these measures solely in scientific or medical terms, as a kind of prophylaxis, is to miss the larger project. Such an approach can explain the state's urgency and even criteria and methods of selection, but it fails to apprehend what totalitarian regimes were seeking to accomplish by these excisions. As Sander Gilman (among others) has suggested, the image of illness and its obverse, that of the whole, healthy body that is to be protected (a body that is invariably also understood as beautiful), encompass *both* scientific and aesthetic paradigms. In Gilman's words, "science often understands and articulates its goals on the basis of literary or aesthetic models, measuring its reality against the form of reality that art provides . . . both perspectives are essential for examining complex social and cultural functions of the image of disease."[18] The Soviet project encompassed both the scientific and aesthetic registers. To give but one example, Maxim Gorky explicitly identified the revolutionary ideal to be "man, the physically strong, handsome beast; but his physical beauty was in complete harmony with spiritual power and beauty."[19] Several decades later, a 1952 Soviet article on "The Aesthetic Category of the Beautiful" insisted that "The idea of communism, as the highest, most harmonious, most complete form of human existence on the earth, represents the culmination of human representations of the beautiful. . . . In an era when 'all roads lead to communism,' the existence of parasitic classes becomes an ugly dissonance. . . . The very division of society into classes, the oppression of some people by others, is a fact of scandalous disharmony."[20]

To be sure, the Soviet state used violence to excise [*iz"iat'*] those individuals it had determined to be "socially harmful." It did so, however, not merely to ensure society's health and integrity but equally to realize an idealized, fundamentally aesthetic image of society and each individual in it.[21] As Peter Fritzsche has noted for the Nazi project, National Socialism's "constructive program of national health was accompanied by a stern eugenics administration that sought progressively to weed out alleged biological dangers to the German Volk. From the very beginning, the regime applied measures to identify, segregate and eradicate debilitating or supposedly foreign matter." But one cannot appreciate the full nature of this project unless one also grasps "the fantastic vision of the National Socialists. . . . A useful way of thinking about the links between the administration of modern reform and the extraordinary measures of National Socialism is to consider modernism in aesthetic terms."[22] To emphasize this underlying aesthetic project in the Soviet case, I have chosen Shklovsky's term *technique* rather than a more technical term like *scalpel* for Soviet state violence.

The Emergence of State Violence as Technique

"A great many of the practices we associate with the Revolution had had precedents in the treatment of the people by the government during the last two centuries of the monarchy. The old régime provided the Revolution with many of its methods; all the Revolution added was a savagery peculiar to itself."[23] Alexis de Tocqueville of course was speaking of the French Revolution, yet his observation holds equally true for the new Soviet regime emerging out of 1917. There is now a tendency to displace all responsibility for the emergence of state violence onto Bolshevism as an ideology. But for its own ends, Bolshevism expanded upon existing practices. There were certainly specificities to Bolshevik applications of violence. Yet the very possibility of applying state violence to the politicosocial body was predicated on two earlier developments: the emergence over the course of the nineteenth century of the "social" as a realm for state intervention; and the fashioning of particular tools for operating on this realm, particularly in the course of the First World War.

To conceive of a politicosocial body upon which to operate, one first has to conceive of a polity in social terms. This was new in the nineteenth century. The very term *social science* was not coined until the first years of the French Revolution. And this new way of seeing encompassed both a model of science (thus allowing for the conviction that the methods of science are applicable to human affairs) and a definition of the social field (providing a specific view of society and of the nature of social processes to which the scientific model can be applied).[24] This social field explicitly related the individual to the larger politicosocial body. Emerging disciplines increasingly shifted from the traditional imagery of a metaphoric relation between the individual body and the social body, to an argument that there existed an actual correlation between the two.[25] This binding of individuals to specific social categories contributed to the development of state measures to act on these individuals. The European state in the latter half of the nineteenth century devoted increasing attention to identifying and removing the social threat such individuals represented. Thus "a *scientific* approach that included careful and constant documentation—or scientific observation" was developed. "Evidently, the demands of bourgeois society for intellectual and moral 'hygiene' were inseparable from the practice of violent policing."[26]

As in the rest of Europe, the emergence of a social way of seeing affected how the Russian imperial state came to view and treat its population. In particular, the discipline of military statistics emerged as one of the essential conceptual models for conceiving of imperial society.[27] Military statistics originated among reforming bureaucrats in the mid nineteenth century and were modeled upon similar European studies. Military statistics transformed the empire's hitherto amorphous "people" (*narod*) into a well-defined "population" (*naselenie*) through an intensive statistical study of its inhabitants. And, of equal significance, military statistics came to express an aesthetic preference (registered in a scientific language) for homogeneity. Thus even prior to the First World War the imperial state was mapping the population in accord with idealized images of the politicosocial body. Military statistics constituted a particular social field upon which the state could act.

Nor were these studies of merely academic interest. In the course of the First World War, the imperial state translated these modelings of the population into actual policies. The forced deportation of Jews, Germans, Balts, and other groups from the western borderlands during the war merely transcribed into practice what military statistics had been teaching for years.[28] Some estimates place the total number of deportees at one million. During the First World War, the deportation of unreliable elements simply became part of the conceptual landscape—a landscape that had been mapped by military statistics.

And the First World War practices of deportation prefigured many of those identified as somehow intrinsically "Bolshevik." Increasingly, threats to the state were described in prophylactic terms: the Jewish 'element' in the western borderlands was "pernicious" (*zlovrednyi*) and "harmful and dangerous for the Russian people."[29] (Although different adjectival modifiers were employed, the expression "an . . . element dangerous to the . . . people" was the precise formula for later Soviet mass operations.) After the May 1915 anti-German pogrom in Moscow, when crowds had demanded the expulsion of all imperial subjects of German background, the appointed head of the city expressed regret that there were simply too many German subjects to fit them in a concentration camp [*sic*] on an island in the Volga.[30] Punitive detachments, which were to become ubiquitous in all armies during the Russian Civil War, operated extensively during the 1916 Steppe uprising. The imperial state in its total war manifestation thus elaborated an entire repertoire of practices for managing and operating upon the population, practices that were to be carried across the revolutionary divide.[31]

The First World War therefore represents a crucial watershed, as the imperial state moved to fashion its vision of a body politic as much by excision as by acculturation. The First World War did not introduce such aspirations. Military statistics (and Russian colonial policy) had long suggested such "solutions" were possible. But total war was the context within which these practices emerged as a regular part of state policies. In this environment, the appeal of scientistic solutions intertwined with an ethos of violence.[32]

In this light, the violence of the Russian Civil War appears not as something sui generis but rather as an expansion of state violence first massively employed in the Great War. Sharing a common conceptual matrix for population politics and emerging from the experience of total war, Whites just as much as Reds reflexively disaggregated the population into "elements" of varying reliability.[33] They then employed a prophylaxis of violence on those elements deemed to be malignant or harmful. Whites termed Jews "microbes" or "bacilli"; Bolshevism was presented as "a social disease." And, pace many existing treatments, this violence was not "wild" but very well structured: White commanders sifted their POWs, selecting out the undesirables and having them executed in groups later, a process the Whites described as "filtering."[34] The Bolshevik application of state violence had its own specificities; but it was hardly unique.

Soviet State Violence as Prophylaxis

So the preconditions for the application of violence to the politicosocial body predated the Bolshevik regime. But the Soviets then employed violence as a technique to fashion society in their own image. And the Soviet state did so as an explicitly ideological regime.[35] Applying Lefort's observations on the centrality of the body's image in totalitarianism, one can discern the Soviet state's constant devotion to the sculpting of its raw, human material, a project diligently pursued even in the years preceding the better-known violence of the 1930s. Seen from this vantage point, the measures of the 1930s are not some anomaly or deviation but only the largest and most ambitious effort in a project stretching back to 1917.

From the very first, the Soviet regime sought to rework the politicosocial body. In 1919, in the midst of a civil war for its very existence, the Soviet state engaged in a policy of "de-Cossackization."[36] This attempt to remove an entire segment of the population (the term employed again was *element*) was not a defensive reaction to a hostile group but instead an attempt to foster an idealized image of the politicosocial body by excising those elements determined to be harmful. In a policy review, I. I. Reingol'd, a senior Party member, summed up the means and ends of de-Cossackization. Its goal had been "to make the Don [Territory] healthy" (*Don ozdorovit'*). To this end, Reingol'd suggested that the Soviet state "will sooner or later have to exterminate, simply physically destroy the vast portion of Cossacks."[37] The Party decree delineating this policy explicitly called for the instrumental use of "mass terror" and the outright and total "extermination" of the Cossack elite. As a direct consequence of this decree, upwards of ten thousand people were judicially executed.

Yet within several months de-Cossackization was abjured, and the Cossacks became normalized as a component part of the Soviet population. This abrupt shift in policy has several lessons. First, while essentializing sociopolitical categories was a critical precondition for de-Cossackization, so too was the role played by political authorities who had sanctioned and pressed de-Cossackization. As Detlev Peukert has argued, the principle of selection and even elimination had long been present in scientific thought. But measures such as de-Cossackization become possible only when states—especially ones pursuing an explicitly ideological agenda—endorse one single branch of modern social thought and grant it supreme state backing.[38] De-Cossackization was not so much the product of scientific models themselves but the result of an ideological system extending scientistic reasoning as a universal template for dealing with perceived threats. The abrupt shift in policy toward Cossacks also demonstrates that what was important was not the category itself but a framework that sought to identify opposition in terms of malignancies to be removed in order to bring about the healthy, pristine, and beautiful society. De-Cossackization was not an anomalous event but represented a Soviet propensity for fashioning visions of society by subtraction as much as by addition.[39] Periods when the regime resorted to such measures were not deviations but those conjunctures when it thought it possible or necessary to act on a long-standing goal—to create a socialist society through managing and sculpting its human as well as its raw materials.

This project of politicosocial fashioning even framed the conduct of military campaigns in the midst of the civil war. Soviet anti-insurgency campaigns in the Don region in 1920–21 and against the Antonov movement in Tambov Province in 1921 aimed as much at operating upon the politicosocial body as at smashing military opposition.[40] Existing treatments merely portray Soviet anti-insurgent policies as repressive measures intended to eliminate political threats. In fact, the campaigns aimed at much more. Soviet forces did not seek to "pacify the people" (*usmirit' narod*) or "suppress the insurgency" (*podavit' vosstanie*). Soviet measures sought instead "to remove and eliminate the bandit element" (*iz"iat' i istrebit' banditskii element*) and "to cleanse those regions infected by banditry" (*ochistit' raiony zarazhennye banditizmom*).[41] That is, they did not seek simply to pacify the countryside and enforce obedience. Banditry (described variously as "a dangerous epidemic" and "a psychological illness")[42] was merely a symptom pointing to the presence of malignant and dangerous elements. The goal was to remove such tumors, whether they be active or benign: once the symptom of banditry revealed the presence of dangerous elements, cleansing was required whether the insurgency itself had continued or not.

Defining its task as excising malignant elements from the population led the Soviet state to apply different measures than if the goal had simply been to enforce obedience and order upon a territory. The goal was not just to secure obedience and order but explicitly "to cleanse" (*ochishchenie, chistka, ochistit'*) the population of pernicious threats, to secure its full health and recovery (*polnoe ozdorovlenie*). It is in this light that one must see Soviet orders insisting that "we must strive by all means at our disposal: 1) to capture all those individuals who have participated directly in bands and to capture those who have offered any aid to individual bands, and 2) then mercilessly eliminate a portion of them and settle the remainder beyond the boundaries of the territory"; or to execute all insurgents except the lowest rank and file, who were to be exiled from infected regions with their families.[43] Thus the goal of these anti-insurgency measures was not simply to pacify territories but to secure the proper condition of the population either by physically removing or simply exterminating "harmful elements." And similar policies, albeit at a lower intensity, continued to be conducted throughout the supposedly benign New Economic Policy (NEP) years of the 1920s.[44]

The drive to identify and then to remove "harmful elements" was not limited to antibandit operations. As Soviet forces prepared in 1920 to storm the last stronghold of the Whites in the Crimea, Stalin informed Trotsky that an order would soon be issued directing the "total extermination of the Wrangelite [General Peter Wrangel commanded the last anti-Bolshevik army, operating out of the Crimean Peninsula] officer corps." After the Red Army had seized this last base of the White movement, Soviet authorities secretly awarded one Bolshevik "hygienist" the Order of the Red Banner for (in the words of the commendation) "having cleansed the Crimean peninsula of White officers and counter-intelligence agents who had been left behind, removing up to thirty governors, fifty generals, more than three hundred colonels and as many counter-intelligence agents, for a total of up to twelve thousand of the White element."[45] This frantic search for the "officer element" within the Soviet population would continue for several decades.[46]

Nor was this process of "cleansing" limited to the fields of battle. Indeed, "questions of purity plagued the Party throughout the mid-1920s and the battles for power within it were fought along a discursive axis preoccupied with corruption," leading the Party to operate with a particular "inoculatory logic."[47] At the close of the civil war, Soviet authorities pursued a systematic "filtering" of unreliable elements from the population. As the military threat receded and the NEP was being introduced, the Bolsheviks had dispatched all potentially harmful elements to concentration camps. These camps cannot be understood merely as detention points for suspects or holding pens for enemies. For an explicitly self-styled Marxist regime, they were a space where those who were redeemable could be reformed through labor.[48] But the camps served equally as a "filter," a space where those who could be redeemed through collective labor were separated out from those who were incorrigible and resistant to labor's ameliorative effects. Suspect elements were removed from the general population while their true nature was determined in the camps through a detailed hermeneutics of the self. Nor were these camps a minor affair. Orel Province had four camps intended not only for compulsory labor but also for the filtration of suspects. In the course of four months, over thirty-five thousand individuals passed through Orel camp #1 alone.[49] The Moscow Cheka (the Soviet secret police agency, predecessor of the KGB) devoted itself to "the massive work in filtering out the enormous numbers of White Guard prisoners," processing twenty thousand White officers just in the summer of 1920.[50]

It is no exaggeration to describe the filtration process as a detailed hermeneutics of individual selves. All students at the Soviet Petrograd Naval Academy were required to present themselves before a filtration commission in August 1921.[51] The commission interviewed each person individually and then divided the entire academy into groups of twenty-five. Andrei P. Belobrov was one of the elements to be filtered. After the initial interview, his group was transported by train to Moscow. (Given the dismal state of Soviet transport at the time, the use of a train for this purpose represented a major resource allocation.) From Moscow this group was then transferred (again, by train) to Vladimir-on-Kliazma, where the suspects were interred in a concentration camp. Three months later, after intermittent interrogations, Belobrov was taken individually to Moscow, where he was photographed and fingerprinted at the central secret police prison, the Lubianka. From there he was deposited in a "political isolator" in Moscow, where he remained until December. At that time he was again summoned to the Lubianka, where he was required to write a detailed autobiography, and again returned to the "isolator." He was summoned back to the Lubianka in February 1922, where he was issued a slip instructing him to present himself to Red Fleet headquarters for further assignment. Belobrov had successfully passed through the filtration. The entire process of hermeneutic probing so as to determine the true nature of this one man had required six months.

Belobrov was fortunate to emerge from the process of filtration. With the civil war already won, the regime was busy discarding all that had been trapped by its politicosocial filters. In early 1920, the Soviets captured and filtered Vasilii Khripunov and his two sons, all three of whom had served as officers in the anti-Soviet Don Army. The Soviets executed Vasilii but dispatched his two sons, via Ekaterinodar and Moscow, to a concentration camp in Tula, from whence they were soon released. (However, due to this blemish in their records, both of Vasilii's sons were executed in 1937.)[52]

One of the most revealing accounts on filtration comes from comrade Rychkov, the head of the Tambov concentration camp, to a July 1921 closed gathering of Party members who had just participated in suppressing the Antonov insurgency. Rychkov insisted that "we must reeducate [the former 'bandits'] so that we can release them as conscious individuals." Other Party members chided him for coddling his charges by setting up plays and choral societies and demanded instead that "one should eliminate the enemy . . . shoot them—period!" Rychkov responded:

> That is an entirely incorrect error, we've heard it repeatedly. It wouldn't take long to shoot them—unlike the bandits, we'd have enough cartridges. But to turn our recent, inveterate enemies into good, strong friends—that's what we need to do. Of course, if any barons or other wealthy sorts ended up there, they'd soon be a head shorter. Also, if a fervent, murdering bandit does not respond to political enlightenment, insists on his own way, his song won't last very long. But we must have an absolutely different approach for those who fell into error and deeply repent. Not for nothing did we, on orders from above, release an entire echelon back to their homes. . . . No, we destroy some, others—those who are able—we reeducate, turn to our side. Such are the conclusions we've come to in our camp.[53]

Rychkov strenuously insisted on the camp's corrective rather than exclusively punitive functions before a closed Party gathering packed with those demanding merciless vengeance. Yet his account also reveals the obverse of this corrective policy: the camp was intended to winnow out those who were redeemable from those who were not. Those detainees determined to be incorrigible were slated for destruction ("we destroy some"). This policy was not limited to the Tambov camps. In March and April 1921, just as the NEP was being introduced, over 540 officers were executed in the Arkhangel'sk concentration camp alone.[54] As a result of this assiduous filtering, one scholar estimates, Soviet power executed over twenty-five thousand people in the eighteen months following the end of the civil war.[55]

These examples from the civil war and early 1920s demonstrate that the project of fashioning society by excising particular "elements" was an intrinsic aspect of Soviet power from the very first. To be sure, repression in the 1920s, during the NEP, was obviously much different than repression in the later paroxysms of interwar state violence, most notably those of 1929–33 and 1937–38. Violence in these "hot" periods was distinct both in its extent and in its lethality. However, the violence during these years was not so much an anomaly in Soviet history as it represented conjunctures of perceived political and geostrategic crisis when the Soviet state massively extended the logic of existing practices, overriding any previous constraints.[56] Indeed, violence during the NEP, although not as extensive or lethal as earlier, during the civil war, or in later instances, was nevertheless a prevalent feature of the time.[57]

The better-known and more widely practiced applications of state violence of the late 1920s and 1930s operated within the same conceptual framework, that of excising malignant "elements" in order to safeguard the rest of society. Indeed, the arrests and executions in 1937–38 often proceeded according to lists drawn up during the 1920s, some as early as 1920–21. To be sure, in the later period the targeted "elements" comprised a much larger portion of the population, and the proportion of those deemed incorrigible (and hence subject to execution) was incomparably higher, particularly in 1937–38.[58] But the later policies represented the extension and expansion of preexisting ways of viewing and acting upon the politicosocial body. (For the continuation of this endeavor in the postwar period, see Amir Weiner's contribution to this volume.)[59]

Seen in this light, the 1929–30 dekulakization campaign represents no anomalous shift in Soviet policy but rather the conjuncture at which the regime sought to implement existing aspirations to practice "social prophylaxis" (Solzhenitsyn) and "prophylactic cleansing" (Molotov). Soviet directives on dekulakization proclaimed the campaign's goal to be "to cleanse the collective farms from kulak and other counterrevolutionary elements" and "to cleanse the farms of the elements that are infecting them."[60] A March 15, 1931, OGPU (successor to the Cheka) "Memorandum on conducting the mass expulsion of dekulakized peasants" stated forthrightly that the goal of deportation from all regions was "*to totally cleanse [them] of kulaks*."[61] And the measures used to secure dekulakization replicated those employed earlier in de-Cossackization and especially in antibandit operations. Indeed, one can view dekulakization as an all-encompassing, unionwide antibandit operation.[62]

As with the earlier bandit and counterrevolutionary "elements," kulak elements were identified within the general population and then further disaggregated into the more and the less harmful. The February 2, 1930, OGPU directive no. 4421 on dekulakization identified, within its three categories of kulak, two classes of kulak within the first category and sanctioned different measures for each group. As in earlier antibandit operations, the most harmful category was to be "immediately liquidated." Soviet activists declared that "We will exile the kulak by the thousands and when necessary—shoot the kulak breed"; "we will make soap of the kulaks"; and "Our class enemy must be wiped off the face of the earth." This was not mere rhetoric. More than twenty thousand individuals were sentenced to death in 1930 alone, and this figure covers only those tried by the OGPU.[63] The remaining, "less harmful" category was deported from their home regions, whether merely from their districts or to distant "corrective-labor colonies" and "special settlements." And when they arrived at their places of detention, kulaks were again filtered. Immediately upon their arrival in Magnitogorsk, dekulakized peasants "were interviewed extensively for their biography, which was thought to be an indication of the degree of danger they posed."[64]

Thus the Soviet state's "Great Terror," can be viewed as expanding upon existing aspirations and even practices. The infamous Soviet "mass operations" of this period were again directed against "elements," this time "anti-Soviet," "counterrevolutionary," and "socially alien." As geopolitical tensions increased and Bolshevik eschatology pointed toward the "final, decisive struggle" promised by the "Internationale" (sung ritualistically at Party gatherings), the February–March 1937 Party plenum devoted particular attention to the supposed presence of a great number of "anti-Soviet elements" in the politicosocial body.[65] Consequently, the Politburo passed the July 2, 1937, resolution "Concerning Anti-Soviet Elements," a concern directly addressed by NKVD (successor of both the Cheka and OGPU) order no. 00447 of July 30, 1937.[66] This order, framing the most massive of the "mass operations," listed nine target populations (e.g., former kulaks, socially alien elements, former members of anti-Soviet parties, former priests, recidivist criminals) and divided them into two categories:

> To the first category belong all of the most hostile of these elements. They are to be subject to immediate arrest and are to be shot upon examination. . . . to the second category belong the remaining less active but nevertheless hostile elements. They are subject to immediate arrest and detention in camps for a period of 8–10 years, and the most malicious and socially dangerous are to be held in prisons for that period.

NKVD Order no. 00447 specified regional quotas for each category, decreeing 259,450 arrests, of whom 72,950 were to be shot, a total comprising well over 10 percent of all those executed during 1937–38. And the regional list was incomplete, because the quotas omitted a number of regions. In any case, from late August to mid-December 1937 the Politburo, at the request of local authorities, sanctioned increases in the totals for execution by a further 16,800 people.[67]

As should now be clear, the oft-drawn distinction between "purges" (*chistki*) as a purely administrative practice limited to Party members and a "Terror" that swirled among the general populace only in 1937–38 is untenable.[68] Indeed, the very term *terror* seems not to have been employed by the historical actors at the time. (Not that Bolsheviks were opposed to the term:

they employed it self-consciously and extensively in the civil war.) Instead, the Soviets proclaimed that they were "cleansing" society, protecting it through the use of the "supreme measure of social defense"—execution. Thus the various Party purges were only one aspect of the overarching drive to cleanse the entire politicosocial body, both within the Party as well as outside it. Indeed, the vast majority of victims in the years 1937–38 were not Party members or state officials.[69]

The argument that Bolshevik applications of state violence sought to eliminate classes but not people is clearly wrong. Soviet attempts to eliminate classes meant the very real, intentional and physical elimination of individuals. Although their category was primarily class, Marxists too spoke of degeneracy and the need to improve the population.[70] But the Soviet project was not simply to excise and eliminate; it was to do so in order to realize an idealized image of the politicosocial body, of the People-as-One. How did the Soviets know what that was to be, and who did and did not belong?

The Human Archive: Of Each and All

"Two new devices for political organization and rule over foreign peoples were discovered during the first decades of imperialism. One was race as a principle of the body politic, and the other bureaucracy as a principle of foreign domination. . . . Both discoveries were actually made on the dark continent."[71] Arendt's observation has been solidly demonstrated by a wealth of literature on colonial rule and domination.[72] Such "colonial" techniques then became embedded within the practices of the colonizing states and became increasingly deployed within Europe as well.[73]

Race, however, is not the only all-encompassing macrocategory through which populations can be refracted. Class is another axis for aligning and explaining the social world, and it too purports to be universal truth. Both nationalism and socialism can thus be seen as the playing out of a more general tendency to homogenize polities, one on a national, the other on a class axis. If race and bureaucracy came powerfully together in the nineteenth century in Africa and India, in the twentieth century class and bureaucracy intertwined on the Eurasian land mass, in the Soviet Union.[74] The social field had emerged in the nineteenth century; in the early twentieth century, a state for the first time sought to catalog and then act upon a specifically socialist vision of it.

Using the prism of Marxist analysis, the Soviet regime attempted to map its politicosocial body in toto and situate every single individual component part of it. In so doing, the Soviet state sought not only to compile a vast human archive but then to act upon its human material (again, in aggregate and individually).[75] These practices strove to make the individual and the collective politicosocial body intersect—here was the place where Lefort's People-as-One was forged out of concrete individuals. But in this attempt to correlate an increasing individualization with the reinforcement of totality, the Soviet project is not some anomaly but rather a particular playing out of the principles of modern political rationality.[76]

Through its censuses, through discriminatory legislation, through its ubiquitous detailed questionnaires, the Soviet state sought to know and order the world.[77] And this world was sculpted along the lines of Marxist analysis. From the very first years of the regime, authorities determined each and every person's "social background" and on this basis assigned each of them a place in their ordering of the politicosocial body.[78] The censuses of 1926, 1937, and 1939—each accompanied by a press campaign promoting it as an event of vital politicosocial importance—delineated the boundaries and constitution of the Socialist polity, a polity constituted by its individual component parts (hence the census).[79]

The "passportization" of the population was the most intrusive and effective device for cataloging the population and impressing upon each and every individual the proper station within the newly emerging socialist society. In the midst of the civil war, Emmanuil Enchmen had (in a pamphlet published under Party auspices) proposed that "the communist society of the future will be founded on a system of 'physiological passports' for all human organisms," which were to serve simultaneously as a type of ration card for consumption and to determine the amount of joy its holder was to have.[80] Although Enchmen's proposal for physiological passports now strikes us as bizarre, German health officials in the early 1920s actually instituted a system of "health passports" and worked on "pyscho-biograms" for relating the population's physical and mental qualities.[81] And though Bukharin criticized Enchmen's proposal as excessively biologistic, Bukharin himself (elaborating on August Bebel and European socialist thought in general) entertained plans in the same period for statistical bureaus to regulate the work of everybody in the new Socialist state.[82] In the course of the civil war the Soviet state implemented a form of passport system—labor books—that encompassed aspects of both Enchmen's passport ideal and Bukharin's enthusiasm for work bureaus.[83]

Labor books passed with the end of the civil war. It was not until 1932 that the Soviet state moved to realize a more total "passportization" of the population. Scholars have noted that a primary object of passportization was the regime's desire, in the wake of collectivization and the ensuing famine, to keep starving peasants on the land and out of the cities.[84] Alongside this task, the passport legislation was explicitly intended "to cleanse" the newly emerging socialist spaces (new cities, constructions sites, worker dormitories) by distinguishing authentic citizens from those elements polluting the pristine new areas. The decree setting out the new passport system justified its introduction by invoking the need "to cleanse these populated points from kulak, criminal and other anti-Bolshevik elements who are hiding there." An accompanying editorial elaborated that a major goal was "to cleanse, to deport these parasitic elements from our cities, building areas, and workers' settlements" and that "the passport system is designed to help the immediate cleansing of these anti-Bolshevik elements from the cities."[85] And it was in precisely these terms that Soviet citizens understood passportization. As passports were introduced to Moscow, Stepan Podlubnyi, the son of a dekulakized peasant, who had moved from Ukraine to Moscow under false documents, confided to his diary that only a miracle could save him from identification and expulsion. Yet he commented with evident approval that "not only institutions, but also the population follows this work with suspense. . . . All in all, [passportization] is a sorting out, the newest model of a human cleansing machine" (*v obshchem, sortirovka, liudechistil'ka noveishei konstruktsii*). (Despite his reservations, Podlubnyi survived this round of "sorting," although the OGPU soon after revealed that it knew of his true background.)[86]

As Podlubnyi himself suggested, passportization was intended to identify "socially harmful and socially dangerous elements" and to facilitate their surreptitious marking and excision. The government established secret bureaus, the purpose of which was to register "the kulak, criminal and all other anti-Bolshevik element" and aid in their removal.[87] According to records of the militia, more than 6.6 million passports had been issued in Moscow and ten other major cities through April 1933. Yet another 265,000 people had been denied passports, among whom the militia had identified over 67,000 "kulaks in flight and dekulakized individuals"; nearly 22,000 individuals whose civic rights had been revoked (*lishentsy*); and 34,800 individuals "not occupied in socially useful labor"—all of whom were subsequently subject to expulsion.[88]

By 1934, passportization had encompassed more than twenty-seven million people in the Russian Federation alone. Of these, Soviet authorities had refused passports to nearly 400,000 as "criminal and socially alien elements."[89] Thus compiling a human archive correlated individual bodies within the larger politico-social body and facilitated the application of violence as technique by identifying those "elements" against whom violence (as either forcible deportation or outright execution) was to be directed.

In addition, these passports served as devices for impressing the state's matrix of meaning upon citizens, for fashioning each one individually as a socialist citizen. Both Rogers Brubaker and Fran Hirsch argue that censuses and especially passports played a critical role in fostering a sense of personal nationality among Soviet citizens by forcing individuals to proclaim a national affiliation and thus fit themselves within a national grid.[90] Such devices created a highly ideologized matrix within which individuals operated.

The cataloging project enforced a new and powerful correlation between individual images and the imagined collective ideal. Photographic representations were inextricably intertwined with sociological profiles as individuals were cataloged into the People-as-One.[91] Carrying over the Bertillon cataloging system from the imperial regime, Soviet dossiers on "criminal elements" and "enemies of the people" integrated photographs and autobiographical expostulations alongside sociological data keyed to the master class grid.[92] For some, this linkage extended to their very last hour and even after death. Execution lists in Leningrad for 1937–38 instructed executioners that upon taking possession of their charges at the prison, they were to interrogate each of the condemned, and to check each against his or her photo card, and only then to shoot them.[93] For their human archive, the Gulag administration supplemented the Bertillon system of photographs with the fingerprint system devised by Sir Francis Galton: the identity of some dead detainees was confirmed through postmortem fingerprints.[94]

The link between the particular and the universal, the intertwining of an individual self and the politicosocial body, was not reserved solely for criminals. The attempt to correlate individual life trajectories with that of the Soviet politicosocial body explains the format of the ubiquitous questionnaires the Soviet state required its citizens to fill out. Such forms asked for one's social and economic standing at significant moments in Soviet society's trajectory: prior to February 1917; prior to October 1917; before and after collectivization.[95] In October 1937, the Soviet state introduced photographs to its internal passports (with a second photograph retained for the police's shadow archive), thereby adding the individual's image to the sociological profiles contained in their internal passports.[96] Here the macrodescription of a healthy and beautiful society (recall the justification for introducing passports) intersected with individual likenesses. Passports, criminal dossiers, and workbooks simultaneously portrayed individuals while constituting them within the idealized projection of the socialist People-as-One.

This cataloging of individuals was central not only to situating them within the idealized Bolshevik image of society but also to the deletion of those who failed to correspond to this image. Although the exact timing of arrest, and the precise charges filed, depended on particular conjunctures, the individuals targeted for arrest and elimination had been identified long before through the cataloging process. This process had already begun with the 1921 filtration campaign and continued throughout the 1920s and 1930s.[97]

In the USSR, as throughout Europe, the human archive came to play a major role in identifying the specific individuals against whom state violence was to be directed.[98] In 1927, Mikhail N. Pokrovskii had proclaimed that "the archives' role is particularly great as a kind of arsenal, from which one can take those weapons that one uses until the moment one comes to use weapons of iron and steel."[99] One archival official elaborated upon this point in 1931, declaring proudly that one of the archives' functions was to cooperate with Soviet repressive organs. This task became nearly the sole pursuit of the archivists in the 1930s.[100]

How could archivists help the Soviet state? By compiling card indexes. In 1927, a secret decree from the archival administration ordered employees in the Central State Archive to maintain card files on individuals identified in the holdings of the tsarist police. Two years later, the northern bureau of the Party's history section, in collaboration with the local state archival department, combed through the collections of the regional tsarist gendarme agency and the holdings of the regional anti-Soviet government from the civil war. From lists of commendations, transfer orders, and pay scales in the archive, they drew up a card file of twenty-five thousand individuals.[101]

And, as state violence intensified in the 1930s, archival information was in even greater demand. From the mid-1930s archives contained special sections that were staffed exclusively by OGPU employees. But the wave of requests for information that followed Sergei Mironovich Kirov's death in 1934 was so great that it swamped the OGPU workers, requiring them to work twelve- to fourteen-hour shifts, prompting the Party to mobilize student Communists and Communist pensioners for work in the archives. By 1937, archivists were instructed to respond only to the NKVD, to which the archival system was totally subordinated in 1938.[102] By the late 1930s, thirty archivists in the Central State Archive and forty in the State Military Archive were charged with the sole task of compiling card catalogs on people identified in the files of White military and civil institutions. By 1938, they had produced a card file with 105,000 names; an expanded search the next year identified a further 500,000 people.[103]

Nor was this information of an antiquarian nature. The NKVD circular ordering the work explained that such searches were necessary to identify "anti-Soviet elements" still living on Soviet territory. In response, the Central State Archive drew up a list of 34,990 "active enemies of the people" and turned it over to the NKVD "for operational realization." Archivists identified 108,694 enemies of the people in 1939. Due to frantic combing through the newly acquired Baltic and Ukrainian archives, and in part also to the archivists at the Central State Archive, who overfulfilled by 100,000 their quota of card files, archivists identified a further 1,399,217 enemies in the following year.[104]

Such operations continued on after the 1930s. In the aftermath of the Second World War, the Soviets seized the Prague Archive, containing holdings deposited in the 1920s and 1930s by the White movements in emigration, and shipped the documents off to Moscow. There they were winnowed for "use in the operational work of the Interior Ministry and the Ministry of State Security." An extensive card file on the Russian emigration was compiled on the basis of these archival collections. For this very reason, these collections are among the most professionally organized in the former Soviet archival system.[105]

It was these preexisting card indexes and lists that served as the reservoir for arrests and executions upon demand from Moscow. Local organs of the NKVD had files encompassing 10 to 15 percent of the total adult population, usually broken down into three categories of perniciousness. (Both the 1930 OGPU dekulakization directive and the 1937 NKVD order on "anti-Soviet elements" divided their target populations into two categories of "more" and "less harmful," with the more harmful slated for execution.) When local officials received orders from the Center for arrests and executions, they simply worked off such lists. If the quota exhausted the first list, they simply moved onto the second list and then the third.[106]

For its campaign against anti-Soviet elements (as per NKVD order no. 00447), the most massive of the mass operations, the Soviet state relied upon its human archive. Two weeks before the operation commenced, local NKVD branches received an order "to register and classify all hostile and anti-Soviet elements according to their degree of activity and social danger," who were then further subdivided into two categories: those to be executed and those to be exiled.[107] State security organs then proceeded with this operation on the basis of the NKVD's card files. Only after these files had been exhausted did the NKVD resort to sweeps of marketplaces and the fabrication of counterrevolutionary organizations.[108]

The Soviet cataloging venture was inextricably linked to the larger project of sculpting an aestheticized politicosocial ideal. Violence-as-technique required a mapping of the politicosocial body, to indicate what was to be preserved and what was to be eliminated; the cataloging of society did precisely this. In doing so, it united the images of the individual (both visual and narrative) with that of the politicosocial body. This linkage forged in a dossier often outlasted the actual individual. The Soviet regime retained its mountains of documentation on those it had excised from the politicosocial body for decades after the individuals so documented had been executed.

The Axis of Universality: Sociological Versus Biological Paradigms

Clearly, the Soviet state's use of violence as technique shares much in common with the practices of Nazi Germany. Many of the reasons traditionally invoked to distinguish Soviet and Nazi violence now seem untenable: that the Soviets sought "only to industrialize" rather than sculpt society; or that the Soviet use of violence was the product only of Stalin's paranoia, or some contingent political disequilibrium. Both regimes employed violence to shape society according to some idealized image; both invoked a medicalized language to describe their eliminative project as prophylactic; and both relied on an extensive cataloging project to correlate individuals with the larger corporate body and as a tool to sculpt the corporate body both by addition and by elimination. Even some of the target populations were identical, most notably, "career criminals" and social enemies ("asocial" in Nazi Germany and "socially alien elements" in the USSR).[109]

Yet, although both systems share a common morphology, it would be nihilistic and ahistorical to present the two regimes as fundamentally identical. The criteria traditionally advanced are unsatisfactory, but there nevertheless remain critical differences in the operations of these specific concretizations of totalitarianism.[110] Most critically, the central role that the physical elimination of the Jews played in the Nazi program has no analogue in the Soviet project. Although the Soviets sanctioned the removal of "anti-Soviet elements" and "liquidation of classes" as essential to building socialism, they did not imbue it with the metaphysical and positive significance the Nazis did to the extermination of the Jews.[111] Additionally, if the Nazis sought, as is classically defined, (1) the total physical elimination (2) of an entire race (3) by industrial means, the Soviets differed on all three counts. While not averse to killing people, the Soviets did not see their task as intrinsically related to the total physical annihilation of a particular group. Second, even when they targeted specific groups, they required the elimination only of those who had been incorrigibly shaped by their sociological background (see below) rather than the outright physical elimination of every living being in that category. Finally, the Soviets did not engage in industrial killing. In short, if

Nazism was both necessary and sufficient cause for the extermination of the Jews, Soviet Socialism was a necessary but not sufficient condition for an ongoing project of mass extermination. In the face of this comparison, "we must keep in view a crucial *analytical* contrast: there is a difference between regimes that exterminate people in the inhuman pursuit of an arbitrary objective and those whose objective is extermination itself."[112]

Lefort insists that we attend to how the particular principles of legitimacy and ways of apprehending reality inform the idealized image that totalitarian regimes seek to realize.[113] That the axis of definition in the Soviet Union was class rather than race, and that the scientific discipline that served as its discovery procedure was sociology rather than biology, does not make the USSR less totalitarian than Nazi Germany. But it does mean that it operated in significantly different ways.

The historical actors themselves distinguished between the different scientific models for apprehending the politicosocial body. In the midst of the 1919 de-Cossackization campaign, its opponents within the Party denounced it not for its violence but because this violence was not deployed "within the parameters of class struggle" and had thus "degenerated into an amorphous zoological struggle." Valentin Trifonov, a plenipotentiary dispatched from Moscow, similarly condemned the policy—not because it was violent but because it was being conducted in a "non-Marxist" fashion.[114]

Several years later, in a popular textbook on historical materialism, Bukharin elaborated on the proper tools for a Marxist analysis of society:

> Among the social sciences there are two important sciences that examine not individual arenas of social life but all social life in all its complexity; in other words, they don't take one series of phenomena . . . but study society's entire life in its entirety [*sic*]. . . . Such sciences are *history* on the one hand and *sociology* on the other. . . . Since sociology clarifies the general laws of human development, it serves as the *method* for history. . . . The working class has its own, proletarian sociology, known as *historical materialism*. . . . With the help of [historical materialism], the proletariat navigates the most knotty issues of social life and class struggle. With its help, Communists correctly foresaw the war, the revolution, the dictatorship of the proletariat and the conduct of various parties, groups and classes in the great transformation, which humanity is now experiencing.[115]

The sociological method extended far beyond textbooks, for it was used not only to "navigate" but to define the class struggle. The Gorky volume on the Belomor Canal project—the first great Soviet "corrective labor" project—emphasized repeatedly "that there are no inveterate criminals, no inveterate rascals, but there were once abominable and odious circumstances which manufactured criminals." Consequently, the volume ridiculed Cesare Lombroso's notion—portrayed as representative of capitalist penal policy—that there existed "inborn criminals."[116] This Lamarckian predisposition helps explain the prominence of Nikolai Marr's ideas in the early 1930s and Trofim Lysenko's in the postwar period.[117]

Even prior to the Russian Revolution, the more virulent strands of biologistic and racialist thought had difficulty finding a firm purchase in Russian culture and Russian professional disciplines. Although of course not entirely immune to such paradigms, "biological theories of social and sexual deviance . . . seem to have encountered strong cultural resistance as they crossed the [Russian] national divide." In Russia, even the advocates of Lombroso's methodologies "tended to emphasize the interaction between biology and society rather than the absolute priority of biology, and to stress social policy initiatives rather than the isolation and treatment of the delinquent as the most effective response to crime."[118] (This disciplinary tradition was significant, for many prerevolutionary specialists in the social disciplines, such as the leading psychologist Vladimir Bekhterev, continued to shape their disciplines into the Soviet period, and many indeed embraced Soviet power.) Even in regard to Jews, the most virulent forms of *racial* anti-Semitism were much less pronounced in Russia than in Germany or France.[119]

With the rise of the Nazis, the Soviets explicitly contrasted their Marxist-inspired sociological approach to the National Socialists' racial-biological model. Throughout the 1920s and 1930s, Soviet authorities viewed "any suggestion of genetic ('racial') determinism as an attack on the revolution." Soviet physical anthropologists posited that races "existed 'objectively in nature' (not just in people's minds), but their reality was 'superseded' . . . by social groups based on class and ethnicity."[120] Nazi racial science served as an explicit countermodel for Soviet thinking, with even "short stories for children about the [1937] census depict[ing] good Soviet Russia as the antithesis of bad capitalist Germany where people were characterized by an objective assessment of race."[121] Perhaps the most famous expression against biological determinism was Stalin's assertion that "a son does not answer for his father."[122]

In his final written works, composed while in prison awaiting execution, Bukharin returned to the contrast between the Marxist sociological method and the fascist "zoological thinking." "When we speak of an individual, his growth and so on" wrote Bukharin, "we speak not of a *biological* but about a *sociological* category, with a specific 'internal content.'"[123] But perhaps most revealing are Stalin's statements in the midst of the maelstrom of 1937–38. Speaking to members of the military council on June 2, 1937, the day following the arrest of twenty members of that body as plotters (soon to be executed), Kliment Efremovich Voroshilov summoned the officers "to cleanse the army literally to its very last crevices." Stalin then spoke, describing how one could identify the "evil" that was to be "rooted out": "when we speak of nobles as a class that is hostile to the laboring people, we mean a class, an estate or a layer—but that doesn't mean that certain individual persons who are from the nobility can't serve the working class. Lenin was of noble origin. . . . Engels was the son of a factory owner—non-proletarian elements, if you will." But to condemn all nobles and bourgeois as hostile to the working class

> is not a Marxist approach. That, I would say, is a biological approach, not a Marxist one. We don't consider Marxism a biological science, but a sociological one. So these are the general criteria, totally accurate concerning estates, groups, layerings, but inapplicable to individual persons who are of non-proletarian or non-peasant origins. . . . One must judge each individual occurrence by his deeds.[124]

Stalin's elaboration clarifies the oft-noted disjunction between his claim that "the son does not answer for his father" and the continued persecution of "socially alien elements," former officers, former priests, past members of anti-Soviet parties, as well as "former kulaks" and even "former Party members." By this phrase Stalin did not mean, as is frequently interpreted, that one's class and social background was immaterial but that an individual's background alone was insufficient to determine his or her nature. A person's background was significant insofar as it elucidated an individually determined, sociological reading of that subject's life trajectory.[125] This Marxist-inspired sociological method accounts for the immense significance of the Soviet human archive project (with questionnaires invariably inquiring after, and passports indicating, one's "social origin") and the prevalence of archival inquiries. They were intended to correlate individual attitudes with their past actions in order to determine their life trajectories.

If Rudolf Hess proclaimed National Socialism as nothing more than applied biology, one can portray Bolshevism as massively applied Marxist sociology.[126] Instead of a rigid and generic biological evaluation, the sociological paradigm required a reading of each individual's past and its effect on that person's development.[127] Rather than a discovery procedure predicated on race (in which the only question for the individual is whether he or she did or did not biologically belong to the national community), the Soviet regime pursued a discovery technique predicated on the life trajectory of individuals. Marxist sociology presumed it possible to correlate a person's disposition with his or her background—but with the corresponding corollary that one's actions revealed the significant and relevant aspects of one's background.[128] Thus a person's merchant or noble background might or might not be relevant, depending on his or her current disposition and what it suggested about that particular life trajectory.

Whereas National Socialists believed a person's biology determined their biography, in Soviet Russia, Gorky argued, one's biography literally became etched into one's "skin and muscles."[129] Even so, a person's exterior alone never reflected the internal content, which had to be probed by other means. Hence, instead of asking after one's race, Soviet questionnaires inquired after one's social background—but also after one's actions prior to February 1917, in October 1917, and in 1929. Dekulakized peasants at Magnitogorsk underwent selection not on the basis of race or age, but on the basis of their biography. Noncriminal workers were judged not on the basis of supposedly objective racial or national criteria but according to their social origin, political past, and work history.[130] And, whereas National Socialist authorities might retain administrative records on an individual's detention and deportation, they did not engage in the Soviet-style individual hermeneutics for each subject, a practice that often generated literally volumes of information on each particular case.[131] As the previous section demonstrated, the Soviet state kept meticulous card catalogs and lists. But this data was intended to correlate individual backgrounds with subsequent behavior. In the Soviet discovery technique, one's past background in itself was of less significance than the perception that one was covering up or hiding one's past. That failure to be authentic or transparent in the present (as corroborated by materials on one's past life trajectory) was the true sin.[132]

The individual nature of Soviet discovery techniques produced a different form of mass death. The Soviet state interred its victims in mass graves, many of which are now being identified. One in Leningrad contained forty-six thousand victims, forty thousand of whom were shot for political reasons, and a Leningrad city cemetery contains another twenty thousand victims.[133] Often, victims were executed in the prison. But even when shot at mass grave sites, Soviet citizens were executed individually. The Soviets judicially executed millions of people, but at no time did they engage in industrial killing.[134]

And different scientific paradigms also suggested different solutions. The Soviet Marxist sociological paradigm suggested that although some enemies were indeed incorrigible and thus must be eliminated, others were redeemable. Extending a line of Western penal thought, the Bolsheviks divided inmates not according to their crimes so much as according to the dispositions that such crimes revealed, thereby seeking to determine the potentiality of danger lying hidden in the individual and which had been manifested by his everyday conduct.[135] Hence, the Bolshevik judicial inquiry was actually less a test of guilt or innocence but rather an inquest into whether one was redeemable (and hence subject to detention and correction) or incorrigible (and hence subject to elimination).

Thus the Soviets did not believe that an individual was irrevocably tainted by his or her biological composition. (This outlook changed in certain ways in the years following the Second World War: see the contributions of Norman Naimark and Amir Weiner in this volume.) Yet, although the Soviets did not believe individuals were organically malevolent from birth, they believed one could *become* irreparably influenced by one's environment. At times Soviet categories operated in similar ways to deterministic racial categories (the dynamic of ethnic repressions bearing the greatest similarities), but the sociological model did account for significant differences in application of violence. The conviction that some bad elements were correctable through labor explains the fundamental difference between Soviet concentrative labor camps and Nazi camps of industrial killing.[136] Soviet camps were not simply reservoirs of cheap labor, although there was obviously a component of economic exploitation.[137] To help cure people of bad sociological influences in their past, Soviet authorities practiced "political enlightenment" in their camps. Although the political enlightenment departments were chronically underfunded, the library of the Belomor camp system in Karelia nevertheless had over 300,000 books valued at over 500,000 rubles. The state then periodically released individuals "cured" through the ameliorative effect of labor—as Gorky put it, the "healthifying of socially sick and dangerous individuals."[138] This Soviet emphasis on sociological influence rather than biological pollution likewise explains Soviet decrees sanctioning the arrest and preventative-ameliorative detention of wives and children of enemies of the people. They had been sociologically influenced but (because "being determines consciousness") could be redeemed. Children were removed from their parents, but rather than being deposited in labor camps or shot, they were raised in NKVD orphanages.[139]

The Soviet persecution of people as "individual occurrences" also created very different possibilities for survivors or the relatives of victims (or, as some would have it, different avenues for working through trauma). First, unlike those deported and exterminated by the Nazis en masse, Soviet citizens were able to appeal and to contest specific judicial or even extrajudicial rulings on themselves or their relatives *as individuals*. And such appeals were filed by the hundreds of thousands from the 1950s on (there were over 600,000 appeals in 1956–57 alone).[140]

This difference in forms of persecution also produces different possibilities for commemoration. In post-Soviet Russia a new genre has developed to commemorate the "victims of Stalinist repression": memory books (*knigi pamiati*), books of often several volumes that list each victim by name, place of origin, charge, and date of sentencing and execution.[141] One unfortunate, if unintentional, consequence of this form of commemoration is that it continues to situate the victims entirely within the matrix of Soviet prosecution. Even their titles echo Soviet administrative parlance: one, titled *Not to be forgotten* (*Ne podlezhit zabveniiu*), is a play on the prevalent Soviet administrative terms for documents from the period—"Not to be announced" and "Not to be destroyed" (*Ne podlezhit oglasheniiu, Ne podlezhit unichtozheniiu*). In short, the individual, even in commemoration, has become coterminous with his or her dossier. Others protest the involvement of the Federal Counterintelligence Service—the KGB's successor—in the memory book project.[142] Nevertheless, the Soviet human archive project and sociological disposition for individual forms of investigation and punishment create greater possibilities for Anna Akhmatova's appeal (from her *Requiem*) "to recall them all by name." Thanks to the Soviet propensity for documenting and photographing individual victims, from December 1990 the newspaper *Vecherniaia Moskva* could publish a weekly column of photographs with short biographical sketches of the victims.[143]

This chapter has sketched a number of points. First, it has suggested that the Nazi and Soviet regimes, pace treatments by historians both of Soviet Russia and National Socialist Germany, benefit from a comparative treatment as totalitarian projects. Second, it has proposed that although Bolshevism as ideology was critical for determining how state violence was to be applied, state violence did not originate with the Bolsheviks. In significant ways, the Bolsheviks expanded upon state practices developed in the late imperial period and massively implemented in the First World War. Third, it has argued that the Soviet regime's application of state violence is better understood as a fundamentally aesthetic project to sculpt an idealized image of the politicosocial body rather than as a narrowly understood medicoprophylactic pursuit. Fourth, this endeavor of sculpting society was essential to Soviet policy from the very first; the Great Terror of the 1930s was an extension and expansion of this aspiration, the conjuncture when the regime sought to act on long-standing goals to sculpt society's human as much as its raw material. Fifth, the regime's drive to order and classify its population was central to its larger endeavor of creating a beautiful and pure society by enforcing criteria of excision as well as inclusion. And this chapter has concluded by arguing that although the oft-invoked criteria for distinguishing Soviet and National Socialist violence are questionable, there remain critical differences in each regime's concretization of the totalitarian project. While sanctioning mass violence, the Soviet regime never set the extermination of people as an objective in itself. Specifically, in contrast to the National Socialist regime's biological-racial standard, the Soviet regime employed a fundamentally sociological paradigm to key individual experience to its universal class matrix. Among other significant consequences, this sociological paradigm resulted in an individualized reading of subjects' lives, an attempt to determine how unique constellations of past events influenced individual subjectivities. This sociological discovery technique did not make the Soviet Union any less totalitarian, but it accounts for significant differences in the application of Soviet state violence.

ELISABETH DOMANSKY 2

The Transformation of State and Society in World War I Germany

WORLD WAR I was neither the first world war nor the first total war in history. It was, however, the first total war between industrialized nations. At war with each other were not—as during the cabinet wars of the eighteenth and nineteenth centuries—individual states; rather, whole societies mobilized against each other.[1] This combination of the industrialization and "socialization" of warfare produced violence, death, and destruction on a theretofore unprecedented quantitative and qualitative scale. Worldwide, nine million soldiers died, and another eighteen million were wounded.[2] A staggering number of those casualties resulted from battles that can only be described as "industrialized slaughter": The battles of Verdun, the Somme, and Passchendaele each produced hundreds of thousands of casualties within a mere few months.[3] Moreover, these battles continued for weeks and months after it had become evident that their original strategic objectives—decisive breakthroughs—could not be achieved.

This kind of mass slaughter was not the only hallmark of the new type of modern warfare. The novel technique(s) of war also provided a new rationale and, at the same time, new opportunities for waging war against civilian populations. As in numerous previous cases, warfare included not only spontaneous outbursts of violence by individual soldiers but also systematic and well-orchestrated attempts at forcing populations into surrender through starvation or through psychological terror, including atrocities against civilians.[4] In World War I, such maneuvers were, on the one hand, the result of the political and military logic and logistics of a total war that resulted *from* and *in* the collapse of the barrier between the military and civil society. On the other hand and at the same time, these techniques of total war, as I want to argue in this chapter, were subordinated to the logic and logistics of a new type of "population management"[5] and of violence that gradually developed over the course of the nineteenth century. The genocide of the Armenian people in Turkey is certainly one of the most shocking acts of brutality that occurred in World War I.[6] It is also one of the most revealing incidents of the character of this kind of population management that constituted *one* of the characteristic elements of World War I and, later, *the* defining element of the National Socialist war project.

The enormously destructive and, at the same time, deeply transformative nature of World War I resulted in a virtual obsession of almost all postwar societies with "making sense" of that war.[7] This obsession was by no means triggered solely or even mainly by the war's diplomatic, political, social, and economic results. To be sure, empires collapsed, new national states were established in their place, and the boundaries of the global spheres of power were fundamentally redrawn. At the same time, the class, ethnic, and gender structures of major belligerent nations were radically reconstructed.[8] Consequently, the postwar years saw many officially launched projects that aimed at discovering the "causes" of World War I, not least in the interest of establishing—internal or external—"guilt" and justifying the war's political consequences—or the resistance against them.[9] However, there were many more attempts at coming to terms with what had happened *during* the war and with the war's moral and ethical consequences for the psychological makeup of individual human beings, as well as for the social fabric of whole nations. The image of the nineteenth century's "death" on World War I's battlefields is most indicative of the sense of loss, the feeling of shock, and the melancholy but—in some cases—also the hope that pervades the innumerable artistic, literary, religious, philosophical, and spiritual efforts of the postwar years of grasping the meaning of World War I for the new century that was born on that war's battlefields.[10]

These attempts resulted not only from the unfamiliarity of the new postwar order. Nor did they reflect solely the inability to grasp the staggering numbers of those who had been killed and wounded in battle, of those who had died from war crimes and genocide, and of those who had lost their lives at the "home fronts." Rather, almost all postwar societies seem to have been deeply traumatized by the war's revelation of individuals' and societies' capacity for unrestricted violence, unlimited destruction, and, at the same time, the concomitant discovery of the extreme vulnerability of human bodies and souls. Although in some cases the horrors of World War II seem to have buried that discovery under their own weight, the shock waves of World War I's great disillusionment can still be traced in some of the former belligerent nations to this day: in Britain, France, Australia, and Canada writers and filmmakers who were themselves children or adolescents during the Second World War have entered a new phase of "working through" the legacies of the First in the 1980s and 1990s, and Australia even created its own memorial of the "Unknown Soldier" of World War I as late as in 1994.[11]

Historical explanations of World War I's violence and brutality have mostly focused on technical, strategic, and political explanations. The "industrialization" of warfare, including new weapons and their consequences for military strategy and tactics and for the role of the individual soldier, is certainly one of the major components of the escalation of violence during the First World War.[12] So is the—especially during the years of 1914 to 1916—obvious incongruence between the applied nineteenth-century military tactics and the challenge of twentieth-century conditions of mechanized warfare.[13] And coercion and propaganda certainly played an important role in preventing military and civilian resistance against the ongoing slaughter. All these arguments certainly help us understand why states entered World War I with the support of majorities of their societies. They also inform us about the technical and strategic conditions for the escalation of violence. In my opinion, however, they do not suffice to explain why this war could *last* as long as it did. The war's long duration was neither self-evident nor unavoidable.

We have to ask, then, why military commanders, such as Sir Douglas Haig, Joseph Joffre, Erich von Falkenhayn, and Erich Ludendorff; politicians, such as Theodor von Bethmann-Hollweg, David Lloyd George, and Georges Clemenceau; and, moreover, broad sections of the economic and cultural elite of the combatant nations were willing to accept, to justify, and to propagate the breach of international laws as well as the use of unrestricted violence.[14] The German chancellor von Bethmann-Hollweg, for example, openly admitted in the German Reichstag (parliament) in August 1914 that the violation of Belgian neutrality constituted a "wrong."[15] And leading intellectuals and artists as well as numerous anonymous members of the warring societies lent their talents to the cultural battles that contributed to prolonging total war.[16] Technological innovations of weapons systems were by no means limited to the production of firearms. Rather, film and photography turned out to be the technologically most advanced weapons of World War I's cultural operations, and psychological warfare was the new strategy that linked these operations to those on the battlefields at the front.[17]

Moreover, millions of citizens of democratic (and not so democratic) societies were willing to endure and to practice mass and massive violence—and for an astonishingly long time at that. To be sure, opposition movements and protests against the war developed in many of the combatant nations, and military mutiny did not only occur toward the end of the war.[18] However, in all of the belligerent nations there was strong support for the war and for its continuation beyond the bloodbaths of Verdun, the Somme, and Passchendaele. This support cannot be explained by referring solely to coercion or manipulation "from above." Rather, the new levels of morale that were characteristic of the Great War's fronts and home fronts alike resulted from a "mobilization of the imagination"[19] that was an indispensable element of the (self-)mobilization of whole societies against whole societies.

This "mobilization of the imagination" was certainly one of the results of the political and military propaganda efforts that accompanied World War I's escalation into total war. However, those efforts themselves were supported by an astonishing willingness of numerous private and professional organizations to participate in the mobilization of society for the war effort. Among such groups were veterans' organizations, economic interest groups—including the leadership of working-class organizations—professional associations, and patriotic women's organizations.[20] Even these combined propaganda efforts of state and parts of society during the war could hardly have been as effective as they were if the "mobilization of the imagination" had not been under way since the late nineteenth century. This mobilization had many different roots and manifested itself in many different intellectual projects and institutional structures.[21] There can be no doubt, however, that "war"—internal or external war—became a central element of European societies' self-perception and self-production during the second half of the nineteenth century.[22] In this sense, World War I was, or so I would like to argue, a much more ideological war than has been traditionally assumed. I will try to explicate this argument by focusing on Germany without, however, claiming that parts of German society pursued a "special path" in moving war to the center of their social visions and politics long before the First World War took place.

Science, Professionalism, and War

The transition from absolutist states to modern civil society that occurred in Europe over the course of the nineteenth century was a complex and uneven process. A key element of this development was the creation of a distinctive social sphere that was seen as separate from the political and the economic domains. Throughout the nineteenth century—and beyond, as it were—political bureaucrats, legal theorists, and practicing professionals engaged in defining the boundaries between these spheres as well as the rules of their interactions.[23] In this context, various groups in civil society competed with each other as well as with the state about shares of control of the social and, thus, of its relationship with other sectors. These groups often tried to limit the role of the state to simply providing the legal framework that endorsed and guaranteed their own "takeover" of arenas of power that had formerly been the domain of the absolutist state. This project was pursued in a variety of fields, such as in the economic sphere; in education and training; in the spheres of public welfare, public health, and the family; and also in the realms of war and peace.

Increasingly, the legitimating source of such attempts was constructed as stemming from "science" and "professionalism."[24] This discursive shift toward a "culture of scientism" can best be described as growing attempts—of very different political actors and agencies—to reorganize all economic, cultural, social, and political relations on the basis of "applied science."[25] It is this definition of politics as "social engineering" that is, in my view, inextricably linked to World War I's violent transformation of the social body as well as of individual bodies in Germany. In order to illuminate this connection, I would like to discuss two of the arenas in which the shift toward the culture of scientism occurred. These two arenas, which intersected with each other in several important areas while pursuing different paths in others, are population management and the struggle for or against class and gender domination. An examination of both as well as of their interrelatedness may help us understand the connection between violence, science, and modern political culture.

It is well known that toward the end of the nineteenth century ever-growing segments of European societies began to construct links between internal social as well as external national tensions on the one hand, and a perceived decline in their respective national populations on the other. Innumerable books and pamphlets on the issue were published; demographic, eugenics, and "racial hygiene" associations were founded; and their warnings increasingly found the ear of politicians, the military, and the public.[26] Demography, eugenics, and "racial hygiene" became mainstream political concerns for numerous reasons. Among them were changes in the European foreign political system, especially the unification of Germany and of Italy, and the spread of national independence movements, all of which raised or exacerbated fears of quantitative "population decline." Such fears reached particular heights in France—which had indeed had a declining birthrate for a long time—after the defeat in the Franco-Prussian War. In England, the British Army's poor showing in the Boer War raised grave concerns about England's "qualitative" population decline, and in Germany, too, concerns about Germany's capacity for international competition were increasingly linked to its success—or failure—to maintain or regain a qualitatively and quantitatively satisfying birthrate.[27]

Fears of "population decline" were also connected with the growing strength of socialist and feminist movements. Many of the mostly middle-class demographers and eugenicists began to argue that the political power balance in society might be adversely affected by a sheer overproduction of offspring among the lower classes, especially because those offspring were considered to be of "lower quality" than those of the middle class. This situation was exacerbated in such views by "modern" middle-class women's refusal to fulfill their reproductive obligation toward their class. The resulting reproductive imbalance between the lower and the middle classes was seen as having grave consequences for the German nation's "health" or "strength" on which its fighting power (*Wehrkraft*) depended. That fighting power, or lack thereof, guaranteed or jeopardized the nation's capacity to "survive" fierce international competition for resources. Thus, the lower classes' production of too many offspring of "low quality" and modern middle-class women's underproduction of offspring of "high quality" endangered both the middle class's dominant position in society and, therewith, the survival of the nation. These were views that demographers, eugenicists, and racial hygienists shared with military experts.[28]

I would suggest to read such constructs as (re)conceptualizations of the relations between class, gender, and nation; between state and civil society; and between the realms of the social and of the family. First, the "survival" of the nation was depicted as depending on the "survival" of the middle class. That survival, in turn, hinged upon the middle class's capacity for controlling its own women's as well as the lower classes' fertility. Thus, within the framework of such concepts, class struggle as well as gender conflicts were displaced from the sphere of production and transferred to the sphere of (biological) reproduction. This transfer meant that class and gender conflicts were deconstructed as interest conflicts over access to economic and cultural capital between classes and between women and men and, instead, reconstructed as conflicts over individual (reproductive) versus national (security) interests: class and gender wars were turned into internal wars not simply against another class or another gender group but also against the nation.[29]

The biologization of class and gender conflicts that formed the basis of this complex ideological reconstruction process regarding the relations between class, gender, and the nation had a series of consequences. First, it provided new rationales and new tools for fighting class and gender wars: class and gender conflicts *had* to be suppressed in the security interests of the nation, and they *could* be suppressed, albeit not by applying political force but by using "scientific" tools. Thus, this transfer of class as well as gender conflicts from the realm of ("subjective") interest politics to the realm of ("objective") social engineering allowed middle-class men—via their role as "scientific" professionals—to increase their power over the lower classes in general and over middle-class women and families while, at the same time, limiting the state's control of these arenas. Class and gender politics were, in such views, not solely issues of (juridically) "policing" but increasingly also of (medically) "treating" parts of the population. In addition, by linking biological reproduction to the security interests of the nation, reproduction was removed from the *control* of the family—within which it was normally still *performed*—and subjected to that of the social realm, thus, redefining the boundaries between those two.[30]

The simultaneous biologization of class and gender conflicts on the one hand and, on the other, the politicization of biological reproduction brought forth a new image of the nation. The nation turned into a male (middle-class) body whose "manhood" and, therewith, military strength had to be constantly protected from the "degeneration" resulting from declining national fertility rates. Consequently, the nation and its reproductive "defense experts" had to be in a state of constant alert using individual bodies as *tools* as well as *sites* for their operations on the national body. This—actual, not metaphorical—fusion of individual bodies with the national body constructed the relationship between the two as one of (individual) subjugation and (national) domination.[31] Given the dominant gender hierarchy, the nation was, thus, constructed as "man," while individual bodies and the sum total thereof, the population, were constructed as "woman." The fusion of individual bodies with the national body helps explain, in my eyes, why German society was willing to sacrifice so many lives in the interest of maintaining or remaking the national body in World War I.[32] The construction of the population as "woman" helps explain why so many individual *male* bodies could be used up in that war, although male life was traditionally considered to be of higher value than female life. I shall return to these aspects later.

It is obvious that the above-mentioned strategies were, in part, directed against the German bourgeois women's movement. Interestingly, that movement used very similar strategies in order to claim for itself a share in the social power of the middle class while contributing to the overall project of securing the middle class's domination in society. I will sketch out some of women's lines of reasoning in order to explain internal differences and overall similarities in the middle-class project of biologizing class and gender conflicts while politicizing biological reproduction. Far from relying on universal suffrage as the main venue to their share in power within the middle class in particular and in society in general,[33] and far from directly competing with middle-class men in the male public sphere, middle-class women chose to create a separate female public sphere that would be acknowledged as being of equal importance as the male sphere. This was, in part, a tactical move in internal middle-class gender conflicts aiming at pacifying middle-class men. More important, however, this strategy resulted from the convictions that women and men were indeed fundamentally different and that this difference constituted an invaluable source for society's improvement, because many female qualities were actually considered to be superior to those of men. Unlike male demographers and eugenicists whose concepts I have discussed above, members of the bourgeois women's movement argued that women could apply their "natural" faculties of caring, sharing, and nurturing not only within their own families but also in the public professions of healing, education, and social welfare. Motherhood, or so they argued, had not only a biological but also a spiritual component.[34]

This line of reasoning separated women's reproductive work from biological motherhood, a move that constituted an important stepping-stone in women's (bourgeois) emancipation. However, this applied only to middle-class, not to lower-class, women. Although, in theory, women had a choice of becoming (biological) mothers or of becoming spiritual mothers who taught other women the required "know-how" of responsible motherhood, in practice, this choice existed only for middle-class women—provided, of course, that middle-class men would grant them access to some of the same cultural capital (education) that was available to them. This meant that, in actual fact, middle-class women would control lower-class women's reproduction. Thus, middle-class women participated in the project of securing the middle class's position of power over the lower classes. This they tried to do without competing with middle-class men in their (scientific) domains, by linking their own status as "reproduction experts" to their (innate) qualities as spiritual mothers. However, by claiming expert status for women, they redefined the concept of the expert as an authority that could not be constructed as solely "male."

As in the theories of middle-class eugenicists and racial hygienists, such concepts separated women's reproductive work from the control of the family and transferred it, instead, to that of the social realm. By trying to *resolve* gender conflicts within the middle class and to *displace* class conflicts between the lower and the middle classes through the creation of a female sphere of social engineering, bourgeois women also contributed to the ongoing project of limiting the power of the state over the control of the social realm. In addition, they also linked the "survival" of the middle class to that of the nation and the survival of both to internal as well as external war. Biological motherhood and spiritual motherhood were compared to men's military service. This service was to be performed in order to guarantee the defense of the nation. This task, however, was a shared enterprise between men and women: men were to defend the nation against external enemies, while women had to guard the "national body" against internal enemies, that is, physical and moral degeneration.[35]

The image of the nation that emerges from these concepts is also that of a middle-class body. This body, however, is one that possesses male (soldierly virility) as well as female (soldierly motherhood) characteristics. Like their male counterparts, bourgeois women saw this body as one that was, at the same time, endangered and in need of mobilizing its own defenses. Because the national body needed to be remade through the (re)production of healthy individual bodies, this concept also fused both male and female bodies with the national body in a state of permanent mobilization. And the relationship between individual bodies and the national body was constructed as one of domination and subordination. Thus, the national body as well as its defense experts bore male and female traits at the same time, whereas individual bodies and the population were consistently constructed as "woman."

These middle-class reconceptualizations of the relations between class, gender, and nation; between state and civil society; and between the realms of the social and the family were solidly grounded in social Darwinism that moved reproductive competition to the center of the construction of society as well as of global power relations. To be sure, not all members of the middle class subscribed to such views. Catholics certainly embraced this ideology, if at all, to a lesser degree than Protestants, and there were differences between the urban and the rural middle classes as well as between different social strata within the middle class. However, substantial parts of the educated economic, political, and cultural middle-class elite in Germany chose social Darwinism over traditional liberal political theories as the ideology that met their needs during the period of rapid industrialization at the end of the nineteenth century.[36]

Traditional liberal theories could neither explain the continuation of old and the development of new inequalities in society, nor could they justify the bourgeoisie's claim to domination.[37] Social Darwinism, however, could. This ideology not only championed notions of inherited (racial) inequality within a nation and among nations but, at the same time, legitimized attempts by social groups and by societies to use all means to win the struggle that resulted from such inequalities. In addition, social Darwinism could be constructed as a "science" that analyzed "objective" facts rather than constituting a specific (class and gender) interest-oriented interpretation of economic, cultural, political, and social relations. German society's penchant for science endowed social Darwinism with the potential of becoming an ideology that crossed class as well as gender boundaries—which, in fact, it did.[38]

Thus, many German members of the middle class subscribed to and developed an ideology that envisioned society as a national body, that moved biological reproduction and war to the center of the construction of society, and that fused individual bodies with that of the nation. I consider this to be the creation of a totalitarian ideology. It was developed not at the fringes but in the center of modern bourgeois society, and it aimed at creating not a totalitarian *state* but a totalitarian *society*. In this case, totalitarianism was not developed as a countermodel to bourgeois society but as one that secured its claims toward political and cultural domination.[39]

Does all this lead to the conclusion that war was inevitable? Certainly not. There is no such thing as a "semantic logic" that leads automatically from certain ideological constructs to actual political events. However, the widespread acceptance of social Darwinism in German society helps delineate the mental universe within which a *new type of war* was thinkable as well as acceptable.[40] Although the enthusiasm of the "August Days" of welcome for the war belongs in the realm of historical fiction rather than fact, there were definitely not only young (middle-class) men who entertained fantasies about war, manhood, and the regeneration of a "rotten" bourgeois society. Rather, a substantial and influential part of German society greeted World War I as an opportunity to heal the national body by remaking it.[41] However, although the overall climate in German society was certainly conducive to war before 1914, the actual decision for war was made by diplomats and military experts. The question remains, then, whether social Darwinism had also infiltrated their way of thinking.

Until relatively recently, that question seemed to be of little relevance, because most historians believed that the German military succumbed to the "short-war-illusion."[42] Recent research, however, has revealed and continues to reveal more and more evidence showing that this "illusion" belongs in the realm of historical and historiographical myths. Not only a few observers, as conventional wisdom would have it, among them the elder Helmuth von Moltke, Friedrich Engels, and Ivan Bloch, warned about the carnage of a future war; rather, members of the prewar German general staff as well as numerous high-ranking officers, among them the younger Helmuth von Moltke, Falkenhayn, Ludendorff, and Alfred von Tirpitz, were all convinced that a future war would be a long-lasting "war of the people" (*Volkskrieg*) with a rather uncertain outcome.[43] In fact, far from regarding war as a preventive strike against revolutionary tendencies in society, these military experts entertained the thought that a future war might actually *lead* to unrest and revolution and, perhaps, even to the extinction of traditional European culture (*Kultur*).[44] The famous Schlieffen Plan was not seen as the blueprint for a whole (short) war but, rather, as the design for the opening battle of a prolonged war. Moreover, the German general staff seems to have been convinced that Germany was neither economically nor militarily prepared to fight a prolonged "people's war."[45]

Such insights were not limited to high-ranking members of the German military. On the contrary, the military and the general public were very familiar with the lessons of the American Civil War and, above all, the Boer War and the Russo-Japanese War. Consequently, concerns and fears about the nature, the length, and the outcome of a future war were widespread even among those who advocated the inevitability of such a war.[46] How, then, do we explain the fact that the German general staff pressed for a war of such uncertain outcome, was able to convince Germany's political leadership of the necessity of entering such a war, and could even be sure of the support by a majority of the German elite for an enterprise that constituted an incalculable risk?

Germany's political and military leaders decided to go to war for a variety of foreign as well as domestic political reasons, and different parts of German society decided to support that decision for yet other sets of complex motives, most of which have been discussed at great length in the available literature.[47] One of the reasons of politicians and military experts was certainly the attempt to fight a war at a point in time when there was still a chance—miniscule though that may have been—to preserve war as the domain of political experts of strategy and military experts of tactics. In other words, the decision to go to war in 1914 resulted in part from the endeavor to secure the state's monopoly over definitions of the goals and means of warfare and the desire to exclude the social realm from any infringement upon this monopoly: not *although*, but precisely *because* any future war was envisioned to be a "people's war."[48] Falkenhayn's famous statement of August 4, 1914, "Even if we are going to perish because of this, it was nevertheless wonderful,"[49] may be read as an expression of a self-congratulatory attitude of the member of a profession that played a high-risk game in order to maintain its professional status. The statement may also be interpreted as one of the many formulations of the famous "politics of cultural despair" that Fritz Fischer has so eloquently conjured up.[50] In the light of the widespread acceptance of social Darwinist ideas among German military elite, Falkenhayn's words—as well as many similar statements of members of the military profession—may also be viewed as an expression of the conviction that war was inevitable and that its outcome, uncertain though it was, nevertheless bore the potential of renewing the German nation in particular and European culture in general.[51]

The question remains, then, whether the imaginary war that was fought in many people's minds before 1914 had any bearing on the actual war that began in 1914. I will pursue that question in the following section of this chapter.

The Formation of a National Body

Under the law of siege that was decreed with the beginning of war in 1914, civil society was subjugated under the realm of the state and its military authorities. Both, however, were still separate from each other. This situation underwent a radical change in 1916. The ascent to power of the Third Supreme Command under the leadership of Paul von Hindenburg and Ludendorff in that year is usually described as the beginning of a "new age of strategy."[52] Because the preceding two years had shown that the war could not be won without mobilizing all of German society, Hindenburg and Ludendorff gave up the traditional notion of warfare as the realm of military and political "experts." Instead, they chose to incorporate social forces into military strategy. This meant that strategy was no longer a mediating element between the means—determined by military experts—and goals—determined by diplomatic experts—of war. Rather, it now became an "explanation and legitimation for total war."[53]

This new type of strategy resulted in the creation and mobilization of an—actual, not metaphorical—"home front" that was as essential a part of the war effort as was the front.[54] Both operated in separate yet interdependent spheres. Thus, total mobilization of German society dissolved the barrier that had separated the military and civil society throughout the nineteenth century, thereby also ending the relationship of domination and subjugation between wartime state and society. While society became thoroughly militarized, war—previously located exclusively within the state's sphere—became thoroughly socialized. Thus, total war eclipsed the boundaries that had until then separated the political, the social, and the economic domains and radically altered their interactions with other sectors in society. The "military-industrial-complex" that emerged out of the fusion of the economic and political realms, and that found its representation in the image of the "war machine," is certainly one of the best understood aspects of the simultaneous "socialization of warfare" and "militarization of society" that occurred in World War I.[55]

Less clear are the ramifications of the dissolution of the boundaries between the political and the social domains. Historians agree that with the advent of total war, civil society ceased to exist. But so did the state. The characterization of the Third Supreme Command's rule as a "(silent) dictatorship" comes, in my eyes, closest to grasping the nineteenth-century state's demise in World War I.[56] Nevertheless, the term *dictatorship* still connotes a state that—more or less—suppresses a somewhat separate society. However, when the political and the social ceased to exist as separate spheres, or so I would like to suggest, they melted into a new hybrid formation: the sociopolitical realm. This new sphere was, at the same time, materialized and represented as a "national body" at war. Because of the simultaneous fusion of the economic with the political, and the political with the social spheres, the boundaries between the "the war machine" and the "national body" were diffuse. In addition, both continued to exist beyond the war's end.[57]

The emergence of the National Body during World War I had grave consequences for two key institutions of nineteenth-century civil society:[58] the family and the individual. According to liberal nineteenth-century philosophical and legal theory, society was the voluntary association of autonomous (male) individuals, and the family was the institution through which civil society reproduced itself. Because of the relationship between state and civil society—the state providing and guaranteeing civil society's legal foundations—the family was also considered to be the foundation of the state.[59] With the transition from war to total war and the concomitant collapse of the social and political domains, the family lost this function. For a variety of technical as well as historical reasons—prominent among them the existing gender system—total mobilization could not be based on the family unit; rather, it had to destroy it. The National Body reproduced itself through its constant and continuous fusion with individual bodies. This required, as I have argued elsewhere, a rearrangement of the spheres of production, destruction, and reproduction: together, all three of them constituted the center of society's self-organization for total war.[60] Thus, the formation of the National Body constituted German society's first large-scale experiment with totalitarianism. As a result, both the family and the individual lost their autonomy. However, the family's additional loss of its reproductive function vis-à-vis civil society was the individual's gain vis-à-vis the National Body. The mutual fusion of both entailed the simultaneous loss of autonomy and gain of power for the individual. This is, in my eyes, one of the main reasons why total war found so many supporters.

In order to clarify my argument, I would like to point out that precisely because of their key role in state and society neither the individual nor the family had been *completely* autonomous during the nineteenth century. The state regulated property, sexuality, marriage, the relationship between family members, and also children's work and education. At the same time, the economic sphere, too, infringed upon the individual's and the family's autonomy. However, as compared to the absolutist state, the individual and the modern family had gained a high degree of self-control vis-à-vis institutions such as the church, landowners, guilds, and so on.[61] In World War I, this (relative) autonomy was not simply subordinated to the exigencies of industrialized warfare. Rather, it was abolished. The continued existence of marriage as a legal institution or of legally guaranteed private property rights should not make us overlook or underestimate the radically changed frame within which actual individuals and actual families operated, when state and society merged into the National Body. Of course, this change did not affect every individual and every family in the same way. And a substantial part of German society resisted the new sociopolitical formation.[62] However, there was hardly anyone who could escape it—at least as long as the war lasted and in many cases beyond its end. In the following text, I will examine more closely how the National Body was made and remade during World War I.

If we want to understand the simultaneous transformation process of state and society, we have to bear in mind the fundamentally gendered nature of waging total war. Total mobilization dissolved the barrier that had previously separated the public (male) from the private (female) sphere. At the same time, however, total war erected a new boundary between men and women by gendering the war effort into a male combat zone at the front and a female noncombat zone at the home front. Thus, total mobilization of men and women occurred within the overall framework of differently constructed gender camps. The home front itself, in turn, was divided into different camps as well. They, too, were constructed along gender but also along age and ethnic lines. The mobilization of children and young adults, for example, was often organized on a peer group basis and not as part of a familial enterprise.[63] This organization of the war effort had immediate and drastic consequences for individual families as well as for the family as an institution.

In World War I, Germany was among the countries with the highest mobilization rate of its male population: about 80 percent of all men of military age were mobilized. That meant that thirteen million men spent at least some time at the front. About two million of them were killed. Of those two million, one-third had been married. Millions of men were wounded, and close to three million soldiers returned from the war mutilated.[64] Thus, the war literally tore millions of families apart: wives were separated from husbands, children from fathers, parents from sons, and siblings from brothers—some only temporarily, others permanently. Women wearing black made the absence of the fallen and, thereby, the enduring violation of previously intact families most visible during the war and its aftermath. So did organizations representing war widows and orphans in the Weimar Republic.[65]

In similar ways, the war permanently inscribed itself on the bodies and souls of those soldiers who returned from the war mutilated, and, thus, war also marked their families. Women, children, and other relatives had to live with—in some cases severely—disfigured men; with men who—as a result of their loss of limbs—had lost their capacity to provide for their families in the same way as they had before the war; with men who would regularly succumb to bouts of shell shock; or with men who needed constant care. State compensation for disabled veterans, war widows, orphans, and parents notwithstanding, the social costs of war were to a great degree privatized.[66]

This was also true in the case of many of those men who returned from the war physically unharmed and without showing conclusive evidence of what nowadays has come to be called post-traumatic stress disorder.[67] In many families, husbands and fathers did not regain the same kind of authority that they had held before the war, either because they returned as broken men or because the radically different war experiences of front and home front had led to estrangement between family members. However, the war experience could also be the source of a new kind of male authority. Rather than being grounded on men's roles as husbands and fathers in their families, this authority was grounded on men's role as soldiers. The postwar construction of the mythical "community of the trenches" is one of the most palpable indicators of this new foundation of postwar male identity. Friendships with war comrades and membership in veterans' organizations became important channels for this kind of (re)fashioning of male identity after the war.[68] Thus, in many different ways, wartime ties between individual male bodies and the National Body were not completely severed when men returned home but kept, instead, infringing upon individuals as well as on the postwar family.

The economic consequences of the gendered mobilization for war also contributed to the formation of the National Body as a material and, at the same time, representational entity.[69] When men were sent to the front, many families lost their principal breadwinner or a family member who had contributed to the family income. In most cases, this loss could neither be balanced by state compensation payments for soldiers' wives, war widows, and orphans, nor by the wages of women and young adults who moved either into new workplaces or entered the workforce for the first time.[70] As a result, many families, especially of the lower middle class and the working class, immediately experienced a sharp drop in the family income.

This had several consequences. Drastically reduced incomes severely restrained the possibilities of taking care of individual bodies' needs regarding food, shelter, and rest. For a variety of reasons, this situation worsened quite dramatically after 1916.[71] Consequently, the war marked the bodies of those at the home front, too. Women, men, and children lost weight as a result of malnutrition. Many succumbed to, and close to half a million died of, war-related diseases.[72] In addition, malnutrition also caused the cessation of menstruation, and many women found themselves unable to conceive or breastfeed children.[73] Together, malnutrition and lack of sleep led to an increase in work accidents, affecting especially women and young adults. Work conditions in chemical plants could even result in discoloration of hair and skin. Thus, in many ways the National Body swallowed individual bodies at the front and home front alike. From a post–World War II perspective, nothing expresses that perhaps more clearly than the collections of women's hair that were organized by the Red Cross and other institutions during World War I. Total war consumed men and women, body and soul, or, as the German saying has it, "mit Haut und Haaren" (with skin and hair).[74] This experience was incorporated and, thus, prolonged into the Weimar Republic in various ways. There were definitely long-term medical consequences of wartime social conditions. In addition, Weimar fashion with its emphasis on lean female bodies and short hair aestheticized this war experience retroactively and, therewith, kept it alive.

This is not the whole picture, yet. Rather, the drop in family income also resulted in a loss of economic autonomy of the family as an institution. During the war, more and more families became dependent on state and private or semiprivate welfare organizations. There can be no doubt that without such organizations, social conditions in wartime Germany would have been even worse than they actually were and that the home front might have had a much higher death toll than it did.[75] However, this should not conceal the fact that because of the way in which welfare was organized, external (welfare) agencies and agents directly interfered with the family budget. Unlike during the American Depression, when families received lump sums of money that they could use at their discretion, compensation and welfare payments in World War I Germany consisted most often of basic sums and additional allocations for specified purposes (fuel, winter coats, etc.).[76] Moreover, welfare was constructed not as an individual right but as a restitution for wartime sacrifices, thus forming yet another bond between the well-being of individual bodies and that of the nation.[77]

All these developments, dismal though their consequences for the lives of those at the home front were, also possessed another side. Both the movement of women and young adults into formerly "male" occupational sectors and the—partial—replacement of male breadwinners by welfare agencies contributed to the erosion of patriarchal authority and thus, at least to some degree, to an empowerment of women and young adults that occurred parallel to their overall loss of autonomy. This was similarly true for yet another aspect of the economic erosion of the family. During the war, "housework"—traditionally defined as the women's domain within the (bourgeois) family—was increasingly deprivatized and incorporated into the national war economy. The production of previously bought goods and the careful management of scarce resources turned into matters of national survival.

On the one hand, this development allowed even more external agencies to interfere with individual women's and the family's economic autonomy.[78] On the other hand, this "nationalization" of housework also constituted a source of a (potential) augmentation of women's influence. Their status definitely rose when household management became a national affair. Moreover, their actual power over other family members increased as well. Household management included, after all, the control over the family's consumption of goods.[79] Access to these goods had to be allocated in different ways to different family members, balancing off, for example, the (perceived) needs of those who were actively engaged in the war effort (the working, the pregnant) against those who were not (the elderly).

Parallel to their loss of economic autonomy, individuals and the family also experienced the loss of their—traditionally limited—reproductive freedom. Because, at the time, biological reproduction could not be separated from sexuality, this also entailed the erosion of individuals' and the family's sexual autonomy.[80] This happened on many different levels. First, and quite obviously, the gendered organization of war itself, that is, the temporary or permanent separation of men and women, severely restricted individuals' sexual and reproductive freedom by subordinating them to the nation's needs of male and female bodies. Second, and more important, the enormous loss of male lives in World War I required an even deeper interpenetration of individual bodies and that of the nation. The massive expenditure of male lives constituted neither an unforeseen side effect of total war, nor simply or solely an unfortunate result of strategic and tactical mistakes. Rather, as military experts of the time continued to argue, (male) bodies were an integral part of industrialized warfare. Soldiers not only used weapons; rather, their very bodies turned into weapons that were flung against the enemy lines.[81]

Consequently, the quality as well as the continuous supply of soldiers' bodies had to be secured in order to ensure the National Body's survival.[82] This meant that women's *and* men's (biological) reproductive work had to become an integral part of the organization of total war. Reproduction's new role not only fused *male* and *female* bodies with that of the nation, but also *present* and *future* bodies, thus establishing the National Body—which was, by definition, a body at war—as a timeless material and representational entity. The steps that were taken in order to ensure this multiple fusion consisted of a variety of positive and negative pronatalist measures. Soldiers were encouraged to use condoms when visiting prostitutes, while access to contraceptives was made more difficult at the home front in order to achieve a high birthrate. Labor protection laws were reintroduced for women workers, and pregnant and breastfeeding women were granted higher food rations. Most of these measures targeted men and women, not the family unit.

Of all the pronatalist measures, the attempt to end the legal discrimination against illegitimate children is perhaps the most indicative of the family's obsoleteness for the reproduction of the National Body.[83]

There can be no doubt that individual men and women—and children, at that—profited in some ways from such pronatalist politics. However, these politics did not primarily aim at improving men's and women's health but, rather, that of the nation. This was similarly true with regard to men's and women's sexuality. The satisfaction of soldiers' sexual needs as well as the protection of their sexual property at home were considered to be important aspects of maintaining troop morale and, therefore, the nation's fighting power. Consequently, men were provided with opportunities for sexual encounters, whereas the policing of women's sexuality increased. Their surveillance, however, aimed not only at preventing women from betraying their husbands. Rather, control of women's sexuality also aimed at protecting and preventing them from having forced or voluntary sexual encounters with the enemy. Such relations were perceived as contaminations of the National Body.[84] Such notions clearly demonstrate that the fusion of individual bodies with that of the nation went both ways. When individual bodies became part of the nation, the nation simultaneously became part of them.[85]

As in the case of their economic freedom, men's and women's loss of reproductive and sexual autonomy exposed individuals to new forms of coercion. At the same time, the "nationalization" of biological reproduction and sexuality also constituted a source of (potential) power. Elevating men and women to "fathers and mothers of the nation" clearly affected the previously existing gender hierarchy. Patriarchy, or so I have argued elsewhere, definitely came to an end. This does not mean that male domination over women ended; however, it was no longer linked to men's role in the family but to men's role as soldiers in the service of the nation. Conversely, women, while gaining status as "mothers of the nation," needed to be controlled more tightly, precisely *because* of their elevated status.[86] Nevertheless, their new role—potentially and actually—provided women with access to social resources—such as welfare—from which they had previously been excluded. The new status could also free some women, for example illegitimate mothers, from traditional restrictions. In addition, the "nationalization" of reproduction could become a source of empowerment for both men and women, because the fusion of individual bodies with that of the nation was not an indiscriminate, but a restricted and selective, process. Not all individual bodies were deemed worthy of partaking of the National Body. Rather, some had to be rejected, isolated, and even eliminated.

The creation of the National Body as a "community of the Volk" (*Volksgemeinschaft*) in World War I was based on an all-encompassing reevaluation of lives with regard to their usefulness for the war effort. Such reevaluations were by no means abstract constructions. Rather, they decided over access to—ever scarcer—resources and, therefore, often determined one's chances to survive. Thus, prewar gender, class, and age hierarchies, although not being completely abolished were, however, thoroughly suffused with a new hierarchical order that divided the population into discrete entities according to their usefulness for the National Body. Soldiers as well as male workers in armaments-related industries were, at least in general, ranked higher than other men and women and, consequently, materially (food rations) and spiritually (honor) better provided for. Similarly, women of childbearing age were considered to be more valuable than those beyond that age, and pregnant and breastfeeding women had more advantages than childless women or women with older children.[87]

Virtually and actually rejected from the National Body were the elderly, the sick, the very poor, and, among them, especially those who were (much) too young to fight. Consequently, mortality rates were especially high among these parts of the population.[88] Biological, medical, or social conditions were, however, not the only grounds on which the inclusion or exclusion from the National Body rested. Lack of support for or opposition against the war effort could also make access to welfare difficult or even lead to an almost certain death sentence. Not infrequently, "patriotic women" in welfare organizations judged other women's worthiness for receiving help according to their enthusiasm for the war effort, and striking male workers were often "punished" by being sent to the front. Whereas other men had the privilege to sacrifice themselves for the national good, these men were sacrificed to this end by others.[89]

During the war, there was also a growing tendency to construct "ethnic" groups that did not fit the national body. The increasing emphasis on the production of "healthy" offspring and the concomitant link between the health of individual bodies and that of the National Body undoubtedly legitimized racist concepts that had already been championed in social Darwinist constructions of social relations.[90] Ludendorff argued this point most clearly when, in 1935, he expressed his conviction that "war and politics not only serve the survival of the people, but war is the highest expression of the racial will of life."[91] It would be too simplistic to dismiss this statement as an ex post facto reinterpretation of a war that got out of hand. Rather, social Darwinist as well as apocalyptic visions suffused the ideology of Germany's strong prowar movement and also the politics of military authorities already during World War I.[92]

This became evident in the war aims that numerous groups promoted during the war. A consistent feature of those aims was the construction of

Eastern European populations as "inferior."[93] Official anti-Semitism also increased. Military authorities, for example, conducted surveys that were meant to prove that Jews tried to avoid military service, thus proving their national unreliability. Although those surveys failed to unearth the desired results, they nevertheless contributed to the construction of Jews as an identifiable and distinct part of the German population.[94] In addition, over the course of the war, fantasies about Germany's cathartic internal renewal gained ground. This "rejuvenation," as it was often called, was perceived as endowing Germany with the strength and determination that would allow it to pursue its "cultural mission" in the world: the defeat of the "ideas of 1789" and their replacement by the "ideas of 1914."[95] In that regard, the image of the National Body seems to have transcended—at least for some groups—nineteenth-century definitions of the nation-state. This is an aspect, however, that needs further investigation.

Is this picture that I have painted of the emergence of the National Body too homogeneous? It certainly is. Not all women and all men experienced the transition, first, from peace to war and, then, from war to total war, in the same way. The fundamental changes that occurred had different effects upon members of different classes, of different age, gender, religious, and ethnic groups, and it did matter if one lived in the countryside or in an urban area. One of the most important factors was certainly whether one was sent to the front or not. There was also early on an opposition movement, anchored mainly in the working class and backed especially by working-class and lower-middle-class women, that resisted the fusion of individual bodies with the national body and, instead, developed a discourse that linked individual bodies and class interests. This opposition movement contributed in a major way to ending the war, at least temporarily.[96]

There was, however, also strong and growing support for the project that I have described, although the emergence of the National Body killed, wounded, and mutilated individual bodies in unprecedented ways and numbers. To be sure, for many contemporaries, the experience of the horrors of total war meant that World War I had to be the last of all wars.[97] Others, however, saw the physical and mental disabilities that the war had produced as proof that not the "fittest" had survived but those who were too cowardly to "go over the top" first or who were too weak to withstand the battles for too long. Consequently, they bemoaned the loss of their "best" after the war,[98] and many of them concluded that the war was, by no means, over. They believed that rather than demobilizing the National Body, it had to be remobilized during a period of "militarized peace" so that it would be better prepared to fight the next war.[99]

In my eyes, the National Body that emerged in World War I was not completely dismembered at the end of the war but rather remembered—in more than one sense of that word—and, thus, connected with the project of National Socialism. Therefore, I have focused in this essay on those implications of the wartime restructuring of social and political relations that connect World War I to World War II, without claiming, however, that there was a causal, let alone monocausal, link between total war and National Socialism. A link, however, there was. And this link also connects National Socialism not simply to "modernity,"[100] but, more important, to bourgeois conceptualizations of a totalitarian *society*. Totalitarianism cannot simply be understood as the antithesis to bourgeois society. Quite obviously, it can also express and result from the desire to gain or maintain not autonomy but power. Those societies that constructed themselves in the wake of the Enlightenment developed not only, as Max Horkheimer and Theodor W. Adorno argued, a cold eye.[101] They also possessed, as Joseph Conrad showed, hearts of darkness.[102]

DANIEL ORLOVSKY

3

Corporatism or Democracy

The Russian Provisional Government of 1917

WORLD WAR I and the Russian Revolution each transformed the social and political landscapes of twentieth-century Europe and indeed the world. Revolution in Russia has left its own stunning legacy as worked out in the tragic seventy-four year history of the Soviet Union, with its distorted and even grotesque achievements and excesses and its attempts to fulfill the Soviet project of overcoming the bourgeois phase of history and establishing its opposite, socialism. Since the demise of the Soviet Union, much ink has been spilled on the prospects of "democracy" in the new post-Soviet Russia. A new discourse of democracy has appeared, with insiders and outsiders alike using the concept to fill the space—as a project—much as the concepts of communism and socialism were used in the past. Still the possibility of democracy in Russia is problematic as a theory and as practice. So it was with the February Revolution of 1917, Russia's first, though dishearteningly short-lived period of democracy. Refocusing the lens away from the master narrative of 1917, scrapping, even for a moment, the categories of class conflict that so dominated the contemporary discourse and subsequent historiography and memory of the era brings into view new layers of memory and images of that early democratic experiment. These images appear more corporatist than democratic, a fact that may lead us toward deeper truths about Russian democracy and its potential. Several examples drawn from the 1917 political and social landscape reveal a fresh terrain, very different from that explored through the more familiar categories of class conflict and either Bolshevik triumphalism or demonization.[1]

Even these brief glimpses suggest the possibilities in a fresh look at 1917 that moves away from the categories of class and the habitual focus on the major parties, toward broader social, occupational, ethnic, and national movements and a reconceived sense of the meanings and institutions of democracy and the state in 1917.[2] Reopening the study of 1917 invites further speculation on what needs to be done. One might begin with the recognition that the February and October Revolutions were part of same historical process, with roots deep in the Old Regime (but particularly in the social, political, economic institutions, and conflicts of its final decades).[3] The Provisional Government experience crystallized these conflicts and projected them onward into the Soviet period, that is, into Soviet state and society building. In short, Soviet history begins neither with Lenin and the Bolsheviks, nor with Stalin alone. And, indeed, Bolshevik ideas of power and practices did not begin either with Lenin's early writings or post-October with the civil war. Many features of the new Soviet state and society had their roots in the politics and new institutions of World War I and the February Revolution.

The master narrative of 1917 obscures more than it reveals. This is a story whose main features are well known—the February Revolution, the creation of dual power, Lenin's return and his April theses, the April Crisis, the first coalition, the First All-Russian Congress of Soviets, the June demonstrations, the July Days and crisis of power, the failed offensive, Alexander F. Kerensky's rise, the Moscow State Conference, the Kornilov affair, the ongoing crisis of state power, the internal Bolshevik debate about revolution, ongoing internecine conflicts and unraveling of all other parties, the failure of the unified Socialist government alternative (the democratic alternative) at the Democratic Conference, and the final coalition and rapid onset of the October Revolution. All of this, of course, is plotted against the backdrop of deepening social and national/ethnic conflict as well as the ongoing dissolution of traditional power structures in the armed forces. It is a challenge to step outside or go beyond this story line that has been shared by the Bolsheviks and standard Soviet historiography itself—as well as by opponents then and now—and even the more recent social historians—largely labor historians, that for a time in the 1970s and early 1980s succeeded in giving the master narrative a social dimension, without changing the plot at all.

Democracy was an ambiguous category in the February Revolution and throughout 1917. Its meanings included the democracy of the liberals, the Kadets, Octobrists—rule of law, the discourse of antibureaucracy, self-government, self-determination of peoples, civil rights, the commitment to Parliament via the Constituent Assembly. A second powerful meaning was somewhat hidden in a large-scale, quiet (not often headline-making), but highly popular form of democracy that signified the opening of politics and institutional life to the plebeians—workers, peasants, employees, white-collar workers—and higher up the social scale to the professionals and protoprofessionals, people of education and skill, laborers of the mind, or to use the language of the time, the "laboring intelligentsia." This democracy also embraced the self-determination and growth of national consciousness among non-Russians in the borderlands and in the deep spaces of Russia itself. In practice this meant many things: participation in all forms of new committees, factory, village, food supply, land, the Soviets themselves, army. It meant the opening of opportunities in education, the workplace, the professions for women. In the professions themselves it meant heightened strivings for status and power for the lower strata of professionally trained groups and occupations—paramedical personnel (*fel'dsher*) in relation to doctors, pharmacist assistants in relation to pharmacists, surveyors in relation to agronomists, sacristans and deacons in relation to priests, and so on. All of this took place within the context of a burgeoning, rapidly growing infrastructure that would carry over into the Soviet period.

A third vision of democracy was more firmly centered in the Soviets (that were themselves organized along corporatist lines as much as the "class" lines of the master narrative with separate worker and peasant national and local organizations that were quite distinctive and expressed very different interests in 1917) and the Menshevik and Socialist Revolutionary (SR) Parties. This was plebian democracy rooted in class-based or broader-laboring, mass-based organizations and parties, and it really signified democratic Marxism or populism. Finally there was the government itself—the amalgam of ideas and policies and pieces of legislation passed through and by the cabinet or ministries, which represented the working out in practice of party visions transformed under the influence of location within the state structure and traditional Russian *vedomstvennost'* (the idea that specific institutions had their own culture, interests, and social support).

Thus, this was the first Provisional Government cabinet, a government that derived its legitimacy from the revolution, attempted to break with Old Regime institutions, and set out the liberal democratic agenda—a truly revolutionary program that called for rule of law, self-government, civil rights, and national self-determination. Perhaps its most cherished goal was to break the hold of bureaucracy and police and administrative power on Russian political life. It certainly aimed to transform Russia. Similarly, the Mensheviks in May took over the new Ministry of Labor while Viktor Chernov, the SR theoretician and leader, found himself at the head of the Ministry of Agriculture (MZ), a post from which he promptly launched an SR interpretation of administrative procedure that gave much wider power to grassroots land committees and fostered the demise of property rights and land transactions in the countryside.

Had the Provisional Government survived as either a coalition or a unified Socialist government, or the "democratic government" of Iulii Martov's later formulation, the evidence indicates that Russian democracy would have taken on certain forms that were more corporatist than the avowed goals and democratic ideologies of either the liberals of the first cabinet or the various parties and groupings of the Left. This corporatism was driven by occupational and economic interests, by the lower middle strata, and by the bureaucracy. Here comparative history highlights these developments. When Russia is placed in its European and Eurasian contexts, contemporary crises of capitalism and democracy illuminate Russia's own revolutionary experience. Especially important was the experience of World War I, with its legitimation of violence and statecraft of mobilization, the growth of nonmarket and antiparliamentary forces, the articulation of a new politics and economics. In France, Italy, and Germany, the language of class conflict and socialism and of the restoration of bourgeois structures also masked the more important social, political, and institutional developments.[4]

The well-documented corporatism of Europe has great resonance in the Russian case and more specifically in the Russian Revolution of 1917. After World War I, Europe witnessed a process of stabilizing institutions, reconsolidating the social order. A variety of social groups participated in this process. The old conservative Right, new radical Right (distressed farmers, retired officers, intellectuals and university youth, clerical employees, hard-pressed small businessmen, and shopkeepers), and even those progressives not on the Right at all—in other words reformers—all attacked socialism and liberalism, and in fact saw the former as having been spawned by the latter. The image and language and categories of prewar bourgeois society were stated as the goals, but what was created was new institutional arrangements and distributions of power—a displacement of power from elected representatives or a career bureaucracy to "the major organized forces of European society and economy, sometimes bargaining directly among themselves, sometimes seeking influence through a weakened parliament—and occasionally seeking advantages through new executive authority. In each case corporatism meant the growth of private power and the twilight of sovereignty."[5] Most conspicuously, this evolution toward corporatism involved a decay of parliamentary power. And indeed developments along these lines in Russia during 1917 did not auger well for the power of the Constituent Assembly or any successor legitimate parliament even had it been elected prior to the October Revolution.

Corporatism in Russia in 1917 involved the bargaining for power and scarce resources between the traditional Russian ministerial bureaucracy—under the banner of *vedomstvennost'*; new economic institutions within and outside the bureaucracy called forth by economic development, World War I demands, and the revolution itself; and a host of "social" or "public" institutions and interest groups, professional associations, and the like that often had little to do with party dogma or politics—though the public debate in 1917 made reference to "parliament." These references were to parliament either in the form of the defunct state Duma of the Old Regime (still sitting in 1917 and holding "private" sessions), the proclamations and program of calling a Constituent Assembly as enunciated by the first Provisional Government cabinet and shared by all major factions, or the Provisional Government's actual halfhearted attempts to create legitimacy through pseudoparliaments (or advisory bodies based upon principles of corporate representation). These pseudoparliaments included the Moscow State Conference of August, the Democratic Conference of September, and most tellingly the Council of the Republic, or "Pre-parliament," of October.[6] It is instructive to read in the archives the appeals of organized interests or social groups for representation or more representation in those successive attempts to align the politics of interests and occupation with democracy as the revolution's stated goal. For example, the Moscow Council of Laboring Intelligentsia on October 7 wrote to the Chair of the Pre-parliament complaining about the low number of intelligentsia representatives permitted in the Pre-parliament. "We have 25 representatives at the Moscow State Conference, but now only a few of the 388 strong democratic bloc."[7] The Moscow Council saw this as a plot of the Soviets to keep it and the intelligentsia out of the Pre-parliament. They argued that the workers now have representatives through the soviets, unions, and cooperatives, but the intelligentsia only have representation through several small discreet unions and in a quantity not in accordance with their relative numbers. The appeal was for independent representation like that of the soviets of workers, soldiers, and peasants. Similarly, on August 8, the women of Sergeev Posad, organized into a Women's Economic and Governance Union, wrote directly to Kerensky asking for representation at the Moscow State Conference. They proclaimed that "we the women were in the majority of those left behind (that is not at the front) and had made the most sacrifices during war and revolution."[8]

The point is that the real legacies of the Provisional Government and the democratic revolution may have had more to do with the Main Committees on Cotton, Leather, and Metals; the Economic Council; the new supply networks and cooperatives; the organized congresses of professionals and specialists; and the fact that the peasants (and more particularly their spokespeople) gravitated (consciously, recognizing that the peasantry as a corporate estate needed a political representation equivalent in status to the Soviet of Workers and Soldiers Deputies) toward the All-Russian Congress of Peasants Deputies and its Executive Committee rather than the populist parties that spoke in their name and for decades had espoused "socialization" of the land. And there is the fundamental fact, often overlooked in discussing the Constituent Assembly (but revealed in the archives of the commissions charged with creating it), that the creation of such a parliament meant the end of the Provisional Government with its plenitude of powers. It is telling that on October 24, the twelfth hour so to speak, F. Dan, a Menshevik leader in the Pre-parliament, and others proposed a resolution (essentially a vote of no confidence in Kerensky and his cabinet) calling for immediate peace, land to the land committees, the creation of a Committee of Public Safety (with Provisional Government participation), and, most important, advancing in time the Constituent Assembly elections. The actual resolution that passed, however, left out the idea of a Committee of Public Safety and the call for earlier elections.

Later, under Soviet power itself, corporatism would take on a socialist caste even as elsewhere it was integral to fascism. Political developments in Europe were echoed in Soviet political and social arrangements. In the 1920s the Socialist state proclaimed the New Economic Policy (NEP), even as it promoted goals not altogether dissimilar to Mussolini's formulation of Italian Fascism. These included the overcoming of class conflict in the new Socialist polity (as a form of depoliticization), the extension of the state downward to embrace the people (producers, or proletariat, as members of the commonweal), the trusts and cartels of the NEP, the emphasis on productivity, the organization of interests into unions and corporations, the culture and promotion of youth, the glorification and militarization of the nation, a growing leadership cult, and emergence of a national Bolshevism.[9]

These themes are illustrated by several visions of 1917 drawn from the archives and the SR Party press (*Volia naroda*—a centrist publication) from June, roughly the midpoint of the process that would culminate in the Bolshevik victory in October.[10] On July 22, 1917, the Union of Simbirsk Landowners wrote to the minister president of the Provisional Government, Kerensky, complaining about the Provisional Government's July 12 decree forbidding land transactions.[11] The landowners proclaimed that this had destroyed fundamental principles guaranteed by the French Revolution: freedom, property, and security and freedom from oppression.

On June 29 the lead article covered the brilliant victory of the SR Party in the recent Moscow municipal elections. "What is the secret of our victory in the CITY, when the countryside is our real territory?" asked the article's writer. The usual answer, the writer continued, is that Russia is a peasant country and we, the SRs, are the voice of the peasants. But now Bolshevik propaganda is even more oriented toward the peasants than is ours. But the issue is victory in the city and also why we are so popular in the army and wide circles of nonclass or outside class (the classes of current political discourse) intelligentsia. The answer is our populism (*narodnost'*), our closeness to the social being and life (*byt*) and to the historical currents of Russian thought. We are the party of not only general socialism, but of *Russian* Socialism par excellence, a national party in the full sense of the word, and that is what makes us popular among the most varied layers of society. We are in full harmony with the historical composition and structure of the nation. This is not unique to Russia. Socialist movements everywhere take national forms. Social Democracy in the West is based on class conflict and the proletariat, an abstract vision that spilled over into SD attitudes toward nationality. These were described as based upon abstract bourgeois legalisms as opposed to SR federalism, which was based on the uniqueness and individuality of each nation, each people as they necessarily remained part of the *Russian* state.

The point was developed in another piece by the eminent SR sociologist Pitirim Sorokin, who proclaimed that events in Russia no longer indicated a class model and continuing differentiation by classes. No, he claimed, many other factors along with class were significant. Now, he argued, there were at work three principles of social differentiation—class, state, and nationality. Sorokin was far ahead of his time. In fact, it would take decades and the collapse of the Soviet Union and the reemergence of nationalism as both creative and destructive force for historians to elevate the nationality question and the larger issue of national identity to status even remotely equivalent to social factors as causal agents of the revolution.

Just a few days earlier, on June 23, the paper discussed the issue of Finland and Russia.[12] The issue here was the Finnish Parliament's (*Seim*'s) refusal to accept payment for factory orders or to pay for Russian troops in Russian currency. The Finns, still very much a part of the Russian Empire, demanded *valiuta*, or Finnish hard currency, a demand that would place the Provisional Government in a large bind.

> The Russian people [*narod*] expect help from all peoples in the RUSSIAN state now that it has overthrown Tsarism, and most of all from Finland. The Best of the Russian people have long protested the treatment of the Finns and one of the first acts of the Provisional Government was the restoration of all Finnish rights. Finland has already received the widest possible autonomy and final decisions on the nature of that autonomy were to be decided by the Constituent Assembly. So, the Seim's action and hostility to Russia is unjust.

For the editorial writers a major point seemed to be that the current Russian state was a new democratic Russia and not the Old Regime. Finnish attitudes, therefore, "could only be explained by hypertrophied nationalist sentiments, national exclusivity which is the opposite of our notion of solidarity." Even more ominous for the moderate SRs was their conclusion that "the Finns are helping German Imperialism, which is swallowing small nations. Only the victory of the Russian Revolution over its external and internal enemies can save Finland."[13]

These ideas were echoed at the All-Russian Congress of the Trudoviki (the Laborites Duma faction) meeting on June 21.[14] There the mood was largely against the demands of the Finns and Ukrainians, a fact that once might have been considered surprising coming from moderate populists who had no prior record of Great Russian nationalism or hostility to the aspirations of the nationalities to security and incorporation of the worst features of the late Imperial regime's Russification policies. Speakers at the Trudoviki Congress argued that to give in to what were perceived as separatist demands would return Russia to its "primordial" condition. Russia (said F. A. Vol'kenshtein expressing the dominant mythology of Russianness) was constructed as a united, cohesive state, and it is criminal now to break it up into pieces (especially because many peoples want Russian protection).

Two further points should be made about the nationality question. First, after the July crisis of power, which in fact extended into August and beyond, there was not so much dual power or even coalition but "many powers," as the Provisional Government in some cases gave executive power to nationality organs as in Ukraine, or passively witnessed such devolution as in the case of the Ozakom (a Petrograd-based committee that administered the Transcaucasian nationalities) in the Caucasus.[15] Second, the need to hold the empire together became a driving force behind Provisional Government statism, precisely because of the attitudes and beliefs about national identity expressed above by moderate Socialists. These notions of Russian identity were in their own way imperial. They continued the long Russian tradition of conflating state and empire. That they were shared by the interstitial Left that supported the Provisional Government as well as the liberal and more conservative wings of the Constitutional Democratic Party speaks volumes about the capacities of the Russian "democracy" in 1917 to sustain democratic institutions.

Another vignette is drawn precisely from the Menshevik sources, the unification congress of the Mensheviks held in August 1917—the last congress of that ill-fated party prior to October.[16] In a fiery speech, Iu. Martov, the great theoretician and leader of the Menshevik Internationalists (which is to say the sector of the party that was against the war and which by August—prior to the Kornilov affair—had turned against the defensist or prowar coalition Provisional Government), called for a decisive drive to wean the petty bourgeoisie, the mass of non-Soviet democratic intelligentsia, away from the bourgeoisie and toward a renewed revolutionary socialism (before the Bolsheviks captured them). Martov had already argued in July against the new Kerensky-constructed coalition, whose members were not responsible before either Soviet or party. Martov wanted a united Socialist government (*odnorodnoe sotsialisticheskoe pravitel'stvo*) based upon the legitimacy of the Soviets and other democratic institutions.[17] Later in September and October, Martov would continue to argue for a "democratic government" that would embrace the lower middle strata and even the peasantry. And he had his followers, even among the Bolsheviks, where the idea of a Socialist or democratic coalition was espoused by a number of leading figures. It is this alternative of a united Socialist or democratic government that must be explored because these labels mask an entire complex of party, occupational, and other organizational life hitherto obscured by the categories of the standard narrative.

Finally, on the Provisional Government's powers, we have the testimony of the legal scholar A. Bogolepov writing in July in the principal journal of the liberal legal profession, *Pravo* (Law). In his article "The Contemporary State Structure of Russia," Bogolepov described how in the "country of unlimited possibilities" with surprising suddenness, the apparently impossible state reversal (revolution—*perevorot*) happened. The old structure was destroyed, but what are the basic outlines of the new? His analysis offered two main points. First, the Provisional Government had taken the "plenitude of powers"; that is, it was the heir to both the tsar's personal power and to the power of the old Council of Ministers, and that embodied both legislative and executive authority. The only limits upon it were its inability to renounce its founding declaration (its pledge to civil rights and electoral laws, etc.) and its temporary nature, that is, its right to exist only until the Constituent Assembly, which alone had the right to formulate basic laws. Of course, the government was empowered to issue all manner of decrees and edicts "for the functioning of government."

Second, Bogolepov pointed out that "the supreme judge of whether the Provisional Government oversteps its powers is now public opinion, which in contemporary conditions can reach the Provisional Government with extraordinary ease through resolutions of meetings, petitions and presentations of various types of groups and organizations." Bogolepov closed on a somewhat pessimistic note, claiming that in government there still was no consistent practice. Things were becoming more structured, but the future was uncertain; the *stroi* (institutions) were built very quickly and in some regions law does not yet prevail, he wrote. We have not a legal or law-governed regime, he pointed out, but one governed by the facts of life. Events are moving so swiftly that what is here today may not be practice in a few days and the entire enterprise may be the subject of historical and juridical analysis, he argued.[18]

Fresh and revealing visions of the revolution can be found not only in new archival sources but also in the little-read press of the interstitial Left, the splinter Populist and Socialist Parties, and the traditional thick journals with their sophisticated political analyses (unfortunately here the revolution moved so swiftly that the lead time for publication of monthlies or quarterlies barely gave them time to react to the events of 1917). On the eve of the revolution, one of these journals oriented toward the community of professional educators published a readers' survey for late 1916 that posed the question, What did people actually read? The answers were suggestive. According to the survey the vast majority of *obyvateli*—that is, literate ordinary citizens—preferred the popular press: *Peterburgskii listok*, the illustrated magazines, *Niva*, and the like. Highbrow newspapers and journals were far down the list.

Now it is true that the February Revolution resulted in a flood of new publications that expressed a heightened political consciousness on the part of journalists and readers alike. But it is also at least possible, given the crescendo of complaints about *obyvatel'shchina* (the predominance in the revolution of mundane or vulgar values and those who held them) and indifference during 1917, that we have lent too much credence in our histories of the era to the wide influence of the party press. How did the thick journals (very definitely meant for sophisticated audiences but not necessarily party oriented) and popular newspapers tell the story of the revolution? What were their categories, how did the language of the revolution fit with the appetites of the ordinary reader? What if all those ordinary types were paying little attention to the party press, to the story as told by the parties and political activists of 1917? And another question: Why had such sources been largely ignored? No major work on 1917, apart from general histories that skim the surface of this question, have stepped outside the circle of party sources to compare the points of view and assess the influence of party publications in relation to each other and to the popular press. All of this suggests that new sensitivity is required to the language of the revolution, the categories of public discourse and propaganda.[19]

If the general public, the *obyvateli*, as indicated by the 1916 reader survey, was not reading the party press, the highly charged ideological discourse written in the codes of party visions of the events of 1917, what did they read? And how did they possibly perceive the rapidly unfolding revolution? A few observations based upon reading the popular journals and the press offers some clues.

The journal *Niva*, an early Russian middlebrow version of a large-format, photo-illustrated weekly, for example, offers a running commentary on events from February through October. In the earliest days of March, the journal lauded the February Revolution and Provisional Government, which it tended to conflate with the Duma and its Temporary Committee. The driving theme was "freedom" and "all the Russian people" as creators of a new era.[20]

The weekly column "Political overview" began on March 25 with Professor K. Sokolov's analysis of the "overturning of the state" (*gosudarstvennyi perevorot*). He began with an analysis of power and claimed that the enormous power of the tsars had depended not just on force but on the wishes and warm sympathies of the Russian people. The idea here was that the *obyvateli* for so long believed that all was in order, that the institutions and rituals of order were in place—the policeman on the beat, and so on—that all was well (*blagopoluchno*), and that the state was healthy and strong. Yet the facts were just the opposite, and though the revolution quickly brought down the regime, the state was still intact precisely because the "wishes and warm feelings" of the Russian people had been transferred to the Duma, now in the process of organizing "free Russia."[21]

Around the Tavrichesky Palace, a new Russian state was in the process of creation. The 1905 Revolution and its aftermath had proven that Russia had outgrown its political forms—had united all layers of the Russian people, in their strivings toward freedom and self-government. One of the first features concerned the new *Mirovoi sud*, or popular courts, in Petrograd. The "new" in this case consisted of the previous court supplemented by an elected city Duma representative and one elected member drawn each from the workers and soldiers. The court was to pass judgment on acts against personal safety and property and attacks on public order and quiet. The punishments included various formulaic "findings," small fines (not more than two rubles), arrest (with no more than three months' incarceration), and prison (not more than eighteen months). The courts had to insure that no one was held without legal edict from the Provisional Government. All judges whose actions did not support the new program were to be removed immediately. The probity and industriousness of the courts working in the name of the people were to be guaranteed by long and constant working hours—all day until 5 P.M., including Sundays and holidays. The proceedings were to be open with oral arguments, and sentences were to be issued in the name of the Provisional Government and quickly carried out.

A telling piece then followed on the sad appearance of "revolutionary *obyvatel'shchina*." It should be noted that the role of the *obyvatel'* is little noticed in the historiography, either the active role of real people, who remained largely undefined—or the rhetorical role, role in the discourse. We have no answers or even speculation as to why newspapers always mentioned, why contemporaries referred constantly to a shapeless mass of urbanites, a group described in the populist *Zemlia i Volia* as a "counterrevolutionary threat," as Russia's "gray hundreds" that appear as human dust (the paper backed off a bit by claiming that although they could act as a brake upon the revolution they could in no way be a "countervailing force"; that is, by themselves they couldn't be a major organized political force—they could only play a negative role or be combined with other "forces."[22] *Obyvatel'shchina* was an important part of the discourse, a necessary explanation for a very obvious social reality (which can be seen in the appeals in journals such as *Niva*—namely, the existence of a mass nonparty audience that cared little about the theoretical concerns of centrist and leftist politicians).

The journal described *obyvatel'stvo* as a part of society that understands nothing and cannot take joy in anything, believes in nothing, and wishes nothing well—a talk with one reveals *grekh* in the spirit/soul—because it is now forbidden to relate to life in the *obyvatel'* manner. The *obyvatel'*, the journal maintained, must disappear along with the autocracy. This was an appeal for active citizenship and participation, "for it is now necessary to be involved, be in affairs, to agitate, argue, battle or with double the energy get into one's own work believing in Russia, because without such belief it is not possible to live now." There is no justification for a person to live now skeptically behind one's own four walls. We must understand, the journal stated, that civil and cultural construction is not only meetings, elections, and speeches; we must also relate cautiously (*berezhno*) to the revolution's gifts (*darovaniia*) and to work. Russia in any case awaits personalities. Let those called to politics take part, and others more than ever must turn to work.

In May, after America's entry into the war, *Niva* carried a photo spread of a squadron of American Navy ships, including one dreadnought that carried the caption—"This ship has on its crew the flower of American wealth—900 millionaires' sons volunteered for the navy and do the work of simple seamen."[23] And this was stated as a matter of fact, with no irony.

In May, the journal also addressed the first coalition. It correctly pointed out that it was not a coalition in the strict European sense, because it had no parliament and the twelve ministers are often jokingly referred to as the twelve autocrats (a play on "down with the bourgeois ministers"), and it pointed out that the Provisional Government was not a ministry in a strict technical sense either. It also noted that even first Provisional Government ministry had members of different parties. The new coalition was just a move to the Left and an expansion to include six representatives of democracy or socialism (the terms are used interchangeably almost in an ironic sense). The writer concluded that the struggle for power would continue this time within the government, which is only a compromise between several social and political groups. "The Provisional Government is now the supreme power and doesn't inform the Duma of anything."

By June the political viewpoint writers had cried out for help in the face of growing anarchy. The journal emphasized the fact that people's power had taken a primitive form and was itself becoming a shadow government—it was by arrests, searches, and deliverance of *samosud* and *samoupravstvo* justice (i.e., willful rule and a sort of vigilante popular justice) that revolutionary collegial organs of all types had taken state power, employing censorship, and blocking meetings. Committees everywhere, including in the army, the writers observed, appointed and replaced personnel, spent government money, and requisitioned goods and buildings. Local authorities in some cases had become fully independent, refusing to recognize the Provisional Government. "They have become dictators (one is reminded of the recent reports from Turkmenistan). Little republics are declared, the latest of which is in Iziumskoi District of Kharkov province, where the militia head, a *podporuchik* [second lieutenant] Shilov, has taken power." The Provisional Government, it warned, is losing the authority under its feet. The authority of its institutions is now only formal, with no real content. And here was the real argument: the Provisional Government had to win over the *obyvatel'*, and to do so it needed to provide security. The *obyvatel'* had to see real police who could keep order and not a government of professors and philosophers, heroes and political leaders (an effort to deflate the heroic image of the revolution). The government must provide real courts administration, rule of law. And finally, the journal's writers warned, it was time to stop looking for counterrevolutionaries, to stop attacking obsessively the Plehves and Protopopovs (tsarist ministers of Internal Affairs). It was time to fight anarchy, the mother of reaction. *Niva* understood well the hold of language, the revolutionary discourse on public opinion.

Finally the "political viewpoints" column was brilliant in its deconstruction of the Moscow State Conference in August of 1917 (this hastily called conference was Kerensky's attempt to call a pseudoparliament—an advisory body to legitimize the regime).[24] *Niva* labeled it an old Muscovite type of institution based upon the "formless" representation of social organizations, forces from the "land,"—it would only be as in Muscovite times *gromozdko*, or not proportional, *neskladno*, or formless. *Niva* noted with great irony that in the revolutionary "newness" of Russia in the twentieth century, we get Muscovite "antiquity" (*starina*); we move to build the most progressive and most democratic new government in the world, and the subjectivity (*stikhiia*) of our political life turns us from fashionable political slogans of the latest times to the ancient and modest overtures and order of the provincial Moscow statehood (*gosudarstvennost'*). The columnists slammed the Provisional Government and Kerensky for moving from party to national support base in this form—in the form of a corporate Muscovite assembly of the land (*zemskii sobor*), which is not a real reading of public opinion or based upon European practice.[25]

The Professions and the Revolution

The revolution involved and embraced many layers of Russian society besides the familiar workers, peasants, soldiers, and sailors. There was the vast army of white-collar workers and protoprofessionals, the lower middle strata.[26] But higher in the social hierarchy were the professionals themselves, another powerful and little-studied force, with roots in the late tsarist period, that came to the fore in 1917. They saw the opening of great vistas to further professional "projects," and although they ultimately did not share the political viewpoints or ideologies of the Russian Left, they still viewed the post-October Bolshevik regime as a supporter of developmental agendas and a possible patron. Many professionals in such areas as public health, the natural and social sciences, and engineering and education would work through the revolutions of 1917 and continue on to help build Soviet power. The participation of professionals in the Russian Revolution and building of the Soviet state was the culmination of an ongoing process with roots in social and economic developments of the late nineteenth century and more specifically in the 1905–7 upheaval and the history of the Union of Unions.[27] In addition to political activism and a tradition of organized corporate interest group activity, the Russian "free" professions were distinguished by an exceptional degree of connection to the state through location of professional activity, career patterns, and even education within state ministries.[28]

Professional projects had been vigorously promoted as a result of economic development, of the exponentially increased demands brought on by World War I, and then by the February Revolution itself. The post-February democracy promised much to professional projects of all sorts: from universal education to public health to electrification, vast public works and the planning or demobilization of the wartime economy.[29] On April 30, I. Pokrovskii, for example, spoke at the All-Russian Union of Jurists. He claimed,

> We do not represent a class or a profession and that is the problem in Russia today. Everything is interests—of classes or of individuals, there is no thought of the whole, and the destruction of the sense of law and justice. Our first and most basic task is to renew and educate in Russian society respect for the very idea of law. Right now the revolution has only replaced one arbitrariness with another.

Similarly, the engineers quickly formed unions and claimed that their active role in the February events and their knowledge entitled them, as S. D. Kirpichnikov put it in the journal *Vestnik inzhenerov*, "to a major role in its life."

At the Moscow meeting to create a Union of Engineers, the project (task) was described this way: Engineers must take an active part in the construction of that new life and state. The new union had to be different from its 1905 predecessor—in that its members must organize sections and be visible in the factories, on the railroads, and so on; must take part in decisions involving the labor question; and have a decisive voice in Ministry of Trade and Industry policy. In short, the engineers organized in a professional union/interest group were to turn into political activists working through the ministerial system and through the public organizations to fulfill both self-interest and professional projects.[30]

The antiparty attitude of the engineers was expressed at a meeting of the All-Russian Union of Peat (*Torf*) Affairs on July 2: "The nature and tasks of mental labor (of the engineers) is located between the workers and the entrepreneurs—the workers join the socialist parties and the owners, the liberal or conservative parties. We do not fit, we have no party"; "And we have no unified political platform. But this does not preclude our acting in politics through organizations such as the Council of Deputies of Laboring Intelligentsia to which we ought to send representatives."[31] The first example mentioned here was electrification, already long on the agenda. New legislation was required, and the Old Regime Duma drafts were regarded as wholly inadequate. The revolution would and could help the engineers realize their development dreams—as indeed would turn out to be the case after October under the Bolsheviks. The same could be said for the medical profession, long connected to the bureaucracy in the realm of public health and long imbued with (an ethos of) ideologies of public service.

In the arena of medicine and public health, the February Revolution brought about a major attempt to wean the profession away from the state and particularly from the Ministry of Internal Affairs (MIV)—and to reestablish the public health project on the basis of decentralization and collegiality.[32] D. N. Zhbankov, a leader of the Pirogov Society termed February the "cleansing hurricane." The Pirogov leaders, steeped in visions and traditions of community medicine, however, did not grasp the Provisional Government's own brand of statism—and its bargaining with the army, navy, Red Cross, and other public organizations involved in public health. Nor did they grasp the fact that wartime service with the public organizations had converted many doctors to the advantages of centralized, planned public health.

At the Pirogov Congress in April, opinion had shifted to support for a Central Medical Sanitary Council. The argument was that the revolution had made the old hostility to centralized medicine superfluous. The revolution had provided now a "broad field for creative activity." The Provisional

Government abolished the Rein Commission with its plan for a centralized bureaucratic Public Health Ministry, but at the same time MVD health officials attempted to regain ground lost to the public organizations and army during the war, by proposing that the medical council be placed within the MVD. The post-February months also witnessed a major push by *fel'dshers*, pharmacists and veterinarians, and other lower-ranking medical personnel to gain a voice and more power and status within the profession. Such was the nature of democratization within the professions and indeed the very basic meaning of the revolution for significant numbers of educated Russians.

The Pirogov Congress adopted a resolution calling for the public organizations to take over management of medical and public health affairs until the creation of a new form of government by the Constituent Assembly and calling for creation of a Central Council of Representatives of the Public Organizations with local affiliates (this, a new form of centralization!). Almazov, a physician and Kadet Duma deputy, was the Provisional Government Commissar, whose own council proposal differed from the Pirogov version in having more corporatist representatives—for example, from existing government departments and the War Industries Committees—and fewer from the *zemstvo* (provincial and district organs of self-government) and community medicine sector. As a Provisional Government official, he also viewed serving the army and war needs as paramount. The MVD opposed both projects, especially fearing its own subordination to Almazov's council. In May, Almazov called a conference of medical officials to ward off the MVD. There he proposed a modified council and managed to sweep away the prerevolutionary structure. Tellingly, the Pirogovtsy (those attending the Pirogov Congress) also backed mobilization of all physicians, thus falling back once again upon statism and centralization. These commitments to essentially bureaucratic or statist solutions to further interests were based, as was so much activity in 1917, on the faith that this was "good" bureaucracy in support of proper and desirable interests and that February signified the onset of a "new" regime.

The Soviets as institutions also entered the medical and public health arena. The Petrograd Soviet had established its own Medical and Sanitary Section. From this base, health professionals advanced the struggle against epidemics, childhood mortality, and venereal disease and worked also to improve working conditions through promotion of medical funds and measures for workplace protection of labor. Pressure brought on by epidemics and the logic of state and public organization involvement in public health led inexorably to centralization, and the Provisional Government created the often-discussed council finally on July 16. This council took up duties two months later than might have been expected and then spent its time on bureaucratic reorganizations and financial questions rather than health reform.

The council's August meetings revealed an agenda that lagged behind the times. Actual medical demands were overwhelming, and grassroots professional activity was continuing to gravitate toward socialist models of public health care. The council appealed to the Provisional Government for more power, but this was futile because even the zemstvos were growing weaker by the day, and the peasants were abandoning them or at least not accepting the *volost'* (administrative unit, below the district level, in the countryside that encompassed a number of villages) *zemstvo*. The result was a new wave of radicalism in the profession spearheaded by the Pirogovtsy in late August and directed against the bureaucratized establishment of the Provisional Government, mainly the War Ministry and Medical Council. Though many rank-and-file physicians no doubt did not adopt this radical stance, they did espouse professional agendas and a firm belief in insulating medicine from the marketplace and providing it with a sound institutional base either within the state itself or in organs of self-government broadly conceived. This facilitated their easy, even willing, mobilization for the public health projects of the Bolsheviks after October. (Lenin was a moderate here, preferring to win the support of the Pirogovtsy, rather than bludgeon them into joining the Bolshevik cause.)

Teachers also viewed the February Revolution as the harbinger of the "new," as a cleansing force that would permit the transformation of primary and secondary education in Russia. As important as pedagogy was in the worldview of teachers and their activist union representatives, the very idea of doing educational business, or administering the system on the basis of self-government, decentralization, and democracy, was even more enticing. This is just one more example of popular perceptions of the revolution as involving goals and categories other than class interests as depicted in the master narrative of 1917.[33]

The teachers were an influential and already highly politicized group when February swept them up into the politics of creating a new world. Their aim too was the establishment of democracy in primary and secondary education. And the main target was the long-hated heavy bureaucratic hand of the Tsarist Ministry of Education, with all of its deadening control mechanisms, procedures, and outright hostility to the teachers as professionals (especially if they were politically active and perceived as members of the opposition) and to the local societies that education was meant to serve. It should be remembered, however, that teachers in 1917 were not denizens of particular parties as much as proponents of their professional interests and educational mission. The teachers, who moved quickly in Petrograd to form a large union, were at first enthralled with the appointment of the Kadet (member of the Constitutional Democratic Party) A. A. Manuilov as the Provisional Government's first minister of education. Manuilov had impeccable credentials as an opponent of tsarist conservatism and the former Ministry of Education. Before the war he had been ousted, in fact, as rector of Moscow University for his oppositional politics.

The record of debate among the teachers at their earliest union meetings reveals an absolute certitude on their part that February meant a clean break with the past, the creation of a "new order," the "liberation of teachers from *obyvatel'shchina* and inertia, the creation of an organized body of teacher opinion to pressure the Ministry of Education," and "a cleansing of the Augean stables of the Old Regime in education."[34] Teacher aims included opening of the schools to all social and national groups and broad decentralization. Their aim was to get the Ministry of Education in order to nourish teacher organizations, encourage openness and pedagogical debate, and bring the schools into the revolution as crucial shapers of the new citizenry. As one leader put it, "to subordinate ourselves together to the idea of the state under the banner of the popular sovereignty."

The revolution, as in so many areas, outpaced the still stodgy operational scheme of the Provisional Government's Ministry of Education. Manuilov, the apparently well-suited new minister, proved to be a far cry from what was desired in the way of a minister from the now organized denizens of the "new." In a highly symbolic meeting on March 29, Manuilov addressed the teachers.[35] He appeared to a standing ovation, as it was unprecedented for the minister of education to appear before an organized professional body. The traditional practice, after all, was one of teacher supplication before a distant and impersonal bureaucracy. In answer to the agenda and pleas just noted, Manuilov delivered a dry speech calling for democratization and decentralization, as well as instruction in native languages alongside the obligation to learn the state Russian language. Manuilov, however, proclaimed that much would be decided in the councils of higher education, and in this he revealed an elitism that very much disturbed the teacher activists. It was immediately apparent that he came from another world, that of the universities and academicians, and that he had little knowledge of or sensitivity to the needs of popular education. Almost from that very moment, Manuilov and the Ministry of Education were perceived of as opponents of or at least obstacles in the way of "the new."

Indeed the Ministry of Education of the "new" free Russia began to behave much like its predecessor. The result was pressure for a third force, soon created as the State Committee on Education, with broad democratic and soviet representation (along with the organized teachers). Its mandate was to legislate the new in the face of ministry intransigence and at times outright hostility. During the months remaining before October, this committee was one of the primary arenas for the new politics of interests—state, public, and social. It was just one of many such new political locations that functioned more or less as an open laboratory of politics. Its mission to prepare an entire legislative program to transform primary and secondary education in time for the new school year in the autumn could serve as a microcosm of another kind of 1917 narrative. It too carried over the October boundary with strong impact.

Popular perceptions of the revolution were often focused on "legality"—which included the breakdown of order or the competing legalisms of the liberal Kadet rule of law symbolized by the Juridical Commission of the Provisional government—and the revolutionary—dictated by local interests and conditions, by moral imperatives symbolized by samosud, and by the actions of peasants themselves as supported by Land and Food Supply Committees and the like.

On July 24 the Balashov District Land Board (*uprava*) wrote to Kerensky and to MVD Tsereteli as follows:[36]

The provincial commissar has sent us the MVD telegram of July 18 (announcing the end of land transactions), and it is now in the hands of almost all the landowners and in a few days will be known to laboring peasants. It will undoubtedly call forth harsh feelings of undeserved injury and danger for the future of the agrarian question. According to our civic responsibility, the land board considers it necessary to inform the government of the actual situation. The political revolution has left the laboring peasantry disorganized and unprepared in civic and spiritual terms. Still, they met freedom and the new conditions of a lawful and just life with rare dignity and with prayerful faith in the coming happiness of the entire people, with quiet faith in the future. The peasantry is virtually the only estate in Russia that did not rush to satisfy its material or class interests, and it bore the enormous sacrifices in the war for the motherland and the army at the same time that the cities witnessed a bacchanalia of private passions and personal interests. This could not help but demoralize and anger the village. The peasantry still suffers the most from the war in terms of casualties and materially. They fight desertion and send their sons to the front despite the desperate need for labor. Now the peasantry is accused of forceful seizure of land, but 90% of this is lies to sow panic and call forth anarchy. We accuse the landowners and speculators of not using the land and even of destroying grain. In such cases the peasant committees take the land and the meadows for hay into their hands, to be sure not always in legal form. But the landowners make oral agreements with the committees and then the next day accuse them of seizures. Food Supply and Land Committees are then indicted in court, and the peasants feel that their only friends are under attack and that the landowners want to deny them their voting rights in the Constituent Assembly. The fact is that the land committees cannot support the old servile [*kabal'nye*] relations. We appeal to you the ministers as Socialists for immediate approval of Chernov's law (on land committees) and the turning over of all land to the land committees until the Constituent Assembly convenes. This is the only way to secure peace in the village.

(The letter was signed "Chair of Board, N. Aref'ev.")

Similarly, the representative of the all-Russian professional forestry organization wrote on measures to end the fuel crisis. He claimed that the peasants believed that the forests would soon be theirs and that their local committees had imposed taxes and obligations at all levels. The result was the complete disorganization of lumber and firewood procurement. Here again was a clash of moral and legal orders within the government itself—because the forestry professionals in the government were demanding open procurement above norms and without land committee permission, if local government officials deemed it necessary.[37]

On October 16 the Provisional Government commissar for Smolensk Province sent in a report (requested on September 1 but only delivered on the eve of the revolution) on conditions in the province from October 6 to October 15.[38] First he noted that the volost zemstvo elections had been held quickly and with little agitation and that elections for the district zemstvo had been held on October 1. He followed with a list of murders and robberies of *khutoriane* (peasants who had taken up Pyotr Arkadyevich Stolypin's prerevolutionary opportunity to leave their commune and set up independent farms), lawless clearing of forests, and the like. "We district commissars are supposed to stop it and we would call for force if possible, but the militia is ineffective and if troops come and stop it, it only starts up again quickly. The population sees no result. What kind of militia is it that acts by writing up a protocol? Nothing more will come of it for us." It is not a secret, he continued, that the population now firmly believes that there are no courts, and there is a basis for this because the militia protocols go unfulfilled. In such matters we need rapid judicial action; the *mirovye sudy* (justices of the peace) are afraid of losing popularity. They fear the illiterate, dark, ignorant masses whipped up by so many Bolshevik slogans. We need an individual with full power and authority including arrest and exile. Then the commissar turned reflective. "I well understand that this is a return to the old, that is, the administrative order for all convicted, but we have already returned to the old order with the death penalty and when it is a question of the fate of the motherland and revolution versus the destruction of both from disorder and pogroms, there is only one choice."

The food supply crisis brought similar appeals. On October 16, the Sevastopol Food Supply Board (*uprava*) reported to the Minister of Food Supply that workers and employees of the Sevastopol port had passed a strong resolution against speculators.[39] The Food Supply Board pointed out that speculation indeed existed and that its only legal remedy at present was to "requisition" goods from the speculators while keeping a certain percentage for the "people's treasury." Such measures were ineffective, the board argued. The only workable solution was complete confiscation of all goods. Therefore, the Board asked for the authority to search (*obysk*) and confiscate. The workers' protocol incidentally had called for not just confiscation powers for the state (which they equated with the *uprava*) but also arrest and prison terms meted out by a revolutionary court. Here the ministry rejected the claim, answering that the board ought to use available legal remedies to prosecute speculators.

Another rich source on competing legalities is the materials of the Main Land Committee.[40] Again we see the pattern of appeals from the grassroots to the provincial and district commissars and the commissars' own sometimes impassioned appeals to the central government. On August 31 a congress of clergy in Kherson District denounced the illegal activities of the volost' land committees, which on August 13 took over church and parish land, declaring that the clergy could no longer give the land out for use without land committee approval and that the rents on the land were not to be more than five rubles per dessiatine for the agrarian year. The rents were to remain in the treasury of the district land uprava to be used to retire land payments. The clergy used legality as a defense, claiming that MZ decrees would not be followed or recognized as legal if they were not approved by the entire Provisional Government. Here began a typical Russian bureaucratic paper chase. The clergy appealed to the local commissar, who sent it on for decision to the central MVD, which sent it to the MZ, which sent it to the Main Land Committee. Which is to say that what passed for the government sent the matter to a quasi-government legislative commission with no executive authority!

In Kaluga Province the land committees reported that peasant clearings were taking on a mass character in the absence of clear government directives (the report was dated October 24—with the claim that they had never received a directive asking for information).[41] They reported that there were few disorders but serious shortages of fuel and construction materials. Although there had been "some misunderstandings" during the harvest, these had been solved by the various levels of land committees, which had tried and largely succeeded in keeping order without resorting to compulsion.

A. M. Krasnousov, a member of the executive committee of Peasants Deputies, reported on the work of the Commissariat of the Soviet of Peasants Deputies in the western Siberian city of Omsk. Most of the Commissariat's work had been instruction on the organization of local self-government and militias and "working through the huge mass of misunderstandings which have emerged in the villages as a result of the lack of information. Though many institutions had participated in such organizational work—it and the sending of individual commissars has not achieved the goals. The mass of the population is completely unable to imagine the new order and continues to be an uninformed mass."[42] The commissar viewed the rapid organization of self-government as the best weapon against counterrevolution and noted that twenty-one instructor units had already been at work toward this goal. In many places the old civil servants had been replaced by new public organizations, but there was great disorder as a result.

Yet legality intersected with the bifurcated model of the revolution as bringing about a "new order" that had already replaced the "old." The revolution produced an imperative on the part of the Provisional Government and representatives of interests alike to judge the "old order" and its denizens and to protect and promote the new. This even took the form of institutionalized procedures and courts set up to identify and prosecute enemies of the new order from ordinary walks of life.[43]

Finally a few words should be included about the leader, or leaders: Prince Georgii Lvov and Kerensky.[44] In a recently published diary, Prince Trubetskoy, the younger, gave firsthand contemporary evidence of what had long been known, namely, Lvov's weakness and unwillingness to back principled positions taken by well-meaning high officials. It is striking to see just how easily he was willing to undercut the authority of his own government while espousing neo-Slavophile, though liberal, visions of a "Russian way." But on Kerensky there is much new to be said, most of it at odds with his own self-portrayal and R. Abraham's recent biography. The archives are full of material addressed to Kerensky from all sectors of Russian society (this tradition of direct communication, of petition, remained very important also in Soviet times). There are abundant new archival sources as used, for example, by Sheila Fitzpatrick in her book *Stalin's Peasants* and many others. These sources, of course, must be read carefully.

From Kiev on August 30 (in the immediate aftermath of the Kornilov affair fiasco) one Anna Khalemskaia sent a "hymn to our glorious leader A. F. Kerensky":[45]

You are our true sunlight
The mind and heart of the native Russian revolution
You are our titan, you are our savior
of freedom for our holy motherland
With all the heart and thoughts of the citizens
greet you, Great Citizen
Before your glorious courage

Similarly, the radical publicist Lydiia Armand produced in mid-September a little pamphlet on the great leader, claiming in the introduction that this was only the beginning, that soon "they will build legends and sing songs about him."[46] Armand began and ended with the image of a wounded lion, in this case wounded by slander and demagoguery. She portrayed Kerensky as a dedicated revolutionary going back to 1906, 1913, 1915, and the February days, when he pushed the Duma to take leadership and stand at the center of the revolution. Where is he headed—she asked—Olympus or Golgotha? Sure, he made mistakes but the great ones always do. Then she described the Moscow State Conference—how when he was out of the hall there was fear, but when he appeared all calmed down. Many thought at the time, "What if we lose him?" And all saw what great feelings were illuminated by this severe (stern) masterful authority. The Democratic part of the conference loved him as a man and had faith in him as a minister, but there is a loss of heart after the state conference (and as a result of Kornilov).

These views must be contrasted with the views of the ordinary citizens writing in from the vast Russian expanses. A moving echo of the past came from one of the few living peace mediators (of the first call-up in 1863—the group of public spirited idealists charged with working with the peasants to implement the emancipation of the serfs). Here the voice was accusatory: "What have you done with our motherland after the February Revolution that we had all greeted with such rapture?"[47] You have seized power with the help of dark irresponsible forces and your four months in power have seen the beginning of the collapse of Russia (and here especially the reference was to the loss of Ukraine and Finland with the Trans-Caucasus only awaiting the right moment to follow). Other letters in the files cover the spectrum from accusations that Kerensky was a Jew, to Theodore Roosevelt's congratulations from Oyster Bay and his admonitions that Russia had to stay the course and that building democracy was a difficult business. For Roosevelt self-government was the key, and he wrote, "Only that nation may embark on the path of democracy that has mastered its passions." "Russia," he continued, "needed self-control, which if not provided, would be served up to the Russians by someone else."[48]

That someone else turned out to be an internal force, that potent combination of Russian traditions of bureaucracy and autocracy, the nature of Russian society, and the catalyst of ideology that combined to create a new order, named socialism, such as the Russians and outsiders alike had never imagined. The various democratic possibilities called forth in revolutionary Russia were subsumed under the power of the executive and its cult-generating capacity as well as administration broadly conceived. This returns us to corporatism and its relationship to the theme of our volume: the control of populations in the twentieth century. The Provisional Government's experience, or, put more broadly, Russia's democratic experiments in 1917, reveal again the very close relationship between the transformative politics of both the Great War and the Russian Revolution and forms of democracy that included alternatives to parliamentary institutions. In 1917, many in Russia were indeed eager to honor the long-cherished goal of a Constituent Assembly. Indeed the story of how the elections to that short-lived assembly were held under the most difficult of circumstances after the Bolsheviks had come to power in October is powerful evidence of the spread of notions of popular sovereignty among broad strata of the population.[49] But the popularity of the Constituent Assembly must be measured against the much deeper political and social power of administration and interest groups that could be mobilized by the state.

MARY LOUISE ROBERTS 4

The Dead and the Unborn

French Pronatalism and the Abortion Law of 1920

ON JULY 23, 1920, a *proposition de loi* came before the French Chambre des deputés aimed at repressing propaganda for abortion and contraception. It imposed stiff penalties for any means of propaganda—advertisements, articles, lectures, posters, the sale of objects—that encouraged abortion and the use of contraceptive devices.[1] The proposition met with little vocal opposition in the Chamber, except from two Socialists, André Berthon (Paris) and Paul Morucci (Bouches-du-Rhône), who contested it on both practical and moral grounds.[2] Questioning the imprecise wording of the law, Berthon asked if its text included "a condemnation of the prophylactics you see visible in every pharmacy window?"[3] In light of the law, he wondered, what might the Chamber do with the letters of Madame Sévigné, which, "as we all know, in fact give particularly precise advice on the way in which one should behave in the conjugal bed."[4] Not surprisingly, these remarks caused an uncomfortable stir in the room. "Let us not forget that this debate is public," one member of the Senate felt called upon to say.[5]

Nonplussed, Berthon went on to object to the law on practical grounds, reminding his colleagues that "in order to have numerous children, one must first be able to feed them. Society must give assistance to single mothers, organize domestic assistance, and provide leaves of absence during pregnancy and after birth."[6] Berthon insisted that although he wasn't against the idea of legislative action to encourage natality, he objected to the hasty, badly conceived, and overly negative way it was being dealt with here. These views were seconded by Deputy Morucci, who continued Berthon's verbal attack with a bad pun. "The good faith of our colleagues today is no doubt indisputable," he conceded, "but the ground on which they are standing seems to me to be hardly favourable to fertilization." He accused his colleagues of crude economic calculations and of seeking national health and happiness in "big numbers." Like Berthon, he demanded that "the state prepare the cradle before demanding the child." Finally, he defended women who aborted, arguing that they were not "criminal recidivists" intent on breaking the law but instead the desperate poor, driven to any risk rather than face another mouth to feed.[7]

Despite these objections, however, which were met by an increasingly hostile, impatient audience, the law passed in the Chamber the same day by an overwhelming majority of 521 votes to 55.[8] It was approved by the Senate without discussion six days later and became known as the *loi scélérate*, the most oppressive of its kind in Europe.[9] The apparent ease with which the law passed the Chamber and the Senate is misleading, for it had already languished in Parliament for almost a decade.[10] In 1918, however, the bill was brought to light, voted on, and passed in a matter of months. This sudden, somewhat surprising victory articulates two distinctive traits of postwar pronatalism: first, the pervasive, almost universal, support it enjoyed in French society; and second, the new willingness of the French state to legislate on its behalf. Far from being limited to the world of practical politics, pronatalist values and ideals permeated all elements of postwar French culture, from novels and short stories to the discourses of social reform, from sociological studies of French society to inquiries on demobilization, from editorials in the popular bourgeois press to medical literature in professional journals.[11] In fact, pronatalist values were so pervasive that counterdiscourses that might challenge their cultural authority almost did not exist.[12] As we have seen, only the most politically marginal figures, such as Socialist deputies Berthon and Morucci, dared to openly denounce them. Pronatalist legislative victories in the 1920s included another even more severe law against abortion, in 1923.[13]

How can we explain this sudden legislative sweep? Historians have interpreted it in two ways. First, they have seen pronatalist legislation as a logical gesture of the postwar conservative, nationalist Bloc National, which came into power in 1919.[14] Yet while leadership from the more conservative wing of the Bloc National was no doubt important in bringing the bill to the Chamber floor in July 1920, it alone cannot account for its passage once there. As the Chamber vote shows, the pronatalist cause found widespread, almost unanimous support across the political spectrum; only Socialists as a group spoke out against it.[15] Similar widespread support characterized the Senate vote as well. Clearly, then, its appeal was not specifically politically based.[16]

Second, historians see the 1920 pronatalist victory as a response to an already serious demographic problem made infinitely worse by wartime casualties.[17] Although postwar demographic realities were admittedly grim, and no doubt played an important part in spurring legislators to action, this explanation also becomes only partial when we consider the way the law of

1920 was constructed. As Berthon was right to point out, the law, for all its severity, did nothing to curb the two most widely used methods of contraception: coitus interruptus and the condom. Although the first of these was clearly beyond the legislators' control to legislate, prophylactics did remain widely available to men, "visible in every pharmacy window," supposedly to prevent venereal disease. Nor did the law provide in any way for the reduction of child mortality, the other of Berthon's objections, a serious problem and a major goal of social legislation in the past.[18] In its punitive logic, the law of 1920 was exceptional; most postwar pronatalist legislation took the more positive form of trying to stimulate births and lower infant mortality.[19] Prohibitive rather than protective, the law of 1920 sought specifically to bring women's sexual practices under legislative control by attacking both abortion and specifically female forms of contraception.[20]

Given the widespread use of coitus interruptus and male prophylactics as contraceptive practices in France, the deputies who voted the law must have known all too well that it would have no effect (as it didn't) on French population decline.[21] A widely respected expert on childbirth, Radical deputy Adolphe Pinard, told his colleagues in the Chamber: "If you were bringing us the certitude of raising French natality both in quality and quantity, I would vote for your proposition with two hands; but what you bring is only the shadow of a repression."[22] Given Pinard's sterling reputation and his angry condemnation of the bill as merely repressive, why did the deputies vote for it in such large numbers?

The answer to this question lies in the specific historical meanings attached to concepts such as "contraception," "abortion," "depopulation," and "natality" in postwar France, as well as the particular rhetorical context in which they were articulated. Far from being transparent or transhistorical in meaning, *depopulation* and *abortion*, as terms used by legislators to debate social policy, were deeply embedded in the trauma of the war and the tensions of postwar recovery. In many ways the pronatalist rhetoric used by members of Parliament replicated that used by depopulation groups from the turn of the century onward; they attributed depopulation to "egoism" or excessive individualism and the degradation of paternal authority in French law.[23] At the same time, concepts such as "depopulation" and "abortion" changed subtly in meaning in the 1920s. In short, they became intimately associated with the war, caught up in an identity of holocausts, which gave them unprecedented force and power.

The parliamentary debates leading up to the passage of the 1920 law were inscribed within a specific horizon of meaning. They relied on a certain collective knowledge of the political system, a common conceptual understanding of the problems at hand (such as the "crisis of depopulation"), and even a communal set of metaphors. This political culture, shared by all deputies and senators who participated in postwar Parliamentary debate, made possible political exchange and decision-making. Parliamentary debate was based on belief in *persuasion* as the ultimate arbiter of political decision-making. Parliamentary persuasion, in turn, was grounded in the assumption that those involved in the debate inhabited the same universe of meaning. If not, they could not understand the terms of the argument being put forth, nor be aroused by the rhetorical and metaphorical devices used to convince them. In short, they could not be persuaded of an argument if it was not, in some sense, culturally intelligible.[24]

Thinking about the debates in this way transforms them into objects of cultural history, a series of texts that can be analyzed by the historian for the specific cultural economy they articulate. Such a historical analysis would define social policy (such as the law against propaganda for abortion and contraception) as a cultural construct, inasmuch as it is grounded in a certain conceptual ordering of social relationships. To give attention to this specific cultural economy—what "depopulation" or "abortion" meant to the legislator in all its historical complexity—is to illuminate a web of signification that, in turn, can explain his rationale in policy making.

Demographers and historians of French depopulation have often argued that the drop in the birthrate was central to France's loss of political, military, and economic hegemony in Europe and that it resulted from some moral or economic decline in French society.[25] In part, this interpretation of French depopulation reflects contemporaneous pronatalist views. As we shall see, it was common among late nineteenth- and early-twentieth-century pronatalists to make apocalyptic statements about France's future and to ascribe depopulation to moral decadence. More recently, the tendency has been to see French depopulation as not necessarily a bad thing but rather a rational response on the part of the French to the demands of industrialization and urbanization.[26] In this light, the fact that depopulation was nevertheless seen by many postwar Frenchmen as a profound crisis that threatened the very existence of France gains significance—not simply as a "wrong" perception—but as a cultural reality in itself, a means of understanding what kinds of social practices inspired fear, anger, and anxiety in the postwar French. In the cultural economy of the parliamentary debates, why was depopulation seen as a matter of life and death? Were other fears and anxieties about war losses (not merely or exclusively demographic) linked to concern about depopulation? If so, can these other losses explain the sudden passage of the law against abortion and contraceptive propaganda in 1920?

Senate debates concerning the law against propaganda for abortion and contraception were spread over three sessions, the first taking place on November 21, 1918, only ten days after the armistice, and the other two shortly afterward, in late January, 1919. These debates became virtual theaters of anxiety, with senators often using hyperbolic and apocalyptic language in order to make their arguments. In the first debate, on November 21, conservative Dominique Delahaye (Right, Maine-et-Loire) argued that "If France does not produce more children, our country is destined to gradually disappear."[27] When Henry Chéron (Union républicaine, Calvados) declared that Malthusian propaganda militated "against the very existence of the country. . . . This is a question of life or death for France," he received enthusiastic signs of approbation from his colleagues.[28]

Although the need to establish the "urgency" of one's cause is important to any social movement, the "crisis" of depopulation, with its proliferating death sentences and obituaries, must be understood as more than a means of self-legitimation. Here "depopulation" as a rhetorical concept was forced to bear responsibility for a variety of other displaced anxieties, in particular, military vulnerability. The rapporteur-général of the bill in the Senate, Paul Cazeneuve (Radical, Rhône) began his opening statement in November by quoting, again, Pinard: "If our population had been equal to that of Germany, we would probably not have been victims of an invasion."[29] Making a similar argument, Senator Jénouvrier (Gauche républicaine, Ile-et-Vilaine) referred to denatality when he argued: "If we cannot put up a sufficient barrier against it . . . it will be in vain that our sons will have been killed."[30] The phrase *sufficient barrier* (somewhat ironic in this context) itself evokes the need for physical protection, a military barricade or Maginot Line. These senators fused postwar fears concerning depopulation, military weakness, and German revenge, and they appealed to the often intensely pacifist sentiments of the French public in support of the pronatalist cause.

In this way, the "crisis" of depopulation became the master narrative of postwar military and political anxiety. This, of course, would explain the debate's apocalyptic tone, alone able to bear the intellectual and moral weight of depopulation's burden of rhetorical meaning. The tone of the debates was also heightened by the senators' tendency to construct an image of France as a sick, anemic, or wounded body. The popularity of this pronatalist image of France as a dying body in need of medico-legislative attention was no mere coincidence: Emile Goy and a sizable number of other Senators were physicians (for example, Paul Cazeneuve, the *rapporteur-général* of the bill).[31] In the January debates, Senator Reveillaud (Radical, Charente-Inférieure) referred to a book, *Les malades sociales*, by Paul Gaultier, and claimed that "the number of . . . social diseases is, alas, considerable." Their root cause, in his view, was the issue at hand, contraceptive propaganda: "France has suffered a great deal from this propaganda," he argued, terming its principles "theories of death."[32] Goy (Radical, Radical-Socialist, Haute-Savoie) created this Spenglerian image of a dying French civilization: "Civilizations are subject to the same processes as all things of this world: they have their moment of youth, of blossoming, and of maturity; then the germs of death which they contain within them, like any other living thing, develop little by little and lead to decrepitude and death."[33]

To save France from this fate, Goy argued for "the addition of foreign, ethnic elements," which "younger, more robust" would "infuse" her with "new blood."[34] Goy exploited sexual images to give his argument force and meaning. If France could be compared to a dying old man or a desiccated old woman beyond her "reproductive years," immigration would recharge him (or her) with new vigor, virility, and life.

It was as managers of life and death, of bodies and the French race, that legislators passed the law against abortion and propaganda in 1920. These efforts were fraught with ambivalence for two reasons: first, because they threatened to undermine *la puissance paternelle* (the authority of the male household head), and second, because of their horrifying implications in the war just passing. As the historian Sylvia Schafer has shown, prewar social legislation gave the state increasing power to intervene in family life when parents were believed to be morally corrupt and hence unable to care for their children. In this case, the state justified its own intervention through the metaphor of the French state as a *père universel* or "metaparent." However, as Schafer points out, the social and political agenda of republican politics demanded that the private, familial ideal as well as the paternal authority of the *chef de famille* (enshrined in the Napoleonic Code) be respected. Hence the senators needed to justify state intervention in the family in a way which did not threaten *la puissance paternelle*. The fiction of private, familial authority had to be upheld as the precondition for the state's increasing control over this same terrain.[35]

In the case of the law of 1920, the senators justified intervention as both members of Parliament and as physicians; they considered it their duty to parent/doctor the child—in this case, not even yet born—whom the morally corrupt mother had endangered by her wish to abort. They also equated the endangered child with the future of France itself. Chéron, for example, described propaganda for abortion and contraception as "propaganda against French natality, that is, against the nation."[36] Seen in this way, from within the larger history of the republican social policy, the law of 1920 revealed the state's increasing confidence to act as the père universel of the French family.

The senators' efforts to act as managers of life and death were fraught with ambivalence for a second reason. Nowhere had such powers to decide matters of life and death been more tragically displayed than in the war, when the state had drafted hundreds of thousands of young men and sent them to their death. These senators must have been acutely aware of such powers in these debates, some of which took place only weeks after the armistice. Consider, for example, these impassioned words of Léon Jenouvrier:

> If we cannot put up a sufficient barrier against [depopulation] . . . it will be in vain that our sons will have been killed; it will be in vain that France will have offered this most horrible holocaust that history has ever known to the defense of liberty and of civilization—1,400,000 killed, others say 1,800,000, a million severely disabled, all of which made three million victims out of eight million mobilized, more than a third, and what a third! The most young and the most courageous, the majority of whom should have been *chefs de familles*, fathers of a family. How can we heal such a wound? How can we fill such a deficit? We must persuade the country that nations are depopulated less by men being killed than by men not being born.[37]

The specter of a wounded, bleeding France, exhausted by "the most horrible holocaust that history has ever known" haunted these debates. Most recently, several historians have shown how the 1920s was a period of acute mourning, in which the peoples of Europe glorified the war dead and grieved their own personal losses.[38] The legislators, then, were all too aware that their power to decide life and death in the family had caused the death or mutilation of millions of potential chefs de famille, in all their youth and virility. If France had become an emasculated nation, which had lost the best third of its "most young and most courageous," was the state responsible? The rhetorical cadences of Jenouvrier's speech here bring into alignment those Frenchmen killed and those not able to be born, the "wound" that France has suffered from the loss of its virile core, and the "deficit" that numerically must be filled. The word *deficit* takes on more than a strictly demographic meaning here and becomes as well a repository of guilt, a reparation to be paid for the slaughter of innocents.

Inasmuch as the war was also a matter of life and death, something about abortion and Malthusian propaganda became unbearable after the war. In the cultural economy of postwar France, depopulation became linked to a whole other set of meanings that concerned the war, its traumas, and its sacrifices. In the eyes of the senators, haunted by the wounds of war and their own growing powers, abortion and Malthusian propaganda became searing affronts to the dead. When the senator and physician Cazeneuve was called upon to defend the principle of medical confidentiality, he conflated the "terrible holocaust" of the war with the threat of abortion or Malthusian propaganda: "I am among those who believe that after the great ordeal that our country has suffered, after the attacks which certain criminals by profession inflict on the population," the doctor must tell what he knows.[39] In Cazeneuve's phraseology, "the great ordeal" of the war and Malthusian, criminal "attacks" were again aligned and identified with each other. France was once again the (emasculated, female) victim-body of both: having "suffered" the war, she must now endure what abortionists "inflicted" upon her. Cazeneuve's identification of abortion with the war's ordeal explains his graphic and highly emotional language in condemning the rise of abortions in recent years. Quoting a physician, he said: "I advise all persons who are upset about the future of our country, from the point of view of its natality, to go look at the number of fetuses which are dredged up [*ramènent*] by sewer boats. Go see the thousands of victims who are carried away to the Seine, or which, on the way, become stuck in the iron bars of the sewers."[40]

It is tempting to connect Cazeneuve's tortured description, which formed a climactic moment in an already emotionally charged opening speech, with the "thousands of victims" to which Jenouvrier referred.[41] The power of a state to guarantee the life and health of the social body was joined in these legislators' minds to the other power of the state: to expose an entire population to danger and death. Victims of war or victims of abortion—both were marked by their innocence and struck down in mind-boggling numbers. Both were perceived as bearing upon "the future of our country" and the "defense of civilization"; both represented "a matter of life and death." Both "inflicted" emotional and sexual "wounds," which somehow needed to be healed. In the minds of senators such as Cazeneuve, Malthusian propaganda was joined to the war at its most raw and deadly core: as a set of "theories of death," the propaganda, too, inflicted upon France a most horrible holocaust, that is, the slaughtering of innocent victims.

This flashing back and forth between the cradle and the tomb also characterized the conception of the law in the Chamber.[42] The *exposé des motifs* (statement of purpose) of the first, original version of the law, deposed on January 22, 1920, argued that "in a France which is wounded in her flesh, the situation calls for certain measures which will give her not only her former vitality, but also a power of expansion."[43] Once again, the language of the exposé suggested a war-wounded and emasculated body-nation, whose virility and life force ("power of expansion") could only be recovered through pronatalist measures.[44] The second *exposé des motifs*, presented by Edouard Ignace in July, also directly aligned the war with abortion and contraceptive propaganda: "On the morrow of a war in which nearly 1,500,000 Frenchmen sacrificed their lives so that France had the right to live in independence and honor, it cannot be tolerated that other Frenchmen have the right to make enormous amounts of money from the multiplication of abortions and from Malthusian propaganda."[45]

This identity of holocausts could have had a particularly mobilizing effect in the Chamber, which was dubbed the Chambre Bleu Horizon because so many of its deputies, freshly returned from the front, still wore the sky-blue army uniform. These deputy-veterans were particularly aware of the sacrifices made by their comrades so that France "had the right to live in independence and honor." They must have felt keenly the "intolerability" of those who made "enormous amounts of money" from death, a stock resentment of the poilu toward the rich war capitalist.

"Depopulation" and "abortion," as concepts used by senators and deputies to debate the law of 1920, were historically embedded not only in the economic and military anxieties of a rocky postwar period but also in the trauma and guilt of the holocaust just passing. How could one heal such a wound? To Cazeneuve the path of action was clear: "Messieurs, after the great ordeal of this war, which has reduced by so much the number of our sons, that is, the most active element of our population, and in the presence of the appalling losses that we have suffered, we have the duty to do everything we can so that the country can be regenerated and repopulated."[46] Given the cultural economy of postwar France—the specific horizon of meaning within which these parliamentary debates were inscribed—Cazeneuve could not have picked a more persuasive rhetoric. By framing the pronatalist argument within "the great ordeal" of the war, Cazeneuve and the other legislators exploited a set of metaphors that enjoyed unequaled cultural force and which would resonate strongly with, and thus convince, their colleagues. If France lay wounded and dying, then the senator's role, as both legislator and (in the case of Cazeneuve, Goy, and others) as doctor, was to regenerate it by passing the law of 1920. The law itself had an ironic, double effect: on the one hand it extended the state's right to control the family and the human body; on the other, it also reversed, or at least seemed to reverse, the state's exercise of its right to kill. In this law, at least, the senators would be saving victims rather than creating them, at the same time that they reasserted their power to decide a matter of life and death. The law represented both a reassertion of the state's confidence in its own power and a way to appease what troubled that confidence, that is, the slaughter of 1.5 million men in the war.

In addition, the law provided a clear path of action to resolve what appeared to be a bewildering array of problems plaguing the state in the postwar era. The French state emerged from the war as much exhausted as it was victorious, and beset with unprecedented economic, social, and diplomatic problems, among them runaway inflation and the scarcity of even basic foodstuffs.[47] Yet the legislators charged with solving the fiscal and monetary problems at hand were woefully unprepared for the task before them. Most were economically illiterate and had little or no experience dealing with shaky currency.[48] This sense of inadequacy and anxiety felt by legislators in dealing with the economic situation was compounded by fears of Germany and the rising Soviet state.[49]

French legislators in 1919 to 1920 were thus faced with enormous and complex tasks, many of which they felt incapable of solving and even of understanding. As P. Bernard and H. Dubief have argued, many of them coped by retreating into a web of illusions: believing that Germany would totally repay reparations or that France would be able to return to the gold standard.[50] Not least among these illusions, I would argue, was the belief that France would be healed, reborn economically and militarily through a simple increase in her natality. Although the problems facing legislators were confoundingly diverse, when they were linked together as various symptoms of one "social disease"—depopulation—they were rendered magically coherent. Pronatalist discourse itself generated anxiety but only to manage it with its own reassuring logic: "If we only have children, many of these problems will be solved." The logical movement of pronatalist discourse was therefore cathartic: it mobilized anxiety only to resolve it, raising it to a fevered pitch (of the like we have seen in the Senate debates) only to produce a clear, uncomplicated path of action, including the law against abortion and contraceptive propaganda.

Once again, however, not everyone was convinced that raising the natality rate would magically cause belle epoque stability to reappear. Radical feminist Nelly Roussel evaluated the effectiveness of pronatalist efforts in this way: "Once again, all these gentlemen are wasting their time. No matter how stupid the people are . . . you would nevertheless be hard-pressed to get them to admit that in the state of economic, financial and physiological 'collapse' in which we find ourselves . . . and at a time when our shaken, exhausted race has hardly begun its convalescence after the terrible shock, that a multiplication of births would be a benefit for the country!"[51] Like Berthon, Roussel tried to point out the feeble logic that underwrote the pronatalist argument. But even among feminists, most of whom were strong pronatalists themselves, Roussel's view was largely condemned.[52] Did this make feminists, and the French in general, "stupid" as Roussel claims them to be? Perhaps the answer to this question lies in Roussel's own use of language, her evoking, no less than Goy, the "shaken, exhausted" body of France, which "has hardly begun its convalescence" after the war. If the French were "stupid" about pronatalism, it was perhaps because of its magically healing effects, its power to soothe "the terrible shock" of war. And if the French legislators were "wasting their time," as the ultimate failure of the 1920 law indeed demonstrated, they at least had found a way to understand the bewildering problems the war had left to them.

Using the family as a means to work out social anxieties had a long history among the legislators and politicians of Third Republic France. Because the family was considered to be an essential foundation to a good republic, its inner workings were afforded an extraordinary amount of attention and came increasingly under legislative control beginning in 1870.[53] But tinkering with the French family was by no means the exclusive domain of republican politicians, as the Vichy slogan "Travail, Famille, Patrie" reminds us. The historian Cheryl Koos has persuasively shown how the conservative vision of gender relations promulgated by Vichy, as well as its measures to increase the French birthrate, both found their origins, at least partially, in interwar pronatalism.[54] Most fundamentally, pronatalists shared with Vichy politicians a belief in the state's right to control the body and the family—to decide matters of life as well as death. These new powers, forged in the crucible of the Great War, were enabled in peacetime by the ideological work of gender. Conventional gender norms served to naturalize the newly expanded ambitions of the state by cloaking them in such regulatory fictions as the ideal domestic mother.

CLAUDIA KOONZ 5

"More Masculine Men, More Feminine Women"

The Iconography of Nazi Racial Hatreds

EUGENIA SEMYONOVNA GINZBURG, after years in Stalin's Gulag, reflected on the fragile line dividing victim and perpetrator. "After all, I was the anvil, not the hammer. But might I too have become a hammer?"[1] Several chapters in this volume examine the capaciousness of "victimhood" as public memory transforms, in Omer Bartov's words, the "boundless definitions of purity and pollution." We see, too, the speed with which the defining terms of "the enemy" can shift, for example, from class to ethnobiological qualities, as in the case of heroes and victims in Soviet ideology at the close of Stalin's rule that Amir Weiner investigates. Gazing backward from our scholarly remove, we easily perceive the tragic arbitrariness of policies that mobilize communities against "outsiders" who have been neighbors for decades and even centuries.

However, at the time when individuals carry out their deadly mission of ethnic, political, or class "cleansing," they cannot afford to harbor any doubts about the utter separation between themselves and their "enemies." The "Hammers" must not suspect that they share human qualities with "anvils." Lev Kopelev, one of a handful of perpetrators who have acknowledged their crimes, recalled that when, as a twenty-year-old Communist, he terrorized helpless peasants in the name of Stalin's collectivization drive: "Everything was so clear and simple: I belonged to the only true party, was a fighter in the only just war for the victory of the most progressive social class in history and thus for the betterment of all human kind."[2] The ideals that shaped this young soldier's identity were specific to Stalin's USSR, but his indoctrination for extermination was, in its fundamentals, typical of military training everywhere. In the language of the contemporary United States military, instructors apply sophisticated "desensitization" techniques to inculcate the difference between "murder" (a sin and crime) and "killing" (a historical necessity). By dehumanizing the "enemy," recruits are converted from "ordinary men" into "ordinary soldiers."[3] The Nazi indoctrination that converted ordinary soldiers into ethnic warriors prefigured the techniques used to prepare soldiers and civilians for ethnic war at the close of the twentieth century.

Compliance with Nazi racial edicts depended not only on relatively small numbers of Storm Troopers, Gestapo agents, Einsatzkommando units, and order policemen on the Eastern Front, but on grassroots compliance within Germany. Uprooting fellow citizens from their communities and subjecting them to racial "actions" required a network of dedicated civilians. As Robert Gellately's research reveals, a veritable "culture of denunciation" motivated Germans to watch zealously over neighbors' and colleagues' attitudes and behavior.[4] Self-righteous enthusiasm fired the thousands and thousands of average Germans who targeted "suspicious" neighbors, tabulated statistics on "defectives" in their care, reported on malicious gossip, spied on "degenerates," and identified Jews. What factors account for such widespread compliance?

Starting with Allied portrayals of "the German character" during World War II through recent depictions of a uniquely German hatred of Jews, many historical accounts have cordoned off Nazi genocide beyond comparative analysis. Paul Rose concluded that "Only if an entire culture were permeated—not always malevolently—with anti-Semitic sensibility could it allow itself to initiate and participate in such a process as the Holocaust."[5] John Weiss, estimating that about half of all German citizens "rejected the racist violence of the Nazis," nevertheless asserts, "It was the singular path of modern German history that ultimately gave anti-Semites the power to destroy the Jewish community."[6] Daniel Goldhagen takes the argument a step further: "Indeed, the evidence indicates not Germans' 'indifference,' but their pitilessness. . . . Germans flocked to watch the assaults on the Jews . . . just as spectators once flocked to medieval executions and children flock to the circus."[7]

At the other interpretative pole, psychologists have searched for the transcultural roots of genocide, either in particular character traits, such as those suggested in Max Horkheimer's and Theodor Adorno's "F-Scale" experiments, or in late-twentieth-century presentiments, such as Robert Jay Lifton's "Holocaust Mentality."[8] Still others locate the "modern" origins of the Holocaust in the Enlightenment. Following the interpretation of the Frankfurt School, Richard Rubenstein suggested that a distinctively modern ideal has inspired states to "improve" the citizens they are charged to protect.[9] Sociologist Zygmunt Bauman extended the interpretation. "The Holocaust is a byproduct of the modern drive to a fully designed, fully controlled world" that is halted only by pragmatic inhibitors (such as political pluralism and guarantees of civic rights).[10] Peter Holquist, in this volume, uses the verb *to sculpt* in describing leaders' violent attacks against minorities. For Bauman, the gamekeeper and the gardener provide apt metaphors. Unlike the leisurely gamekeeper of earlier ages, who merely watched over his realm, the modern state is like a diligent gardener who is "armed with a detailed design of the lawn, of the borders and . . . [seized] with the determination to treat as weeds every self-invited plant which interferes with his plan and his vision of order and harmony."[11] Bauman's metaphor of the gardening state, while useful in highlighting the role of instrumental reason in genocide, misleads us by directing our attention only to weeds and gardener—while ignoring both the "desirable" plants and the gardener's zealous apprentices.

In this chapter, I describe the aesthetic and scientific components of Aryan identity, in other words, the gendered racial "blueprint" that inspired the design of the Nazi garden and supplied the core imagery that popularized it. Apprentices, weeds, and valuable plants formed part of a racialized "imagined community," to use Benedict Anderson's phrase. But although Anderson (like Terrence Ranger, Eric Hobsbawm, and Craig Calhoun), operating within this scholarly framework, ignores gender and barely notes race, these two terms formed the core of Nazi discourse on the national body (*Volkskörper*).[12] Historians have scrutinized every dimension of Nazi racial policy, but they have only begun to notice gender. Perhaps Nazi policies on the family and "woman question" seemed sufficiently ubiquitous that scholars failed to consider (much less "problematize") them. Yet Nazi doctrine on gender provided commonsense support for a logic that connected characterological differences to anatomical traits. Assumptions about physiologically fixed sexual character reinforced the linkage between external racial markers and individual value. If male and female displayed contrasting personality traits, as virtually everyone at the time believed they did, then did it not follow that genetically defective or racially alien individuals also bore the marks of their difference? Focusing on the gendered dimensions of stereotypes of these two "outsider" categories, I will trace one dimension of the transformation of prejudice into murderous hatred. Although much about Nazi racial propaganda was distinctive, its basic goal differed little from genocidal discourse elsewhere: to incite the strong to attack the weak.

The capacity of a modern state to mobilize national solidarity across the premodern divides of class, religion, region, and political belief had already become visible before World War I. Two experiences in particular presaged ominous future developments. At the close of the nineteenth century, as Elisabeth Domansky demonstrates, Western European reformers launched campaigns to "improve" the quality (and quantity) of their own "racial stock" by intruding into citizens' reproductive choices and child-rearing practices. During these same decades, conservative politicians discovered the mass appeal of colonial conquest in the "Heart of Africa" and deployed imperialist rhetoric as a strategy for mobilizing broad segments of newly enfranchised electorates behind patriotic themes. In the first days of August 1914 many of these same conservatives were astonished at the power of the sentiment they had inspired when they saw even the most internationalist socialists and feminists rush to join the war effort. In wartime propaganda, "enemy" Europeans replaced dark-skinned "savages," and reports recycled adjectives from colonial "outrages" in Carl Peters's and David Livingston's southern Africa and in Henry M. Stanley's and King Leopold II's Congo.[13] In the discursive practices of the day, the vocabularies of race and gender exaggerated fissures between "enemy" and "friend" and marked the superiority of the "us" against the "other." The very success of the "mobilization of imagination," again following Domansky, allowed "industrialized slaughter" to continue.[14] In all belligerent nations except Russia, high morale facilitated vast social-engineering projects that recast the masculine-feminine and public-private divides of prewar society.

Throughout the twentieth century, the discursive formulas that solidified the "us" against the "other" in the rhetoric of empire and of war provided the templates for the state-sponsored mass killing of civilians at the close of the century. However, the paradigms of us and them shifted according to the particular context. The tropes of dehumanization that marked the "savage" in Africa stocked the "enemy" imaginary in Europe, and both together contributed to the symbolic universe of a nation threatened by "vermin" within its borders. On a parallel trajectory, the identity of the perpetrators underwent a transformation from arrogant civilizer, to righteous defender of the nation, to endangered body politic. Nowhere was this transformation swifter than in Germany.

Germany, as political historians routinely point out, straddled the geopolitical divide between East and West. Chronologically, Nazi genocide lies at a midpoint on the line connecting colonial conquest, the First World War, the Stalinist purges, the Soviet Gulag, and the ethnobiological slaughter in the postwar and contemporary world. Nazi racial programs also developed in a crucible between two cultural and economic blocs. With its sophisticated communications network, a fully literate population, and a technologically advanced infrastructure, Germany in the 1930s resembled the Western European democracies. But Nazi rule bore strong affinities with the dictatorships of Josef Stalin and Benito Mussolini, and Francisco Franco and Jósef Piłsudski in less industrialized states. Upon seizing power, only Hitler, of all the interwar dictators, inherited an efficient bureaucracy, a disciplined police force, and a sophisticated communications network. A well-organized Nazi Party utilized this potential to both impose and incite an extraordinary degree of compliance from German citizens. The Nazi case, although atypical within interwar Europe, was prototypical of genocidal assaults that occurred a half a century later in ex-Yugoslavia, Rwanda, East Timor, and Azerbaidjan.[15] To maintain their tenuous hold on political power, some authoritarian leaders (such as the ones examined by István Deák) have exercised their monopoly over the media to incite ethnic war. In far too many cases, paraphrasing anthropologist Robert M. Hayden, imagined communities have produced real victims.[16]

In this chapter I examine the tools by which Nazi specialists crafted an "Aryan" identity powerful enough to inspire pride and yet vulnerable enough to make the threat of racial dangers credible. Racial qualities became coterminous with demographic zones of safety and danger. Nazi administrators underwrote the creation of a modern, secular language that blended aesthetic tastes with the authority of science to isolate minorities within the larger national community. The expert replaced the clergyman, and the fanatic displaced the politician. From this it does not follow that zealots necessarily provided the "hard core" of Einsatzkommando killers. Rather, the importance of experts and fanatics lies in their role within the Nazi Party.

In his analysis of ideology, Claude Lefort described the function of the fanatic in totalitarian states. Produced by the mass party, "fanatics" provide a crucial element of both stability and dynamism. In their roles as community leaders, they mediate between (in Lefort's terms) the "imperative of activism" and the "threat of inertia." By embodying the principles of the state/party, the fanatic opens up to himself a range of choices that he experiences as liberating. "He draws from it (the party) the possibility of freeing himself from the conflicts to which he is exposed . . . embodying in his person the generality of the social." Upon entering the party, the fanatic is a "man without specific features, who acquires his definition as fascist or communist man; a pure social agent."[17] Lefort's focus on activism and inertia, however, ignores the danger that the fanatic (motivated by excessive zeal or disillusionment) may escape the chain of command that directs his activism. Norman Naimark remarks on this danger in his discussion in this volume of Soviet leaders' chronic difficulties in both inciting and controlling the population. Nazi Party indoctrination was more successful in tempering fanaticism with constraint. From the earliest days of the Nazi Party, its guidelines routinely paired "propaganda" with "organization." The party obsessively monitored its control over party members, from the 1930s, when the Party Court maintained discipline (without purges), through the Second World War, when Heinrich Himmler obsessively worried that "his" SS men would yield to the temptations of corruption and/or sadism. One element in the relative orderliness of Nazi forces, as I will suggest, was the restraint built into the masculine ideal. In addition, Nazi racial and gender ideology had the advantage of appealing directly to the preexisting prejudices. Whereas the justification for Stalin's collectivization derived from an intellectually elegant Marxist-Leninist orthodoxy, no such constraints bound Hitler, who fashioned his doctrines from commonplace völkisch (folk or ethnic) beliefs and cloaked them in the authority of modern biology.

As Hitler repeated in *Mein Kampf*, leadership does not mean imposing ideas on the audience as much as it does listening to what the audience wishes and then telling it to them. Nazi propaganda addressed every aspect of an individual's public and private life in the most ordinary terms. Polarized gender stereotypes defined the racial superiority of "more masculine men and more feminine women," while "unhealthy" or "distorted" gender behavior stigmatized the "dangerous" and "inferior." Conventional stereotypes about biologically defined human nature formed the vocabulary on which the experts drew. At its most successful, the racialized social universe did not reveal itself as ideology at all, but rather as entertainment, education, or public service. Looking back, historians call this "indoctrination." To Germans in the 1930s, "popularization" would have seemed like a more accurate term. The very ordinariness of the Nazi imaginary disguised its ideological goal so well that contemporaries too seldom found Nazi racial projects alarming and too frequently admired the revival of national racial pride announced by Nazi rulers.

"Political" ideology, in their minds, might refer to the *Führerprinzip*, revenge against Versailles, demand for Lebensraum, or publicity for organizations such as the Labor Front. Racial and gender doctrine, by contrast, appeared within the "apolitical" context of magazines, festivals, films, educational exhibits, textbooks, and news broadcasts. Of course, this wide array of productions remained under tight censorship, but a wide diversity within allowable public speech and images masked the exclusion of "unwanted" ideas. The concept of state-sponsored popular culture may seem like an oxymoron. It is not. Under Joseph Goebbels's Ministry of Propaganda and Popular Enlightenment, scores of educators, filmmakers, artists, writers, racial experts, and scriptwriters responded to mass audiences' hunger for culture. As Alice Kaplan reminds us, during the 1930s, the rapid expansion of audiences meant that there was more culture out there to be enjoyed. In the Western democracies, the private sector supplied it; in Germany the state and party led the way. From the earliest months of the "Third Reich," police (*Sicherheitsdienst*) officials gathered morale monitor reports to test the acceptance of all manner of policies and propaganda. Much as advertising firms in industrialized democracies experimented with market research and opinion polls, Nazi experts calibrated their messages to audience reactions.

Audiences may not have recognized racialized popular culture as "propaganda," but Joseph Goebbels and his deputies certainly did. By his lavish sponsorship of writers, filmmakers, sculptors, artists, and composers, his Ministry of Propaganda and Popular Enlightenment transformed the "nation" into the "racial community" (*Volksgemeinschaft*). Goebbels congratulated himself, "This is the really great art—to educate without revealing the purpose of the education . . . which is also indeed the real purpose of propaganda. The best propaganda is not that which is always openly revealing itself; [but] that which, as it were, works invisibly, penetrates the whole of life without the public having any knowledge at all of the propagandist initiative."[18]

In fact, visual images constituted the most "invisible" propaganda of all. Although a veritable mini-industry has developed around Nazi art interpretation, the centrality of visual texts to racial indoctrination has gone virtually unnoticed.[19] As historian Gerhard Paul notes, the stunningly effective emotional persuasion techniques (*Gefühlspropaganda*) were deployed via speeches and powerful visual images, yet most scholars have trained their sites on the turgid volumes turned out by the likes of Alfred Rosenberg, Hans F. K. Günther, and Walter Darré.[20] And even when historians interpret racial propaganda, they routinely ignore gender. Perhaps the Nazi picture of racial health depended on gender markings and racial prejudices so conventional they scarcely seemed noteworthy. That kind of ordinariness, Homi K. Bhabha reminds us, is the very essence of a nation's modernity, which is written as both "the event of the everyday and the advent of the epoch." He notes that "the feeling of "national belonging comes laden with atavistic apologies."[21] In Nazi propaganda for a racial utopia, "atavistic" concepts retain their currency by appearing as "timeless."

Many cultural critics and not a few political scientists have used the term *banality* when analyzing fascism and Nazism. Few recognize the way Hannah Arendt transformed its connotations when she appropriated "the banality of evil" in her Adolf Eichmann portrait. Kaplan, however, reminds us that, as used by Walter Benjamin and other intellectuals in the interwar years, "banal" referred to plebeian taste, without overtones of moral judgment. Sentimental, hackneyed, and derivative—banal art could be (for those very qualities) democratic, "'open to the use of the entire community.'"[22] Utilizing mechanical mass reproduction, Nazi popular culture made the great classical traditions (which the avant-garde had long since abandoned) available to a wide audience via postcards, films, radio shows, museums, art appreciation books, and sculpture. While Goebbels oversaw the expulsion of degenerate and modernist influences from public view, members of the various official chambers under the Ministry of Propaganda and Public Enlightenment produced a pure alternative—nostalgic images of healthy Aryans—hardened soldiers, peasant Madonnas, stalwart youth. The reworking of eighteenth-century German drama in Nazi cinema opened up to viewers a holistic new social imaginary within which they could shape their own identity.[23] Clement Greenberg, writing in 1939, deplored the outpouring of derivative art as "Kitsch" and commented on its political effectiveness. Kitsch "keeps a dictator in closer contact with the 'soul' of the people. Should the official culture be one superior to the general mass-level, there would be a danger of isolation."[24] In Nazi Germany, a state-sponsored culture industry imitated, duplicated, reproduced, and standardized an aesthetic of the racially "fit."

Aesthetics and science blended to form a racialized popular culture that pulled spectators into the narrative of safety and danger, purity and pollution. Pure Aryan types, defined by radical separation between masculine and feminine, defended their superiority against confusion (*Verwirrung*). In this visual discourse, ambiguity became anomaly; and anomaly spelled danger.[25] The juxtaposition of aesthetically clear-cut and putatively scientific markers separating healthy Aryans from racial and genetic "others" instilled pride in the "us" even as it incited anxieties about the "other." Positioning itself against chaotic and decadent Weimar values, the Third Reich promised a new clarity as it restored the "natural" body. Science provided a shield of objectivity, careerism supplied abundant incentives, and appeals to a historic tradition enhanced moral rectitude. Educators, cultural critics, popular writers, and filmmakers called for a return to "authentic" völkisch (ethnic) values, praised the *Heimat* (the regional, rural homeland) over the metropole and celebrated the collective above the individual. Although crusading vigorously against modernity, state and party leaders stood on the authority of modern science and mimicked the techniques of Hollywood and Madison Avenue. The Nazi Party and the state lavishly sponsored the culture industry that imitated, duplicated, reproduced, and standardized the aesthetic experience of all "fit" citizens. "Atavistic apologies" saturated technologically advanced propaganda.[26]

At the heart of racial health lay polarized gender images. "More masculine men and more feminine women" constituted the norm against which biological danger was identified. In the Nazi aesthetic canon, the salient characteristic of degenerate art lay in its distorted representations of the human form and its blurred gender distinctions, as in Otto Dix's 1926 painting *Drei Weiber* (Figure 1). By publicly displaying "degenerate" art, rather than hiding it from view, Nazi ideologues incited repugnance, which they believed would deepen average Germans' gratitude to the purifying state. Two stereotypes pervaded Nazi painting: gentle female nudes and rugged uniformed men. *The Four Elements* (Die vier Elemente; Figure 2), the triptych above the fireplace in Hitler's Munich residence, features four nudes by painter Adolf Ziegler against a black-and-white tiled floor that recalls the perspective of Renaissance painting. Oskar Graf's *Aphrodite* (Figure 3) stands modestly alone amidst

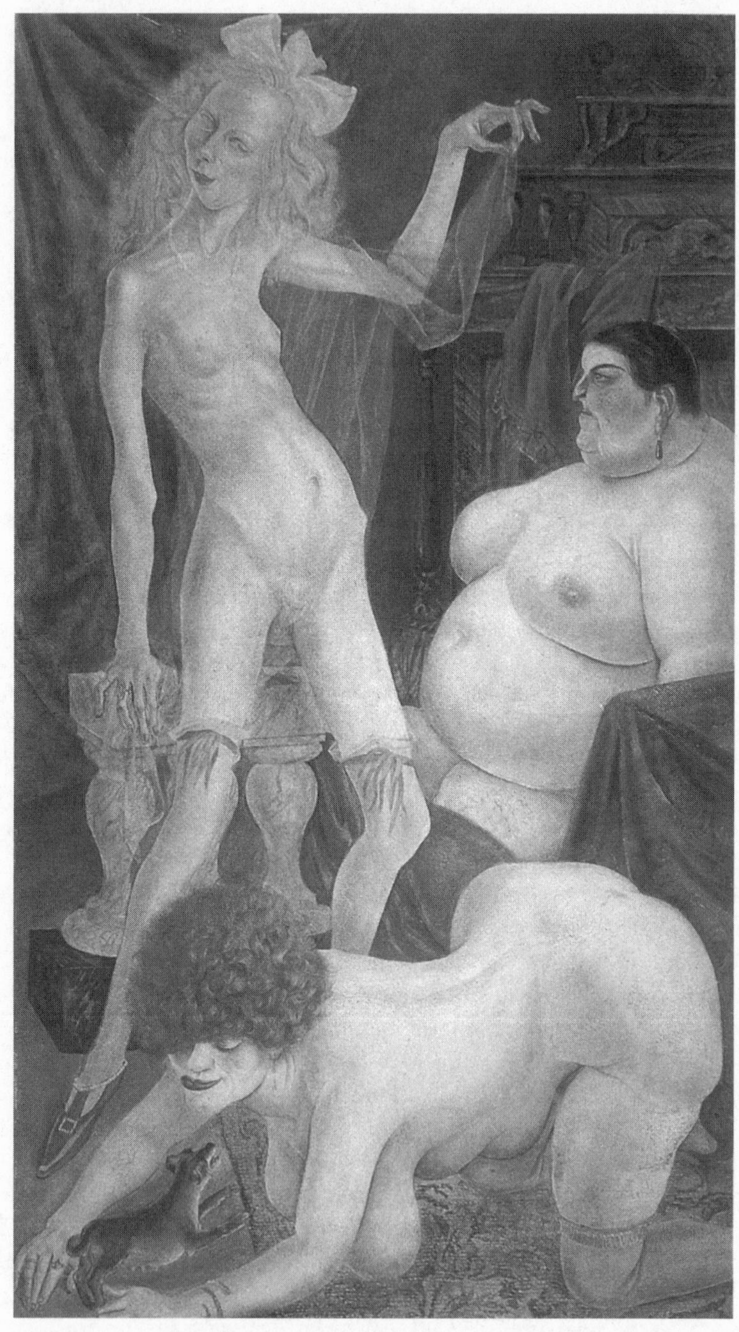

Figure 1. Otto Dix, *Drei Weiber* (Three Females), 1926. Galerie der Stadt, Stuttgart.

Figure 2. Adolf Ziegler, *Die vier Elemente* (The Four Elements). This painting hung in the living room of Adolf Hitler's Munich residence. Bayerische Staatsgemäldesammlung, Munich.

Figure 3. Oskar Graf, *Aphrodite* (Aphrodite), 1941. Deutsches Historisches Museum.

the ruined Greek columns, flat sea, and billowing clouds. Many nudes in the canon of Nazi art draw on Renaissance conventions, in which the utterly unclothed female nude (*nuda veritas*) represents wisdom made available to the scientist or philosopher. In Marina Warner's elegant formulation, "The wholly naked human body, carrying with it multiple meanings of nature, integrity and completeness, transmitted by the allegorical tradition, generated a personification of truth as a female form, often entirely naked, because Truth has nothing to hide and can never be less than whole."[27]

Literary critic Ludmilla Jordanova connects female nudity to the democratization of national personifications and gendered conceptions of science and nature. Representations of nude females, starting with the Renaissance, suggest that access to Truth and Nature have been democratized.[28] Although the connoisseur might look contemptuously at this vast outpouring of derivative art, it expanded membership in a national cultural community.

The Madonna provides a prime example of one way Nazi art blended classical themes with Nazi biological aims. Appropriating imagery from Renaissance art, such as Ambrogio Lorenzetti's *Madonna del Latte*, painters underwrote "timeless" natalist virtues—a common theme in Nazi art was a mother clad in Madonna blue against a rural backdrop. Rudolf Warnecke's woodblock print *Mother Breast-Feeding Her Child* (Stillende Mutter) replicates the theme in Reformation style. Not surprisingly, fathers were routinely excluded from depictions of mother and child. When painters depicted males in historic settings, they moved to medieval times, displaying Hitler or ordinary soldiers clad in armor as in this painting by Hubert Lanzinger (Figure 4). Females never appear in these settings.

However, in some Nazi paintings, a male figure (usually fully clad) would dramatically set off female nudes. As in the classical Greek tradition, these female nudes in the presence of males represent the erotic attraction of Aphrodite (in contrast with the Renaissance "wisdom") luring male viewers to contemplate them without inhibition. Here access to the female body itself is being democratized. In the *Leda and the Swan* paintings by Karl Truppe and Paul Mathias Padua, the relationship between male and female is violent (although Leda is depicted as ready to enjoy the rape that is about to occur). In *The Judgment of Paris* by Ivo Saliger, a fully clad Paris gazes on a completely naked woman while two other women dress.

These prolific artists depicted well-worn (many would say "worn out") conventions. Like the creators of the windows at the cathedral in Chartres, who clothed biblical figures in the dress of their day, Nazi painters gave their nudes several markers of 1930s culture—such as updated hairstyles and gestures common in fashion photography. In Johann Schult's *Waiting* (Erwartung; Figure 5), two nudes with 1930s hairstyles lounge in the woods. Constantin

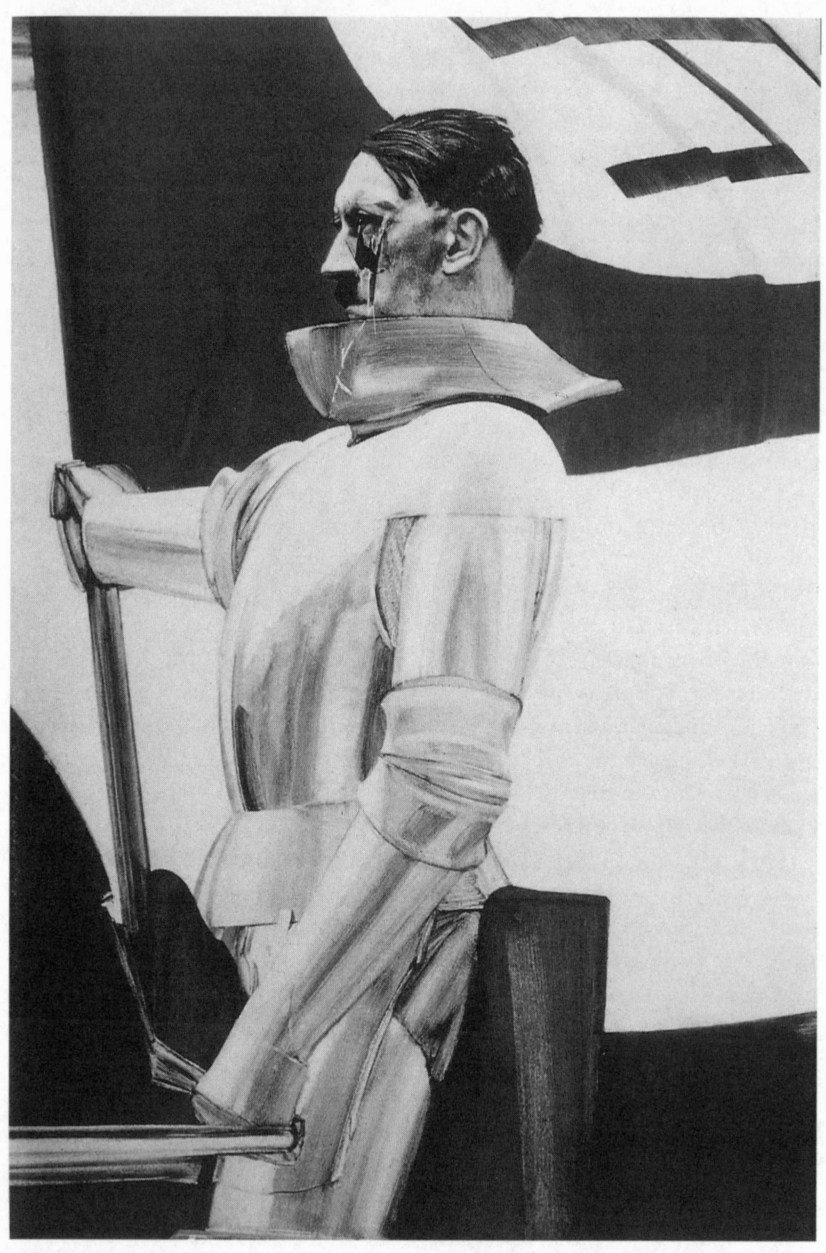

Figure 4. Hubert Lanzinger, *Der Fahnenträger* (The Flag Bearer). Courtesy of Army Art Collection, U.S. Army Center of Military History.

Figure 5. Johann Schult, *Erwartung* (Waiting), 1942. Reprinted with permission of the Deutsches Historisches Museum.

Gerhardinger's *A Sunny Day* (Auf sonniger Höhe) portrays two seminude women of the 1930s. Several paintings take popularization a step further by placing a lone female nude in her peasant bedroom, next to the bed, as in Oskar Martin-Amorbach's *Peasant Venus* (Bauernvenus; Figure 6). But more recent inspirations were at work in Ernst Zoberbier's *Reverie* (Träumende), a reclining nude posed in the manner of Édouard Manet's *Olympia* but without the cat, the maid, or the flowers. Even elements of the "degenerate" art banished from Nazi museums reappeared within the stilted and formalist "masterpieces." Hans Gött's *Girls at the Water's Edge* (Drei Mädchen am Wasser) mimics Paul Cezanne's brushwork and palette. Nazi painters of nudes broke a classical convention when they depicted pubic hair, thereby allowing viewers to sample a taste of the risqué modernity that marked "degenerate" paintings by, say, Egon Schiele. One of Hitler's favorite painters bore the nickname the "Master of Pubic Hair" (Meister des Schamhaars).

Given the official natalism, the relative absence of families from the oil paintings of the period seems surprising. In the relatively few family portraits painted, the subjects do not display mutual affection and often hardly pay attention to one another. Rather, the viewer's gaze is directed at a Nazi object, as in a cartoon of an ideal couple, Hitler and a devoted female follower, rendered by the Nazi tabloid *Der Stürmer* artist FIPS (Philipp Rupprecht). In Adolf Wissel's *Kahlenberg Peasant Family* (Kalenberger Bauernfamilie), the strongest gaze links the father-husband to his mother, while the wife's closest attachment is to her daughter. Often a larger motif such as an eagle or swastika or Hitler's portrait dwarfs the family. In one celebrated painting, *The Art Magazine* (Die Kunstzeitschrift), by Udo Wendel (Figure 7), family members' attention is drawn to a nude sculpture in an art appreciation book. Subliminal messages underscored the understanding that same-sex bonds among the racially superior anchored social and aesthetic stability; that the most important male-female bond tied mother to son, not husband to wife. In Hans Schachinger's painting used as a magazine cover, *The Austrian Peasant Family* (Ostmärkische Bauernfamilie), no family members make eye contact, not even with the soldier-son who is the centerpiece of the composition. Generations rarely mix. Except for an occasional pietà, such as Hans Adolf Bühler's *Homecoming* (Heimkehr), same-age heterosexual couples virtually never appear among the hundreds of paintings produced by "official" artists.

So complete was the visual segregation between masculine and feminine spheres that gender was "color coded" in Nazi posters, with blues predominating for females and browns or blacks delineating males. Men appeared in uniform, women in conventional dress. Although swastikas regularly adorned masculine posters, they rarely appeared in posters designed to inspire female viewers to join an organization, contribute to charity, cook a stew (*Eintopf*)

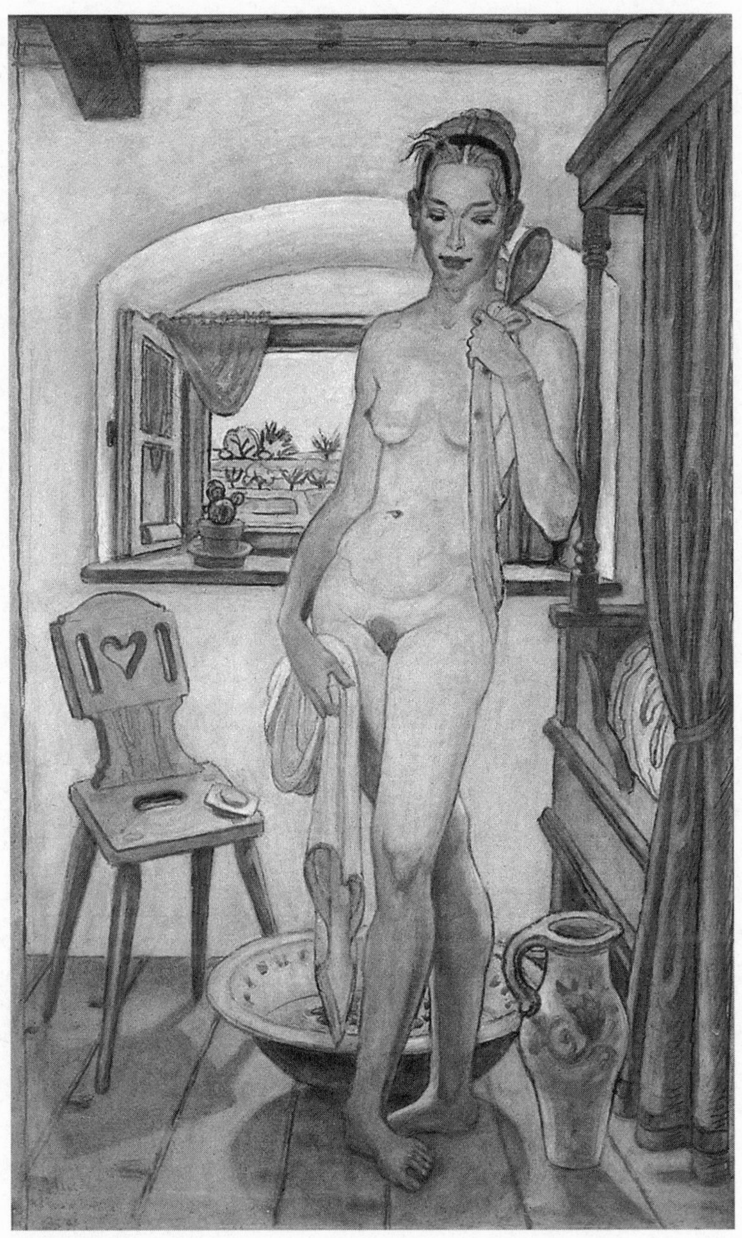

Figure 6. Oskar Martin-Amorbach, *Bauernvenus* (Peasant Venus). By permission of Christoph Stenger.

Figure 7. Udo Wendel, *Die Kunstzeitschrift* (The Art Magazine).

for the *Vaterland*, or attend a rally. Rather, women saw themselves called to serve under a national symbol, like the eagle, or under a special women's organization "rune," a cross with its arms angling downward. Girls wore uniforms that resembled Girl Scout or Girl Guide garb in other countries. In the *Organizations-Buch* of 1937, for example, no adult women's organization merited a picture, whereas dozens and dozens of males displayed the uniforms of the various male party organizations. The only female in this book of uniforms was a BDM youth leader. Visual images conveyed the silent message: girls shared "masculine" qualities such as physical vigor, arrogance, and courage, but women "Aryans" served the Führer in docile and loving maternal roles. Among "superior" civilizations, as Hitler put it in his 1934 Nuremberg Rally speech, men inhabit the "big world" of public affairs while women tend the "little world" of home and family.

But within the sex-separated depictions of strongly gendered men and women lurks a subtle ambiguity. Battle-hardened soldiers occasionally weep in the company of other men, as in Felix Albrecht's *War Memorial* (Ehrendenkmal; Figure 8) painted in brown hues, of a soldier mourning his dead comrade. Gentle women, at least in mythology, could take up arms, as in the case of the helmeted Athena who gazes happily on while S.A. (storm trooper) men remove "degenerate" paintings from the temple of German art (Figure 9). The female gymnasts on the German Olympic team stride forward with military seriousness. In Leni Riefenstahl's *Triumph of the Will*, amidst columns of identical marching men, we glimpse "he-men" frolicking together and hardened young women athletes marching in lockstep. The ambiguity conveyed by rare images of disorderly men and disciplined women did not break stereotypes but rather served as exceptions that enhanced the typologies that dominated the film. Far from representing androgyny, these brief departures from rigid and monolithic gender stereotyping allowed for a "safety valve" that permitted individuals faced with extreme situations to display a certain amount of "inappropriate" behavior. In war (against degenerate art and racial enemies) women can become warriors and men can weep. These "inappropriate" responses sustain the fundamental gender divide inherent in "Aryan" racial superiority. After the German defeat at Stalingrad, when impending catastrophe loomed large, posters for the first time included men and women (still in blue). With military calamity on the horizon, Hitler's image receded from the central place it held during the 1930s. As in World War I propaganda, the perfidious English in the West and the savage *Untermenschen* (subhumans) in the East menaced the German (not "Aryan") nation at war. The "us" appeared as embattled homeland, unified, strong, and single minded.

Throughout the Third Reich, the vision of an Aryan utopia emanated from Goebbels's Ministry of Propaganda and Popular Enlightenment.

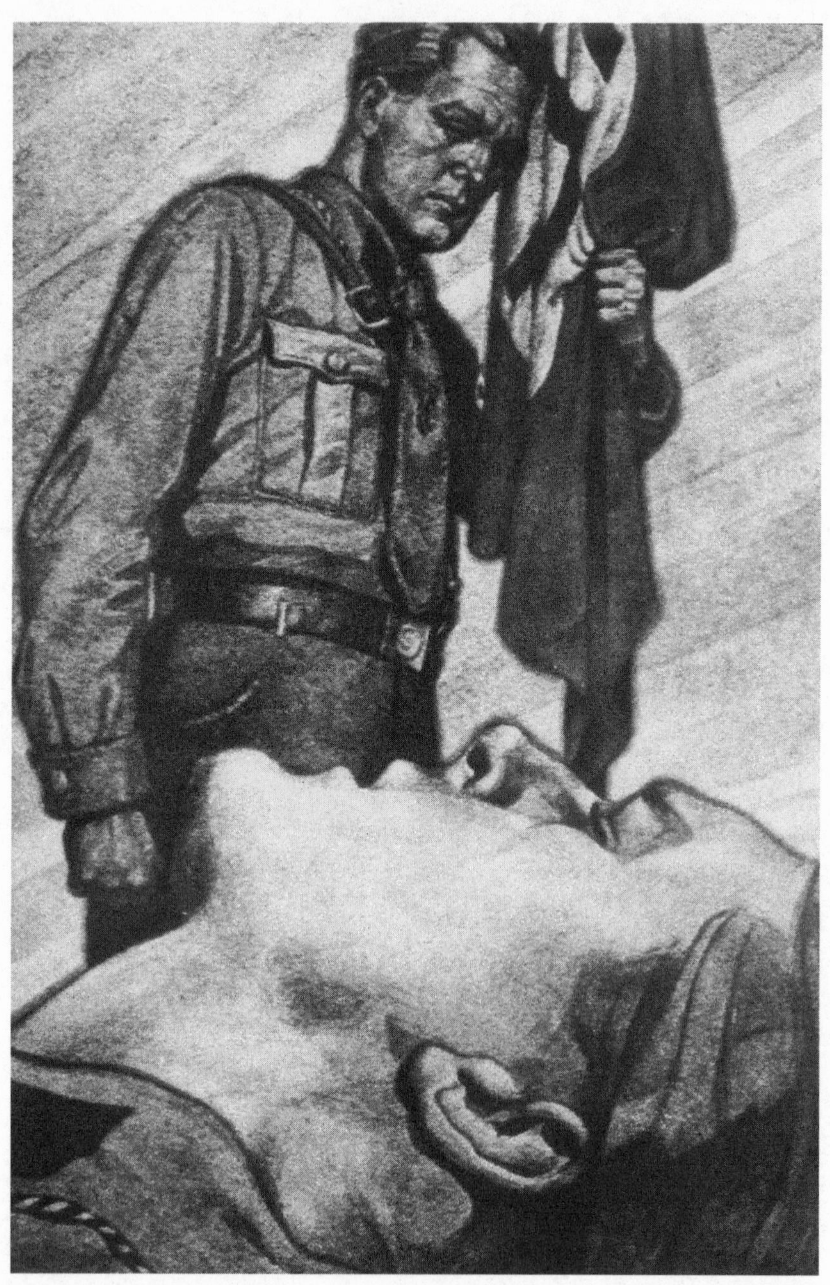

Figure 8. Felix Albrecht, *Ehrendenkmal* (War Memorial).

Krampf und Dreh war all' umſunſt,
Sieger bleibt die wahre Kunſt

Figure 9. Der Stürmer cartoon, July 1937, on the removal of "degenerate" paintings from the Temple of Art. "Tricks and deceit were all in vain, true art has triumphed once again."

Goebbels, the diarist, bureaucratic survivor, and flamboyant self-advertiser, occupied center stage in his own lifetime, and he has dominated the historiography as well. Scholars have credited him with astonishing victories as creator of "Hitler's secret weapon" and called propaganda "the war Hitler won." The easy availability of Goebbels's own copious writings and speeches, combined with a well-cataloged and vast archival collection from his Ministry, make this focus easy to understand. But hate propaganda was "mainstreamed" from many sources.[29] Interior Minister Wilhelm Frick supervised the national health bureaucracy, which assumed major responsibility for drafting legislation related to eugenics and race as well as publicity campaigns. The immense labor and youth bureaucracies produced their own booklets, racial awareness programs, instructional manuals, and slide shows. Walter Groß, director of the Nazi Party Office of Racial Policy, coordinated racial policy and publicity and monitored public responses to it.[30] Under Gertrud ScholtzKlink, the Women's Bureau included racial health information in motherhood and home economics courses. Gerhard Wagner, chief of the Nazi Doctors' League, supervised medical research and training. Specialists within the Ministry of Religion served as liaisons between racial experts and the clergy. Well-funded research institutes launched lecture series, sponsored monographs, publicized their findings, broadcast their opinions, and awarded prizes for important work.

In doctors' waiting rooms, patients read lavishly illustrated medical magazines with articles about Aryan beauty and distorted Jewish physiognomy. Medical journals carried bioethical treatises on the morality of racial purification, that is, sterilization and euthanasia. Average citizens smiled at caricatures of bossy housewives and cartoons of greedy Jews, marveled at breakthroughs in genetic research, and shuddered at lurid posters alerting them to racial dangers. Racial knowledge circulated in these visual and written texts as public interest, humor, educational, or scientific material. The Jewish Question and genetic degeneration appeared as knowledge and truth, not ideology or propaganda.

Glowing photographs of happy Aryans played against the sinister remnants of the despised Weimar democracy. The binary pairing of Weimar versus Nazi itself yielded up a split in the image of "Weimar," as often occurs in negative stereotypes. On the one hand, Weimar was too "soft." Overprotective welfare policies and institutions nurtured too many "weak" individuals whom in earlier times a harsh Mother Nature would have allowed to die. As a result of this kindness, the overproduction of "inferior" citizens had weakened a healthy *Volkskörper*. But Weimar also represented the power of a "Jewish conspiracy" to undermine the healthy racial spirit (*Volksgeist*). In this case, Weimar had become too "hard." During the mechanistic, soulless "Era of the System" (*Systemzeit*) unbridled ("Jewish") capitalism gutted the social cohesion of bygone days. While visual representations of the healthy "Aryan" body provided the ideal for which "fit" citizens must sacrifice, the split image of Weimar brought them face to face with the twin "dangers" of "damaged genes" and an "alien race." This "threat," like the "degenerate" art, did not disappear from view but on the contrary formed the centerpiece of racial purification discourse.

Literary critic Linda Schulte-Sasse, in her study of popular Nazi films, described audiences' enthusiasm for the lurid, the dangerous, and the frightening: "The painful history Nazism dredges up can be enjoyed because it is organized in the form of stories guaranteeing harmonious closure; hence, the greater the pain, the greater the pleasure."[31] Filmed images of leering Jewish men or violently insane "Aryans" terrified audiences but at the same time held out the prospect of a happy resolution because a strong state would excise such racial dangers. In earlier eras, public executions provided masses of spectators with a feeling of safety as they watched "dangers" removed from their midst. Until the cultivation of bourgeois respectability, Europeans displayed little inhibition against staring at such outcasts as lepers, madmen, deformed people, and flagellants, the "unfortunates" in their midst. On weekend outings, Londoners would gaze at the inmates in Bedlam and other asylums, for entertainment. But by the early twentieth century, although medical students saw photographs of "genetic damage" and ordinary people frequented freak shows, asylum walls shielded most physically disabled individuals from public view. By publicizing photographs of severely disabled individuals, racial experts broke a taboo. They reassured "healthy Aryans" of their own superiority. Racial education exposed "dangers," and racial laws excised the threat.

By not only allowing but inciting audiences to gaze at subjects that previously had been outlawed from polite society, Nazi racial propaganda broke old taboos, unleashing old hatreds and generating new revulsions. Popular culture, generously funded from the national treasury, packaged both the threat and the solution as a drama of transgression and salvation. Social fantasies of "genetic damage" and "racial danger" not only repulsed viewers but fascinated them as well. As literary theorist Slavoj Zizek observed, "outsiders" serve as the very frame within which the utopian social fantasy can exist.[32] In the Nazi case, the persistence of "genetic damage" and "Jewish influence" called for constant watchfulness. Although racial hygienists often linked these two sources of degeneration, actually the etiology of each was quite distinct. Anti-Semitism racialized ancient Christian Judeo-phobia, but the drive against "genetic damage" emerged from anxieties that barely existed before the turn of the century.[33] While, as Raul Hilberg noted in his introduction to *The Destruction of the European Jews*,[34] each anti-Semitic measure in Nazi Germany had precise parallels in early Christian doctrine, no eugenic legislation had passed in Germany before 1933.

The "genetically dangerous," as the moral obverse of pure Aryan men and women, bore the distinctive marks of "inferiority." From the choice of genres to the images selected for display, visual propaganda underscored the subhuman status of the genetically dangerous. Director of the Nazi Party Office for Racial Policy, Walter Groß, explained, "the values [*Werte*] of blood and race" to his female listeners in 1934. "You [*Du*] are a link in the chain of life, a droplet in the mighty blood stream of your People [*Volk*]."[35] The harsh laws

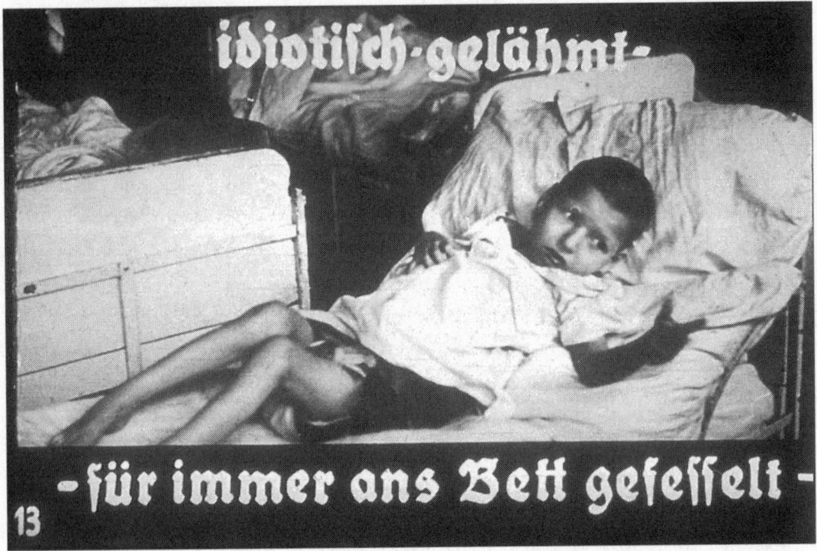

Figure 10. Hitler Youth Education Slide, "Idiot, chained forever to his bed."

that dictated the death of "trees that cease to bear fruit and roses that lose their fragrance" also governed human society. The duty of Germans, he admonished his audience, was to look squarely at genetic threats. Rhetoric quickly became law.

Within weeks of Hitler's takeover, Joseph Goebbels gloated, "With the Nazi Revolution, the year 1789 is stricken from History."[36] As if to underscore the world historical magnitude of the Nazi Revolution, Bastille Day, July 14, 1933, was chosen as the date to promulgate sweeping policies concerning citizenship, the flag, the Hitler salute, relations with the Vatican, the one-party state, and the destruction of the last vestiges of federalism. This consideration must have figured in the passage of legislation that allowed physicians to sterilize individuals who might carry "damaged genes" for "inherited" conditions (blindness or deafness, spina bifida, Huntington's chorea, Down's Syndrome, alcoholism, mental illness, epilepsy, or severe bodily disfigurement).[37] Because the law was kept secret for two weeks, there had been no rush to draft it. Passing it guaranteed that in the German tradition, the sterilization law became known as the law of July 14, 1933. Beginning in January 1934, social workers, health professionals, and teachers were required to identify potentially "damaged" individuals—which could well mean, Interior Minister Wilhelm Frick predicted, that up to 20 percent of all Germans would be sterilized. How could the regime popularize so drastic a eugenics program that, in dramatic contrast to the early anti-Semitic legislation, had no precedent and very little public support in Germany?[38] For the full institutionalization and popularization of the program, years of concerted effort would have been needed.

The highly developed German communications system held out the potential for changing public opinion at a speed hitherto undreamed of. Mass-circulation magazines featured learned articles on genetics, complete with illustrated graphs and dramatic photographs. Radio broadcasts warned about the genetic dangers within the *Volkskörper.* One of the most effective methods of transforming consciousness anywhere is to begin with teenagers and their teachers. The Nazi educational administration lost no time setting youth in motion. Under Bernard Rust, minister of education, and Hans Schemm, leader of the Nazi Teachers' Union, a national initiative organized high school students to compile their genetic health family trees (and submit them for inspection to a national genetic health data bank). Weekend workshops provided "catch up" courses to teachers of all subjects, not only biology. Math teachers, for example, were instructed to integrate racial thinking into their homework. "If the construction of an insane asylum requires six million Reichsmarks, how many housing units for normal families could be built at 15,000 RM apiece for the amount spent on insane asylums?"[39] Regional and local leaders of Hitler Youth groups learned how to narrate the official traveling slide show for their peers. Its three parts (Aryans, Jews, and genetically damaged), illustrated with seventy-six black-and-white images, show how aesthetics and biology underwrote the logic of dehumanization. Against the background of starkly beautiful and strongly gendered Aryan athletes, soldiers, and peasants, photographs of feeble-minded adults, a severely deformed child chained to its bed, and mentally retarded siblings shock the viewer (Figure 10). A "picture may be worth a thousand words," but each of these photographs required a phrase to preclude viewer compassion. In these images of the "lives not worth living" (*lebensunwertes Leben*), gender is virtually erased by institutional dress, shaved heads or short disheveled hair, and vacant gazes.

Blurred gender qualities continue as the visual imagery moves to the second theme: expense to the taxpayer. In this section, the photo captions convey the annual cost of maintaining "inferior" individuals, the price of decent housing for a hardworking low-income family, photographs of institutions in immaculately landscaped settings juxtaposed with slums where hardworking "Aryans" lived, and the numbers of out-of-wedlock children produced by a single mentally ill woman. In a similar fashion, magazines and newspapers warned of genetic decline in illustrated graphs that grossly overestimated the rate of reproduction among the "defectives" in comparison with the "healthy." The final section in the slide show moves beyond aesthetic repugnance and taxpayer concerns to ethical questions about the value of "life without

Figure 11. Hitler Youth Education Slide, "God Cannot Have Wished Infected Individuals to Pass on Their Illness to Future Generations." Courtesy of the National Center for Jewish Film, Brandeis University.

hope . . . life without meaning." The concluding image of a grotesquely deformed infant invokes Christian values with the caption: "God cannot have wished infected individuals to pass on their illness to future generations" (Figure 11). From biology to economy and theology, an aesthetic of revulsion and danger constructed forced sterilization as a call to idealism. A photograph from an S.S. recruiting pamphlet sets off genetically superior marching under the motto, "My honor is my loyalty" (Figure 12).

Documentary films enhanced the discursive world of genetic danger that threatened Aryan health. Audiences would view such educational "shorts" between the coming attractions and the newsreel before the feature film began. In the silent film, *The Inheritance*, bold texts carry dire warnings. The voice in the sound documentaries is invariably the deep, masculine movie tone of a racial expert in a white lab coat. Feminine qualities have been muted in images of the "inferior." The photos of male inmates with large ears, leering smiles, and shaved heads in documentary films such as *Victims of the Past* (Opfer der Vergangenheit) (1935) recall scenes from the original Dracula film, F. W. Murnau's *Nosferatu* (1922). Here, although gender is muted, pictures of emaciated men with open mouths and vacant eyes suggest an anomalous and eerie femininity, evoking a sense of the *umheimlich* (eerie or uncanny) com-

sich so viele junge Deutsche zur Waffen-SS melden, ist ein sprechendes Zeugnis für das Vertrauen, das von der heutigen jungen Generation gerade der Waffen-SS, ihrem Geist und vor allem ihrer Führung entgegengebracht wird. Es ist aber auch ein stolzer Beweis für die weltanschaulich sichere Haltung dieser deutschen Jugend, daß sie den Sinn des Kampfes der SS verstanden hat und genau weiß, warum die Waffen-SS eine dem Führer besonders verpflichtete Gemeinschaft bildet. So wird auch auf deinem Koppelschloß der Wahlspruch stehen, den der Führer selbst am 1. April 1931 seiner SS verliehen hat:

MEINE EHRE HEISST TREUE!

Das sind unsere Männer!

5

Figure 12. S.S. Recruiting Image, "My Honor Is My Loyalty." Hoover Institution Archives, Poster Collection.

mon in horror films. The visual and written texts pushed "damaged" individuals beyond the edge of the *Volksgemeinschaft* and beyond the limits of moral consideration.

However, confusion at the margins of the degendered images of the "inferior" plagued this propaganda. Important constraints curbed too-obvious insults against "genetically ill Aryans" because however "imperfect" they were, these disabled people nonetheless belonged to the superior race. They could not be openly ridiculed and certainly could not be mocked in cartoons or caricatures. Official dogma sometimes likened the involuntarily sterilized to conscripted soldiers who died on the battlefields of World War I (a parallel drawn in Oliver Wendell Holmes's 1926 Supreme Court decision in favor of compulsory sterilization in the United States). Many professionals and distressed relatives wondered, Why, if sterilization was an honorable sacrifice for the national good, were sterilized people deprived of the joys of married life so celebrated in Nazi values? Why did sterilization constitute grounds for divorce from a fertile spouse? Or, if sterilization were heroic, why were "patients" promised confidentiality in the first place? Social workers pointed out that, in fact, the ban against marriage of infertile people required a violation of the promise of confidentiality. From its inception, the publicity intended to popularize eugenic purification exposed the central inconsistencies it was designed to mask. Not even the "slickest" media campaign could both dehumanize and valorize "inferior" members of the "superior" race. Dissonance built doubts into images and rhetoric, even though, paradoxically, the sterilization program was the only Nazi racial project to win foreign acclaim—and it continued, after the defeat of Nazism, in the United States, Sweden, France, Japan, and West Germany. The fuzziness of this binary scheme, in other words, did not function as it did with gender binaries, to allow for flexibility and still sustain the dominant themes. The propaganda designed to clarify the division between "worthy" and "unworthy" lives could backfire and spread anxiety among Aryans that they might harbor secret genetic damage. Unsuspecting Aryans worried that they might become targets of the laws designed to protect their "genetic inheritance" (*Erbgut*).

Anti-Semitic indoctrination did not suffer from the particular form of cognitive dissonance that riddled the eugenics education campaign. Vile caricatures and the "big lie" portrayed "the Jew" as irrevocably "other." As in the polarity between masculine and feminine, Nazi anti-Semitism drew on stock stereotypes that equated physical appearance with inner character. Nazi propaganda, built from historical and transcultural antecedents as well as contemporaneous prejudices ubiquitous in Europe, deepened conventional hatreds by both increasing the quantity of propaganda and reconfiguring the nature of the "Jewish Question" itself.

The sheer volume of anti-Semitism overwhelmed readers of the popular press as negative images were "mainstreamed" into every conceivable cultural setting. No longer did such scurrilous allegations appear mainly in nationalist and conservative publications. The Nazi Party newspaper, with local editions in all urban areas, the *Völkische Beobachter*, fed growing numbers of readers a steady diet of caricatures. The demeaning cartoons in *Der Stürmer* continued to dehumanize "the Jew." As the paid circulation figures (from 50,000 in April 1934 to just under 500,000 in 1937) indicate, many more readers viewed them.[40] Nongovernmental publications (which required censors' permission to publish) expanded their coverage of the Jewish question under such diverse rubrics as the economy, culture, biological research, urban life, domestic politics, diplomacy, and military affairs. Vigorous efforts at building a racial consensus undercut liberal constraints and reduced self-censorship as well.

Simultaneously, the images of racial hate themselves underwent a shift to accommodate new laws and a more racialized anti-Semitism. Drawing on a visual vocabulary that predated Nazism, writers and racial experts highlighted physical markers, like bowed legs, large noses, and bowler hats.[41] And, as in nineteenth-century visual rhetoric, "the Jew" epitomized both international finance capital and international Bolshevism in the kind of bifurcation typical of stereotypes. At every point, despite the virulence of visual and verbal attacks on Jews, Nazi leaders curtailed unsanctioned violent anti-Semitism. In late March 1933 Hitler ordered a halt to individual S.A. units' random violence against Jews. To discipline his ranks, he requested Goebbels to call for a boycott on April 1 against all Jewish businesses and to lift it only when foreign journalists stopped filing reports critical of the Nazi regime. After only twenty-four hours, the boycott ended, attesting to its failure within Germany. In its place came the more "legal" measures: exclusion of "non-Aryans" from the civil service, reduction of physicians and lawyers allowed to practice to the ratio of local "Aryan" to "non-Aryan" populations, and exclusion of "non-Aryan" children from public schools. These bureaucratic policies were designed to give an image of fairness and improve the Nazi image abroad and in Germany.

Accordingly, the imagery of Nazi visual language shifted slightly to emphasize putatively "objective" qualities. For example, "The Jew" became more apelike and hairy (Figure 13). While Nazi publicity exhorted health conscious "Aryans" to refrain from smoking, visual images linked Jews with cigarettes and cigars, as in this apelike gargoyle (Figure 14). Throughout the 1930s the personifications of "hostile" foreign nations assumed "Jewish" qualities. In the

Figure 13. *Der Stürmer* cartoon, "The Ape and the Jew."

wartime film *The Eternal Jew* (Der Ewige Jude), Jews were likened specifically to hoards of rats—and one scene in particular quoted the *Nosferatu* scene in which rats swarm out of the hold of Dracula's plague-bearing ship as it approaches the Bremen harbor.

Because the Nazi utopia promised so total a solution to life's large and small problems, "the Jewish menace" expanded as the repository for all sources of failure. When people grumbled that the Third Reich had not lived up to Hitler's extravagant promises of harmony, security, material prosperity, and national pride, the Jewish question as a catchall (*pauschal*) scapegoat appeared.[42] By locating sources of failure in racially "alien" qualities (urban, cosmopolitan, greedy, capitalist, aggressive, and ruthless) in the "Jew," anti-Semites could blame failure on persistent remnants from the despised Weimar democracy.

Figure 14. Cartoon, "Above Parisian Rooftops" from the Nazi humor magazine, *Die Brennessel*, (6:9) February 1936. "The famous sculptures of the Notre Dame need repair. The Devil, nevertheless, is in good shape, although he has changed his form a bit."

During the Weimar Republic a major image of the Jew had been the "string puller," who lurks behind the scenes of all events that critics saw as dangerous to Germany.[43] Nazi images deemphasized the power behind the scenes and foregrounded the Jew as the source of moral and sexual corruption. Schulte-Sasse notes the ways in which the protagonist in the film *Jüd Suss* epitomizes the Nazis' contradictory attitude toward modernity by appearing both careless and organized, sloppy and efficient. "Hence Jews do not merely represent capital; they come to personify its intangible, pernicious power."[44] But it was also true, as Ian Kershaw notes, that hatred of "the Jew expanded to become the abstract (and intellectually more respectable) 'Jewish question.'"[45] Goebbels in 1940 distinguished his hatred of Jews from mere prejudice. "Films in which Jews appear are not to be labelled as anti-Jewish. We want it to be made perfectly clear that such films are not determined by any tendentious considerations, but reflect historical facts as they are."[46] Even as the Jew's physiological, "racial" character became more central to anti-Semitic doctrine, the "danger" represented became more abstract.

In many of their caricatures, Nazi artists depicted so-called racial dangers using the collage and expressionist styles that Goebbels had outlawed as "degenerate." Unlike the characterizations of the "genetically damaged," which muted gender contrasts, "the Jew" became hypermasculinized. Jewish women and children virtually disappeared from view, with the important exception of cartoons designed to underscore that *all* Jews, even the apparently innocent women and children, belonged to a "separate race." In contrast to the restrained and obedient masculinity attributed to Aryan men, Jewish males were represented as aggressive outlaws whose removal required vigilante action. Avaricious bankers, lecherous seducers, deceitful charlatans, ranting politicians, and murderous physicians provided familiar tropes in the anti-Semites' visual vocabulary. By equating unrestrained sexual and financial corruption with "Jewishness," these images warn "Aryan" men to "stay in line." As a counterpoint, an effeminate hedonist or indolent shirker occasionally flanked the dominant hypermasculinized "Jew." Sometimes this "weak" type was joined by an equally dissolute Jewish woman.

In anti-Semitic cartoons we see most dramatically the fusion of class- and race-based identities into a grand melodrama of a racialized national fantasy. The evil Jewish male threatens a fair Aryan maiden, who represents Germany (usually represented as the virile Vaterland) as in the picture of Satan hypnotizing his victim (Figure 15). Implicitly, the drama behind the caricature calls on the courageous masculine viewer to leap to the rescue. In this genre, male aggression is located in hypermasculinized "Jews," who bear the responsibility for "Aryan" female impurity. Masculine "Aryan" (read "guilt-free") aggression is both incited and channeled into hatred for the "enemy Jew." This scenario,

Figure 15. Der Stürmer cartoon, "Germany's Hypnotic Slumber."

too, was not without ambiguity. Despite an occasional individual who "looked Jewish," the victims of anti-Semitic attacks appeared quite average and actually behaved "normally." Moreover, it was well known that divorce, crime, and alcoholism rates among Jews were very low, while their income and educational levels were well above average—as was their reputation for philanthropy and civic spirit. Images so scurrilous that they bore no resemblance to friends and neighbors risked losing credibility. Equally threatening to the racial project was the fact (obvious not only to us but also to racial researchers in the mid-1930s) that no blood type, head shape, or other physical trait could be discovered that would identify Jewishness. Even the most vicious Jew haters in the Nazi leadership admitted the weakness of their propaganda. Himmler agonized about the possibility that even an ardent anti-Semite might decide to protect this one friend, an "exception" Jew from his fate.

Genocide (whether ethnonational or ethnobiological) can occur only in modern contexts where a leader (or political elite) has the potential to mobilize one community against another. Along with the ready availability of the weapons for mass slaughter, genocide requires a monopolized and sophisticated media network. The relative nature of "adequate" is illustrated by the case of Burundi, Rwanda, and the Congo, where transistor radios and machetes functioned as effectively as Croatian and Serbian television and modern weapons. Whether they are motivated by passionate hatreds or political cunning, genocidal leaders deploy popular media to redraw their followers' ethical map. The most effective method of desensitizing perpetrators is to convince them of their victims' malice. As in the military strategy of a preemptive strike, visual and verbal messages project aggression onto the targeted category. Conventional ethnic prejudices, reinforced by gendered assumptions about "human nature," define the line between the "us" and the "them." The goal of racial persuasion is to widen the gap that separated the "racially" chosen people from "others." This chasm simultaneously immunizes perpetrators from the ethical consequences of their actions and assures them that they personally will never be endangered by the massacres that have been unleashed. Rigid polarities, marked by gender and ethnonational traits, form a vital part of the technologies of the self by which leaders shape the perpetrators' moral universe.

OMER BARTOV 6

Defining Enemies, Making Victims

Germans, Jews, and the Holocaust

THE DISCOURSE on enemies and victims, its effects on our conduct in and perceptions of war and genocide, and the extent to which such perceptions have in turn redefined our views of victimhood and identity can be viewed as among the most crucial issues of this century. This is a vast topic, and in the present context I do not presume to cover it all. Rather, I will limit myself to two related issues: first, German self-perceptions and attitudes toward Jews, especially in the Third Reich and the Federal Republic; second, Jewish self-perceptions and attitudes toward real and perceived enemies in the past and the present, in Europe, the United States, and Israel. That there are numerous connections between the German discourse on nationalism, identity, and Nazism, and the Jewish discourse on identity, Zionism, and the Holocaust, indeed, that the two have a complex reciprocal relationship, is both obvious and in need of further elaboration. Moreover, although this relationship has been crucial in defining national and individual identities, it has retained a persistently pernicious potential that has often led to obfuscation, repression, and violence, rather than to understanding and reconciliation.

Even this narrower focus is obviously too large to allow a comprehensive analysis. Hence the following chapter merely presents some ideas and conceptualizations that will hopefully provoke further discussion. This is a synthetic essay that offers no new documentation, although some of the literature it cites may not be known to all readers. My aim is not to provide any definitive answers but to raise questions, reformulate assumptions, and sketch out links that are not commonly recognized. I am well aware of the danger that although some readers may find my generalizations open to criticism, others will be familiar with at least some of the material. But I hope that they will keep an open mind to the main thrust of this chapter, which is to make us think about whether, at the end of the twentieth century, we have succeeded in breaking out of the vicious circle of defining enemies and making victims, which has characterized much of the last hundred years and has been at the root of so much violence and bloodshed. Because historians have been implicated in much of this discourse in the past, I believe that they would do well to think about its ramifications for their own time as well.

The Great War of 1914 to 1918 came at the end of a long process of domestic consolidation and outward expansion of the great European powers. Indeed, among the most distinct features of the new nation-state was the eradication of inner resistance to its claim to sovereignty and control, and the ceaseless striving to expand either its proper borders or its overseas empire. This in turn tended to create a mechanism of self-definition and legitimization based on two mutually dependent conceptual and material requirements, namely, the need to define enemies and the urge to make victims, even if the intensity and severity of the application of these requirements depended on specific circumstances in each individual state. From the state's point of view, those seen as belonging to it had to be integrated, either willingly or by coercion; whereas those seen as not belonging to it had to be excluded or eliminated, no matter whether they wished to belong to it or not.[1] Hence the definition of both foe and friend, compatriot and nonpatriot, entailed the making of victims, that is, compelling people to conform to a definition they might not share, based on categories imposed on them by a larger community or a political regime. In the course of this process, some ethnic, religious, or linguistically distinct minorities within these large entities retained an especially ambiguous status. Paradigmatic of such ambiguity were the Jews.[2]

If the legal emancipation of the Jews coincided with the emergence of the modern nation-state, it was this very same process that brought about a profound transformation in the age-old anti-Jewish prejudices of Christian Europe into modern political and racial anti-Semitism. And if the Jews increasingly welcomed their economic and political integration into gentile society, the efforts of assimilated Jewish communities to retain some features of their specific identity and some links to their coreligionists across national borders made them into a symbol of the "insider as outsider." Thus the Jews served as both proof of and metaphor for the immense integrative powers of the new nation-state; simultaneously, they came to symbolize its exclusionary potential.[3] Ambiguous identities produced tremendous social, political, and psychological tensions, which in turn made for that complex relationship between creativity and disintegration, ingenuity and annihilation so typical of our century. In this sense, the Jews can be seen as the paradigmatic example of the preoccupation with identity and solidarity, exclusion and victimization, that numerous states or at least some of their agencies have manifested in the modern era.

As it consolidated its domestic and international status, the nation-state was simultaneously beset by visions of decadence and degeneration, chaos and anarchy, disintegration and subversion, invasion and destruction. Europe on the eve of the Great War was a society haunted by inarticulate fears and anxieties just as much as it was propelled forward by a fervent faith in progress and science. The hard-won domestic unity seemed to symbolize and facilitate the eternal grandeur of the nation; paradoxically, it also appeared to be in imminent danger of social, political, and moral upheaval. A source of confidence and security, the national community also generated anxieties about its potential dissolution, seemingly under attack from all quarters: organized labor "from below"; destabilization of traditional gender roles "from within"; and deterioration of international relations "from without." Moreover, confidence in European superiority vis-à-vis the rest of the world, rooted in the newly conquered vast colonial empires, was undermined by fears about the West's vulnerability to infiltration by other races and civilizations and alarm about the biological degeneration of the white race.[4]

With the outbreak of the Great War it seemed at first that rumors of approaching internal disintegration had been greatly exaggerated, as all the aggressive potential of fear and anxiety and the dehumanizing and demonizing imagery of prewar domestic enemies were mobilized against the foreign enemy at the gate. The German *Burgfrieden* and the French *union sacrée* were explicit attempts to create solidarity at home by focusing attention on the danger from without. Moreover, in Germany (as in other nations) those sectors of society that had remained to a greater or lesser degree excluded from the nation, such as the Socialists, the Jews, and the Catholics, rallied to the flag in a show of patriotism meant to legitimize them as full members of the national community. Similarly, disgruntled intellectuals, skeptical bohemians, disengaged artists, and detached scholars all seized the opportunity of this uplifting event of cataclysmic military confrontation and took up the national cause. If the enemy was now clearly defined and easily identifiable, so too the victims of the war were obviously all those who fought for one's own nation. For a moment, then, the fog and confusion of war was accompanied by a miraculous clarification of identities.

Yet as the casualties mounted at the front and deprivation and mourning increased in the rear, the classifications of foe and friend, victim and perpetrator, began shifting once more. This was a fundamental transformation, occurring simultaneously with the unprecedented expansion of the state's powers of mobilization and production, control and surveillance, propaganda and coercion. It has had far-reaching consequences for the rest of the twentieth century.

While propaganda and the brutalizing effects of the fighting enhanced a view of the world as divided between demonic foreign enemies and one's own victimized nation, the peculiar conditions in the trenches of the Western Front created a sense of solidarity between the fighting troops on both sides of the line and a growing resentment of the rear. Moreover, the scope and relentlessness of this new type of industrial killing also created a sense of breathless, if often morbid fascination, and for some even an overpowering enchantment and intoxication with the horror being perpetrated on the battlefield. The soldiers could thus both hate the war and experience a sinister attraction to its desperate camaraderie and ruthless, indifferent, wholly unambiguous, outright destructiveness; they could both hate the men across no-man's-land and appreciate that they alone could empathize with their own predicament, due to that bond of blood and suffering that had been sealed between them. The "real" enemy was therefore to be found in the rear, among the staff officers, the noncombatants, the politicians and industrialists, even the workers in the factories, all those who were perceived as having shirked the fighting and thus having excluded themselves from that community of battle, increasingly celebrated by the fighting troops. This was a grim, probably inevitable glorification of one's helplessness, of pain and death, just as much as of heroism and sacrifice; it was, that is, a glorification of victimhood.

The community of solidarity both crossed over the border and shrank into itself. Precisely by fighting the enemy across the line, combat soldiers shared a front-line solidarity and a sense of alienation from their respective civilian hinterlands. This imaginary battle community continued to exert a tremendous influence on postwar society long after the fighting had ceased. Made of embittered, at times silent, at times rebellious and violent survivors of the front, this community was torn between a desire to be reintegrated into society and a sense of being separated from those who had not been "there" by what appeared to some, and was mythologized by certain extremist organizations, as an insurmountable barrier, more difficult to traverse than even that no-man's-land into which the soldiers had stared with horror from both sides of the front for four long years.[5]

A sense of victimhood and alienation breeds an urge to look for culprits, for those who had perpetrated the slaughter and in the process both eschewed the suffering and profited from it. Hence the transformation of front-line solidarity into a quest for the "true" enemy, the "real" cause of evil. And because the evil was so keenly felt and of such vast dimensions, so too should be the punishment of the guilty. And yet the identity of that true enemy remained elusive, making for still greater rage and frustration, expressed both in passivity and listlessness, and in violence and brutality. If the foreign enemy had become one's comrade in suffering, if the glorious war for which one had sacrificed so much had been in vain, and if patriotism had been whipped up by a lying propaganda conjured up by gutless intellectuals safely closeted in the rear, then how was one to make sense of it all?[6]

Disaster can be more easily confronted if traced to a cause, to human culprits, superhuman agency, natural forces. Destruction may not always be rooted in identifiable evil, but it often creates imaginary carriers of perdition. Scapegoats have the advantage of being readily accessible and defenseless, and if slaughtering them may not prevent future catastrophe, it can have a powerful psychological effect. For bewilderment and inaction in the face of catastrophe sap the will to hold out, while identifying a cause and acting against it helps cope with trauma, creating the illusion of fighting back and generating the energy and determination needed to ensure survival. Hence imagination and metaphor are crucial in liberating man from the perceived stranglehold of uncontrollable, invincible forces. In other words, the aftermath of disaster may have less devastating psychological and physical consequences for survivors if they can in turn victimize their real or imaginary enemies.

The search for those guilty of the massacre in the trenches, the "real" enemy, began in Germany even before the deteriorating military situation at the front and its ultimate collapse made for open accusations of subversion against those least capable of defending themselves. The legend of the "stab in the back" was preceded by the notorious *Judenzählung* ("Jew count") of 1916, an official inquiry aimed at gauging the alleged underrepresentation of Jews in the army. If before the war many generals had feared that the growing numbers of working-class recruits affiliated with the Social Democratic Party (SPD) would undermine the army's reliability as a tool against social unrest, during the war the notion of casting doubt on the loyalty of millions of fighting soldiers stemming from the lower classes would have obviously been counterproductive and might have seriously demoralized the troops. But turning against the Jews, a numerically almost irrelevant minority actually striving to demonstrate its loyalty to the regime by dying with frightening zeal at the front, was an almost foolproof way to direct the people's growing anger and frustration away from the political and military leadership without undermining morale (an old method employed often enough in the past by the czarist regime). Moreover, reports by Jewish soldiers indicate that they were encountering anti-Semitism even among their own comrades, a sentiment also reflected in the diaries and correspondence of the officer corps, some of whose members eventually became Hitler's generals.[7] In this respect, the legendary *Kampfgemeinschaft* (battle community) was already in the process of becoming a *Volksgemeinschaft* (racial or people's community), from which the Jews were excluded by definition. The rapid and vast growth of the populist, ultranationalist, and anti-Semitic *Vaterlandspartei* (Fatherland Party) during the latter part of the war is also instructive in this context. The domestic enemy, whose presence could explain the military disaster and whose elimination would herald national salvation, was thus becoming an indispensable factor in the national imagery even before the fighting finally ended.[8]

The German sailors and soldiers who rebelled against their commanders were primarily motivated by a desire to put an end to the pointless carnage at the front and the navy's plan of a suicidal attack against the British. The widespread disenchantment among the troops would indicate that by the last phase of the war, the myth of the battle community hardly reflected the rank and file's perception of reality. But revolutionary situations are a highly fertile breeding ground for fantasies and distorted perceptions. The legacy of the immediate postwar years in Germany was one of seething animosities and mutual victimization, violence, and terror, all crucial elements in the subsequent rise of the Nazi Party. The extremists on both the Left and the Right, but also to some extent the more moderate liberals and Socialists, tended to view their political opponents as sworn enemies; the militants also often perceived themselves as victims. It is true that the Weimar Republic provided more opportunities for German Jews than ever before in the past, as can be seen from the growing prominence of Jews in the arts, academe, the media, and politics. At the same time, however, this was also a period of growing anti-Semitism, in which the Jews came to be viewed by much of the radical and conservative Right as the main cause and beneficiary of the military debacle and the collapse of the imperial regime and all that it had stood for. The impact of this atmosphere on German Jewry was just as significant, although reactions were anything but unified. Some Jews turned to accelerated assimilation, others sought to recover their Jewish identity, others still made efforts to emigrate; but most were aware of the mixed signals given them by Gentile society and beset by a sense of crisis.[9] Conversely, if the Socialists could be accused of adhering to a pernicious ideology, the working class as such could never take the place of the nation's foreign enemies, because the future army expected to undo the humiliation of the Versailles diktat would eventually be raised from its ranks. To be sure, the carriers of "Bolshevism" had to be eliminated, but their followers were to be won over, not destroyed. Those on the lookout for domestic enemies needed a target group that would be both sufficiently visible and more or less universally disliked, both perceived as all-powerful and numerically marginal so that its elimination from society would not have a major detrimental effect on the nation—both an easy target for victimization and generally accepted as the chief instigator of its persecutors' own victimhood. An enemy was sought, that is, whose very persecution would serve to manifest the power and legitimacy of the victimizer, while simultaneously allowing the persecutor to claim the status of the "true" (past, present, and potentially future) victim.[10]

Toward the end of the 1920s, and with much greater vehemence following Hitler's nomination as chancellor in 1933, increasing numbers of Germans began to identify the Jews as their most pernicious domestic foe. And precisely because the Jews were the elusive enemy par excellence, they served as a metaphor for all other domestic and foreign opponents of the nation (and the regime that claimed to represent it), making it appear possible to wipe out political opposition without casting doubt on the inherent unity of the *Volk*. Hence the image of "the Jew" as constructed by the regime played an important role in consolidating the Nazi state and preparing it for the existential struggle for which Hitler had always striven.[11]

While a consensus over the identity of the enemy was being reached, however, the enemy's elusive nature, as presented by the regime, meant that he might lurk everywhere, not only in one's social environment but even as a constant threat to each individual's alleged Aryan purity. Paradoxically, just as the Reich was declared progressively "Judenrein" (free of Jews) the specter of Jewish presence seemed to haunt people's imagination all the more; it was as if the Jews had simply gone underground or had merged into the innocent Aryan population so well that they might be discovered even among Hitler's most obedient followers. At the same time, "the Jew" came to represent also the entirety of Germany's foreign foes, serving as the incarnation of Bolshevism and plutocracy just as much as the cause of the *Dolchstoss* ("stab in the back") and all the misfortunes that followed it. Hence individual psychological anxiety, domestic social threats, and foreign military opponents were all merged into the image of that elusive yet all-powerful enemy, "the Jew."[12]

The image of "the Jew" as the state's most insidious enemy by dint of being both distinctly and irreversibly alien, and capable of such mental and physical dissimulation that made him appear "just like us," was a legacy of late-nineteenth-century political and racial anti-Semitism. The rapid transformation of European society in the wake of the industrial revolution, whose immediate outcome for much of the population was often poverty, disorientation, and fear, created the need to isolate and identify the evil forces lurking behind such an unprecedented upheaval. Simultaneously, the emancipation of the Jews, which, along with industrialization, accompanied the creation of the new-nation state, while providing the Jews with new opportunities created unease and animosity within a gentile population still permeated by anti-Jewish prejudices.[13] And because the Jews appeared to be the main beneficiaries of the process, they quickly came to be identified as the instigators of the suffering it caused. Thus, especially among the threatened old middle class of small shopkeepers and artisans, the argument could be made that by putting the Jews "back in their place" all the confounding and wretched realities of modernization would go away and the good old order would return.

If the new economic forces were anonymous and faceless, Jewish emancipation and assimilation created a new kind of Jew, who could no longer be identified as such with the same ease as in the past. Seemingly indistinguishable from his gentile neighbors, "the Jew" as an identifiable "other" was disappearing, at the same time as his power, according to the anti-Semitic logic, was expanding immeasurably. Modernity and the Jews thus shared the same elusive qualities and could be presented as inextricably linked. To be sure, a rather significant leap of the imagination was needed in order to conclude that an international Jewish conspiracy was at work, where "real" Jews, stripped of their modern, emancipated garb, were plotting in the dark to take over the world. But both in popular and elite circles the idea was gaining ground that behind the mask of the new Jew lurked the "Asiatic" features of the proverbial Jew of medieval lore and Christian imagery. And, as in all nightmares, this elusive enemy generated much greater anxiety than the easily identifiable one. The notion that the enemy is amongst us, yet cannot be unmasked, has always been the stuff of fear and paranoia and the cause of destructive imaginings and violent eruptions.[14]

Modernity brought with it also a belief in science and progress, accompanied by fears of physical and mental degeneration. Scientific racism soon asserted that humanity was divided into higher and lower species, thereby positing racial purity as a goal and miscegenation as racial pollution. According to the skewed logic of racial hygiene, the Jews were both the lowest and most insidious race and the most zealous guardians of their own racial purity, even as they threatened to contaminate the higher races with inferior blood. Yet the same scientists who claimed to have identified the different strands of the human race were haunted by the protean nature of "the Jew" and his ability to defeat scientific diagnoses. This implied that every individual was potentially a carrier of precisely those Jewish qualities one was striving to eliminate, that is, that everyone was suspect of belonging to the enemy's camp even without being aware of it. Indeed, anti-Semitism was imbued with this fear of "the Jew within," just as the glorification of masculinity was pregnant with anxieties regarding one's feminine predilections. The most nightmarish vision of the elusive enemy was, that is, to discover that he was none other but oneself.[15]

The Great War strengthened the state's ability to identify, control, and supervise its population to an unprecedented degree; it thereby also greatly contributed to the spread of anxiety about the presence of a seemingly inexhaustible number of elusive enemies in society's midst. The modern surveillance techniques developed in that period were designed to acquire *knowledge* about the population, *influence* it in ways deemed necessary by the regime, and *eradicate* domestic enemies. This does not mean, of course, that such techniques and policies were employed in the same manner everywhere, and there is a vast difference between the development of surveillance in the Soviet Union, Fascist Italy, and subsequently Nazi Germany, and in countries such as interwar France and Britain. Yet the potential was definitely there, expressed, for instance, in postal control; mass public opinion surveys; lists of political suspects to be arrested at a time of emergency; and even the proliferation of popular fiction and film on spies, treason, and infiltration of the state by foreigners disguised as patriots. Indeed, by acknowledging the difficulty of identifying the enemy within, the emerging surveillance state, which reached its fully fledged form in the Third Reich and Stalinist Russia, asserted that anyone was a potential foe, however well-integrated and assimilated he or she seemed to be.[16] A society of doppelgangers, where each individual might discover in himself an unknown Mr. Hyde, or be metamorphosed overnight into a repelling insect, was also one being prepared to apply the most powerful insecticides to rid itself of its perceived monstrous traits.

Obsession with "the Jew within" was also the lot of many assimilated and even baptized Jews, who often internalized the anti-Semitic imagery of their environment and consequently forged a highly ambivalent perception of their own identity. This could be expressed in self-torment and ultimate self-destruction, as was illustrated, for instance, in the celebrated case of Otto Weininger.[17] It was also, of course, apparent in the thinking of the fledgling Zionist movement, whose desire to create a "new Jew" in his own (home)land was accompanied by urgent calls to purge the Jews of what had made them into a Diaspora people, or of what the Diaspora had made of them, namely, those very insidious traits proclaimed by the anti-Semitic movement, which both created the occasion for Zionism and provided it with much of its anti-Diaspora rhetoric. Zionism pledged not only to take the Jews out of the Diaspora, but also to take the Diaspora out of "the Jew." The assimilated Jew's "discovery" of his monstrosity or abnormality consisted in his awareness of the discrepancy between his alien "essence" and his conventional outer appearance, whereby he ended up as neither Jew nor gentile. For just as the Jews were abandoning most, but not quite all, of what had made them into Jews, and saw themselves as almost but not wholly indistinguishable from their environment, they were increasingly reminded that it was precisely these remnants of their identity that made them appear all the more suspect to the rest of society. The proverbial "self-hating Jew" was predicated on this condition of almost, yet not quite complete, assimilation. And the conclusions to be drawn from this predicament were either self-annihilation, whether by physical or cultural suicide, or self-assertion, whether by return to Jewish tradition or by Jewish nationalism.

If in Germany many Gentiles both before and after the Great War could still say that some of their best friends were Jews, many German Jews discovered that some of *their* best friends still preserved anti-Semitic sentiments. Indeed, the socially elusive enemies of the Jews were precisely those liberals who, while supporting Jewish emancipation and integration, insisted that they must eventually disappear as a distinct religious or ethnic category. This meant in turn that especially in Central Europe, Jews in this period were torn between the desire to enter into Gentile society as equals and their reluctance or inability to wholly give up their own sense of history and identity. Tragically, just as German and Austrian Jews were desperately and often creatively seeking a solution to this dilemma, their environment was rapidly edging toward a total rejection of the Jewish-German symbiosis for which they had striven.[18]

For Adolf Hitler, the destruction of the Jews was a sine qua non, a fundamental precondition for the re-creation of the Germans as an Aryan herrenvolk in a new thousand-year Reich. What he meant by his calls for eliminating the Jewish influence in Germany may have changed over the years, but he always maintained that "Judaism" must be removed, uprooted, or annihilated in order to preserve Germany from degeneration and decline. This was an extreme position, espoused even in the 1920s by a relatively small minority. Hitler himself was hardly in a position to envision Auschwitz when he wrote *Mein Kampf.* But many others of his generation in Germany and elsewhere were haunted by exterminatory fantasies. Moreover, if most Germans in the 1920s were probably not particularly preoccupied with the "Jewish question," anti-Semitic sentiments of varying intensity were becoming increasingly prevalent in the Weimar Republic, fed by economic hardship and political turmoil in the aftermath of the Great War and soon thereafter the Great Depression of the early 1930s.

The tendency to perceive the Jews as somehow related to all the evils that beset postwar Germany greatly facilitated the Nazi Party's anti-Semitic propaganda and the popular appeal of the Third Reich's subsequent anti-Jewish policies. Eventually it meant that the regime never faced any difficulties in recruiting personnel to organize, administer, and perpetrate genocide and that it could count on the implicit support for, or at least general indifference to, these policies by the rest of the population. This was achieved in part thanks to the regime's ability to present the Jews as the real, albeit elusive, enemy lurking behind all other evils that plagued Germany. Thus, while widespread circles in Germany saw Communism and Bolshevism as the greatest domestic and foreign danger, the Nazi argument that the Jews were the "real" instigators of Bolshevism could both popularize anti-Semitism and offer the not insignificant minority of Communist Party supporters in Germany a convenient rationale to rejoin the emerging *Volksgemeinschaft* as they "liberated" themselves from Jewish influence.

Similarly, by arguing that "plutocracy" too was part of a Jewish world conspiracy, the Nazis could attract at least some members of the working class (and apparently more than has been estimated until recently) without thereby antagonizing big capital and industry, on whose cooperation Hitler's expansionist policies were largely dependent. The argument that Hitler had played down anti-Semitism in the years immediately preceding and following his nomination as chancellor because it was far less popular than his promises of economic recovery and national reassertion is insufficient. Rather, the very image of "the Jew" as the "real" but elusive enemy of the German nation enabled the regime to maneuver between contradictory ideological assertions and policies. Hence anti-Semitism, even when it was least discussed, served along with economic anxiety and hardship, fear of revolution, a longing for national unity and greatness, and a generally xenophobic climate as an important adhesive that kept together an otherwise incoherent and irreconcilable ideological hodgepodge.[19]

The elusive and yet ubiquitous presence attributed to the Jews by the regime played an even more important role in creating an inverted perception of victimhood throughout the Nazi era. Although the regime glorified both nation and race, it invariably presented Germany as a victim of its enemies, among whom the Jews stood out most prominently. In January 1939 Hitler "prophesied" that if the Jews were once more to unleash a war aimed at the "Bolshevization of Europe," this time their attempt to victimize the Germans would lead to their own annihilation. He never budged from this position, asserting in his testament that it had indeed been the Jews who had caused the destruction of his thousand-year Reich.[20] The impact of this view could be seen just as clearly in individual Germans' perceptions of reality. Thus soldiers tended to ascribe massacres perpetrated by their own units to Jewish criminality, even when the actual victims of such atrocities were Jews, and civilians in the rear similarly attributed the destruction of cities by aerial bombing to Jewish thirst for revenge. Indeed, fear of "Jewish" retribution was very much at the background of Germany's stubborn resistance in the last and desperate months of the war, when the invading "Asiatic hordes" in the East and the "Materialschlacht" in the West were presented as an expression of the Jewish will for world domination.[21]

In this context it should be stressed that even while they were murdering Jews in unprecedented numbers, many of the perpetrators perceived themselves as acting in their own defense against their past and potential victimizers. That the Jews *appeared* defenseless and helpless seems only to have enhanced the need among the perpetrators to view themselves as the "real" victims and those they murdered as the culprits. The children, if allowed to survive, would take revenge; the women would bear more children; the elderly would tell the tale. Hence Germany's misfortune could only end by means of a terrible, final solution, and genocide was "a harsh, but just atonement of Jewish subhumanity," whose execution merely proved the German nation's determination to survive against all odds and enemies.[22]

Although it is impossible to establish how many Germans shared this view, indeed what proportion of the population was even aware of the Holocaust, it would appear that it was prevalent among those directly involved in perpetrating genocide.[23] Moreover, elements of this kind of reasoning had much deeper roots. For the very fact that the genocide of the Jews was planned and executed by German bureaucrats, soldiers, and policemen, just as much as the manner in which it was both carried out and rationalized, does tell us a great deal about the crucial role played by the fabricated image of the elusive enemy in preparing German society to take the path to inhumanity and barbarism. Indeed it could be argued that the very notion of elusive enemies—who especially in the German case were invariably the Jews—is a crucial precondition for atrocity and genocide, because it postulates that the people one kills are never the people one sees but merely what they represent, that is, what is hidden under their mask of innocence and normality. Thus the encounter of Germans with "real" Jews in Poland and Russia, who conformed to the anti-Semitic imagery of a traditional garb and way of life, only confirmed the suspicion that "their" German Jews were merely hiding behind a Westernized facade. Moreover, even these "real" Jews were not the old men, women, and children they appeared to be but pernicious enemies in no way different from fanatic Red Army commissars and vicious partisans. When asked how he had felt about killing children when he himself was a father, the death camp commander Franz Stangl said that he "rarely saw them as individuals. It was always a huge mass . . . they were naked, packed together, running, being driven with whips." On another occasion he noted that upon reading about lemmings he was reminded of Treblinka.[24]

Central to the "worldview" and functioning of the Third Reich was the assertion that its elusive enemies were ubiquitous, indestructible, and protean. That is why Nazism was not only committed to killing all the Jews but was predicated on the assumption that there would always be more "Jews" to kill. This is the crucial link between the "euthanasia" campaign and the Holocaust, quite apart from the well-documented fact that the killing of the mentally and physically handicapped, which began before the "Final Solution," provided the expertise and experience, as well as the crews and the psychological makeup necessary for the launching of a vast genocidal undertaking.[25] For if there was always a fear of "the Jew within," the urge to cleanse society of all deformity and abnormality was truly a promise of perpetual destruction. In this quest for perfection, everyone was potentially tainted, and no proof of ancestry could protect one from allegations of pollution. Even in a totally *Judenrein* universe, the definition of "health" could always exclude more and more members of society, whose elimination would promise a better future for the rest. The boundless definition of "purity" thus made for an endless pool of potential victims certain to feed the nihilistic dynamics of Nazism for as long as it survived self-annihilation. Nor has this urge for purity and health in modern civilization wholly disappeared with the final destruction of the Nazi regime.

The ubiquity of perpetrators and victims, and the frequent confusion between them, is at the core of the destructive energy characteristic of modern genocide, taking place as it does within an imaginary universe that encompasses every single individual in a cycle of devastation and murder. And because a neutral position is no longer available, both individuals and collectives will naturally tend to present themselves as victims. Thus the unique features of the Nazi genocidal enterprise illustrate an important characteristic of state-organized industrial killing, whereby the fabrication of elusive enemies makes everyone into a potential victim, and the assertion of elusive perpetrators makes everyone into a potential killer.

The question of German guilt was raised already during the war: Were all Germans guilty, or were they themselves victims of a criminal dictatorship? Conversely, although the Jews were acknowledged to have been (among) Germany's victims, the war was not presented as being waged on their behalf, not least for fear of arousing anti-Semitic sentiments among the Allies' populations.[26] This conundrum created a great deal of ambiguity regarding the identities of both victims and perpetrators at the end of the war, much enhanced by the rapidly changing political and ideological circumstances after 1945.[27] The cold war transformed old enemies into allies and former allies into sworn enemies; de-Nazification applied a narrow definition of perpetrators, thereby making for a highly inclusive definition of victimhood. The perceived need of the democracies to unite against communism meant that normalization in the West was accomplished by representing the war as a site of near universal victimhood.[28]

Germany's destruction was there for everyone to see; in the midst of this landscape of utter desolation, the concentration camps easily blended in. Although seen as examples of Nazi depravity and criminality, they did not readily divulge the identity of their victims. Moreover, the death camps were situated far from what had remained of the Old Reich.[29] Whereas the German and Austrian inhabitants of towns in the proximity of the camps had come to think of the inmates as "criminal elements,"[30] in subsequent postwar representations the inmates often appeared as political prisoners who had fought against the Nazis.[31] This supplied the enormity of the Nazi "concentrationary universe" with a false logic, according to which the regime had simply, albeit ruthlessly, suppressed all opposition. It also implied that there had indeed been a tremendous amount of resistance to Nazism. The far more numerous victims who had been murdered in the name of racial ideology without ever presenting any objective danger to the regime were at best relegated to a position of secondary importance, if not altogether ignored. In other words, the genocide of the Jews, which defied the liberal logic by appearing wholly counterproductive to the German war effort, was left largely unexplained for many years following the Holocaust, whether by historiography, legal discourse, documentaries, or other forms of representation.[32]

It has been noted that Germans experienced the last phases of the World War II and its immediate aftermath as a period of mass victimization. Indeed, Germany's remarkable reconstruction was predicated both on repressing the memory of the Nazi regime's victims and on the assumed existence of an array of new enemies, foreign and domestic, visible and elusive. Assertions of victimhood had the added benefit of suggesting parallels between the Germans and their own victims. Thus, if the Nazis strove to ensure the health and prosperity of the nation by eliminating the Jews, postwar Germany strove to neutralize the memory of the Jews' destruction so as to ensure its physical and psychological restoration.[33]

To be sure, the crimes of the Nazi regime became a necessary component of both West and East German identity and self-perception, even if the meanings ascribed to them were very different.[34] But it must be stressed that Nazi criminality itself was persistently associated with the suffering of the *Germans*. Both the murder of the Jews and the victimization of the Germans were described as acts perpetrated by a third party; but although Germans believed they had little in common with the Jews, they naturally felt their own suffering very keenly. Thus the Holocaust was an event carried out by one group of "others" on another such group; whereas the destruction of Germany was perpetrated by (possibly even the same) "others" directly on "us," the Germans. In this manner, the perpetrators of genocide were associated with the destroyers of Germany, and the Jewish victims were associated with German victims, without, however, eliciting the same kind of empathy.

Postwar German perceptions of victimhood entailed both inversion and continuity. In the Federal Republic the Third Reich's population was seen as the victim of both Hitler's terroristic regime and of Stalin's no less criminal Communist order. This was reflected in the so-called *Berufsverbot*, which barred German civil servants from membership in either Nazi or Communist organizations, thereby indicating that both ideologies were of an equally despicable nature. At the same time, however, the view persisted in some quarters that Germany had also been the victim of Western (and especially American) military might and imperialistic policies, now pursued by other means in a campaign of "cultural imperialism" that threatened the German way of life.[35] Conversely, in East Germany, the official view of fascism as the product of capitalism made it possible to deny all responsibility for the Nazi past and to retain pre-1945 prejudices against the West. In both Germanies, therefore, "Americanization" took on the appearance of an elusive enemy, not least because of its appeal for so many young Germans on both sides of the "Iron Curtain," making it thereby also into the enemy within. Moreover, although East Germany presented communism as the destroyer of the criminal Nazi clique and its capitalist supporters, deeply ingrained prejudices against Russians never quite disappeared there either, making them into yet another elusive enemy whose presence could not be openly criticized.[36]

West German representations of the past have often included the figure of "the Nazi."[37] This elusive type, rarely represented with any degree of empathy, retains a complex relationship with its predecessor, "the Jew." Serving as a metaphor for "the Nazi in us," it inverts the discredited notion of "the Jew in us" (which postwar philo-Semitism in turn has inverted into a positive attribute);[38] simultaneously, it presents "the Nazi" as the paradigmatic other, just as "the Jew" had been in the past (and in many senses remains despite "his" newly discovered moral qualities). If the 1935 Nuremberg Laws could define "Aryan" only negatively as having no Jewish ancestry, postwar representations defined "German" as not being (truly) Nazi. Both instances made for an array of "racial" or ideological *Mischlinge* ("half-breeds"). After all, just as in the Third Reich there was always the fear or suspicion that one had some Jewish ancestor in the remote past (quite apart from the fact that many "pure" Aryans did not display the physical attributes expected from Nordic types),[39] so too Germans who had abstained from any affiliation with the various agencies of the Nazi Party and its innumerable offshoots throughout the Third Reich's twelve years were rather hard to come by.

Only the Jews were innocent on both counts, having been excluded from both the racial and the ideological community. But Jews rarely appear in German postwar representations of the past. Hence only those who had, by their actions or words, shown that they were "pure" Nazis, were seen as such by postwar Germans, and even in that case they were rarely pursued and punished with much energy or severity. The innumerable others were said to have been affiliated with the regime unwillingly, unknowingly, naively, innocently, opportunistically, but in any case not out of true conviction. They were not, therefore, "really" Nazi, which left open the possibility that they were "good" Germans.[40]

The new enemy of postwar Germany, "the Nazi," is thus both everywhere and nowhere. On the one hand, "he" lurks in everyone, and in this sense can never be ferreted out. On the other hand, "he" is essentially so different from "us" that he can be said never to have existed in the first place in any sense that would be historically meaningful or significant for "us," namely, for contemporary Germany and especially for the vast majority of individual Germans, who were either not in positions of power in the Third Reich or belong to succeeding generations.[41] Hence "we" cannot be held responsible for "his" misdeeds. Just like the Devil, "the Nazi" penetrates the world from another sphere and must be exorcised; conversely, "he" is a metaphor of the satanic element in humanity. Both faces of "the Nazi" abound in German representations of the Third Reich; and both greatly facilitate identifying with its (German) victims. But the latter view, that of "the Nazi" as an inherent potential in humanity, while it can be construed as apologetic, also generates deep anxiety about the ubiquity of evil even in our own post-Nazi universe.

The public discourse on the Holocaust in postwar Germany has, until recently, largely concentrated either on the social marginality of the perpetrators or on the anonymous forces that made it into a reality. The Jewish victims have rarely featured as anything more than the by-products of this process. So-called ordinary Germans appear to have been either untouched by or irrelevant to genocide, and arguments to the contrary have been seen and condemned as attempts to assign collective national guilt. The largely defensive reaction to such arguments shows the difficulty many Germans still have in accepting that the Third Reich had perpetrated crimes on such a vast scale with the support and complicity of large sections of the population. Instead, it is *German* victimhood, and, in some cases, martyrdom, that tends to be stressed time and again.[42]

This can also be seen by reference to the debate over resistance to the Nazi regime. Notably, the conservative opposition, associated primarily with the plot of July 20, 1944, has received much more attention in the Federal

Republic than the resistance by the Communists and Socialists especially during the early years of the regime. This is partly related to the available documentation, partly to the ideological inclinations of postwar historians, and partly to the circumstances of the cold war. It should be pointed out, however, that the Nazi regime tended to associate Socialist and Communist opponents, both domestic and foreign, with the Jews, and persecuted them from the very beginning. Indeed, the early concentration camps housed mainly members of the left-wing opposition, along with a variety of "asocials." Conversely, the conservative opposition came from the social and military elite and often had impeccable anti-Semitic credentials and a record of early support for the regime that turned sour only when Hitler appeared to be taking Germany on a dangerous war course, or even later, after it became clear that, for all intents and purposes, the war was lost. This is not to cast doubt on the moral motivation of some conservative conspirators, nor on the fact that they were appalled by the crimes of the regime. Yet it is just as true that they were potentially acceptable allies, and that for a long time they indeed served in that capacity, making possible the creation of the regime and the organization of the army that facilitated the disasters and crimes against which they ultimately rebelled. It should also be remembered that the conspirators were a very small minority that can hardly be said to have been representative of the milieus from which it stemmed. Nevertheless, during the cold war it was as difficult for the Federal Republic to concede that resistance to Nazism had begun on the Left as it was for the German Democratic Republic to admit that the single most dangerous domestic challenge to Hitler had indeed come from the old German elites. Moreover, the very notion of resistance to the regime at time of war remained problematic, because it could be construed as another "stab in the back" along the model of 1918, a point of which the resisters themselves were well aware. Indeed, casting doubts on the legitimacy of the Nazi regime by praising the conspirators threatened the far more numerous officials who defended themselves from postwar accusations by asserting their legal and moral obligation to obey the regime, especially in wartime.[43]

The resisters have therefore retained an ambivalent position long after 1945. Seen as both conspirators and heroes, they represent the ambiguity of resistance to the regime, so well reflected in the treatment by the Federal Republic (FRG) of lesser acts of resistance or subversion by the lower ranks in the army, such as insubordination, desertion, and self-inflicted wounds. While the Wehrmacht (armed forces) meted severe punishments for such allegedly political offenses, including the loss of pensions, the FRG, until very recently, has upheld these sentences without consideration for the circumstances of the time (while paying pensions to retired members of the Waffen-SS [Armed

SS] or their families). If the senior officers who rebelled in 1944 have been glorified, rebellious soldiers of the rank and file were for a long time seen as traitors and criminals.[44]

For historians, determining the identity of the Nazi regime's domestic opponents is also a matter of definition, not always corresponding to contemporary perceptions. While scholars engaged in reconstructing the *Alltagsgeschichte* (history of everyday life) of the Third Reich have noted resistance by the population to this or that governmental measure, this type of behavior was not always perceived by the regime itself as outright opposition, especially because it was often accompanied by conformity with or support for other aspects of Nazi rule: if everyone was a potential enemy, complicity was nevertheless pervasive.[45] Conversely, until recently, the everyday life of the regime's declared enemies received little attention, an implicit acceptance of Nazi distinctions, internalized by much of the population, between "Aryans" and Jews. This has been changing in recent years, but it should be noted that there is still a general tendency to write the history of the Germans and the Jews separately, even though many German Jews saw themselves first and foremost as Germans, at least as long as the Nazis did not force them to think otherwise.[46] It could thus be argued that postwar scholarship has institutionalized an ideologically imposed perception, with the result that the historiographies of perpetrators and victims rarely overlap. Although the lives of German Jews and Gentiles were separated by the regime, it is the process of segregation that needs to be clarified rather than accepting its outcome as natural; and although the categories of victims and perpetrators are distinct, it is the encounter between the two that facilitates genocide, and keeping them strictly apart only blurs the fact that persecution, discrimination, and murder, are actions in which one side does something to another side, that is, where there is an encounter, physical and material, mental and imaginary, between the killer and his victim.[47]

The memory of the Holocaust has been constructed as an elusive, unstable entity by both Germans and Jews. Shortly after the war, Hannah Arendt wrote that the past had become a matter of opinion, rather than fact, for many Germans.[48] More recently, the deniers of the Holocaust in several countries have adopted to their own purposes relativist and postmodern assertions regarding the instability or nonexistence of facts about the past, said to be as elusive as memory itself.[49] One of the perpetrators interviewed by Claude Lanzmann in his film *Shoah* admits that Hitler's dislike of the Jews "was well known. . . . But as to their extermination, that was news to us. I mean, even today some people deny it. They say there couldn't have been so many Jews. Is it true? I don't know. That's what they say."[50] Indeed, the very nature and unprecedented scale of the destruction has tended to put into question the capacity to remember, represent, and reconstruct it.[51] Atrocity becomes elusive precisely because it is ubiquitous; inconceivable because it is fantastic; faceless because it is protean. Devastation of such proportions not only destroys the very mechanisms capable of measuring its scale but also the ability to imagine it.[52] It must therefore be reduced to a more manageable size and more conventional nature so that the mind can take it in rather than totally blot it out. Paradoxically, both those who want to keep the memory of atrocity and those who wish to deny it are engaged in a similar attempt to force the event into an acceptable imaginary mold. If their goals are radically opposed to each other, their means are much less so: for both denial and remembrance begin by diminishing the event. Denial starts off by casting doubts on the minutiae of destruction, undermining thereby our acceptance of the whole; reconstruction similarly begins from the details, because the scale of the enormity it so vast that it denies its own existence and vanishes from the mind. Having created a reality beyond its wildest fantasies, humanity cannot imagine what it created. In this context, human agency remains tenuous, the disaster being ascribed either to insane genius or to anonymous forces. Language too, disintegrates; hence the resort, either to medieval imagery of hell and metaphysical speculation or to radical skepticism about reality and a perception of the world as text, complex and elusive, but purged of the inarticulate screams of the millions, inscribed into every word pronounced since the Holocaust.[53]

For the Jewish survivors of the Holocaust, it would seem, there was nothing elusive about the identity of either the perpetrators or the victims. And yet, both the event of the Holocaust itself and the identity of its human agents and victims have remained highly elusive in what has become by now a substantial body of Jewish ruminations on and representations of the event.[54] This has to do both with the inherent nature of the event, and with the fact that its Jewish representation depends to a large extent on the ideological, national, and religious affiliations of the survivors, their offspring, and those who have been spared direct or family-related contact with the event. To be sure, the manner and extent of Jewish preoccupation with the Holocaust, more evident perhaps at present than at any other time in the past, seems tragically both to recapitulate and to invert the urging of the Passover Haggadah to tell the story of the liberation from slavery in Egypt as if they themselves had experienced it. For the Holocaust is not a story of liberation but of annihilation. In this sense, due to the scope of the destruction and the exterminatory aspirations of the Nazis, every Jew is a survivor by dint of having been a potential victim, including those born after the event who would not have seen life had Hitler had his way. But precisely because the Holocaust poses the most profound existential questions to Jewish life since the Exile, any interpretation of it cannot be isolated from its implications for the present. And because the event as a whole defies the imaginative capacities of the human mind, it is open to an array of interpretations and ascribed meanings, whose single common element is that they all agree on their incapacity to "save" it completely from its inherently inexplicable nature. Hence the Holocaust can both serve to legitimize contradictory choices of various Jewish communities in the postwar era and simultaneously to cast doubt on each and every one of them, exposing them as precariously founded on a reading of an event that is perceived to be beyond comprehension. In that sense, the Holocaust is both at the root of the extraordinary revival of Jewish life after the genocide and is the cause of the deep anxiety and bewilderment that characterizes much of postwar Jewish thought and creativity.[55]

In the years immediately following the Holocaust, the two most influential and articulate Jewish communities left in the world, American Jewry and the State of Israel, largely kept silent about the event. While Soviet Jewry, that other major survivor of the Holocaust, found itself under political circumstances that made public, or even private, discussion of the Holocaust almost impossible, American Jews and Israelis, with some important exceptions, largely accepted the very different official state perception in their respective lands. To be sure, both narratives were constructed as a tale of ultimate triumph, either of American democracy and values or of Zionist ideology and Jewish statehood, and both claimed to have discovered the best remedy to the condition of Jewish Diaspora in Europe. Indeed, whereas American Jews were convinced that their country of choice had led the eventual victory over Nazism, Israelis believed that the very existence of their newly founded state constituted a defeat for Nazi aspirations to destroy the Jewish people. These narratives were not wholly consistent with historical reality. The United States did not fight Germany to save the Jews and could hardly be said to have pursued opportunities to hamper the killing process during the war with any conviction. Moreover, the American government had refused to accept any significant numbers of Jewish refugees during the 1930s, a decision which in retrospect proved to have had fatal consequences. Nevertheless, there was little doubt that the United States did play a major role in destroying the Third Reich and thereby put an end to the extermination of the Jews (by which time of course the vast majority of European Jewry had already been murdered). What was just as important for Jewish perceptions of the United States was the fact that following the war, many survivors were allowed to immigrate here and to begin a new and at least materially successful life.

The Zionist/Israeli narrative similarly contained some baffling contradictions. After all, the minuscule *Yishuv*, or prestate Jewish community in Palestine, which numbered just over half a million people during the war, was hardly in a condition to fight Nazism. While the Zionist rhetoric subsequently claimed that unlike the Diaspora, the "new" Jews of Palestine would not have gone as "sheep to the slaughter," the fact of the matter is that had Erwin Rommel broken through at Alamein and reached Palestine, the Yishuv would have probably ended up just like any other major ghetto in Europe. What saved the Jews of Palestine was not Zionism but the same factor that saved British Jewry, namely, the British armed forces. No less disturbing for subsequent reconstructions of the period was the knowledge that while the Holocaust was happening in Europe, the Yishuv was preoccupied mainly with ensuring its own survival and prosperity, building the economic and political infrastructure for the establishment of the future state, and preparing for the anticipated military confrontation with the Palestinian Arab population and the surrounding states. Similarly, American Jewry was extremely slow to acknowledge the reality of the genocide in Europe and was greatly troubled by the prospect that putting too much pressure on the American government to act on behalf of European Jews might have a detrimental effect on the still not fully established position of Jews in the United States. In this sense, the same mechanism of repression functioned in the Yishuv and American Jewry during the Holocaust. Both communities found it difficult to believe the horror tales coming from Europe, and they blotted out for as long as they could the growing amount of information indicating that a whole Jewish world, including the families and towns from which so many American and Palestinian Jews had originated, was being systematically annihilated. Both communities also shared a certain level of complacency and self-satisfaction in view of the fact that their respective choices of residence had been justified by the plight of their brethren in Nazi-occupied Europe.[56]

At this point, of course, there was nothing particularly elusive about the self-declared enemy of the Jews. And yet, even while the Holocaust was still happening, the enemy was also being defined both more widely and more narrowly, closer to local concerns, on the one hand, and associated with traditional images, on the other. Moreover, the nature of the Holocaust itself made for a reluctance to concentrate on its details, an obsession with its implications, and a preoccupation with the relationship between victim and perpetrator, complicity and resistance, individual and community, altruism and self-interest.

Many of these strands came together both in the United States and Israel during the Adolf Eichmann trial, the first major public confrontation with the Holocaust in either country. Until that point, the murder of the Jews was presented in the United States as part and parcel of the World War II, and specifically of the political persecution that had characterized the Nazi regime and had therefore made the struggle against it into a just war. The genocide of the Jews was still not referred to as the Holocaust, and the symbols of Nazi oppression were Bergen-Belsen, Dachau, and Buchenwald, namely, those concentration camps—and not death camps—that had been liberated by the Western Allies and had indeed served during much of their existence for the incarceration of the real and imaginary political, rather than "biological" enemies of the regime.[57] In Israel, of course, the *Shoah*, as the Holocaust was called there, was indeed perceived as the most important event of the World War II, as well as a major disaster for the Jewish people; but public discourse and education tended to emphasize especially such events as the Warsaw Ghetto rebellion and other instances of Jewish resistance, on the one hand, and the eventual *Ha'apala* (illegal immigration) of the survivors to British-occupied Palestine, on the other. The mass slaughter of the Jews was acknowledged but with a distinct measure of embarrassment and discomfort, because although it could be used to justify the Zionist argument about the urgent need to create a new Jewish "type" in an independent Jewish state willing and able to fight for its existence, it was also perceived as a case of national humiliation and highlighted the Yishuv's own vulnerability as well as its inability to defend the vast majority of the Jewish people murdered in Europe by the Nazis. This combined sense of shame and anxiety made it appear all the more urgent during the early postwar years in Palestine and then Israel rapidly to convert the arriving survivors from Diaspora Jews into Zionist Israelis, that is, to erase those qualities in the new arrivals that had allegedly made the victims go "like sheep to the slaughter" and to remake them as patriotic citizens of the Jewish state, new types unburdened by the shadows and ghosts of the past and capable of protecting the Jewish state from any more genocidal assaults. That the state was increasingly made up of survivors, and that the Yishuv itself had been saved from the Holocaust due to circumstances wholly beyond its control, was not, and perhaps could not, be acknowledged in those early and precarious years of Jewish statehood.[58]

The Eichmann trial redefined many of the categories hitherto employed by the two communities in representing the Holocaust. Receiving wide media exposure in Israel and the United States, the trial greatly complicated previous perceptions of the event, both by providing the public with masses of the information that until then had been the domain of only a few specialists and by casting doubt on conventional narratives and interpretations that had been employed in confronting, or in avoidance of confronting, the reality and implications of the Holocaust. This was also the reason for the furor with which Hannah Arendt's controversial reports and subsequent book on the trial were greeted by both Jewish communities, posing (but also dodging) as she did some of the most crucial questions about the significance of the Holocaust for postwar society, issues that in large part have indeed not been resolved to our own day. One major aspect of this controversy involved the nature and identity of both the enemy and the victim.

Jewish interpretations of the Holocaust conventionally assumed that the Nazi genocide was motivated mainly by a particularly virulent strain of anti-Semitism, perceived more generally as inherent to European, Christian civilization. Arendt's argument that the genocide of the Jews was carried out by loyal, law-abiding, and opportunistic bureaucrats, who cared little about ideology and a great deal about their own status and reputation as civil servants capable of executing their allotted tasks flawlessly and efficiently, introduced a highly disturbing element to the debate. Moreover, if previously the Jews had perceived themselves as the main victims of the World War II, Arendt claimed that Jewish traditions of compliance and accommodation in the face of adversity, and the inability of community leaders to recognize the true genocidal intent of the Nazis, led to fateful complicity of the victims in their own annihilation. Although infuriating her critics, Arendt's assertion also indicated the need for more subtle analyses of victimhood and complicity. Conversely, while American public opinion had previously subsumed the murder of the Jews under the regime's persecution of its political enemies, the Eichmann trial heralded the emergence of the Holocaust in the United States and subsequently also in Western Europe as the paradigm of evil, and the fate of the Jews as the epitome of victimhood.[59]

It should be noted that much of the historical evidence for Arendt's essay was taken from Raul Hilberg's magisterial study on the Holocaust. Interestingly, Hilberg's own study was rejected by the Research Institute of Yad Vashem (Martyrs' and Heroes' Remembrance Authority) in Jerusalem when he asked for assistance in publishing it, mainly because in the view of the institute's staff Hilberg had failed to pay due attention to Jewish fate and resistance and had instead focused primarily on the perpetrators.[60] Indeed, neither Hilberg's work, nor Arendt's important study *The Origins of Totalitarianism*, has been translated into Hebrew to this very day; her *Eichmann in Jerusalem* was finally published in Israel only in 2000. However, this should not create the impression that Arendt and Hilberg were in agreement with each other. Not only has Hilberg voiced strong criticism of Arendt recently; there is little doubt that these two scholars were of a very different cast of mind and were motivated in their work by very different agendas. Thus, whereas Hilberg's focus on the perpetrators was based on his assumption that this was the only way to explain the genocide of the Jews, Arendt's intention was overtly to diminish the centrality of anti-Semitism in explaining the Holocaust and to show the inherent genocidal potential in the modern state. As numerous works (cited above) have since demonstrated, her dismissal of anti-Semitism as a motivating factor among the perpetrators and within German society more generally can no longer be supported; but her insistence on the pernicious traits of the modern bureaucratic state greatly contributed to our understanding of the twentieth century and makes her work into a cardinal text of postwar scholarship.

Conversely, Hilberg's analysis of the Third Reich has had a tremendous influence on all subsequent studies of the period; yet its limited focus has both encouraged the view that the Holocaust can be explained with the victims more or less left out and that Nazi Germany can be analyzed in isolation from other totalitarian and genocidal systems. At the same time, although Arendt took a much wider and less precise view, and Hilberg a narrower and more detailed one, both scholars have implied that the Jews were somehow complicit in their murder and did little to prevent it; they ignored, or did not know about, the numerous instances of Jewish resistance, on the one hand, and, on the other hand, failed to acknowledge the more or less unresisting annihilation by the Nazis (and other regimes) of many other groups not normally charged with "having gone like sheep to the slaughter," such as, most prominently perhaps, the millions of Soviet prisoners of war murdered by the Nazi regime and its associates (but also Tutsi by Hutu, Cambodians by Cambodians, Armenians by Turks, and so forth). Both tried to steer away from the monocausal interpretation of the Holocaust as motivated only by anti-Semitism and in the process minimized its impact more than the evidence warrants. Yet Arendt was apologetic for German cultural traditions, Hilberg accusatory of German bureaucratic mentality. Both works threatened to replace one monocausality with another. But Hilberg was interested mainly in the mechanism of genocide, Arendt in its moral and philosophical implications.

Arendt's criticism of Eichmann's trial in Jerusalem and of Jewish behavior in the Holocaust; her unwillingness to condemn German culture as a whole; her impatience with the simplistic narrative of the Holocaust as the culmination of European anti-Semitism; and her association with, and subsequent defense of, Martin Heidegger cast her in the role of the proverbial self-hating Jew and critic of the newly established Jewish state.[61] Such so-called self-hating Jews were a social and psychological phenomenon related to the secularization and often only partially successful assimilation of European Jews beginning in the nineteenth century, and they were anathema to the Zionist and Orthodox establishments alike. Seen often as the enemy within, they reflected the profound crisis in Jewish identity that Zionism, along with other political movements, had sought to rectify.

Especially in its early years, Israeli society found it much easier to deal with the phenomenon of the Jew as resister and fighter, even if he or she ended up as a victim, than with the Jew as the victim of another's perception, irrespective of his or her actions. In other words, whereas Jewish resisters were glorified, "passive" Jewish victims were treated with greater distance and discomfort. Conversely, the early tendency in the United States to assimilate the Jews as a whole into the view of Nazi victims as the regime's political opponents, while it glorified them, did very little justice to their actual fate and arguably made for an integration into American society based on silence and repression. The Nazi regime, of course, ultimately differentiated only between part and full Jews, and occasionally (and temporarily) between Jews who could work and those who could not. Hannah Arendt, however, proposed yet another category of Jews, namely, those who in one way or another were complicit in their own genocide, whether (and most especially) as members of the *Judenräte* (Jewish councils) or as Kapos recruited to control the Jewish population in the ghettos and camps. Unlike previous distinctions, then, between types of Jewish victimhood, Arendt's notion of Jewish complicity blurred the boundaries between victims and perpetrators. Indeed, it is likely that precisely because there was a tremendous amount of resentment toward such Jewish "collaborators" among both the survivors and the Jewish communities that received them (especially in Palestine), Arendt's emphasis on this phenomenon in a public (Gentile) forum, well beyond the closed Jewish circles in which it was acknowledged, was perceived as a particularly pernicious type of treason.[62]

Arendt's case is related in yet another way to more subtle, albeit not always cautious, distinctions between and within categories of victims and perpetrators. Educated in Germany, and steeped in the German philosophical tradition, Arendt was unwilling to condemn German culture per se or to speak of German collective guilt for the Holocaust. However critical she might have been of early postwar Germany's failure to face up to its murderous past, its tendency to concentrate on its own victimhood and reconstruction, and its lack of empathy for the victims of the Nazi regime, she rejected interpretations that linked Hitler with earlier German history or assertions about the unique (or uniquely evil) German "character." The product of that remarkable, if also deeply troubled Jewish-German (negative) symbiosis of Wilhelmine and Weimar Germany, Arendt was affiliated for a while with Zionism, and she retained a strong association for much of her adult life with Martin Heidegger, the great German philosopher who greeted the advent of the Nazi regime with so much enthusiasm. In this she had a great deal in common with many other German Jews in pre-state Palestine and Israel, whose allegiance to and love for the culture from which they had been forced to flee was expressed in the libraries of German classics they had taken along with them on their way to exile in the Jewish homeland. These were not "self-hating Jews" but men and women who refused to condemn the world that had been part and parcel of their own identity and formation, even if they would never return to it. The survivors of German Jewry knew their enemy better than anyone else, because they had lived in that enemy's midst until they were finally driven out. Their ambivalence resulted from the fact that although enemy and victim were so much alike, having largely shared the same educational and cultural background, they were also ultimately defined as stark opposites, so that their fellow citizens became their potential murderers, and they in turn were transformed from patriotic Germans into often ardent, even if at times somewhat schizophrenic, Zionists.[63]

This was only part of the troubled relationship between enemies and victims within the Israeli discourse on national identity. Zionism had formed in Europe as a reaction to political anti-Semitism, the view that "the Jew" was European society's most dangerous and yet elusive enemy. The Zionists, in turn, presented Gentile European society as the greatest danger to Jewish existence and promoted the idea of a Jewish state, applying to it the very model of Central European nationalism that had increasingly viewed Jews as an alien race but combining it with traditional Jewish attitudes to their non-Jewish environment. Yet the new Jewish state was created in the Middle East, on the rim of an Arab, Islamic world, although the original vision of Zionism was to establish a political and social entity very much in line with liberal or socialist ideas brought over from Europe. This made for a great deal of ambivalence vis-à-vis Europe, seen as both the persecutor of the Jews and the model for an independent Jewish existence. Conversely, although the Zionists aspired to create a "new Jew" closer to the ancient Israelites than to their Diaspora ancestors, the only available example for this figure was the Arabs, who for their part increasingly resisted Jewish nationhood in Palestine. Hence there developed the ambivalent attitude toward the Arab world, which was seen both as a model for a resurrected Hebrew culture and as its worst enemy. Meanwhile, the arrival of large numbers of Sephardim from the Arab lands in the newly established state was also greeted with mixed feelings. For although the "Orientals" appeared closer to the Hebraic precursors of the modern Jew, their traditional culture, social norms, and religious practices seemed positively alien and primitive to the largely secular Ashkenazim, even if it had the exotic appeal of biblical times.[64]

All this made for a complex process of inversion and denial, whereby anti-Semitic stereotypes were employed by Zionism both in order to mold a new type of Israeli Jew and to forge a negative image of the Arab, while the virtues of that very European civilization from which the Zionists had emigrated were both appropriated by the state and set against the "oriental" nature of its Arab environment. At the same time, and in apparent contradiction to this first image, the Arabs were presented as the local manifestation of European anti-Semitism, and fighting them was presented as a continuation of, and this time victory over, the genocidal aspirations of Gentile Europe. Thus, the Israelis could see themselves both as an outpost of European civilization on the fringe of barbarism, and as winning the war against the collaborators of Nazism that their European ancestors had lost. Ironically, if the Arabs saw the Jewish state as a modern reenactment of the Crusaders, to be ultimately destroyed by a latter-day Saladin, the Jewish memory of the Crusaders pictured them as the precursors of Europe's anti-Jewish pogroms, stretching from the Middle Ages all the way to Hitler; and if the Arabs saw the Jews as European colonizers, the Zionists claimed to have regained their ancestral homeland, whence they had been exiled into a two-thousand-year-long existence as the perennial victims of European civilization.[65]

The origins of modern genocide, as well as its long-term consequences, are thus deeply rooted in a history of metaphors of evil, or, perhaps, of evil metaphors claiming to be history. The Israeli case presents only one important aspect of the discourse on persecution and victimhood that has become a central feature of our century. It is no coincidence that while some Israelis have seen the Palestinians as the incarnation of Nazism, Palestinians have presented themselves as the Jews of the Middle East, and some anti-Israeli speakers have compared the Israelis to the Nazis. Whatever the shortcomings of her thesis, Arendt's argument on the elusive nature of victimhood, complicity, and crime provides an important insight into the larger context of the Holocaust. For it is not only an event that defies conventional interpretations but one that has been appropriated by all and sundry and yet ultimately belongs to us all.[66]

The Holocaust has been used to justify the unjustifiable; it has served as a measuring rod for every other atrocity, trivializing and relativizing what would otherwise be unacceptable; it has created an image of an enemy so monstrous that it can be employed to demonize all other enemies (as being the same) or to let them off the hook (as being not as bad); it has created an image of victimhood so horrific, that all other suffering must be diminished in comparison or inflated to fit its standards. Itself the product of the idea of elusive enemies, the Holocaust has by now been repeatedly mobilized to perpetuate victimhood.[67]

For what makes the event so maddening, so frustrating, so resistant to human understanding and to ordinary empathy and emotion, is the elusiveness of its perpetrators and victims—the former because of the bureaucratic and detached manner in which they organized genocide (even if it was ultimately carried out by run-of-the-mill sadists or quickly brutalized "ordinary men"), the latter because the vast majority of them disappeared without a trace, and the few who survived have found it almost impossible to recount their experience, not only because humanity would not, and could not, accept the sheer horror of the event but also because they themselves have been torn between the urgent need to recount the tale and the terror of plunging into infinite despair by evoking it once more. What is so devastating about the Holocaust is that there can never be any acceptable relationship between the crime and the punishment, between what humanity has been able to imagine and what it has wrought upon itself. This was already evident during the postwar trials, where the murderers of thousands, having been given a public hearing, were often let off with the lightest of punishments, while their victims had no voice at all. It was manifested by the necessary normalization of both the perpetrators' and the victims' existence, accomplished by repressing the memory and erasing the traces of a past that could not be assimilated into the present. It was, finally, established through the decision that life must continue after the apocalypse. And as a result of this seemingly inevitable process, much that has been at the root of the original evil has persisted beyond its enactment and extended into the present. Hence the spectacle persists of victims being accused of complicity in their own destruction; of perpetrators enjoying a prosperous postwar respectability; of shattered, disjointed, and guilt-ridden memories of survivors, for whom the categories of victim and perpetrator as we understand them cannot have the same calming effect, cannot order the past into those convenient distinctions that we wish so much to draw in retrospect. For the final and most tragic legacy of the Holocaust is that even the few who survived know that they could have just as easily joined the endless rows of the "drowned" yet at the same time are burdened by the sense that they owe a debt to the murdered they can never repay, the debt of their own lives. This is the atrocity after the event, for although so many perpetrators have neither paid for their crimes nor suffered guilt, the "saved" are doomed to remain their own unrelenting enemies, struggling with the memory and vision of their death for the rest of their tortured lives.[68]

The victim trope is a central feature of our time. In a century that produced more victims of war, genocide, and massacre than all of previous recorded history put together, it is both a trope and a reflection of reality. Yet, at the same time, it is a dangerous prism through which to view the world, for victims are produced by enemies, and enemies eventually make for more victims. Traditional societies often create elaborate rites of vengeance and pacification; modern, industrial societies have the capacity to wreak destruction on such a vast scale that ultimately everyone becomes its victim. This chapter has attempted to examine only one case, that of German and Jewish views of enemies and victims, and the extent to which the legacy of the Holocaust has molded the fate and identity of these two peoples over the past fifty years. Although I have used the past tense, I believe that this legacy is still an inherent part of German and Jewish consciousness. Moreover, this is merely a single, albeit especially pertinent, example of the pernicious effects of the discourse of victimhood in many other parts of the world. By way of conclusion, and without going into much detail, it may be instructive to point out a few more cases in which competing memories and representations of violence have embedded themselves in the historical consciousness and politics of identity of other twentieth-century nations.

The similarities and differences between German and Japanese "coming to terms" with the past have recently drawn the attention of several scholars and journalists. Most relevant to the present context is the tendency of the Japanese, throughout most of the postwar period, to portray their nation primarily as the victim of nuclear annihilation. The shrines erected in Hiroshima and Nagasaki are thus more than symbols of modern war's destructive nature, and they cannot be seen as mere expressions of pacifist sentiments. Rather, by celebrating Japanese suffering, these sites have facilitated a process of long-term repression, if not denial, of Japan's own war of annihilation in China and other parts of Asia, as well as its criminal conduct toward enemy prisoners of war. In a recent ironic twist, the German citizen and member of the Nazi Party who saved thousands of Chinese lives during the "rape of Nanjing" was described as the "Oskar Schindler of Nanjing." Thus another "good German" was discovered just as Japan's war of extermination was brought back to the public consciousness. At the same time it should be stressed that the Chinese government has for long been reluctant to portray its own nation as the victim of Japanese atrocities, both for internal reasons and because of its relations with postwar Japan.[69]

Politics have played a major role also in the case of the Turkish genocide of the Armenians. Whereas the Armenians have seen themselves not only as victims of Turkish extermination policies, but also of many decades of concerted Turkish efforts to repress and deny their veracity, the Turks have asserted that claims about genocide were merely part of Armenian nationalism, which had allegedly sparked anti-Armenian policies during the Great War in the first place. In this case, too, differing views of victimhood have been reflected in controversies over academic politics and educational policies. This was demonstrated, for instance, in the recent debate over the alleged intervention of the Turkish government in an appointment at an American university, as it was in the no-less-embarrassing dispute over teaching the Armenian genocide in Israeli schools. In yet another characteristic twist, recent revelations concerning the involvement of the German government in the Armenian genocide expose the highly complex links between instances of mass murder in the twentieth century, as well as their perception by groups of perpetrators, victims, and bystanders.[70]

Similarly, the genocide of his own people by the leader of the Khmer Rouge, Pol Pot, has been used and abused in political debates and ideological confrontations. Dating back to the American involvement in Cambodia during the Vietnam War, the genocide in Kampuchea has been presented by some as the consequence of Western imperialism, by others as one more instance of communism's destructive urge. It was used by the "revisionists" of the German *Historikerstreit* (historians' controversy) to relativize the Holocaust and has most recently become the focus of an attack on the director of the Cambodian Genocide Program at Yale University, a research project launched by a grant of the U.S. State Department.[71] Meanwhile, in one of the most grotesque, yet not untypical, statements by a modern genocidal dictator, shortly before his death Pol Pot himself was reported in October 1997 to have said to an interviewer what Hitler too might have said had he found refuge in some remote jungle: "I feel a little bit bored, but I have become used to that."[72]

Finally, the two most glaring instances of genocide and "ethnic cleansing" in the 1990s were also deeply mired in a discourse on victimhood and enemies, traced by the protagonists many centuries back and showing few signs of being resolved any time soon. Thus the recent genocide in Rwanda was only the latest in a series of mass killings between Hutu and Tutsi. Moreover, new scholarship has demonstrated how the self-perception of the population in Burundi and Rwanda has been molded by European ideas regarding the supposed "racial" differences between Hutu and Tutsi, very much in the service of colonial and postcolonial powers as well as of the Catholic Church. That the media latched on to the stereotypes propagated by such interest groups indicates how the easy access to information in the electronic age by no means facilitates knowledge and understanding, let alone prevention of atrocity.[73] As for the mass killings and ethnic cleansing in Bosnia and Kosovo, the long memories of South Eastern Europe go much further back than the world wars and the horrendous massacres that have afflicted that region in the course of the twentieth century. As in the case of the Middle East, political discussions in the former Yugoslavia invariably begin and end by evoking the memory of ancient wars and animosities, deeply inscribed in popular lore, legend, and song. Chronological time and detached historiography play a minor role in people's perceptions of reality, especially at times of crisis (produced to some extent by precisely this hiatus of historical perspective). The heroes and martyrs of days gone by reappeared on late-twentieth-century battlefields, reenacting the sacrifices and atrocities of their forefathers. Thus the Croats described the Serbs as "Chetniks," the Serbs called the Croats "Ustashe," and the Muslims were seen as "Turks." The horrors of the past were told, remembered, and repeated. The war, it has been said, was never over; "it was a question of waiting for the right moment to recommence it."[74]

All of this should amply demonstrate that perhaps more attention should be devoted to the process of defining enemies and making victims in future historical work. And yet, just as identifying the similarities between such cases is necessary, no less crucial is the need to make distinctions. Criticizing the recent revival of equating the Soviet and Nazi systems, Peter Holquist notes that "in contrast to the National Socialist regime's biological-racial standard, the Soviet regime employed a fundamentally sociological paradigm to key individual experience to its universal matrix."[75] Hence, he rightly argues, a comparison between Nazi and Soviet state violence indicates that "the Soviets did not see their task as intrinsically related to the total physical annihilation of a particular group," nor to the "outright physical elimination of every living being in that [sociological] category." The Soviets did not "engage in industrial killing" precisely because they viewed extermination a means to a goal, unlike the Nazis, for whom it was the goal itself.[76] Nevertheless, here too the Jews came to play a unique role. As Amir Weiner shows in his contribution to this volume, the post-1945 "twin institutions of hierarchical heroism and universal suffering," which constituted "the cornerstones of the Soviet ethnonational ethos of the war," both erased the Jewish participation in the Soviet struggle against the Germans from official commemoration and historiography and incorporated the Holocaust "into the epic suffering of the entire Soviet population." Indeed, although the Soviet leadership practiced ethnic deportations already in the 1930s and continued them on a much greater scale after the war, following the defeat of Nazism the Soviets increasingly turned to a view of the Jew as an undifferentiated biological entity, an image that combined traditional anti-Semitic features, racial characteristics borrowed from the Nazis, and inherent socioeconomic, class, or "cosmopolitan" attributes that were allegedly impossible to correct. Consequently, despite the Soviet allegiance to sociological categories, the postwar discourse on the "Jewish question" became central to the "fight over the memory of the war and genocide, which was rapidly turning into the dominant point of reference in the articulation of identities in the Soviet polity."[77]

The rapid realignment of forces and normalization of conditions after 1945, and the resulting tendency to blur the distinctions between the numerous victims of war and genocide, thus left Holocaust survivors as defenseless against the ravages of traumatic memory and mental devastation as they had been against the Nazi murder machine.[78] From this perspective, one may view the fate of the Jews under Nazism as especially tragic; for although in the camps action was often either impossible or counterproductive, even those who survived were unable to act against the perpetrators, both in the context of post-Holocaust reality and in their fantasies. In this sense, Holocaust survivors have remained eternal victims, devoid of any recourse to meaningful, even if ineffective and irrelevant, action, trapped within the very conditions of their original victimhood. Conversely, the far more numerous "Aryan" survivors of Hitler's Germany were also faced with the troubling fact that although they perceived themselves as victims (and were therefore on the lookout for perpetrators), they were largely seen by their former enemies, who dominated much of the international discourse in the years immediately following the war, as perpetrators.[79]

As the protagonists of the Holocaust are slowly leaving the scene, we, as historians, are charged with the task of reconstructing the event and surmounting the barriers that had stood in the way of coming to terms with it. Yet we must not become so detached from the horror as to avoid perceiving some of those fundamental factors at its root, which are still very much with us today. In a world obsessed with defining enemies and making victims, we should remind those who would listen that there are other ways to view reality. And the first step in that direction is to study what this manner of perceiving the world had wrought on humanity in the past.

AMIR WEINER 7

When Memory Counts

War, Genocide, and Postwar Soviet Jewry

ORDAINED AS THE ARMAGEDDON of the Bolshevik enterprise, the Second World War precipitated major changes in both the Soviet state and in popular ideology and practices. Nowhere were these changes more noticeable than in the perennial cleansing drives. The war signaled a qualitative and quantitative shift in a polity already consumed by constant campaigns to eradicate internal, elusive enemies that hampered the pursuit of sociopolitical harmony. During the prewar era, the regime maintained differentiation and the prospect of reform and rehabilitation of groups targeted as internal enemies, but in the war's wake it considered such groups undifferentiated, unreformable, and irredeemable collectives.

The result was the unprecedented deportation of entire ethnic communities charged with harboring sympathy for the invading Germans or actively collaborating with them. Internal enemies were no longer differentiated according to their alleged degree of hostility toward the revolution and the Soviet state or according to the presence of family members with the proper politico-ideological background. Deportations that hitherto had been confined to term sentences now meant permanent exile. In essence, these acts constituted severe challenges to what was previously a sacred tenet of the Soviet enterprise, according to which individuals and groups were considered sociological constructs, prone to transformation via Soviet acculturation.[1]

Consecrated as the climactic clash of the revolution that would usher in the era of Communism, the war was also viewed as a final cleansing of the human "weeds" who had survived previous cycles of purges. There was little hope for those stigmatized as having failed to rise to the occasion. The Soviet regime and citizenry may not have possessed the exterminatory impulses and institutions that made the Nazi regime unique. But after the war, they displayed a willingness to discuss and operate on the very same assumptions as their arch enemy, if only temporarily. And this was the position in which Soviet Jews found themselves during the last decade of Stalin's reign, when the antifascist regime to which they pledged loyalty began flirting with racialist thinking and practices.

Conventional wisdom points to the establishment of the state of Israel and the unfolding cold war as primary causes for the deterioration in the status of the Jewish community within the Soviet polity. Indeed, the creation of the Israeli state transformed Soviet Jewry overnight into a Diaspora nation with a highly active external homeland. In the 1930s, a similar situation had cost Polish and German minorities in the Soviet Union dearly. Often glossed over, however, is the centrality of the living memory of the war and the Jewish genocide in shaping the course of Soviet-Jewish relations and providing them with a constant point of reference in the years following the war. Soviet officials were aware of this juncture. Years after the war, when the Israeli poet Avraham Shlonski visited the Soviet Union, he was told by Aleksei Surkov, the secretary of the Union of Writers, that "there were times when we thought that the process of Jewish assimilation was being intensified by dint of the historical logic of Soviet conditions, and that the Jewish problem was being solved by itself. Then came the war with its horrors, then the aftermath. All of a sudden Jews began to seek one another out and to cling to one another."[2] If Surkov is to be forgiven for some self-righteousness, he was not off the mark. From the early stages of the war, the Jewish community found itself pitted against the cornerstones of the Soviet ethos of the war, the twin institutions of hierarchical heroism and universal suffering. Whereas the various nations of the Soviet Union were ranked in a pyramidlike order based on their alleged contribution to the war effort, their suffering was undifferentiated, ruling out any ethnonational distinction, in spite of the awareness of the Nazis' own racial hierarchies and practices.

Pondering the Unthinkable: Racialized Communism?

It comes as no surprise that the totalization of Soviet practices in the quest for purity brought to the fore the inherent tension between the biological and the sociological categorization of the enemy within, and consequently the inevitable comparison to Nazi Germany, the other totalitarian enterprise. Nowhere else was this issue exposed more than in the Soviet policy toward its Jewish minority. Following the war and the trauma of the Holocaust, conducted extensively on Soviet soil with the implicit and often explicit approval of the local populace, as well as a wave of popular and official anti-Semitism that swept the immediate postwar era, ordinary Jewish citizens and activists began to ponder the unthinkable: was there a logical affinity between the two ideologies?

For some there certainly was. In the small town of Nemyriv, angry survivors of the genocide and returning partisans accused the local Party leadership of deliberately impeding the evacuation of the Jewish community to the Soviet rear and of actively collaborating and participating in the extermination of the local Jewish community. They concluded that the Party's policy toward the Jews did not differ from that of the Germans.[3] Following a mass pogrom in Kiev on September 4, 1945, Red Army Jewish veterans complained to Stalin and Lavrentii Beria that the local Communist Party consciously adapted German racist politics. The reference to the "new course" of the Communist Party unmistakably echoed the Nazi New Order. "This 'course,'" wrote the four veterans, "has a lot in common with the one that originated earlier from the chancery of Goebbels, whose worthy transmitters turned out in the Central Committee and the Council of People's Commissars of Ukraine."[4]

This point was also laid out bluntly by Vasilii Grossman in his epic *Life and Fate*, which he started writing at this time. For Grossman there was nothing accidental or temporary about the barbarization of Bolshevism. It was ingrained in the core of the Bolshevik ethos, he argued. The war merely helped to bring this reality to the fore. Grossman chose none other than the triumphant moment and site of Stalingrad to underline the common ethos of the Nazi and Soviet enterprises:

> Suddenly, probably because of the war, he began to doubt whether there really was such a gulf between the legitimate Soviet question about social origin and the bloody, fateful question of nationality as posed by the Germans. . . . To me, a distinction based on social origin seems legitimate and moral. One thing I am certain of: it's terrible to kill someone simply because he's a Jew. They're people like any others—good, bad, gifted, stupid, stolid, cheerful, kind, sensitive, greedy. . . . Hitler says none of that matters—all that matters is that they're Jewish. And I protest with my whole being. But then we have the same principle: what matters is whether or not you're the son of an aristocrat, the son of a merchant, the son of a kulak; and whether you're good-natured, wicked, gifted, kind, stupid, happy, is neither here nor there. And we're not talking about the merchants, priests and aristocrats themselves—but about their children and grandchildren. Does noble blood run in one's veins like Jewishness? Is one a priest or a merchant by heredity?[5]

Indeed, in the wake of the war, Soviet public representations increasingly identified Jews as inherently resistant to Soviet acculturation and, even more threateningly, as an undifferentiated entity. As early as December 1941, during a conversation with a visiting Polish delegation, Stalin found time to reflect on the martial qualities of the warring sides. The Slavs, observed the Soviet leader, are "the finest and bravest of all airmen. They react very quickly, for they are a young race which hasn't yet been worn out. . . . The Germans are strong, but the Slavs will defeat them." Jews, on the other hand, were repeatedly referred to as "poor and rotten soldiers."[6]

The core message of the anticosmopolitan campaign in the late 1940s was that the Jew remained a Jew, an eternal alien to the body national, no matter what the circumstances. As such, Jews had to be stripped of the false layers under which they deceptively wrapped themselves. In early 1949, the Soviet press violated one of the taboos of Bolshevik revolutionary culture when it started disclosing pseudonyms. The birth names of assimilated Jewish figures in the arts were regularly attached to their assumed ones. And so the literary critic Il'ia Isaakovich Stebun learned, along with the readers of the Republic's main newspaper, that at the end of the day, after honorable service at the front and a career of writing in the Ukrainian language, he was still Katsenelson. Similarly, the poet Lazar Samiilovych Sanov found out that his own work in the Ukrainian language and service as a war correspondent did not change the fact that he was still Smulson, just as Zhadanov was still Livshits and Han remained Kahan.[7]

When the anti-Semitic campaign was reaching its climax in early 1953, the alleged Jewish resistance to Soviet acculturation called for the use of uncompromising methods by the authorities. While exposing an accused Jewish embezzler in the town of Zhmerynka who, needless to say, had relatives abroad and managed to avoid the front during the Great Patriotic War ("he fell ill precisely at the end of June 1941"), the satirical magazine *Krokodil* posed a rhetorical question: "To tell you the truth, we became tired of reading your decisions scattered there: 'to reprimand, to point out, to suggest,' etc. Doesn't it seem to you, comrades, that you overestimate the educational significance of these resolutions of yours? And, anyway, who are you trying to reeducate? With such touching forbearance, too?"[8] The Jew, simply put, proved to be the anomaly in the Marxist premise of the primacy of nurture over nature. He was immune to reeducation. In early 1953, with the recent executions of the leadership of the Jewish Antifascist Committee, the unfolding Doctors' Plot (the fabricated charges against Jewish physicians accused of plotting to murder Soviet leaders), and rumors about the inevitable mass deportation of Jews dominating the day, the recommendation to transfer the embezzling case to the regional prosecutor, an office famed for meting out swift and harsh punishments, sent the unequivocal message that there was only one way to deal with such types.[9] As the living antithesis to the core Soviet myths of hard and honest Socialist labor and the martyrdom of the recent war, the Jew was beyond redemption. His nature was immune even to the powerful acculturation of nearly four decades of Soviet life. Similarly, portrayal of Jews in the press assumed an unambiguous racial character. In a biting feuilleton, which could easily be mistaken for Nazi prose, the true physical and psychological traits of an exposed Jewish embezzler came to light once he was caught and stood for trial. The once "handsome, brown-haired, with a felt hat and well-cut overcoat" turned into a physically repulsive creature. "His long, fleshy nose points mournfully downward, his puffy lips tremble with fear, his small ratlike eyes roam uneasily. He only comes to life when he tells how he bought gold and concealed diamonds."[10]

Uncovering the "real" Jew, however, was not confined to the Stalin era. Several years later, it was the turn of the de-Stalinizing Nikita Khrushchev to warn other Communists against the false hopes of acculturating the Jew. While attending a session of the Central Committee of the Polish Communist Party, Khrushchev urged the Poles to correct the "abnormal composition of the leading cadres" as the Soviets successfully had done. Staring hard at the chairman of the meeting, Roman Zambrowski, who was born Zukerman, Khrushchev exclaimed: "Yes, you have many leaders with names ending in 'ski,' but an Abramovich remains an Abramovich. And you have too many Abramoviches in your leading cadres."[11] The meeting with a delegation of the Canadian Workers' Progressive Party on August 29, 1956, provided Khrushchev with a forum to articulate another Jewish trait that he alleged he had discerned through his wartime experience. Jews' contempt for manual labor, coupled with their understanding that this was the domain of "the other," appeared as an inherent trait of the group. "I would like to tell you about one incident which I witnessed myself," Khrushchev told the delegation. "When the town of Chernivtsi was liberated during the course of the Red Army offensive operations, it was extremely neglected and dirty. The town had to be cleaned. It should be mentioned that during the occupation period the Germans gave the town to the Romanians, and that's why its Jewish population escaped destruction. When we dealt with this issue, the Jewish population of the town declared to us that after the arrival of the Red Army all the Ukrainians left for the villages, and so, they said, there was no one to clean the city."[12] Some time later, while reflecting on the evident failure of the Jewish Autonomous Region of Birobidzhan to establish itself as national homeland for Soviet Jewry, Khrushchev concluded that it was the result of historical conditions. Yet his description of the sociological was practically genealogical. "They [the Jews] do not like collective work, group discipline. They have always preferred to be dispersed. They are individualists," Khrushchev told *Le figaro* in an interview in March 1958. Finally, in the crudest, officially ordained, anti-Semitic publication to emerge from the Soviet system, Trohym Kychko's *Iudaizm bez prikras* (Judaism Without Embellishment), Nazi-like vocabulary and illustrations drove home the message of alienation of everything distinctively Jewish from the tradition of progressive humanity in general, from the Soviet family in particular, and even more specifically, from the Ukrainian nation. Portrayed as speculators and hostile to manual labor, collaborators with the Nazis, and murderers of Symon Petliura, the leader of the short-lived Ukrainian National Republic in 1918–19, Jews were entirely excluded from the October Revolution, the Great Patriotic War, and Ukrainian aspirations for independence—all subjects of core myths within the Soviet milieu.[13]

But this complete exclusion concealed a crucial difference between the Nazi and Soviet enterprises. The class-based Soviet theory and practices of social engineering seemed to present an ominous obstacle to the application of uniform social targeting. Classes, strata, and layers were neither faceless nor homogeneous. Rather, they were variegated and arranged in a hierarchical order based on the services their members had rendered to the Communist drive. Responsibility and accountability were assessed on the individual's merit, even though this principle was often compromised in the course of exercising the structuring acts. Moreover, individuals maintained the right to appeal and often did so successfully and, after the initial deadly phases of deportations, throughout the 1930s and 1940s children were either spared the fate of their parents or won earlier rehabilitation.[14] Even when weakened and worn out, the social-class paradigm still allowed for the coexistence of humanistic allusions and the harshest repressions.

These acute differences between the biologically driven Nazi and the sociologically based Soviet cleansing policies came to fore as early as the 1930s, when Soviet terror was reaching a level that compelled the regime to address the inevitable comparison with the Nazi shadow. No one could articulate this dilemma better than Stalin, and for good reason. In a series of speeches delivered as the terror approached its climax, Stalin explained the policy guidelines. Concluding his remarks to the plenary session of the Central Committee on March 5, 1937, Stalin warned the delegates not to confuse sworn and irredeemable enemies with those who recanted and redeemed themselves when they joined forces with the Bolsheviks in the anti-Trotskyite campaign or those "who, at one point happened to be walking along the street where this or that Trotskyite happened to be walking, too. . . . In this question, as in all other questions, *an individual, differentiated approach* is required. We must not treat all alike," concluded Stalin.[15] Three months later, in a speech before the Military Council of the Defense Ministry on June 2, 1937, in the wake of the liquidation of the military leadership, Stalin reflected on the tension arising from the Soviet search for the enemy within. Reminding his audience of Lenin's noble and Friedrich Engels's bourgeois origins on the one hand, and of the proletarian origins of Leonid Serebriakov and Iakov Livshits (former Central Committee secretary and Deputy People's Commissar of Communications, respectively) who turned out to be bad apples on the other, Stalin concluded:

> Not every person of a given class is capable of doing harm. Individual people among the nobles and the bourgeoisie worked for the working class and not badly. Out of a stratum such as the lawyers came many revolutionaries. Marx was the son of a lawyer, not a son of a *batrak* [agricultural laborer] or of a worker. Among these strata can always be found people who can serve the cause of the working class, no worse, [but] rather better, than pure-blooded proletarians. We consider Marxism not a biological science, but a sociological science. Hence this general standard is absolutely correct with regard to estates, groups, strata, [but] it is not applicable to every individual who is not of proletarian or peasant origins.[16]

And indeed the Soviets persistently rejected the primacy of the biological over the sociological. The principle of human heredity and its potential practices, whether exterminatory euthanasia or constructive eugenics, were officially repudiated in the Soviet Union from the early 1930s on. What is more, the Soviet Union was practically alone among the major countries in the 1930s in its rejection of euthanasia or sterilization of the mentally retarded, a practice that was embraced, often enthusiastically, on both sides of the Atlantic. In such an atmosphere, Alexis Carrel, the French-American physician who won the Nobel Prize in medicine for his work on blood vessels, transfusion, and organ transplantation, could call on modern societies to do away with the mentally retarded and criminals who cost a fortune to maintain in asylums and prisons. "Why do we preserve these useless and harmful beings? why should society not dispose of the criminals and the insane in a more economic manner?" asked Carrel. The worst criminals (including the insane and people who misled the public in important matters), he concluded, "should be humanely and economically disposed of in small euthanasic institutions supplied with proper gases. . . . Modern society should not hesitate to organize itself with reference to the normal individual. Philosophical systems and sentimental prejudices must give way before such a necessity."[17] In Nazi Germany, as several scholars have reminded us recently, euthanasia was a key element in ideology and practice, and the forerunner of the persecution of the Jews, gypsies, and homosexuals, in sharp contrast to the Soviet purification drive, which at no point was anchored in genocidal ideology.[18] Without it, the operation of industrialized killing—the aspect which set the Holocaust apart from other genocides—was inconceivable.[19]

The same logic applied to eugenics, the constructive twin of euthanasia. In his 1935 *Out of the Night: A Biologist's View of the Future*, H. J. Muller, the chief advocate of eugenics in the Soviet Union, argued that with artificial insemination technology, "in the course of a paltry century or two . . . it would be possible for the majority of the population to become of the innate quality of such men as Lenin, Newton, Leonardo, Pasteur, Beethoven, Omar Khayyam, Pushkin, Sun Yat Sen, Marx . . . or even to possess their varied faculties combined . . . which would offset the American prospects of a maximum number of Billy Sundays, Valentinos, Jack Dempseys, Babe Ruths, even Al Capones."[20] But when Muller forwarded a copy of his book to Stalin in May 1936 and assured him that "it is quite possible, by means of the technique of artificial insemination which has been developed in this country, to use for such purposes the reproductive material of the most transcendently superior individuals, of the one in 50,000, or one in 100,000, since this technique makes possible a multiplication of more than 50,000 times," he practically sealed his fate and the fate of eugenics in the Soviet Union for the next three decades. Stalin read the book, and although he did not respond in writing or verbally until June 1937, his actions spoke for themselves. Muller escaped the Soviet Union by the skin of his teeth, but his cohort was wiped out. The Institute of Medical Genetics was disbanded, and the era of Lysenkoism and its doctrine of acquired characteristics was ushered in. In the long process of constructing a Socialist society, acculturation prevailed over biology as the means of both the expansion and purification of the polity.

And indeed, there was not, nor could there be, a highly placed Jew such as Lazar Kaganovich in the Nazi leadership; nearly half a million Jews could neither serve in the Wehrmacht nor become members of the National Socialist Party. Nor did it matter if they had excelled in the ranks of the German Army in the First World War. There was only one Jew, and he could not be Nazified. The Jew was an enemy not because of a role he played or a position he represented. He was evil incarnate, irredeemable, unreconstructed, and as such, had to be exterminated. The basis on which the extermination of the Jewish "lice" took place (was) neither that of religion nor law but the racial biopolitics of genetic heredity.[21] That was not the case in the Soviet Union. True, living by the motto "sons are not responsible for their fathers" proved difficult. Just two years after Stalin's famous dictum, NKVD (the political police) and Party investigators started busily plunging into the records of members of the Communist Party, resurrecting from oblivion the original sin of the wrong social origin to destroy scores of true believers and their families. In the wake of the Terror it appeared as if the stain of bad social origin was permanent and incurable. It took the war to realize and institutionalize Stalin's dictum in Soviet political life. Nevertheless, even at the height of the officially endorsed anti-Semitic campaign, there were hundreds of thousands of Jews in the ranks of the Party, the army, and scores of other political institutions. Restrictions on the number of Jews in state institutions (*numerus clausus*) could and did coexist side by side with Jewish high officers, Heroes of the Soviet Union, and Party activists.[22] The Nazi example was still a powerful deterrent, especially regarding the Jews. The United Nations draft resolution of the Genocide Convention on November 21, 1947, provided the Soviets with the opportunity to elaborate their own definition of excisional and exterminatory ideologies and practices. In his comments on the treaty, Aron Trainin, then the leading Soviet authority on international law, agreed with the prevailing notion of genocide as the extermination of national or racial collectives. His points of disagreement, however, were telling. First, argued Trainin, however extreme the persecution of opponents based on political motives may be, it does not constitute genocide.[23] Second, the definition of genocide should not be confined to physical extermination but applied to the curtailment of collective national-cultural rights as well. "Of course, in the land of the Soviets, where the Leninist-Stalinist national politics triumphs and the cooperation of nations is a political reality, there is no problem of national rights and national minorities," wrote Trainin. There was a problem, however, in the capitalist world, where class exploitation could be identified with national oppression. Not only lynch trials but also a dense net of national-cultural barriers separate "Negroes" in the United States from the white population, Trainin continued. "Accordingly, international law should struggle against both lynch trials, as tools of the physical extermination of Negroes, and the politics of national-cultural oppression. Therefore along with physical and biological genocide, the notion of national-cultural genocide must be advanced, a genocide that sets for itself the goal of undermining the existence and development of national and racial groups."[24]

In essence, these were the twin pillars of Soviet population policies: the application of state violence anchored in political rationale and the simultaneous cultivation of ethnonational particularism. Without them, one could hardly understand the simultaneous eradication of entire groups of national elite and intelligentsias along with the persistent delineation of particularistic identities.[25] In this light, total excision in the Soviet polity was not necessarily exterminatory, nor did it operate by a racial and biological code. And this, in turn, shifts the focus of our discussion to another political arena within which the Soviet socioethnic body was delineated, the commemorative politics of cataclysmic events.

When Memory Counts

Ironically, none other than Vasilii Grossman pointed to memory as key in shaping the postwar quest for purity. As the driving force behind the failed projects of the *Black Book* and the *Red Book*, the works celebrating Jewish martyrdom and heroism, respectively, which were never published in the Soviet Union, Grossman offered keen insight into a new mechanism for engineering the Soviet body social. The postwar construction of ethnic hierarchies of heroism and the simultaneous leveling of suffering underlined the power of commemoration in the shaping of an ideal-type community. This mechanism was fateful in particular for the Jews.

The refusal to recognize any distinctive Jewish trait pervaded all spheres of Soviet society, notably including the Gulag. When the head of a cultural-educational department in one of the camps drafted a working paper that advocated methods to redeem inmates toward the end of the war, his exemplary cases included a Jewish inmate. Samuil Goldshtein, whose ethnicity was not mentioned, was an exceptionally difficult case, refusing to work regardless of the consequences. Yet, instead of resorting to harsh penalties, as others advocated, the author summoned Goldshtein for a talk about the war. "Do you know what goals the fascists pursue in the war against us?" M. Loginov asked Goldshtein. "I don't know," Goldhstein uttered quietly. "I explained to him who Hitler was and what his goals were. I showed him several pronouncements of the fascist bandits on world domination. I explained the essence of racial theory and the Hitlerite new order in Europe," wrote Loginov. In all likelihood, the NKVD man informed the Jewish inmate about the fate of the Jews under the Nazis, but in 1944 a spade was certainly not called a spade and the Jewish genocide was not mentioned explicitly. The tale, however, did not stop here. "The war will end. The happy life of our people will flourish once again. Every decent man will say: 'I shed blood and sweat fighting for this life.' What would you say? How would people look at you?" Loginov scolded the stubborn inmate and appeared to push his buttons. The conversation, claimed Loginov, was a turning point for Goldshtein, who after digesting the information turned into an exemplary worker in the camp and later volunteered for the front, where he heroically sacrificed himself in battle. Back in the camp, his combat exploits and letters from the front were paraded before the inmates. Loginov concluded with a dedication to the "eternal memory of Samuil Goldshtein" but not the faithful son of the Soviet Jewish people, just one Goldshtein, a convict who redeemed himself by answering the motherland's call.[26]

Like the Gulag, the rest of Soviet society would recognize neither unique Jewish suffering at the hands of the Nazis nor their distinct contribution in the war against the invaders. With the emergence of the war as the core legitimizing myth of the polity, Jews were separated as a *group* from the Soviet family. This incident outlined the twin institutions of hierarchical heroism and universal suffering, the cornerstones of the Soviet ethnonational ethos of the war. Whereas the various nations of the Soviet Union were ranked in a pyramidlike order based on their alleged contribution to the war effort, their suffering was undifferentiated. More so than any other ethnonational community, these aspects of the Soviet ethos were evident with respect to the Jewish community. Jewish participation in the trials of combat service were ignored in public and denied in private. By the time Stalin addressed the commanders of the Red Army, Jews had disappeared from public representations of the war. Hand in hand, the Holocaust was incorporated into the epic suffering of the entire Soviet population; its uniqueness for the Jews was ignored.

Hierarchical Heroism

> *Petrenko:* You grew up eating Russian bread, you received an education paid by the Russian people, and now you betray your motherland? For you and your whole people I fought at the front for four years.
>
> *Shcharansky:* My father also fought at the front. He spent four years there as a volunteer. Perhaps he did that for your son and your people?
>
> *Petrenko:* Your father? In the army? What division was he in?
>
> *Shcharansky:* Artillery.
>
> *Petrenko:* Artillery? I also fought in the artillery, but I didn't see your sort there. What front was he on?[27]

This exchange took place in March 1977 at the Lefortovo prison in the course of the interrogation of the Jewish dissident Anatoly Shcharansky by a KGB colonel named Petrenko. This exchange might have looked surrealistic had it not engaged a core issue in the myth of war. Back then in a speech at the second meeting of the Jewish Anti-Fascist Committee held in Moscow on February 20, 1943, Il'ia Ehrenburg limited himself to one issue that he argued was a burning one: the need to publish a book that would detail Jewish heroism at the front. "Such a book is required," said Ehrenburg, "for the peace of mind of the Jewish soldiers at the front who received letters from their relatives in Uzbekistan or Kazakhstan telling them that people there say that the reason one does not see Jews at the front is because they don't fight." To illustrate this point, Ehrenburg told the attendants the following story:

> I was paid a visit by an old Jew, the father of a famous pilot, whose heroism was celebrated in the entire military press. He was the only son of this man. He loved him very much. And he told me: "I spoke with a certain civilian official who said to me: 'Explain to me, please, why there are no Jews at the front? Why doesn't one see Jews in the war?' I did not answer him. I found it hard to speak. That was only four days after I had received from the commander the news of my son's death."[28]

What was the rationale behind these harsh and swift accusations? Such comments defied the evidence and contemporary official Soviet representations of the Jews in the war. Contemporary evidence and recognition of the participation of Jews in the war pointed in the opposite direction. A recent and evidently conservative estimate points out, nevertheless, that the number of Jews in active combat service during the war was proportional to their share in the general population, often exceeding it, especially among elite units, which bore the brunt of fierce fighting at the fronts. Even as the percentage of Jews declined with the influx of ethnic Ukrainians and Belorussians into the Red Army ranks after the liberation of the German-occupied territories, their overall share in the armed forces remained proportional to their share in the general population.[29]

Throughout the war the Jewish contribution to the combat effort was visible and rewarded publicly. Jewish soldiers and officers were not discriminated against in promotions or decorations in the fighting Red Army. Official publications that celebrated the friendship of the peoples allegedly cemented under the trials of war allotted the Jews a respected place within the family of the fighting nationalities.[30] Early on, however, a certain pattern began to emerge. Breaking with the established pattern of mentioning the ethnicity of servicemen when celebrating their exploits in the mass media, official reports omitted the Jewishness of their subjects altogether even when their ethnicity was evident, as it was with General Iakov Kreizer, Hayim Fomin, and Yeidl Khaiat, to cite three of the most famous examples. And by the end of the war Jews were no longer marked as a separate group in either public presentations of war heroism or in confidential reports.

The paradox of a large Jewish presence at the front and the industrious denial of Jewish heroism invited several explanations. For one, the notion of Jewish avoidance of military service seemed to be deeply rooted in both prerevolutionary and prewar Soviet society, as was evident in both official reports in the First World War and in private deliberations during the interwar years. Second, the peculiarities of the warfare on the Eastern Front further advanced the perception of "no Jews at the front." Jewish soldiers intentionally concealed their national identity, especially in combat units, as soon as it became clear that Jews faced summary execution by the Germans if taken prisoner. According to some historians, along with the progressing assimilation of Soviet Jewry, soldiers' denial of their Jewishness was a mass phenomenon.[31] The problem of the intentional concealing of identity was exacerbated by the intensive Nazi propaganda at the front, which played on traditional prejudices. The consequences were bluntly conveyed by a Jewish colonel in a letter to Ehrenburg:

> We are all lying in the trenches. Soon I will have to give the command: "attack—up and out!" And then those devils with the black crosses start to fly by one after the other—just like locusts. We bury ourselves in the trenches and wait. The bombs will drop soon and then we'll be in a really tight spot. But they keep flying and there are no bombs, only leaflets—a world of leaflets. Some of them made their way to me in the trenches. They contained only a few words, a message: "Look around you, sol-

diers: Are there any Abrahams or Israels around you?!" And that's all. And that was enough to make soldiers look around, and not knowing who was a Jew, to come to the poisonous conclusion: "there are no Jews at the frontline."[32]

Another explanation for the popular perception of no Jews at the front indicated that Jews made up a relatively high percentage of the refugees and evacuees. This was a combined result of a large-scale flight because of fear of extermination, especially when reports and rumors about the German treatment of the Jews reached Jewish communities, and later of the planned evacuation of industries and bureaucracies that contained a lot of Jews.[33] This phenomenon, which saved the lives of hundreds of thousands of Soviet Jews, was not intentional, and many of the refugees and evacuees were eventually drafted into the Red Army. Nevertheless, it helped the proliferation of the notion of the "Tashkent Partisans," a derogatory term for those who had lived the war in the safety of the Soviet rear.

However, the denial of Jewish combat heroism pointed to some deeper concerns. The authorities fiercely resisted all attempts to carve out a particularistic Jewish space within the all-encompassing myth of the war. Jewish perception of the uniqueness of their wartime experience threatened to undermine the universality of suffering and the ethnonational hierarchy of heroism, the twin pillars of the ethos of the war. If the recollections of Jewish partisans are accepted at face value, then they went out of their way to exact a certain special revenge on the enemy. In the ongoing process of brutalization of public life, Jews appeared determined to present themselves as active perpetrators and not merely passive victims. "Among the [captured] Germans we also found Vlasovites [members of the collaborationist Russian Liberation Army headed by the former Soviet general, Andrei Vlasov]," recalled Zalman Teitelman, a Jewish partisan in the Chechl'nyk district. "Granovskii, I, and several other Jews consulted with the partisans and decided that all Vlasovites should be executed. We staged a military trial on the spot, and we mowed down ten Vlasovites in the local dump, where the Jews were buried."[34] Probably of more political weight were the attempts to parade this particularistic urge in public. In his appearance before the Jewish Anti-Fascist Committee in the summer of 1945, David Dragunskii, two-time Hero of the Soviet Union, described in detail the extermination of his entire family by the Germans in February 1942 and his visit to Babyn Iar and to the concentration camps. The speech, however, was marked by Dragunskii's intense emphasis on the Jews' special reckoning with the Germans. "All of us hate the Germans!" Dragunskii told the audience.

> But I hate them doubly. Once because I am a Soviet man. Once because I am a Jew! I was filled with hate because I saw what the Germans had done to our people. . . . I yearned to get to Germany. I got to Germany. I did my duty as a son of our mother-

land. I fought for all Soviet people. I fought for all Jewish people. . . . The Germans knew that my brigade was headed by a Jew. They posted notices that they would flay me alive. They hated me twice over, for being a Russian and a Jew. That very night [in Berlin] we caught five hundred SS troops whose commander had posted that notice. We made shashlik and beef stroganoff of them all. We caught the colonel of the SS swine. He complained that someone had taken his watch. Take care of his complaint, I commanded one of my men. The colonel is not around any more.[35]

Some time later, a group of Jewish veterans set out to reverse the prevailing order. The Jews, argued the veterans in a letter to Stalin, had more than a legitimate claim to share the glory of heroism with the rest of the Soviet people. After explaining the Jewish contribution to the October Revolution, in which the Jewish people "showed itself as the most revolutionary people," the veterans noted the Jewish contribution at the front, which they argued was exceptional. "During the Patriotic War tens of thousands of Jews fought heroically at the front. Many of them were killed in battles for their Socialist motherland and many became heroes. The percentage of decorated Jews in the Patriotic War is very high," they noted with pride.[36]

Jews sought their own distinctive insignia. On May 19, 1947, *Dos Naye Lebn*, a Yiddish-language journal in Lodz, Poland, carried a short story by Itzik Kipnis, the Soviet Jewish writer. In the story entitled *On Khokhmes, On Kheshboynes*, Kipnis intimated a personal wish "that all Jews walking the streets of Berlin with a sure, victorious step would wear bandannas with decorations and medals and also a small pretty *Magen David* (Star of David) on their chests. It would be our shameful mark. Everyone would be able to see that this is a Jew, and my Jewish and human worth among loving citizens cannot be diminished."[37] The harsh reaction to Kipnis's story made it clear that as a symbol of Jewish heroism, the Star of David needed a different place.[38]

The response to Jewish attempts to set their agenda was telling. Taking on Il'ia Ehrenburg, the Jewish high priest of the Soviet anti-German hate campaign, Oleksandr Dovzhenko, the famous film director, entered in his diary a conversation alleged to have taken place among Soviet soldiers:

When I read him or listen to him being read, I start to feel very sorry for him.
Why is that?
Because he's so full of hatred. A bottomless abyss of hatred.
Where does he get it all? He's covered with hatred like a horse with mange.
Maybe he's just afraid that we don't have enough of those poisonous feelings.
That's what I think. He doesn't believe in our anger and intelligence and awareness of history.
He has no pity for us. We've knocked off four hundred battles all the way to Berlin, and now we've got to find the strength to start a new life.
Strength for our women, friends, and for starting families. He has no pity for us,

> the living, only for the dead. That's why I don't want to read him. I have enough anger in myself and in all the pictures I've seen the last four years. Never mind him. Let him write. It doesn't hurt us, but at least it annoys the Germans.[39]

So even at the very moment when all Soviet men appeared as one undifferentiated whole fighting a common enemy, the Jew remained alien. And it was not simply the additional devotion celebrated by Dragunskii and Ehrenburg. It was the Jew's vindictive nature and his mistrust of his own society that set him apart. Or maybe it was the enduring teachings of his dead religion with its pretense to superiority and utter lack of compassion that alienated his Christian comrades. Unfit for the tasks of war, the Jew did not have a place in the postwar milieu either.

All these representations of the motives behind the fighting spirit of the troops actually outlined various degrees of resilience and subsequent agendas within the Soviet family. The Jews possessed ulterior motives and agendas that were clearly out of step with the Soviet hierarchy of heroism. In any case, Dragunskii's remarks could be related to his fellow Jews only in a closed gathering. By then, any effort to break with the hierarchy in public was bound to be curtailed, as Ehrenburg learned in the summer of 1944. When Ehrenburg tried to advance the *Red Book*, the second part of his planned trilogy on the Jewish fate in the war against the Nazis, which was supposed to tell the stories of Jewish soldiers and partisans, he was bluntly told by a top official in the Soviet Information Bureau that "there is no need to mention the heroism of Jewish soldiers in the Red Army; this is bragging."[40]

Universal Suffering

In the same vein, Soviet authorities had been fairly aware of how the Germans treated the Jews. Moreover, information on the Jewish genocide reached Moscow almost immediately. Also, the regime pursued the punishment of perpetrators of anti-Jewish massacres from the moment of liberation until the disintegration of the Soviet Union, as well as offering material help to Jewish survivors. Having learned about the obstacles put in the way of Jewish survivors in Ukraine, none other than Beria ordered the Ukrainian authorities to take the necessary measures to aid the working, housing, and domestic arrangements for Jews in the liberated territories, "who were subjected to particular repressions by the German occupiers (concentration camps, ghetto, etc.)."[41]

Such actions, however, were kept out of the public eye. There were hardly any references to the Holocaust in the Soviet press, not even in the much-publicized reports of the Extraordinary State Committee for the Study of German-Fascist Atrocities, where the Jewishness of victims was not specified even in testimonies on massacres that were directed solely against Jews.[42] When the veterans we encountered earlier complained to Stalin in the fall of 1945, the erasure of a distinct Jewish catastrophe was already a fait accompli. "No other people experienced as much sorrow and misfortune as did the Jewish people during the Patriotic War. [Yet] not a single article was devoted in the press or in print to their situation [or] their needs," lamented the veterans.[43] By then, this pattern in the myth of the war had already been established. The suffering of the civilian population at the hands of the invaders was universalized, ruling out any ethnonational distinction, in spite of the awareness of the Nazis' own racial hierarchies and practices. When certain space was allowed for the expression of ethnonational particularism, it was limited to a marginal, isolated, and hardly visible tale, such as that of the Romanian occupation.

The Soviet authorities seemed much more troubled by the annual gatherings of Jews commemorating the extermination of their brethren, which they viewed as a pretext for stirring up separatist nationalist sentiments. "The NKGB seemed unaware of the effort of Zionist elements to organize in Kiev a mass demonstration of the Jewish population on the anniversary of the massacre by the Germans in Babyn Iar," charged the Party officials.[44] When a survivor fixed the Star of David on an obelisk erected atop a mass grave, the authorities threatened to bulldoze it unless it was replaced by the five-cornered Soviet star.[45] The reluctance to commemorate particularistic suffering was captured in Khrushchev's memorable retort to Il'ia Ehrenburg. When the latter appealed to Khrushchev to intervene and stop the construction of a marketplace on the site of the massacre in Babyn Iar, Khrushchev advised him "not to interfere in matters that do not concern you. You had better write good novels."[46]

The swan song of the attempt at public representations of particularistic ethnonational wartime suffering came in 1946 with the curtailment of the publication of the *Black Book*, edited by Il'ia Ehrenburg and Vasilii Grossman. Having read the preface in which Grossman echoed the Nazi position that "the fascists placed the Jew in opposition to all peoples inhabiting the world,"[47] Georgii Aleksandrov, head of the agitprop department, shot back in a letter to Politburo member Andrei Zhdanov that the

> preface written by Grossman alleges that the destruction of the Jews was a particularistic provocative policy and that the Germans established some kind of hierarchy in their destruction of the peoples of the Soviet Union. In fact, the idea of some imaginary hierarchy is in itself incorrect. The documents of the Extraordinary State

Committee convincingly demonstrate that the Hitlerites destroyed at one and the same time Russians, Jews, Belorussians, Ukrainians, Latvians, Lithuanians, and other peoples of the Soviet Union.[48]

"There are no Jews in Ukraine," lamented a horrified Grossman when he first encountered his liberated birthplace in 1943. "Nowhere—Poltava, Kharkov, Kremenchug, Borispol, Yagotin—in none of the cities, hundreds of towns, or thousands of villages will you see the black, tear-filled eyes of little girls; you will not hear the sad voices of an old woman; you will not see the dark face of a hungry baby. All is silence. Everything is still. A whole people has been brutally murdered."[49] True, soon after this lament, the Ukrainian terrain was filled again with returning Jews, albeit in significantly lower numbers and settling in fewer places. But already in 1943, Grossman's words rang true with regard to the future as well as to the recent past, and in a way he could not envision at the time. The invisibility of Jews in the Soviet Union in general, and in Ukraine in particular, was not because of lack of presence. The surviving Jews did indeed return but as a mythical antithesis and into political invisibility.

At first glance, there seemed to be nothing unusual in a polity whose official nationality policy envisioned at its final stage the merging (*sliianie*) of its various ethnic and national components into a single entity. The Jews, in this light, were leading the Soviet camp in terms of historical development. But this was an ironic twist. Whereas ethnic groups were supposed to merge in an intense cultivation of ethnic particularism, the Jews were to skip this stage in the wake of the war. And because the date of the final merging remained as elusive as ever, the erasure of Jewish collective identity from the new legitimizing myth of the polity bore grave consequences. In October 1946, merely two years after the liberation of the region, and equally important, two years before the establishment of the state of Israel, the Jewish community in the Soviet Ukrainian Republic joined their German and Polish minorities in political invisibility when Jewish national rural soviets were converted into Ukrainian soviets, side by side with official pressure for increased migration from Ukraine to Birobidzhan.[50]

Deeply rooted popular anti-Semitism coincided with similar sentiments among the local and national leadership, but, more crucially, these attitudes were articulated within the powerful Soviet ethos of a simultaneous search for harmony and purity. A barrage of popular novels portrayed Jewish characters as draft dodgers who lived the war years in the safety of the rear and on the blood of their Soviet compatriots. It was a short step from the exclusion of Jews from the Soviet fighting family to their exclusion from the Soviet family at large. The wartime stereotype of the Jewish draft-dodger occupied an increasingly central place in the anticosmopolitan campaign. This rootless cosmopolitanism was embodied by the worst antipatriotic act of all, deliberate evasion of service at the front when the motherland needed the ultimate sacrifice of each and every one of its sons; the sons responded, except for the rootless cosmopolitans. This did not prevent them from seeking medals for their "sacrifice" when the war ended.

In one of these novels, Vsevolod Kochetov's *Zhurbiny*, the beating of such a Jew (who happened to carry a copy of *The Wandering Jew* in his suitcase wherever he went) was portrayed as nothing less than a cathartic moment that transformed one worthless womanizer into a proud Soviet citizen. And how does the Party react to the recourse of violence? It has two minds. The one mind, the official, views the incident as improper for the modern Soviet society. "Comrade Skobelev," thoughtfully remarks the Party organizer who deals with the incident, "the Stone Age was a good time. Primitive man picked up his club and went off to settle accounts with his neighbor." But then there is the private mind, between men. "You know," the Party organizer intimates to Skobelev, "as a man, I understand you. Such people deserve a slap in the face."[51]

In a polity that associated military service with local, national, and supranational Soviet identities, and sacrifice on the battlefield with true patriotism, exclusion from the myth of the war amounted to exclusion from the Soviet family. A similar outcome, if only through a different practice, emerged from the commemoration of wartime suffering. The mass murder of Jews was never denied in Soviet representations of the war, but in the official accounts and artistic representations, memory of the Jewish catastrophe was subsumed by the larger Soviet tragedy, erasing the very distinction at the core of the Nazi pursuit of racial purity.

Such a policy certainly coincided with similar developments across the European continent. In the restored societies emerging from Nazi occupation, memories of defeat and victimization were set aside in favor of intensive, state-sponsored cults of heroism and resistance. In the ravaged and humiliated societies burdened with the task of national revival, the mobilizing power of the myth of active heroism was undeniably greater than that of victimization anchored in the shame and guilt-ridden memory of defeat. Above all, memories of victimization bore the troublesome particularism associated with the Jewish minority. Jewish particularistic suffering was integrated into an all-national paradigm of victimization and in some cases transformed into one of triumphant heroism.[52] The universality of the activist-triumphant myth was underscored by its predominance in the new Israeli state, where Zionism helped to reconstruct a series of cataclysmic defeats in Jewish history as redemptive triumphs, starting with the rebellions against the Romans in the first two centuries A.D. and culminating with the Holocaust. There, the official commemoration of the Holocaust had been incorporated into the epic struggle for an independent Jewish state.[53]

Such a dilemma and solution were all too familiar to the Soviet scene, and for similarly compelling reasons. For one, the wave of pogroms that swept Ukrainian cities in 1944–45 marked a new development. For the first time in the Soviet era, violent anti-Semitism exploded as an open, urban phenomenon. In such a volatile environment and with the war still raging, identification with the traditionally resented minority was the last thing the returning Soviet power wanted. It was about this time that Khrushchev supposedly said "Here is the Ukraine and it is not in our interest that the Ukrainians should associate the return of Soviet power with the return of the Jews."[54] Yet the wholesale deportations of alleged collaborationist minorities conveyed the message that the Soviet polity would not shy away from opening the Pandora's box of collaboration conceived in ethnic terms. This willingness to confront the ethnic face of wartime collaboration directly, which most multiethnic polities avoided doing, and the enduring denial of the particularistic Jewish fate under the Nazis long after the rest of Europe recognized it, pointed to another motive, one that lay at the core of the revolutionary myth.[55]

The twentieth anniversary of the Great Patriotic War in 1965 marked the transition of this cataclysmic event from a living to a historical memory, and a determined attempt to develop a commemorative canon and a sense of closure. The last vestiges of the socially alien element—the few remaining kulaks—were released and rehabilitated. Ethnic Germans deported en masse during the war received an official apology from the Supreme Soviet of the Soviet Union,[56] and, most notably, all limitations were removed on former leaders and members of underground nationalist movements, the last category to win rehabilitation (and among whom Ukrainian nationalists were the largest component).[57] The reinstatement of the largest, best organized, and most persistent of the anti-Soviet separatist movements into the legitimate Ukrainian body national only fifteen years after it was singled out for permanent exclusion was indeed the most visible marker of reconciliation. By allowing them to return home, the regime showed its confidence in the efficacy of the punitive system and in its redemptive power.

But no olive branch was extended to the Jewish community. On the contrary, Jews were branded as traitors. The community was handed a mass-circulation historical novel, *Tuchi nad gorodom*, by Porfyrii Havrutto, which developed an earlier charge by Khrushchev about treason and the collaboration of a certain Jew-Judas who "betrayed the Kiev underground to the Germans, served as a translator for Field Marshal Paulus, cleaned his boots, helped interrogate Soviet prisoners of war and even shot at his own compatriots." The readers were informed in the accompanying editorial note that the novel was actually a documentary. The Jew was not merely out of the Soviet family. He was its living antithesis.[58]

It was at this time that Stalin's daughter, Svetlana Allilueva, noted that already "with the expulsion of Trotsky and the extermination during the years of 'purges' of old Party members, many of whom were Jews, anti-Semitism was reborn on new ground and first of all within the Party itself."[59] Perhaps Allilueva got it right. The Bolshevik epic had to be purged of its association with the resented minority. By the eve of the war, popular identification of the revolution with the Jews had already found its echo inside the Party ranks. In the early 1930s, peasant uprisings against forced collectivization were often directed against the "Jewish militia" and "Communist kikes." When the Party surveyed its rank and file throughout the prewar years, it found that Jews were perceived as the main beneficiaries of the October Revolution: holders of the best positions and jobs, owners of the apartments, and accomplished draft dodgers.[60]

Victimization often breeds more victimization rather than empathy, and the pogroms of the summer of 1944 are a case in point. Several years after the war, a nationalist activist from Ukraine observed that under the Germans anti-Semitism had become racially rather than religiously based. The exposure to a lengthy, relentless barrage of Nazi anti-Semitic policies left unmistakable imprints on various segments of the local population. As the war progressed and the Nazi occupation became part of the local political scene, anti-Semitic expressions became ever more racialized. And so in the midst of the war, a rabid anti-Stalinist village poet could write this:

> O you, Stalin, the flayer,
> What have you done to us now?
> You expelled Ukrainians from their huts,
> And Jews became the rulers.
> We spend the nights under fences,
> We have no father, we have no mothers,
> Because you, Stalin, a cruel beast,
> Drove them as far as Siberia,
> And to the Jews you gave medals,
> So that they could torture us.[61]

The bestial metaphor was not limited to nationalist circles. The portrayal of the Jew as a parasite living off the blood of decent patriotic people could be found in the expressions of local Red Army servicemen as well. "There are five to seven thousand Jews [in the Ukrainian town of Vinnytsia]," wrote two officers to Khrushchev while they were on vacation in summer 1944.

"They are like worms. A Jew controls the housing administration. . . . In the military-trade store—a Jew. In the office—a Jew, that Kaminskii type. In other commercial establishments it is filthy."[62]

By the end of the war, Soviet society was not free of Jews. But it was a society that came to think of the "Jewish problem" as a legitimate one, and one to ponder in racial terms. The Jew was thought of as an inherently alien organism whom people wished to see removed from their midst. Soviet citizens may not have possessed the exterminatory intentions that made Nazi anti-Semitism unique, but they were open to its arguments. And this tension between arguments and the pursuit of their logic came to the fore with the "Doctors' Plot" in January 1953. By then, as the treatment of enemy nations and nationalist guerrillas indicated, the extension of guilt to entire collectives was the norm rather than the exception in the purification drive, conducted in a brutal and increasingly radical manner. Even one of Stalin's loyal lieutenants, Anastas Mikoyan, was shocked by this evolution of state terror. "Stalin's decision to deport entire nations had a depressing impact on me," recalled Mikoyan. "I did not understand how one can accuse entire nations of treason while they had Party organizations, Communists, peasant masses, and Soviet intelligentsia! Many were mobilized into the army and fought at the front. Many representatives of these peoples were awarded medals as Heroes of the Soviet Union! This was a deviation from the class approach to the solution of the nationality problem."[63]

Mikoyan may indeed have been shocked, and so were many Soviet citizens. Many others, however, had no qualms with the extension of charges to the entire community. In intimate settings and through anonymous leaflets, individuals stressed the elusive and beastly nature of this group ("they live like wolves," "this is not a people, but the anti-people called the 'kikes.' They are not human beings but traitors who sell innocent Soviet victims to America for dollars"), but even more relevant, the Jews were viewed by both believers and skeptics in light of the recent war. Recommending the deportation of the treacherous Jews from the southeastern and southwestern territories of the Soviet Union, one leaflet reminded the people of "[the parallel betrayal] of the Crimean Tatars during the war years, as well as that of the Chechens in the Northern Caucasus." Since all Jews were enemies and a fifth column, "they are like the Kalmyks, Ingushetians and Crimean Tatars," another author charged. "They are American spies, our vilest enemies, there should be no forgiveness. Blood for blood! They deserve this, there is and there should be no mercy for them."[64] The reference to enemy nationalities deported during and after the war on charges of collective guilt underlined the internalization of the other pillar of the postwar purification drive: the abandonment of belief in the prospect for redemption of the enemy within.

Not only did ordinary citizens appear to accept the principle of elusive enemies in their midst but also the worst charges. The treacherous wartime conduct of the Kalmyks and the Chechens was accepted at face value, and in the wake of the announcement of the arrest of the doctors, scores of people refused to be treated by Jewish physicians.[65]

Even more telling were the reactions to the April 4, 1953, announcement by the Ministry of Internal Affairs that the whole thing was a fabrication and that the doctors were fully rehabilitated. Issued only a month after Stalin's death, the laconic statement turned upside down nearly three months of relentless, ferocious announcements. But if the rehabilitation statement was meant as the first signal that the era of mass terror had come to an end, it did not land on fertile soil. If the admittedly limited sample of letters to the press and government organizations is indicative, they revealed a population whose absolute majority was still receptive to the principle of elusive enemies in its midst and, more specifically, the identification of such enemies with the Soviet Jewish community. Once again, righteousness was judged in terms of one's wartime experience. Indeed, more than one letter expressed anger at the official admission of "impermissible investigation methods strictly forbidden by Soviet law." Yet even then, the legacy of the recent war bred skepticism. "Were they subjected to torture like those staunch and true patriots Zoia [Kosmodemianskaia] or Liza Chaikina?" cried one Savel'ev from Moscow in reference to the two young partisans who became symbols of martyrdom after being tortured and executed by the Germans. "Even terrible torture did not break the spirit of heroic Komsomol members and did not provide the fascists with the confessions they sought," wrote a group of students from Iaroslavl'. "And what about our ordinary citizens who stood their ground when stars were being branded on their bodies or parts of their bodies were being amputated. They did not reveal anything," wrote another one from Moscow.[66] The Jews in this light were not only guilty. Just as they had during the war, they once again "managed to get off scot-free." The basic Soviet view of the war was regenerated even when specific aspects were denounced. If the myth of the October Revolution was "Judaicized" beyond repair, then the new myth of the Great Patriotic War would not suffer the same fate.

GORDON H. CHANG

8

Social Darwinism Versus Social Engineering

The "Education" of Japanese Americans During World War II

IN JUNE 1947, Donald O. Johnson, a former teacher at the War Relocation Authority (WRA) Schools at Tule Lake, California, site of one of the internment camps established by the U.S. federal government for the incarceration of persons of Japanese ancestry during World War II, ended his thesis for a Stanford master's degree with a lament tempered by a hopeful admonition for the future. Johnson, who had repeatedly expressed in the body of his unpublished paper sympathy for the internees, concluded:

> The mass evacuation [one of the many euphemisms federal authorities used during the experience] of the people of Japanese descent from the West Coast probably created more problems than it solved. . . . The [wartime security] problem seemingly could have been handled more rationally. The removal of the Japanese under the guise of "protective custody" or under any other term or reason, real or imagined, other than the established necessity for national security is questionable in the light of democratic action. But evacuation, with its resultant evils has happened, and it is only left for us to determine that if *in the future we find it necessary to control minority groups within our population, that we shall do so by democratic methods.*[1]

Evident, despite Johnson's obscurantist and qualified language, are assumptions that reflect administrative thinking that rationalized wartime internment—the interned were "people of Japanese descent" and "Japanese" (although the majority were in fact American citizens) and "national security" exigencies justified nondemocratic action. But further, Johnson, in anticipating possible similar future efforts at mass population control, betrayed no apparent awareness of his highly racialized and contradictory notions about American democracy—"we" should control "minority groups," democratically.

Johnson's way of thinking was not singular or even unusual but represented the way many of his fellow teachers, researchers, camp administrators, and political leaders had thought about wartime internment. Examining their various writings about internment offers a way of understanding not just a group of individuals who were involved in what critics even at the time of their institution called America's "concentration camps,"[2] but also more broadly racial ideologies in America and their connection to various conceptions of social control in a liberal democracy. This chapter seeks to contribute to a discussion about the ideology of social-engineering projects in the mid twentieth century.

In the early spring of 1942, several months after war began between the United States and Japan, the U.S. federal government began incarceration of what eventually numbered 120,000 persons of Japanese ancestry into ten internment centers scattered in desolate locations throughout the West and South. Sixty percent of the internees were American citizens by birth; the remainder were first-generation Japanese immigrants, whom immigration law denied, along with other Asian immigrants, the possibility of naturalized citizenship, even though most had lived in the country since their arrival in the late nineteenth and early twentieth centuries. Most of the internees had lived along the Pacific Coast, which the federal authorities after Pearl Harbor had declared a special military zone from which the army was authorized to exclude any specially designated persons for security reasons. The Western Defense Command, acting with the authority of the president, announced in April 1942 that "all persons of Japanese ancestry, both alien and non-alien" were required to report to military authorities for "evacuation" from the sensitive area into centers operated by the federal government. The duration of "relocation" was indeterminate—internees did not know if their removal was temporary or permanent.[3] With very few exceptions, the targeted population complied with the order; most lived the rest of the war years in what authorities called "assembly" and then "relocation centers," prohibited from returning to their former residences until the last months of the war. Several tens of thousands received permission to leave the camps earlier to enter the army, attend college, or work outside the exclusion zone.

The reasons for the American public's widespread support for internment varied, but many accepted the argument offered by General John L. DeWitt, commander of the Western Military Command, in his official, publicly released recommendation for internment:

> In the war in which we are now engaged racial affinities are not severed by migration. The Japanese race is an enemy race and while many second and third generation Japanese born on United States soil, possessed of United States citizenship, have

> become "Americanized," the racial strains are undiluted. . . . That Japan is allied with Germany and Italy in this struggle is no ground for assuming that any Japanese, barred from assimilation by convention as he is, though born and raised in the United States, will not turn against this nation when the final test of loyalty comes. It, therefore, follows that along the vital Pacific Coast over 112,000 potential enemies, of Japanese extraction, are at large today.[4]

Many in the country and especially in the West, stronghold of fears of the "yellow peril" in America, easily accepted DeWitt's assessment and proposal; many had believed that persons of Japanese ancestry were inassimilable and suspect because of a combination of genetic incompatibility with European Americans and irreconcilably hostile cultural differences. Japanese immigrants and their descendants in America were therefore considered fundamentally different from European immigrant groups, such as the Germans and Italians, neither of whom suffered any group deprivations in the war. As a *Los Angeles Times* editor urging action against Japanese Americans had written in February 1942, "A viper is nonetheless a viper wherever the egg is hatched."[5] Most American political leaders and the public, even as they embraced declared anti-aggression and antifascist purposes, had little problem endorsing the internment of persons of a racial minority at home. They had been nurtured on nineteenth-century and early-twentieth-century assumptions about a genetically based racial hierarchy of humankind and the claims of a "biology"-based social Darwinism that linked social behavior, psychology, and culture to blood.

Others who held less biologically based assumptions about race were still persuaded by the argument of "military necessity." Prominent educators and political figures with more liberal credentials fell into this category. Many in academia had come to accept the cultural rather than "race"-based explanations of social behavior that had emerged in the 1920s and 1930s, but they still found compelling the national security argument that rationalized internment. For example, faculty in Stanford University's School of Education offered this perspective not long after the implementation of internment: "Since the outbreak of war, loyal American citizens of Japanese extraction have been subjected to humiliating insults and indignities . . . [although] the removal of the Japanese from the coastal region was a military necessity, both for the safety of the country and the safety of the evacuees themselves."[6] In fact, the federal government's invocation of "military necessity" was never substantiated by evidence; within the government, military intelligence and law enforcement agencies, such as the FBI, had actually opposed unselective internment of persons of Japanese ancestry. (In 1982, the federal commission appointed by President Jimmy Carter, which reviewed the history of internment, declared that it was "not justified by military necessity. The broad historical causes which shaped these decisions were race prejudice, war hysteria, and a failure of political leadership.")[7]

The view that internment was somehow even in the interests of those affected, that the national body as well as its suspect part both benefited from internment, was never offered as official rationale but did circulate widely among the public. Liberals who expressed support for the extreme measures, albeit with some regret, often believed the measures were somehow in the interests of Japanese Americans. Moreover, such support was often accompanied by forceful denunciations of the "racists," profiteers, and political demagogues, including in Congress, who publicly pressed for more extreme measures against the internees, including wholesale deportation, abolition of citizenship for the American-born, permanent segregation from the rest of the American population, separation of male and female to prevent further reproduction of the population, sterilization, and even death.[8] Such views obviously sounded uncomfortably similar to the racism of the fascist enemy and were rejected by liberal-minded Americans—nevertheless with very few exceptions, American liberals accepted and endorsed the internment order.

The remainder of this chapter will focus on this latter group of liberal, "antiracist" supporters of internment, which included many who were involved in the administration of the camps themselves. These individuals, including Dillon Myer, the director of the WRA, and many of the camp officials and personnel, often thought of themselves certainly not as participants in a disreputable enterprise but as contributors to the battle for democracy and "Americanism." And more, although they may have seen internment as an unfortunate necessity, they also saw many positive possibilities in the experience, with important lessons for understanding problems in human management in the postwar world. The unassuming title of the WRA's own final public report on its work captured this faith in technomanagerialism, *The WRA: A Story of Human Conservation.*[9] Internment, which allegedly served both dominant as well as minority community interests, exemplified the ideology and method of liberal social engineering.

An individual who saw opportunity in the internment camps was John J. McCloy, assistant secretary of war, among the most responsible in government for the internment decision itself, future high commissioner of occupied Germany, and one of the most influential men in cold war America. Not long after the internment camps had opened, McCloy revealed thoughts about their possibilities; he felt sufficiently comfortable about his ideas to share them with prominent civil libertarian Alexander Meiklejohn, former president of Amherst College, McCloy's alma mater:

> We would be missing a very big opportunity if we failed to study the Japanese in these Camps at some length before they are dispersed. We have not done a very good job thus far in solving the Japanese problem in this country. I believe we have a great opportunity to give the thing intelligent thought now and to reach solid conclusions for the future. These people, gathered as they now are in these communities, afford a means of sampling their opinion and studying their customs and habits in a way we have never before had possible. We could find out what they are thinking about and we might very well influence their thinking in the right direction before they are again distributed into communities.
>
> I am aware that such a suggestion may provoke a charge that we have no right to treat these people as "guinea pigs," but I would rather treat them as guinea pigs and learn something useful than merely to treat them, or have them treated, as they have been in the past with such unsuccessful results.[10]

McCloy believed national security interests necessitated internment—as late as the 1980s McCloy continued to defend the decision, arguing that it was "entirely just and reasonable" because of the demands of wartime security—but his view of internment went further. Internment offered an opportunity for something "positive," an opportunity for those in power to study and shape the confined population in the interests of the state. The temptation was too great; the possibilities too attractive for McCloy and others to ignore. The internees, racially defined, incarcerated against their will, and in violation of constitutional practices and principles, were indeed treated as "guinea pigs." Years later after the end of the war, McCloy continued to maintain that "our Japanese/American [*sic*] population benefited from the relocation rather than suffered."[11]

Another individual with very different credentials flirted with conclusions similar to those expressed by McCloy in 1942. Carey McWilliams, chief of the Division of Immigration and Housing for the State of California in 1942, and later prolific and leading author on American minority and labor issues and editor of the *Nation*, at first criticized the idea of wholesale internment of the Japanese when the idea began to circulate publicly in early 1942. In one article for the *New Republic*, he at first characterized the idea as a "dangerous concrete proposal" and opposed it without reservation. In another article for the same journal, he declaimed that if Japanese Americans were relocated, "then obviously one group of citizens will have been discriminated against solely on the basis of race."[12]

After internment actually began, however, McWilliams adopted a very different view, one compatible with McCloy's. "Evacuation and resettlement," as McWilliams put it in the summer of 1942, "can be handled democratically and fairly for the attainment of highly desirable social objectives." He seemed to have been persuaded by what he called the "unique opportunity" relocation offered to develop underutilized lands, to "democratize" the

Japanese, and to improve the economic resources of the Japanese community. "I see in the resettlement of the Japanese," McWilliams emphasized, "a unique opportunity to work out not only new community patterns . . . but the necessary administrative skills and techniques for dealing with the whole problem of rural and urban reconstruction in the post-war period." Like McCloy, he saw the possibilities that internment offered for social engineers. In a major article for *Harper's*, McWilliams, acknowledging that he had originally opposed the idea of relocation, nevertheless praised the government's actual roundup and incarceration of Japanese Americans as "a miracle of effective organization." "There is no reason why the relocation projects cannot be successful," he concluded his article, and "cannot in fact reflect great credit upon us as a nation—provided a majority of the American people will insist upon fair treatment of the Japanese and not succumb to demagogues and race-baiters."[13]

McCloy and McWilliams in 1942 were not alone in sensing the current, and future, social-engineering lessons the camps might offer. A regiment of teachers, social scientists, and government administrators explored the possibilities in scores of internal government reports, published articles, and books. The WRA itself employed some thirty anthropologists as analysts who closely monitored the interned population and reported to camp authorities. The responsibilities of these specialists, most trained at leading research universities, was to help administrators improve social controls. According to one of these analysts, they worked at "sizing up [internment] problems which stood in the way of executing the basic policies, and to a lesser extent at devising means for solving those problems." In typical WRA bureaucratic language that obfuscated the actual social *and* racial relations between the powerless, who were incarcerated, and the authorities, the analyst concluded, "The role of Community Analysis was that of an aid in maintaining communication between a group of administrators and a group of administered people." Years later, this same analyst assumed a much more jaundiced view of the internment enterprise in which he had been involved. He came to characterize camp officials as administrative technicians steeped in the Western tradition of "getting things done." The WRA administrators made decisions for the internees "and then asked for cooperation in accomplishing what they had decided on." The result was a "paternalistic set of decisions." Though still employing euphemistic terms, the former analyst had come to sense not only the antidemocratic nature of internment but the liberal, technomanagerial ethos that imbued the entire experience.[14]

Many of the analysts, teachers, and other WRA camp staff (who were officially called "appointed personnel" or, bizarrely, "the Caucasians," to further the fiction that the camps were not prisons) believed their work carried significance beyond serving the needs of the WRA administrators and, like McCloy and McWilliams, saw their work as possibly helping address what they believed would be American needs in the postwar period. Their outlook, as revealed in their own writings, displays a confidence, even hubris, in the morality of their mission and rationality of their intentions and actions.

In these writings, the authors frequently convey an enthusiasm, a self-consciousness about involvement in what they felt was an enterprise of historic importance. This was an enthusiasm that went beyond inflation of one's contribution to the good war effort. There is the sense that, as pedestrian as some of their specific tasks may have been, they were thrilled not only by the intellectual challenge of their jobs and the research possibilities offered by access to a controlled population but also by their connection to the immense coercive power of the state and the possibilities that power offered to determine the destinies of thousands of humans. They found themselves molding, reshaping, remaking a people in ways they determined best and consistent with their own ostensibly higher values and superior way of life, regardless of the rights and sentiments of the subject population. They could have Mephisto's power but without the consequences or the guilty conscience.

The titles alone of some of their essays, many published in respected social science journals, are themselves suggestive: Emory S. Bogardus, "Relocation Centers as Planned Communities," (*Sociology and Social Research*, 1944); Bureau of Sociological Research (WRA), "The Psychiatric Approach in Problems of Community Management: From a Study of a Japanese Relocation Center" (*American Journal of Psychiatry*, 1943); Wanda Robertson, "Developing World Citizens in a Japanese Relocation Center" (*Childhood Education*, 1943); Monica Kehoe, "Japanese Become Americans: Adult Education at Gila River Relocation Project, Rivers, Arizona" (*Adult Education Journal*, 1944); John U. Provinse, "Building New Communities During War Time" (*American Sociological Review*, 1946); and Edward H. Spicer, "Reluctant Cotton-pickers: Incentive to Work in a Japanese Relocation Center," in E. H. Spicer, ed., *Human Problems in Technological Change* (1952).[15]

One administrator at the Poston Center, which contained eighteen thousand internees, enthusiastically described internment as a part of an "epic drama" testing the country's "moral import." In "Education Through Relocation," John W. Powell, a school official in the prewar years, observed that in the camps, "every relationship is educational, and every [staff] man a teacher. . . . It is hard sometimes to remember not to speak of the Project as the Campus." Education was more than formal training for the young; it sought fundamental reshaping of the lives of all the people. Powell's stated goal was to see that

Poston become "a source of rich production, a school for wise and energetic Americans in years to come." In even more dramatic language that displayed his excitement in the possibilities for human engineering that lay ahead of him and his fellow administrators, Powell explained that their goal must be "to train these people, not just to make a living or to pass the time until the war ends, but to make them ready to *hurl as projectiles* of democracy into the maelstrom of postwar readjustment."[16] Powell, as did many of his fellow administrators, objectified the internees as "docile tools," as human clay for the hands of the social engineer. Nowhere in his article does he reveal self-consciousness of any possible contradiction in his vision that the interned, placed in prison camps as a result of an authoritarian decision, could be used as agents for genuinely democratic purposes in the postwar world.

To achieve such grand ends behind barbed wire, the WRA strove to build what it believed were ideal American communities, with town councils, pseudoelections Americanization classes, and organized celebrations of American holidays. These efforts, occurring within confinement and directed toward those who were already in fact Americans, were by nature highly contrived, artificial, prescribed, and orchestrated. An educational administrator for the camps giddily declared in an Office of Education publication during the war that the camp schools "can become, in a measure often dreamed of by educators but seldom realized, an effective instrument of community planning and building."[17] The WRA teachers' handbook stated explicitly that education should "lead each individual to practice American manners and customs." Instruction was given on proper ways to shop and recreate and on acceptable etiquette and mores. In the prison camp classrooms for children as well as for the adult education classes, teachers were to promote new gender relationships by encouraging "the American ideal of the equality of women."[18]

Although this goal of imbuing the captive Japanese American internees with the trappings of middle America (Americanizing the Americans, so to speak) was high in the minds of staff members, the *method* of attaining such ends was given no less attention. Stanford School of Education professor Paul Hanna and his graduate students helped develop the philosophy and curriculum of the camp schools. They were guided by the latest wisdom of what was known as progressive education, which stressed the integration of school and community spheres to prepare youngsters to become good, productive members of American society. For these educators, the positive opportunities seemed immense. They envisioned the internment camp as a great big school. "Education," one of the planning documents stated, "becomes a process which goes on everywhere in the Relocation Center": "The walls of a classroom cease to be educational boundaries." The whole camp was to serve "education" interests. The "Japanese Relocation Centers," Paul Hanna's associates wrote, "probably offer the greatest opportunity in the United States for the kind of service that the community school can give." Most of the educators in the camps never appreciated the cruel irony of these proposals being advanced under the banner of democracy.[19]

One who was untroubled by his work in an internment camp provides especially interesting insight into the thinking of teachers. Jerome T. Light taught at the Minidoka, Idaho, camp school and was unusually sympathetic to the internees. Light wanted to close the distance between himself and the internees, whom he acknowledged had suffered considerable dislocation and distress. He even sent his own four children to the camp school to try to live as the internees did. After the war, he completed his doctoral degree in education at Stanford, and devoted his two-volume, twelve-hundred-page thesis to an explication of his teaching experience at Minidoka. He dedicated the work to his former students at camp, praising them for conducting "a truly American high school under extremely adverse circumstances."[20]

And yet, Light pursued his educational responsibilities in camp with no self-reflection on the contradictory purposes of his job (educator *and* prison camp staff member), let alone the implications internment had for the high-minded principles continuously propagated in camp. Light, for example, reported that the camp teachers agreed that the promotion of "Americanism" should be an essential part of their teaching efforts. He proudly described their work:

> The educational program itself could be expected to increase the use and appreciation of American social customs. Studies of vocations dealt with occupations in the United States. The science courses, although not exclusively American, pointed out the scientific advances made in the United States. Vocational education, including home economics and commercial courses as well as shop courses, inevitably taught American practices. The reading instruction presented American literature, the books in the library were American. . . . The American History and Government taught in grade 11 was enriched as much as possible for this same purpose. The study of World Problems in grade 12 was oriented inevitably with the American viewpoint. In dealing with the 10th grade theme, The Community: A Human Invention to Serve Human Needs, the American communities were studied most of the time, and when foreign communities were studied they were inevitably viewed through American eyes. The theme in the 7th grade, How Man Utilizes Science and Inventions, illustrated how it was done in the United States more than elsewhere. And, the very method of instruction and the organization of the school were typically American as was realized by the students.[21]

But perhaps most intriguing was Light's description of the approach the teachers adopted in inculcating Americanism within a prison camp school:

> In keeping with these assumptions and recognized facts [the unusual circumstances of instruction, the resentment and suspicion of the pupils, Americanism as a "dynamic and growing ideology"], the faculty agreed to make no issue about Americanism in the school but to act as though there were no question about it.[22]

With these words, Light unintentionally captured much of the spirit governing the entire internment enterprise: faith in the good purpose of the project; pride in the intentions of those in authority; acceptance of the unquestioned value of propagating an idealized Americanism; obliviousness to any contradiction between those ideals and the surrounding reality; confidence in the ability to manipulate the subjects for their own good, as defined by the administrator; and a collective self-consciousness of the need to "act" to further the political ends of the authorities.

Light concluded his exhaustive account of his wartime teaching experience with a high note of optimism and convinced of the useful implications of his work. The educational program at Minidoka, Light wrote, "succeeded to a degree which would justify the repetition of its program in similar situations. . . . The experience herein described demonstrates that a program so formulated in advance can be put into successful operation despite very considerable material and administrative handicaps."[23]

Nowhere did Light reflect upon the possible reactionary consequences of what had happened to the Japanese Americans, but rather, as a good education technician, he took unquestioned pride in his work and set aside troubling questions. He was confronted with a task of managing and shaping the lives of an incarcerated human group and, even years after the original decision for internment and the appearance of wide criticism of internment, he offered his expertise as relevant to a possible, even anticipated, repeat of a similar effort. He was ready to serve the state again.

How did the targets of the social-engineering efforts respond?

The responses of Japanese Americans themselves reflected the conflicting explanations given by the state that rationalized internment and the reeducation opportunities it presented. Most Japanese Americans were confused, angry, and certainly frightened by the 1942 internment order. Their futures were completely uncertain and unguaranteed by the state. But most publicly responded to the order with relatively little opposition and protest. Some believed internment was a necessary evil demanded by a good government, and they complied and cooperated. Cooperation with whatever the state demanded could prove loyalty. For others, internment confirmed the basically racist nature of American society and resistance within the centers, which included political and cultural forms, often frustrated administrators. The differences of opinion and attitudes among the internees ran deep and produced sharp, even violent, conflicts. It was not at all clear to them whether internment was a result of a racism that assumed Japanese biological inferiority and disloyalty or of wartime overreaction to security concerns. Once in the camps, Japanese Americans did not know whether they faced possible future elimination, through deportation or physical extermination (a bleak social Darwinist "fate"), or a benign bureaucratic paternalism that wanted to bestow the blessings of Americanism (a social-engineering "project") upon them. Were they kept in what some publicly called "concentration camps" or had they been simply "evacuated" into temporary "centers" under the care of the federal government, as others described their situation? Plenty of evidence existed to argue for any of these interpretations. That there was no clear answer was itself tormenting.[24]

The recorded experience of one internee, historian Yamato Ichihashi, offers an especially useful vantage point to understand the internment dilemma. Although Ichihashi was untypical among Japanese Americans—he was not a farmer but had been a Stanford professor since 1913 and was perhaps the most eminent internee in the camps—his correspondence with Stanford friends and his diary during the war years provide a complete, day-to-day account of internment. His record is perhaps the only extant complete first-person account of the experience as events actually unfolded.

Ichihashi was also both witness as well as victim. From the beginning of his ordeal, he appreciated the historic importance of internment and recorded his experiences in order to write an account at a future point. He never got there, but his records remain for us today to consult. His observations are particularly valuable, because he was fluent in both English and Japanese, trained as a social scientist (historian and economist), and experienced in research and writing; yet his intellectual skills and wisdom did not prepare him for the years of trial in the camps. Although at the start of internment he believed himself mentally and culturally superior to the tens of thousands of other internees from plebeian backgrounds whom he had to join in the centers, he found that he could not avoid the cost of imprisonment. He thought he could rise above the mean life of camp, but by the end he too was dragged down. When he returned to Stanford in the spring of 1945, he was a bitter, cynical man whose family had disintegrated around him and whose intellectual life had died.

Examining Ichihashi's effort to try to describe his unfolding experience reveals the conflicting ideologies that controlled the camps and the difficulty he had in comprehending exactly what was happening to him and the other internees. There was no clear precedent upon which he could base his interpretation. The internment centers were not prison camps for convicted persons or prisoners of war; they were not reservations for subjugated, indigenous peoples; they were not forced labor camps; they were not reeducation centers for the politically degenerate. They were none of these but also a bit of all of them at the same time.

In one of his first letters to a Stanford colleague after he was "evacuated" to the "assembly center" at the Santa Anita racetrack, Ichihashi tried to describe his circumstances in incarceration by analogy. The choice of his words is revealing. The state, he wrote, had "established in this Center a truly classless community (a Soviet ideal unrealized as yet in Russia). Residents (inmates more appropriately) are not recognized as individuals; we are numbered for identification and are treated exactly alike." "The Camp has a population of 18,400, each of which is numbered for identification; for instance I am No. 5561A." Ichihashi described the abysmal living conditions, including multiple families forced to live in converted horse stalls. "In management of the classless community, the government has apparently adopted the lowest conceivable standard of treating human beings." He also condemned the hypocrisy of officials that administered the center. The administration was supposedly civilian, but in fact it was the army that ran the camps. Channels for complaint and communication from the internees were established, with even a "community council" composed of nominally elected representatives from among a portion of the evacuees. In fact, the administration determined their composition and manipulated their operation. Unexplained arrests, detentions, and harassment of internees were widespread, prompting Ichihashi to write in his diary (again, the language is instructive), "The present setup of the community is illogical and impossible; this is made more so by the attitude and handling of affairs by the management—autocracy enforced by a veritable Gestapo."[25]

As the months wore on, living conditions improved and administrative operations became more routinized, which provided a measure of assurance to the internees. Nevertheless, the state never produced a clear rationale about the camps; the flimsy fictions that they existed as a benign national security precaution or for the protection of the internees themselves continued. But the expressed attitudes of camp officials also regularly betrayed very different feelings toward the internees. "You can't imagine how close we came to machine-gunning the whole bunch of them," a camp official stated to the press after the suppression of a protest demonstration at the Tule Lake center. Speculating about his personal future after the war, Ichihashi wrote his closest friend at Stanford that he did not know what he and his family would do. "Who can tell whether this country will be an agreeable place for us to live, and if one were to believe what is being said at present, no Japanese are wanted here. Naturally we need not stay in a place we are not wanted; unlike the Jews, we have our native-land." (American law until 1952 denied

Japanese immigrants naturalization rights, and they therefore remained Japanese citizens.)[26]

Ichihashi of course did not know what was happening to the Jews of Europe in the Nazi death camps—if he and the other Japanese Americans had known, their feelings about confinement would undoubtedly have been very different. Ignorance in their circumstances was a blessing of sorts for them. How might they have acted if they had known about the industrial murder of the confined in Europe, we of course cannot know. But we do have Ichihashi's reflection, more than a year into internment, about his experience. It is an especially insightful comment on the results of race-based confinement, official obfuscation, administrative hypocrisy and manipulation of the internees, and brutal confinement. Ichihashi wrote a Stanford colleague in late 1943:

> I am naturally touched by the sad nature of events relative to institutions and persons. . . . [During this past year and a half] I have been forced to witness sad aspects of human life without relief; almost daily I have been encountering the death of men and women whose life history of struggle for thirty, forty, fifty years had been known to me. I have attended more funerals during this short period than I had in my lifetime. . . . But it is not death alone that saddens my heart, but the stupid behavior of young and old, resulting in the shattering of families and of controlled domestic relations, in the breaking up of true friendships. Individuals have become selfish, self-centered or egoistic or else so apathetic as to lose a balanced view of life. In brief, men and women have been washed out [of] whatsoever culture and refinement they once had possessed; they have reverted to savages and in many cases to beasts. This is the fruit of a forced communistic life as I see it.[27]

Ichihashi and his wife were finally allowed to leave internment and return to their home in the late spring of 1945. The former professor returned a greatly reduced person, in some ways as he had described others in the above commentary. He, and most of his fellow adult internees, never became "projectiles for democracy" or the model citizens wanted by the state. The ambitious social-engineering efforts never succeeded in transforming them. But this does not mean that they went untouched—they were passed by and ground down. The social engineers devoted little attention to these consequences when they reflected on the contributions internment made to the national body.

Years after internment ended, many who were involved in administration dismissed or excused their involvement by referring to the pressures of war and the demands of national mobilization. The focus of examination here, however, has not been so much about the rationalizations for internment but more about the underlying attitudes toward race and administration of internees. Except for McCloy and Myer, most of the individuals mentioned in this essay were not distinguished or unique individuals but were everyday teachers and academic researchers, with generally liberal inclinations. It is exactly their ordinariness that makes their thoughts noteworthy. In their prewar occupations, they had possessed little power in any conventional sense, but their connection to state authorities that had easily incarcerated 120,000 persons opened their visions to new possibilities and meanings for their lives. Power offered them possibilities for ambitious social engineering, possibilities that were often accepted with alacrity. (On several occasions, Ichihashi even found himself under the authority of young former students of his at Stanford.) They willingly offered their intellectual services to the state's purpose, and one wonders whether the attraction of administrative power over a captive people helped blind them to the ugliness of their endeavor and the contradiction between their expressed democratic principles and the sentiments of the targeted population. (In contrast, some were deeply troubled by their involvement. The first director of the WRA, Milton Eisenhower, was uncomfortable in his position and left the job after just a few months. When asked by Dillon Myer, his proposed replacement, about whether he should accept the position, Eisenhower said, "Yes, if you can do the job and sleep at night." Eisenhower said that had been unable to do so.)[28] The excitement of encountering "scientific possibilities" and the challenge of applying their intellectual worth to "practical" purpose were certainly part of this enthusiasm, but such is precisely the lure of projects of social control.

Functioning as good technoadministrators, as researchers consciously seeking ways to improve social control in the camps, and as conscientious teachers seeking to mold Japanese American students in their own image, these individuals believed they were playing a progressive and constructive role, not only in contributing to the war effort but in positively reshaping an entire population for their own good. They went far beyond merely trying to help a distressed group. Many took pride in their belief that they successfully fought off the racists, for the benefit of democracy and for Japanese Americans. Dillon Myer, himself, in his self-serving account of the WRA, devotes an entire chapter to "The Continuing Battle of the Racists," where he contrasts the WRA's efforts to congressional extremists. And although the differences between, on the one side, the crude racists who believed in fundamental "blood" and genetic differences among peoples and, on the other the side, the WRA educators and researchers was formidable and meaningful, the two groups also shared common ground. They shared a vision of the desirability of an America well ordered and prescribed in middle-class Euro-American values and ways, of the undesirability of Americans who did not fit those definitions, and of the possibility of using state power to reshape the target group. The liberal educators and researchers, perhaps precisely because they held to a cultural and not genetic basis for differences in group human behavior, differed from the crude racists in their greater faith in the ability of modern forms of social control (information management, systematic education, "scientific" administration informed by the insights of social psychology) to shape a subject population. As John Embree, one of the leading academics who worked for the WRA, put it tellingly, the applied social sciences had become essential to any effective, modern management effort, whether it be "for industry, [such as] the Western Electric Company; for colonial government, [such as] the British in New Guinea and parts of Africa; and finally in our American parallel to Colonial Administration, the War Relocation Authority."[29] Dillon Myer, the director of the WRA, was appointed, appropriately, commissioner of the Bureau of Indian Affairs in the early 1950s.

One of the seeming contradictions in the internment of Japanese Americans during World War II is that political leaders such as Franklin Roosevelt and implementers such as Jerome Light were on the whole consciously "antiracist." They did not share the openly racist views of those who retained social Darwinian notions about the genetic differences among so-called racial groups. In fact, those responsible for the camps went out of their way to oppose the open racists—the assumption of the WRA's Americanization programs was that the internees could become just as American as any other people. Any yet, the entire internment enterprise and its operation were imbued with what can only be called racist policies and actions. The original internment decision, which made no distinction between the rights of alien and citizen, separated persons of Japanese ancestry from those of German or Italian descent. The camp education and Americanization campaigns sought to impose regimes that were in fact racially based and similar to efforts long directed against native Indian populations.

Scientific racism, those systematic doctrines of racial inequality and hierarchy espoused by intellectuals beginning in the nineteenth century, largely fell into disfavor by the outbreak of World War II. The mainstream of social scientists and scientists broke from open avowals of racism in the 1930s and accepted culture-based explanations of differences among peoples. The rejection of openly racist language among the educated and liberal members of the Roosevelt administration and WRA reflected this eclipse of social Darwinian notions. But, as discussed above, the emergence of a new, technocratic social-engineering mentality, replete with the jargon of racially neutral terms, code words, and unexamined assumptions, helped sanction and inspire new forms of state mistreatment of a group that was in fact racially designated, in this case Japanese Americans. They would not be alone, of course. The absence of overt racist language in intent and practice did not mean the triumph of egalitarianism but highlighted the emergence of a new faith in the malleability of social groups.[30]

Soon after internment began, the Socialist Norman Thomas publicly condemned the New Dealers and "liberals" who trumpeted the roundup of Japanese Americans solely on the authority of the president; he linked internment to the ominous general centralization of political power in the country. "For the first time in American history," he wrote, "men, committees and publications boasting of their 'liberalism' as against 'fascism' are in the vanguard in justifying the presidential assumption of dictatorial power." More troubling perhaps was the embrace of the possibilities of mass, "scientific" population control by everyday liberal Americans. The enthusiastic use of various methods of technoadministration employed by the liberals directing America's internment camps was a sign of the fascination with state manipulation of populations for their own "interests" that became ubiquitous in the postwar period.[31]

ISTVÁN DEÁK

9

How to Construct a Productive, Disciplined, Monoethnic Society

The Dilemma of East Central European Governments, 1914–1956

IT IS A HISTORICAL POSTULATE that East Central Europe, which is the area lying roughly between the German- and Russian-inhabited lands, has been more prone to violent change than Western and Southern Europe. The region is also known to be backward, both economically and politically, yet rich in creative talent. Many of those who gave the Western world its negative assessment of these backwoods of Europe came themselves from the region and counted among the West's most successful scientists and scholars.

There is no reason to challenge most generalizations that have accrued to the image of East Central Europe, although one could well relativize at least the charge of violence by arguing that violent change in the region was matched by changes in the West of earlier times. It seems to me more important to analyze a third historical postulate directly related to the first two assertions, namely, that the region's answer to political instability and inadequate economic development has always been authoritarian rule and an all-caring, all-intrusive state.

No doubt, Central Europe harbored a strong tradition that led to what Zygmunt Bauman calls the "Gardening State": bureaucracies that claim the right and duty to provide for both the corporal and spiritual needs of their subjects. Let us think only of the paternalistic practices of the Habsburg bureaucracy, which were rooted in the eighteenth-century enlightened ideology of Emperors Joseph II and Leopold II. Extensive state machineries, controlled by a strong man or a strong oligarchy, were common in interwar East Central Europe, not to mention the post–World War II communist era. I would only contend that those who most often wrote about these phenomena, the East Central European expatriates, tended to overemphasize the power of state bureaucracies, and it was this overemphasis that became an article of creed among Western specialists. Consider, for instance, the success of the World War I Czech voluntary exiles Tomáš G. Masaryk and Edvard Beneš in perpetrating the myth of the Habsburg Monarchy as a bureaucratic monster, a prison of the peoples, an oppressive, inefficient, and archaic patriarchy. The writings and speeches of Masaryk and Beneš in exile exercised a crucial influence on President Woodrow Wilson, on his administrator Colonel House, and on R. W. Seton-Watson, an influential British journalist and historian. Yet the two exiled politicians were not in harmony, at that time, with their Czech colleagues at home, who, until 1918, viewed a reorganized Habsburg Monarchy as a viable possibility for the Czechs and Slovaks.[1]

The fact is that what some saw as a much too intrusive state, others perceived as a too weak and too tolerant state. Public demand for less oppression was neatly counterbalanced by public clamor for a more interventionist state. It was only a question of who made such demands and when, as well as why. Others strove for the creation of a new state on the ruins of the old in which the formerly oppressed would occupy a dominant position. Unfortunately, once the new state was created, the former champions of freedom became champions of strong central control, and the former ruling elites complained bitterly of too much control. What we have to deal with here, therefore, is not so much the overwhelming power of interventionist, paternalistic states but the differing perceptions of state power by various contemporaries and by legions of biased historians.

In general, there was more disorder than bureaucratic order in the region; this, at least until the rise of the post–World War II Communist regimes, which alone succeeded in creating a closely controlled society. Yet not even the Communists managed to bring about a new, public-spirited citizenry, or if they did then it was in a negative sense, unifying the citizenry against themselves. The Gardening State has always been more of an ambition than a real thing.

The only genuine success the East Central European governments were able to achieve was in the chilling realm of ethnic cleansing, and that only because ethnic cleansing enjoyed much wider public support than any other form of governmental activity. Unlike other official measures, ethnic cleansing in its diverse forms met with no significant opposition on the part of the ethnic majority in any of the East Central European states. Only a few Greeks and Bulgarians protested the expulsion of Turks from Greece and Bulgaria before and after World War I. Not many Poles, Russians, and Ukrainians objected to the Jewish pogroms perpetrated in the same period. During World War II, thousands of East Central Europeans resisted with arms the German occupation but only a handful of resisters attempted to obstruct the killing of five million Jews. After 1945, in an East Central Europe generally hostile to the Soviet occupation, hardly any voices were raised to protest the Red Army's and its East Central European associates' killing or expelling from the region of some thirteen million Germans. In recent years, within the former Yugoslavia, only a handful of Serbs and Croats protested the rape and killing of the Bosnian Muslims.

The reason for all this must be sought in the traditional superiority—fiscal, educational, and often even political—of some minorities over the majority populations. Germans in Poland, Hungary, Bohemia, Russia, and the Baltic region felt superior to the native populations; they were also treated as superior by the governmental authorities. Jews, although seldom legally privileged, towered over their Gentile neighbors in terms of education, and in more recent times, in business, the professions, culture, and the arts. Hungarians and Germans in Transylvania constituted legally privileged strata against the Romanian speakers, who formed the absolute majority in that province. The same can be said of the Polish minorities in the Ukraine and Belorussia, the Greeks in Turkish Anatolia, and the Italians in Croat-speaking Dalmatia. The history of many minorities in East Central Europe, all of them originating from regions to the west of the habitat of the local majority, is that of mild or not-so-mild domination, interrupted by bloody revolts against this domination. At last, in the twentieth century, mostly during and after World War II, ensued the final defeat, extermination or expulsion of these minorities from East Central Europe. What we are experiencing, therefore, is the triumph of people originating from the native peasantry over the urban inhabitants, traditionally made up of foreigners, and over the farmer-settlers from the West, who had been lured into the region with the promise of privileged treatment and a degree of autonomy.

Fascism, communism, and all other forms of political control turned out to be mere episodes in the history of East Central Europe; witness the remarkable success of democracy in our days and the existence of early parliamentary practices in nearly all the states in the region. The only lasting and irremediable change has been brought about by immoral ethnic cleansing. Neither the Jews nor the Germans, the two peoples who once shouldered the burden of East Central European economic and cultural development, are likely to return to the region. The major reason East Central Europe is so different today from what it was in 1914 is not because the state has succeeded in converting its citizens to one way of thinking or another, but because the state, with the connivance of the majority of the citizens, has succeeded in forcibly assimilating, deporting, or killing most of the ethnic minorities. The consequence is a hitherto-unheard-of cultural and ethnic uniformity that marks every East Central European state.

Let us now cast a glance at the relationship between state and citizenry in East Central Europe before the Great War and proceed from there through the interwar period to some considerations of what the governments undertook in terms of population management during and immediately after the Second World War.

By 1914, the increasingly anarchical Ottoman Empire had been replaced in the Balkans by a number of successor states. Montenegro, Greece, Serbia, Romania, Bulgaria, and Albania all claimed perfect historical justification for their existence but were rather unsure of the developmental road they wanted to take. The new elite, largely of peasant origin, both desired and feared modernization. All the new states possessed elected parliaments, but more power rested in the state bureaucracies.[2] One of the main sources of instability lay in conflicting views on the nation's destiny, mainly in the conflict between what the Greeks called the Megali Idea, the hope of recreating an often mythical medieval or premedieval great empire, and the desire to strengthen the already-existing smaller national state. Serbian politicians and intellectuals, for example, had a hard time deciding whether they wished the continuation and eventual expansion of their national state or whether they should strive for the submersion of the state into a larger South-Slavic unit. What further weakened any unity of national purpose in the Balkans were the urban capitalist practices imposed on a largely self-sufficient, marginal rural economy, and the conflicting ambitions of the major state institutions. Under the circumstances, relatively little could be done to change society. There was no shortage of such controlling organs as, for instance, the secret police, but the police, the military, and other governmental institutions often worked at cross-purposes.

Typical was the case of the Serbian military or, rather, of a group of young officers within the Serbian military who in 1903 overthrew the ruling dynasty and even killed the king and the queen. The same group, in 1914, arranged for the murder of Archduke Francis Ferdinand. This brought about the war against Austria-Hungary, which is what the Serbian officers had wanted. Whether or not the radical Serbian prime minister Nikola Pašić was in favor of such a development is immaterial; what counts is that this decisive act in Serbian history was not the government's doing but that of a group of officers whom the government both distrusted and feared.[3]

The Habsburg state is often described as an authoritarian construct with not much more than a facade of parliamentary practices. Yet nothing could be further from the truth. First of all, the Habsburg state was in reality two states, Austria and Hungary, in which the two partners moved in different, often opposite directions. Increasingly democratic and truly multinational Austria often skirted anarchy and had to be governed, again and again, by ministers recruited from the bureaucracy. They, at least, could assure the survival of the state. Under such circumstances the best that the Austrian state authorities could do in terms of civic education was to propagate the image of a good, all-knowing, and supranational emperor, to whom all owed loyalty: because of tradition, because of respect for the ruler's old age, and because of the prospects of further economic growth and domestic peace. This imperial propaganda was actually more successful than what the World War I political émigrés and later nationalist historians were willing to concede. Witness the surprising loyalty of the monarchy's eleven major and numerous minor nationalities to the emperor during the horrors of the First World War. Masaryk and Beneš always spoke of the sixty thousand Czech legionaries in Russia as proof of the Czechs' alienation from the Habsburg Monarchy. They said less about the close to a million Czech soldiers who did not surrender to the enemy.[4] Admittedly, not every front soldier is in a position to surrender to the enemy, no matter how much he desires to do so. Still, it would have been impossible to stop the simultaneous desertion of hundreds of thousands of Czechs, less even of millions of Austro-Hungarian soldiers of Slavic origin. The Russian tsarist army, for example, was powerless, in 1917, to stop the desertion of millions of Russian soldiers.

Habsburg imperial propaganda was undoubtedly counteracted by nationalist agitation, be it German, Slavic, Romanian, or Italian, as well as by a somewhat outdated but still influential territorial ideology. As a result, rather than being able to impose a single state idea, the Austrian government had to maneuver among many conflicting ideologies. A Czech in Prague, for instance, was allowed to profess loyalty, simultaneously, to the imperial family and historic Austria, to Bohemia as a historical-political unit, to the Czech nation as the mother of all Czechs, and even to the new, fashionable idea of a "Czechoslovak" nation. Add to these the lure of such concepts as proletarian and Roman Catholic internationalism. Or consider the case of a Jew in Prague who was expected to be both a good Austrian and a good Bohemian but was also urged to decide whether he or she was a Czech, a German, and/or a Jewish nationalist.[5] Most subjects of the Austrian Empire exhibited multiple loyalties and did not even feel uncomfortable while doing so. Characteristic was the case of the reserve officers in the so-called Austro-Hungarian Common Army who, while in their civilian occupations, often abominated the entire monarchical setup but willingly wore the emperor's uniform when called up for maneuvers; they embraced the manners as well as the aristocratic, supranational ideology of the professional officers.[6]

In pre–World War I Hungary the situation was both simpler and more complex. It was simpler because the country was efficiently governed by a political oligarchy made up of Magyar nobles and of upwardly mobile non-nobles, who were often of Slavic or German origin. Meanwhile, the Hungarian economy was being successfully developed by a group of immigrants who were German, Swiss, Belgian, and so on, and even more by assimilated Jews. Complexity came from the fact that the government wanted the inhabitants of the country to be simultaneously loyal to Francis Joseph and to the Hungarian nation and state. As a consequence, in pre–World War I Hungarian textbooks, Francis Joseph was described both as the good and gracious Hungarian king and as an evil Austrian emperor who, after 1848, had hanged the best of Hungarian patriots. As for Hungary's ethnic minorities, who made up one half of the citizenry, they were told to be good subjects of the king and to be good Hungarians. Meanwhile, the leaders of the minorities instructed their followers to be more loyal to the emperor than to the king of Hungary. Most of these leaders strove to achieve autonomy for their ethnic group either within or outside Hungary but still within the monarchy, whereas the radical minority saw their nation's future not only outside of Hungary but even outside of Austria-Hungary.

In brief, pre-1914 Austria accepted the fact of its being a multinational state. Following the electoral defeat of the German Liberals in the 1870s, the Vienna government no longer favored the German nationality over the others. Emperor Francis Joseph's only loyalty was to his own family, and he expected his subjects to feel the same way. In Hungary, on the other hand, the political elite argued insistently that everybody in the kingdom, including Francis Joseph as king, was a Hungarian, except that the ethnic minorities spoke a language other than Hungarian. To be a Hungarian was said to be a spiritual condition, independent of language and ethnic origin.[7]

In pre-1914 partitioned Poland, the public developed a lifestyle and a way of thinking largely independent of the political teachings of their Prussian and Russian masters. Austrian presence in Galicia was a somewhat more successful proposition. Nothing proves more the failure of Prussian and Russian indoctrination in Poland than that during World War I, the Polish soldiers of both empires proved largely indifferent or hostile to the state. On the other hand, the Polish soldiers of Austria-Hungary were generally willing to serve in the Habsburg Army, at least so long as the hope existed that the Austrians would help to liberate and to unify the Polish nation. The main trouble with Poland was, especially in the interwar period, the inability of its leaders to decide whether they wanted to build a multinational Great Poland, in which each ethnic group and each province would enjoy certain rights, or whether they preferred a smaller, ethnically Polish state.[8]

World War I brought East Central Europe one step closer to the ethnic purity that is increasingly its hallmark today. The wartime flight of millions of Polish and Russian Jews to Budapest and Vienna simplified the ethnic picture in the former regions; it also contributed enormously to anti-Semitism in Austria and Hungary. More important, every government, whether Austro-Hungarian, German, or Russian, engaged in active ethnic politics during the war, favoring one nationality over the other and spreading nationalist propaganda among the civilians, the troops, and the prisoners of war. The Austro-Hungarian High Command sent soldiers from the reputedly loyal nationalities, such as the German-Austrians, Hungarians, Slovenes, Croats, and Bosnian Muslims, to the most dangerous sectors of the front, where they suffered inordinately high casualties. Meanwhile, reputedly disloyal regions, such as Bohemia, were placed under harsh military rule and some leaders of suspected nationalities were imprisoned.[9]

All governments paid special attention to the status of prisoners of war. Whether in the territory of the Central Powers or in Serbia, Russia, and Italy, POWs were generally segregated on the basis of class and nationality. The favored treatment given to officers aggravated class tensions both in the POWs camps and, because of the prisoners' letters, in the home country. The favored treatment of Slavic, Romanian, and Italian prisoners from the Habsburg army in Serbian, Russian, and Italian POW camps increased ethnic tension both among the prisoners and in Austria-Hungary. Meanwhile, the Austro-Hungarian and German authorities engaged in active anti-Russian propaganda among the non-Russian captives from the army of the tsar.[10] In other words, during the war, the three great monarchies, the Russian, the Habsburg, and the German, prepared their suicide by embracing the principle of nationality.

During the Russian Civil War, in Siberia, "Red" Hungarian, German-Austrian, and German ex-POWs fought pitched battles against "White" Czechoslovak legionaries. At the end of the war, returning POWs from Russia constituted the vanguard, in former Austria-Hungary, of the socialist revolutionary movement and/or of the Slavic, Hungarian, German, and so on, nationalist revolutions.[11]

The collapse of the three great empires, Russia, Germany, and Austria-Hungary, led to numerous civil wars and local wars in East Central Europe. In these conflicts, the combined forces of the Entente Powers and local nationalists easily defeated the amateurish socialist revolutionary governments in Hungary, Bavaria, and Slovakia. Yet it is still worth remembering such a regime as, for instance, the Hungarian Soviet Republic, which, in the spring of 1919, attempted totally to transform society. In its early days, the Hungarian Soviet Republic was not even unsuccessful. Among other things, it rallied behind the red flag almost the entire Hungarian intellectual and artistic establishment. However, the combination of its wild experiments, the Jewish origin of most of its leaders, and its terror measures produced a lasting negative effect not only in Hungary but also in East Central Europe as a whole. From that time on, anticommunism and anti-Semitism were major weapons in the hands of nearly every regime.[12]

Unlike the socialist revolutions, the nationalist revolutions or takeovers were successful everywhere—in part because they built on existing political parties, well-established social classes, and experienced local bureaucracies, and in part because President Wilson and the Western democracies were stronger than Lenin's Soviet Russia.

All the new states in East Central Europe were created by the force of arms. This allowed the victors among them, Czechoslovakia, Poland, Romania, and Yugoslavia, to expand far beyond where Czechs, Slovaks, Poles, Romanians, Serbs, Croats, and Slovenes lived. It also forced the losers, Bulgaria, Hungary, and German Austria, to accept a situation in which millions of their conationals found themselves under the rule of neighboring hostile states. Moreover, the military fait accompli caused such aspiring nationalities, whose political goals had been disregarded after 1918, to bide their time until the opportunity would arise to overthrow the rule of Poles, Czechs, and Serbs. For the Ukrainians, Slovaks, Ruthenes, Croats, Slovenes, Bosnian Muslims, Albanians, and Macedonians, or rather for their self-appointed political leaders, the new geopolitical situation was as much of an anathema as it was for the German Austrians, Hungarians, Bulgarians, and Turks.

The Paris peace treaties of 1919 to 1920 confirmed the demarcation lines originally created by military conquest. Moreover, insult was added to injury by the shameless way the victorious East Central European governments indiscriminately used historical, ethnic, economic, and strategic arguments to legitimize their conquests. From that time on, the peace treaties of 1919 to 1920 determined the policies of East Central European governments and the political sentiments of the public.[13]

Interwar Poland, Czechoslovakia, Romania, and Yugoslavia were miniature multinational empires, which in their politics resembled the prewar Hungarian kingdom more than the prewar Austrian empire or the Ottoman empire of old. The Hungarians' modernist interpretation of nation and nationality became, after 1918, the ideology of every East Central European state. The nationalist ideologies propagated in the prewar years by East Central European politicians, in opposition to the multinational empires, now became state ideologies. Because East Central Europe was divided between have and have-not nations; because enmities existed not only between winners and losers but also among the winners; and because there was poverty and economic stagnation, all interwar governments took very similar measures to strengthen the loyalty of the citizens.[14]

Among such governmental measures were the creation of large armies and police forces. Poland, Romania, and Yugoslavia maintained armed forces in excess of their financial abilities. In this respect, at least, the losers were in a better situation, having been forbidden by the peace treaties to rearm.

Every interwar state attempted to win the loyalty of the population by introducing a number of social reform measures. These invariably led to the expansion of bureaucracies but did not necessarily improve the lot of the population. Land reform, the distribution of large estates, was attempted everywhere, but not always seriously, so as not to alienate the landowning classes or to disrupt production. In Czechoslovakia, Romania, and Yugoslavia, the land reform had a distinct ethnic agenda: its primary targets were German and Hungarian landowners. However, even these remained mostly half measures, and there was little evidence to show that the poorest peasantry, on whose behalf the expropriations had been undertaken, genuinely profited from them. Much more successful were the extension of health benefits, the introduction of a social security system, new labor laws, new housing projects, the building of schools, and so forth, all of which had their roots in prewar legislation. Only the poverty of the state and the protests of landowners and capitalists put a limit to such measures.

The political leaders of the interwar states, even in conservative Hungary, would have wanted to go further in adopting welfare measures than allowed by those who had the money, namely, the local bankers, industrialists, and landowners. Nor were such measures promoted by the foreign bankers and the League of Nations, which had to guarantee the indispensable foreign loans. The reason for the government's readiness to expand social services was not so much idealism, although that existed also, as the perceived need to create a healthy and loyal citizenry for the coming, inevitable armed conflicts.

Behind every major governmental measure taken in the interwar period lurked the perceived necessity to prepare the nation for war. This alone explains the drive for economic self-sufficiency; the enormous expenditures on armaments; the special organizations to train young people in warfare and labor service; the awards given to mothers with many children even though each East Central European country suffered from rural overpopulation, unemployment, and underemployment; and the anti-Semitic propaganda that was motivated, aside from other reasons, by the misconception that Jews made unreliable and weak soldiers. That the East European right-wing governments were not alone in this misconception regarding Jews as soldiers is shown by Amir Weiner in his chapter on the Soviet Union. Among other things, Weiner points to Stalin's repeated references to the Jews as "poor and rotten soldiers." Finally, it is important to note that whereas every East Central European government favored industrialization and urban development, it woefully neglected agriculture and the rural population—all this, despite these regimes upholding what they called "sacred rural values."

The official idolization of peasants, powerfully seconded by much of the urban intelligentsia, must be seen as part of the preparation for war, because the peasants were considered the best soldiers, especially when compared with the physically stunted and "Bolshevik-infected" urban proletariat.

Well before World War I, as Elisabeth Domansky explains in her chapter, Western European governments were haunted by the fear of population decline, both quantitative and qualitative. Especially worrisome in their eyes was the perceived shift of the domestic demographic balance in favor of the less-worthy lower classes. This view should be modified, in my opinion, with regard to Germany and East Central Europe to say that the regimes feared primarily the overproduction of undesirable offspring among the urban proletariat. Meanwhile, these regimes placed their hope, although not their money, in the preservation of the "sturdy, sober, and patriotic" peasant class.

Nationalist propagandists, whether working for or against the government, expanded pre–World War I legends regarding the mythical, semidivine origins of the Hungarians, Romanians, Poles, Serbs, and others. Each nation was said to have entered East Central Europe with a mission to uphold superior moral and martial values. Each could boast of an extensive and highly civilized medieval empire. Each was said to have suffered devastating defeat, between the fourteenth and eighteenth centuries, by a ruthless foreign power aided by domestic traitors and by jealous neighbors. The Serbs were betrayed and defeated at Kosovo in 1389; the Hungarians at Mohács in 1526; the Czechs at the White Mountain in 1620; the Poles through numerous domestic-assisted foreign invasions in the eighteenth century. Each nation experienced greatness in medieval times; each suffered martyrdom later; each went through a period of darkness and stagnation due to foreign rule and domestic corruption, only to emerge, at last, within the aura of a beautiful national renaissance beginning in the early nineteenth century.[15]

Nations were said to have experienced periodic ups and downs, under great and under worthless rulers. As taught by Romanian textbooks in the interwar period (or under President Çeauşescu in more recent times), the Romanians were salvaged from evil forces during the two thousand years of their national existence by the periodic emergence of such great princes as Burebista, Steven the Great, Mircea the Great, Vlad the Impaler, and Michael the Brave. Romanian enslavement between the ages of great heroes was barely worth remembering.

How much effect did such governmental measures and such official propaganda have on the population? In my opinion, they were not completely successful. Take, for instance, the attempt by several East Central European governments to replace the old warrior nobility with a new privileged estate that was to be unconditionally loyal to the state. Czechoslovakia tried to build the new state on the Czech legionaries of World War I fame, who were rewarded with land in ethnically mixed areas and were invited into the officer corps and the administration. Yet the legionaries could not stop either the growing disloyalty of the Sudeten Germans before the Munich Agreement or the secession of Slovakia from the Czechoslovak state shortly after Munich. In Hungary, Regent Admiral Miklós Horthy created an "Order of Heroes" mainly from among middle-class elements and better-off farmers who had actively opposed the Soviet republic headed by Béla Kun. It was expected that this new elite would defend the regent in his hour of need. Yet on October 15, 1944, not a single one of Horthy's Heroes rose to defend their leader against the German SS and the Hungarian fascists.[16]

The rise of fascism in the 1930s presented the interwar governments with their greatest challenge. The left-wing movements, on the one hand, were generally easy to deal with because they lacked popular support; the far Right, on the other hand, appealed to millions of people, with its ultranationalist, anticapitalist, anticonservative, and antiestablishment message. It was in part because of the fascist challenge that the threatened governments of Hungary, Romania, and Poland increased their anti-Semitic sloganeering, strengthened their social welfare measures, and attempted to impose military discipline on society. In other countries, such as Yugoslavia, the fascist movements were much weaker. There, however, it was agitation among the ethnic minorities that caused the government to experiment with harsher measures.

By the 1930s, the conservative governments of Poland, Hungary, Austria, Romania, Yugoslavia, and Bulgaria had adopted some fascist paraphernalia and even some fascist practices so as to take "the sail out of the wind of the radical right." As a result, not a single radical rightist movement was able to seize power in East Central Europe, not at least until the coming of the Germans. But, meanwhile, some conservative regimes had changed to such an extent as to be nearly indistinguishable from their fascist opponents.

The exception to all this was Czechoslovakia, which remained democratic until after the Munich Agreement on September 29, 1938. It is impossible to tell whether a more fascistlike Czechoslovak government would have been able to prevent the dismemberment of the state in 1938 and 1939. In any case, beginning in 1938–39, the governments of both the Czech Protectorate and Slovakia were busy emulating the German and Italian fascists.

World War II brought independence to Croatia and Slovakia as well as at least the promise of independence to the Ukrainians. In these respects, the Germans showed more foresight than the Western powers and the Soviet Union, for even though, after the war, the triumphant Allies allowed the reunification of Czechoslovakia and Yugoslavia, a few decades later the drive for Slovak, Slovene, Croatian, Bosnian, Macedonian, and Ukrainian independence became irresistible.

In the dire emergency of war, every East Central European government attempted to impose iron discipline on the population and to unify the nation. It does not seem that these measures were particularly successful. With or without an authoritarian government, the Polish people would still have defended their country against the traditional German and Russian enemies. Their rather authoritarian regime did not prevent the Yugoslav troops from surrendering to the German invaders, in 1941, in a matter of days. During the Germans' military campaign in the Soviet Union, the soldiers of the Slovak, Hungarian, Croatian, and Romanian armies showed not even a minimum of enthusiasm for the anti-Bolshevik crusade so triumphantly announced by their own governments.[17] Again, it was ethnic cleansing that alone appealed to the population. Masses of East Central Europeans as well as their authorities, whether on the local or the central level, participated in the Nazi extermination campaign against the Jews or in their own government's persecution of the ethnic minorities. Moreover, after the war, the new antifascist governments had no trouble recruiting willing helpers in setting up concentration camps for the German civilians and in driving the Germans, under atrocious conditions, across the border to Germany. It is not at all comforting to learn, especially from Norman Naimark's chapter, that the ethnic cleansing practiced by the Soviet Red Army and its East European auxiliaries against the German population was not more terrible than Stalin's persecution of the Chechens, the Ingush, and the Crimean Tatars in the Soviet Union.

The Communist governments arising in East Central Europe between 1945 and 1948 imitated the Hungarian Soviet Republic of 1919 by attempting to change everybody and everything within the shortest possible time. No doubt, conditions were somewhat favorable for such a drastic transformation because of the presence of Soviet troops in the area, because the prewar regimes had generally discredited themselves, and because the old social and political elites had largely disappeared.

We know only too well what the Communist regimes attempted to achieve, all the way from nationalizing nearly all the means of production and distribution through regulating birthrates to controlling even the chess clubs. Theirs was a project of social engineering carried to its logical extreme. The social and educational achievements of the Stalinist leaders were considerable at least at the beginning; so was the support the Communists enjoyed on the part of the formerly downtrodden, the intelligentsia, and even some surviving members of the old elite. Within a few years, however, much of what the Stalinists had said and done turned against them. It also became clear that the essence of the system was the political police, which, left to itself, decimated not only the anti-Communists and the non-Communists but even the Communists themselves. Millions were sent to jail or to concentration camps; instead of creating a better society, the Stalinist regimes created a system that devoured itself. Not even the political police was efficient: witness the Hungarian revolution of 1956, which took the Party and the police by surprise and against which they proved completely powerless. Again, it turned out that population management and the dream of creating a new, nobler body social, was precisely that: a dream.

Soviet tanks crushed the Hungarian revolution. Thereafter, even though Communism survived for another thirty years, the initial activism and enthusiasm of the Communist leaders and followers gave way to caution and intellectual stagnation. Gradually, the Communist leadership abandoned the hope of educating the public politically and of creating a new society. Now, the sole purpose of the Communist regimes was to survive, but even this failed in a surprisingly short time. Step by step, East Central Europe lined up with the rest of Europe; the age of social engineering had come to an end. Today it is the market, not the government, that changes and rejuvenates society.

NORMAN M. NAIMARK

10

Ethnic Cleansing Between War and Peace

THIS ESSAY EXPLORES four cases of "ethnic cleansing" that took place in the Soviet Union and East Central Europe at the end of the Second World War.[1] It reviews two related Soviet cases—the deportations of the Chechen-Ingush and Crimean Tatars in 1944—and two related East European cases—the expulsion of Germans from the Western, the so-called Reclaimed Territories of Poland, and from the former Sudetenland in Czechoslovakia. How did the respective states involved in these cases justify the deportation and expulsions of former citizens of a different nationality? What did the war have to do with these cases? What do the similarities and differences between the cases tell us about the nature of ethnic cleansing as a state-sponsored means of shaping and controlling populations?

The Soviet Background

From its inception, the Soviet state sought to mobilize its citizens and, at the same time, to control them. These dichotomous goals plagued the Soviet system until its very end. One of the ways to mobilize the large non-Russian populations of the Soviet Eurasian land mass was to grant them autonomy and a measure of self-government. In the 1920s and early 1930s, Soviet nationality policy encouraged among the subject peoples the development of national self-consciousness within finite borders of a geographical unit.[2] The Soviet state built up indigenous national elites within these units and provided them with a structure of governance over their respective peoples. Simultaneously, the Soviet state itself, and especially its police organs, used direct methods of controlling the population. From the institution of the passport system to the development of an elaborate program of residency permits, Moscow increasingly established mechanisms of control over the population as a whole.[3] If the goal was to mobilize the country for the attainment of socialism, then—in theory anyway—no one could opt out or disappear. Control of the borders, control of population movement, and control of the workplace were intended to insure full participation.

As a system motivated by Marxist-Leninist ideology, mobilization also depended on successful combat with and the defeat of the system's enemies. The aristocracy and bourgeoisie were the initial enemies of the new Soviet state, but they were roundly defeated, according to Soviet conceptions, in the civil war. The kulaks—supposedly wealthy farmers and their families—were identified as enemies of the state in the late 1920s, and, in 1932, they were deported en masse—some 1,100,000 people altogether—to the Far North, Central Asia, and Siberia.[4] Engineers, technical specialists, and other remaining bourgeois enemies were similarly dealt with at the beginning of the 1930s.[5] Amir Weiner has suggested that a critical moment in this history of attacks on class enemies came in 1936, with the promulgation of the new Soviet ("Stalin") constitution, which proclaimed the attainment of Socialism and the creation of the legal category of "enemies of the people." From this point forward, Weiner argues, national (or "biological") enemies tended to replace class ones, and deportations focused on enemy peoples rather than enemy classes. In some senses, the categories of class and nation were conflated into one.[6] Part of this process, as Terry Martin has demonstrated, included the elimination of many smaller national units and subunits as reactionary and unnecessary.[7] Already in 1937, 1938, and 1939, large nationality groups were subjected to forced deportations.[8] The Koreans and Chinese were removed from the Pacific region, ostensibly for security reasons, and deported to Kazakhstan. Poles and Germans were removed from homelands in the West and deported to Central Asia, as well.

The war exacerbated in every way Stalin's fears regarding national enemies at home and abroad. In the process of fighting a war with and suffering occupation by the Germans, the Soviet population itself became much more nationalistic. Both officially and unofficially, the language of class all but disappeared; ideas of racial affinity for other Slavic nations grew markedly, and racial stereotypes of Germans, Jews, and Central Asians became characteristic of the Soviets' worldview. The Russian people were exalted above all others; their inherent superiority was incontestably demonstrated by their victory in the war.[9] It may be too much to suggest that Stalin and Hitler learned from one another during the war. But Nazi-like racial thinking, including vicious stereotyping of the Jews, permeated Soviet society in the immediate postwar period and clearly influenced Stalin and the Soviet leadership. In fact, official and unofficial anti-Semitism threatened the safety of Soviet Jews in the last years of Stalin's reign, as demonstrated by the murder of Solomon Mikhoels and the attacks on the Jewish Anti-fascist Committee, as well as the planned deportation of the entire Jewish population to Siberia prior to Stalin's death in March 1953.[10]

The new postwar state ideology included the domination of the Russian (and to a lesser extent, Ukrainian and Belorussian) nations over the others. The multinational Soviet state was to take its cues from "the most outstanding [nation] of all," the Russians.[11] Stalin also emphasized in the foreign relations of the Soviet Union a strong neo-Pan-Slav element. The new Soviet man was to look like a Russian, speak like a Russian, and—if not Russian or Slavic himself—to recognize the inherent superiority of the Russian in the historical development of the lands in which he or she lived and in contemporary affairs. Any nation that stood in the way of this conception was imperiled. The deportations of Chechen-Ingush and of the Crimean Tatars in 1944 can only be understood as part of this story.

Chechens and Ingush

Lavrentii Beria was in full charge of the operation in the Northern Caucasus. He bivouacked army and NKVD (political police) troops among the Chechen and Ingush towns and villages from the end of 1943.[12] Locals were told that the military units were taking a rest from the war and that they would soon be returned to the front. The troops mixed easily with the villagers, often eating and living in their homes, and joining them in their customs. On February 23–24, 1944, Beria ordered the operation to start.[13] He called in Chechen Party leaders and told them about the fate of their people. Comrade Molaev, the representative of the Chechen Autonomous Republic to the Sovnarkom (Council of Peoples' Commissars), wept bitterly, but in the end he offered his services to make the deportations move more smoothly.[14] Troops went from house to house informing the residents that they had a half an hour (in some cases a bit more, in some less) to get themselves ready for transport. Many of the men were rounded up at work or in the fields and taken directly to the railheads.[15] Anyone who resisted was shot; indeed, the NKVD reported only sporadic cases of resistance.[16] Troops assembled villagers and townspeople, loaded them onto trucks—many deportees remembered that they were Studebakers, presumably fresh from Lend-Lease—and delivered them at previously designated railheads.[17] From the railway stations, the Chechen and Ingush nations were loaded into boxcars and shipped to Kazakhstan and Kirghizia, which were to be their homes until the mid-1950s.

The NKVD was ordered to clear all the Chechens and Ingush out of their homelands. No exceptions were allowed. Party leaders, war heroes, and famous intelligentsia writers and artists were sometimes sent separately and in somewhat better circumstances, but everyone had to go. Those who could not be moved were shot. In one particularly grisly case in the village of Khaibakh (Galanchozh District), there was no transportation available, so NKVD troops herded some 730 villagers into a barn, set it on fire, and shot those who tried to break away from the inferno.[18] Despite the careful planning and NKVD claims to a flawless operation, numbers of Chechen fighters escaped to the high mountain passes of the Caucasus. The attempts by specially trained mountain units to flush these Chechens out of their hideouts were studied by military historians of the Chechen war of the early 1990s.[19] But these few fighters aside, the entire Chechen and Ingush nations, 496,460 people, were deported from their homeland.[20] In theory, all the Chechens and Ingush living within the borders of the USSR were designated for deportation. Some thirty thousand Chechens living in northwestern Dagestan were deported, as were Chechens and Ingush living in Northern Ossetia.[21] Whether they were serving in army units or laboring in NKVD camps in the north, Chechens and Ingush were sent with their brethren to Kazakhstan and Kirghizia.

As in every case of ethnic cleansing and the forced deportation of peoples, large numbers of Chechens died in the process. Some three thousand perished even before being deported.[22] The NKVD readily supplied precise (and unquestionably low) figures about the numbers who died in harsh conditions of various transports, mostly the old, the infirm, and the very young. One can extrapolate from these separate figures that roughly ten thousand died in transport, from disease, hunger, and the cold.[23] The largest death toll came in the days and months after arrival, again extrapolating from NKVD statistics, roughly 100,000 in the first three years.[24] The local authorities were simply not prepared for the influx of these special settlers (*spetspereselentsy*, sometimes *spetsposelentsy*), a classification that had been previously used only for kulaks. Despite NKVD orders to Kazakh and Kirghiz Communist Parties to make building and working materials available to the settlers and to provide adequate food and clothing at the deportees' destinations, the Chechens and Ingush found themselves without work, food, clothing, or a roof over their heads.[25] They died by the tens of thousands in fearful poverty.

The official justification for the deportations emphasized the collaboration of the Chechens during the war: "Many Chechens and Ingush were traitors to the homeland, changing over to the side of the fascist occupiers, joining the ranks of diversionaries and spies left behind the lines of the Red Army by the Germans. They formed armed bands at the behest of the Germans fighting against Soviet power."[26] Although it is unlikely that the Chechens were any more enthusiastic about the Soviet war effort than other Muslims of the

Caucasus or Central Asia, it is also unlikely that they were less patriotic. The issue of the exact extent of Chechen-Ingush collaboration cannot be fully answered without a thorough investigation of relevant Soviet and German archives. But available evidence indicates that they did not collaborate in any significant way, that they participated fully in the war effort, and that their war record was like that of many peoples not subjected to removal from their homelands.[27] John Dunlop confirms the observations of other historians of the Chechen deportations, Aleksandr Nekrich and Robert Conquest, that there were no more than one hundred recorded instances of "aiding and abetting" the enemy.[28] Why then *were* they deported? The explanation is twofold and goes back to rationalizations of state (shaping the "body politic") and rationalizations of history (settling old scores), both of which were more easily dealt with during wartime.

Although hardly the collaborators portrayed by the Soviet documents on the deportations, the Chechens and Ingush were unquestionably a thorn in the side of the Soviet authorities. As Muslim mountain peoples, nearly a half million altogether, the Chechens and Ingush maintained much more cultural and religious autonomy than the Soviets liked. Aleksandr Iakovlev maintains that the Soviet authorities felt particularly threatened by the "anti-Soviet" Sufi Muslim brotherhoods that flourished in the mountains.[29] Local *obkom* (regional Party organization) documents speak of the resiliency of the Chechen clan leadership in the face of Soviet education and propaganda campaigns and of the difficulty recruiting Chechens into Grozny's working class, associated almost exclusively with the local oil industry.[30] Chechen women were particularly difficult for the Party to reach, in good measure because their fathers and husbands, in the Party and government and not, refused to allow their participation in public affairs.[31]

Stalin and Beria would not forget easily how difficult it was to pacify the Chechens and Ingush during the civil war and after. Chechen and Ingush resistance to collectivization, which included pitched battles with armed units, also was fresh in Soviet leaders' memories.[32] The attachment of the Chechen and Ingush to their homelands; the difficulty of imposing modern state forms on a resilient traditional society; and the ability of the Chechens to resist both direct pressures from Moscow and the modernization expected from the granting of national institutional forms—all these factors made the Soviet leadership determined to deal once and for all with the Chechen problem.

The fate of the Chechen-Ingush Autonomous Republic also leads one to think that the Soviets were in search of a permanent solution to the Chechen question. The region was officially dissolved in 1944, and neighboring Dagestan, Northern Ossetia, and the Georgia and Stavropol region eagerly seized and absorbed their designated sections of the Chechen and Ingush lands.[33]

They renamed towns and villages, bulldozed Chechen graveyards and monuments, and erased any remaining signs of Chechen presence in the region. No one spoke of the deportations of the Chechens in the newspapers, in meetings, or in public. Postdeportation records of Grozny obkom meetings never mention the peoples who had once lived there.[34] They disappeared even from history books and encyclopedias. In exile in Kazakhstan and Kirghizia, the Chechens and Ingush were not allowed to use their language in schools, nor could they foster their culture in any public way.

Even after the death of Stalin in March 1953, the Soviet authorities refused to allow the Chechens to return to their homelands, though a few began to make their way back to the Northern Caucasus in any case. After Nikita Khrushchev's secret speech in February 1956 called attention to the violations and "excesses" of Stalinist policy in the treatment of Soviet nationalities, thousands of Chechens and Ingush began the long trek back to the mountains. But unlike other nationalities, the Chechens and Ingush were explicitly forbidden to return to their homelands. They were removed from the status of being *spetspereselentsy*, but, stated the directive of the Supreme Soviet, "this does not mean that they have the right to the return of their property confiscated during their expulsion, nor do they have the right to return to the places, from which they were expelled."[35] In fact, the Soviet government intended to prevent the Chechens and Ingush from returning home and to create for them an autonomous region in Kazakhstan. But Chechen and Ingush Party leaders and intelligentsia resolutely rejected any such "solution" to their problems.[36] Despite opposition from the new rulers of the Chechen-Ingush territory, the Soviet government finally relented in 1957. The Chechens and Ingush Autonomous Republic was reestablished, and all the Chechens and Ingush were allowed to return to their homes.[37]

The Crimean Tatars

The deportation of the Crimean Tatars from their homeland to Uzbekistan and Tajikistan in May 1944 was justified, as was that of the Chechens and Ingush, by the alleged collaboration of Tatars during the war. Unlike the case of the Chechen and Ingush lands, the Germans actually set up an occupation regime in the Crimea from October 1941 until April 1944. Trouble was brewing for the Tatars already in 1943, when Russian partisan leaders A. N. Mokrousov and A.V. Martynov accused them of collaborating with the enemy. V. Bulatov, head of the Tatar obkom, forced Mokrousov to recant his statement. There were large numbers of Tatars in the resistance, he insisted. Moreover, many partisan groups, such as Mokrousov and Martynov's, would not allow Tatars to join, and instead of seeking cooperation with Tatar villagers, would attack them and steal their food, thus driving them into the camp of the enemy.[38] Even though Mokrousov and Martynov recanted, local Russians continued to complain about the Tatars and their friendliness toward the Germans.[39] Criticisms of Tatar collaboration under the Nazis found their way to Beria, head of the NKVD, who reported them to Stalin.[40] In the Tatar case, like that of the Chechens and Ingush, it is unlikely that their active collaboration with the Germans was any more noteworthy than that among Russians or Ukrainians of the region.[41] But Stalin and Beria used these charges to deport the entire Tatar nation, roughly 189,000 men, women, and children, from the Crimea.

NKVD and Red Army troops, already experienced from similar operations in the Northern Caucasus, surrounded Tatar villages and homes on the night of May 17–18, 1944, demanding that the Tatars assemble for transport to the east. As in the case of the Chechens and Ingush, every single Tatar had to go, whatever their position in society, whether married to a Russian or not (something that was much more common among the Tatars than among Chechens or Ingush).[42] The rail transport in sealed, unhygienic boxcars, much like the case of the Chechens and Ingush, took a fearful toll in Tatar lives.[43] Although an educated and highly adaptable people, the Tatars also suffered terribly in the special settlements designated for them in Central Asia. After the transport, they were in no condition to work and therefore could find no way to support themselves and their families. The indigenous population refused to help, and they treated the Tatars with brutality and disdain, and the local NKVD warders of the special settlers sometimes beat and exploited them.[44] Many thousands died before the situation stabilized at the beginning of the 1950s.[45] According to Tatar historians, the losses from the deportations and settlement reached as much as 45 percent of the entire Tatar population.[46] The victims were mostly women and children.[47]

Undoubtedly, long-term reasons of state as defined by Stalin and Beria lay behind the deportations. The Soviet leadership wanted a Crimea without Tatars, thus fulfilling a goal of Russian statesmen ever since the incorporation of the Crimea into the Russian Empire during the reign of Catherine the Great. After the Crimean War of 1853 to 1855, the imperial authorities deported 100,000 Tatars from the Crimea.[48] Now, after the liberation of the Crimea in 1944, Stalin and his lieutenants were determined to clean out the Crimea of *all* foreigners, Tatars primarily, but also Greeks (15,040), Bulgarians (13,422), and Armenians (9,621), who were deported soon after the Tatars.[49] Although the deportations of the Tatars had racial overtones, as did those of the Chechens and Ingush, it was not primarily race that was on the Soviets' minds; Tatars from other parts of Russia were allowed to stay where they were.

Tatar residents in the Crimea who were off fighting the war were, however, like their Chechen-Ingush comrades-in-arms, also sent into exile.

When, after the war, a few hundred Tatars managed to return legally to the Crimea, the local authorities reacted with sharp protests to Moscow. Foreign espionage services would inevitably use the Tatar population for their nefarious purposes, they claimed. Thus, not a single Tatar should be allowed to stay in the Crimea. If released from the status of special settlers, then the Tatars should be allowed to settle in other parts of Russia, just not in the Crimea. Stalin is reported to have met with Comrade Bulaev of the Crimean obkom and to have given "the order not to allow Tatars in the Crimea under any conditions, because they serve as sources for foreign spies."[50] Although a few exceptions were allowed for family reasons, most of the Tatars who had filtered back to the Crimea were deported again to other parts country.[51] As in the case of the Chechens and Ingush, Tatar monuments were destroyed, books and manuscripts were burned, and history was rewritten to suggest that Tatars had been nothing but bandits and thieves over the course of modern Russian history and made no contribution to the development of their homeland.[52] Already on August 14, 1944, the Crimean obkom issued an order to change all the Tatar names of towns, cities, regions, *kolkhozes* and *sovkhozes*, "in connection with the changed circumstances of the Crimea."[53] Unlike the Chechens and Ingush, the Tatars were never formally rehabilitated by the Soviet government and never given permission to return to the Crimea. During perestroika, however, many did indeed return and sought to regain rights to their homes and lands, a struggle that continues to this day.

Given the contemporary definitions of *ethnic cleansing*, there can be little question of classifying the Soviet deportation of the Chechens-Ingush and Crimean Tatars in this fashion. Stalin, Beria, and the Soviet leadership forcibly removed these peoples from their homelands and deported them to regions from which there was no escape. That tens of thousands died in the deportations and when they arrived at their destinations did not overly concern the Soviet authorities, though clearly they did not intend to kill off these nations in a genocidal attack. Instead, policies were implemented to reeducate the Chechens-Ingush and Crimean Tatars, forcing them to forget their homelands and their cultures. Unlike other cases of ethnic cleansing in the twentieth century, the Soviets did not insure that a particular nation take the place of the Chechens and Ingush in the Northern Caucasus or the Tatars in the Crimea. Thus, the deportations were not intended to create an ethnically homogeneous region, as in the cases of ethnic cleansing in the Balkans. Nevertheless, the eliminationist attack on the Chechen-Ingush and Tatars was complete; alien elements were violently excised from the body politic.

The East European Background

The war had barely begun when both the Polish and Czechoslovak governments-in-exile began talking about the expulsion of the Germans from their respective countries after the victory. Both governments referred frequently to the ostensibly successful transfer of Greeks and Turks by the Treaty of Lausanne in January 1923. The Great Powers supervised this transfer and provided the financial backing to relocate the exchanged populations.[54] For the Poles and Czechs, the operative principle was the forced relocation of a population under the auspices of international organizations. Indeed, both governments talked to each other about the expulsions of their respective German populations and the need to lobby with Allied governments to insure the acceptance of population transfer in principle.[55]

The Polish and Czechoslovak governments-in-exile did not need to worry. If, in the Polish case, poor relations with the Soviets created a series of roadblocks to the London government's postwar aims, there was nearly perfect agreement all around that the Germans would have to be moved, both out of postwar Poland and out of the former Sudetenland. The vast movements of peoples during the war itself made further mass migrations, especially involving the hated Germans, unproblematic. The Soviet Union's experiences with deporting large numbers of people also made their officials quite receptive to the entreaties of the Poles and Czechoslovaks.[56] Edvard Beneš, president of the Czechoslovak government, claimed that he received the blessings of Churchill and even Roosevelt for the transfers.[57] Stalin and Viacheslav Molotov were also fully informed and offered no objections. Allied agreement with the principle of transferring the Germans was canonized finally at Potsdam. The text of article XIII read: "The three Governments, having considered the question in all its aspects, recognize that the transfer to Germany of German populations, or elements thereof, remaining in Poland, Czechoslovakia, and Hungary, will have to be undertaken. They agree that any transfers that take place should be effected in an orderly and humane manner."[58]

Sudetenland

Although the cleansing of Germans from Czechoslovakia at the end of the war and beginning of the peace was as total and merciless as the cases of Soviet ethnic cleansing, the causes are much more transparent. In addition, in the Czechoslovak (and Polish) cases, the apparatus of state could not directly control the nature of the violence, and thus it was more haphazard and indiscriminate. The Germans in Czechoslovakia, like the Chechen-Ingush and the

Tatars, were accused by the authorities of being traitors to the state.[59] This was more justified in the case of Czechoslovakia, given the activities of the Germans in the interwar Republic, not to mention the widespread Sudeten German sympathy for and participation in the Nazi occupation. As Beneš reportedly put it: "Our Germans . . . have betrayed our state, betrayed our democracy, betrayed us, betrayed humaneness, and betrayed humankind."[60]

It is also interesting that in both the Soviet cases and in the case of Czechoslovakia (and Poland), the government acted to eliminate the rights of a national minority in the name of the modernization of the state. In the Soviet cases against the Chechens-Ingush and Tatars, this rationalization was muted and implicit in the removal of these peoples from their traditional homelands in the Caucasus and Crimea, where they had allegedly held back Sovietization and Socialist mobilization. In the Czech (and Polish) cases, democratic governments justified the elimination of minority rights because they were an impediment to the smooth functioning of a citizen government. During the war, the Czech government-in-exile was ready to grant Czechoslovak citizenship to those Germans with proven antifascist credentials as long as they swore fealty to the new Czech Republic. But, to the consternation of the Sudeten German Social Democrats, who worked closely with the Czech government-in-exile in England, the Czechs refused to grant any minority rights to the Germans, meaning they would shut down their schools and special institutions, the German university would be closed, and the same would happen to Hungarian schools and institutions in Slovakia.[61]

Given the history of the Comintern's support for minority rights in Eastern Europe, the Czech Communists—and other Communists, as well—found themselves in a difficult position when it came to the question of expelling the Germans. During the war, the Communists' position, articulated by Georgi Dimitrov in Moscow, was that those Germans responsible for the war and its crimes should be tried and sentenced, whereas the German workers and peasants should be reeducated. But the Czech Communists quickly realized that the "German question" had tremendous political resonance, and by the end of the war the Communist leader Klement Gottwald, like Beneš, called for the expulsion of the Germans from the Czech lands and of the Hungarians from Slovakia.[62] The Soviets readily confirmed the policy of the Communists in this regard. There was virtually no difference between non-Communist and Communist politicians on the issue of the expulsions of Germans in postwar Czechoslovakia or Poland.

Beneš and the Czechoslovak government-in-exile announced from the very beginning of German rule in Bohemia and Moravia that the postwar state should be reconstructed in its former borders.[63] They were more insistent about maintaining the eastern borders than the western, meaning the inclusion of some three million Germans who resided there. (The Czechoslovak leaders eventually gave in to Stalin's demands for the Carpatho-Ukraine in the East.) Initially, Beneš called for the expulsion of one million German fascists, Henleinists, and their sympathizers. Later, he spoke of expelling two million Germans.[64] In 1943, his deputy, Edvard Taborsky, devised a plan that made it possible for German antifascists, Social Democrats, and those who had suffered at the hands of the Nazis to stay in the new democratic state. Smallholding German peasants would also be allowed to remain if they neither involved themselves in politics nor exploited their Czech neighbors.[65] However, in a meeting with Stalin on December 16, 1943, Beneš made it clear that he wanted to solve the German problem once and for all and create a Slavic Czechoslovak state free of Germans and Hungarians.

> The defeat of Germany presents us with the singular historical possibility to clean out radically the German element in our state. . . . The future republic should be a state of Czechs, Slovaks, and Carpatho-Ukrainians. It should be a state of Slavic nations. From Czechoslovakia should be obligatorily expelled all German teachers, professors, SS types, Gestapo-men, members of the Hitler youth, all active members of the Henlein movement and the entire German bourgeoisie, all rich Germans.[66]

Here and elsewhere during the war Beneš and his advisors talked about some "good" Germans being able to stay in Czechoslovakia. By the end of the war, however, no Czech politician or political party could resist the rising wave of anti-German Czech nationalism that demanded revenge and retaliation for the insults of Munich, the loss of Czech sovereignty, and the trying circumstances of the war itself. As the German armies retreated before the Soviet advance, Czech militia, many recruited from Prague after the uprising, Communist action groups, and the so-called Svoboda Army moved into German areas and attacked civilians in their homes and on the streets.

These armed fighters drew few distinctions between antifascist Germans, plain farmers, or Henleinist sympathizers. In a paroxysm of violence, which shocked even experienced Soviet tank commanders and political officers, Czechs beat up Germans, set them on fire, forced them to do humiliating and life-threatening tasks, and showed them no mercy. In a few cases, there were outright pogroms, where Czech militia rampaged through towns and villages, shooting Germans at will.[67]

It quickly became clear that all of the three million Germans in Czechoslovakia would be forced to leave their homes and that the Three Powers would not stop the process. Not only did Potsdam sanction the transfers from Czechoslovakia and Poland, but the proviso that they should be undertaken in "a humane and orderly fashion" may have cost more German lives than it saved. The flow of refugees was temporarily stopped in order to insure that they would be taken care of when they arrived at their destinations in occupied Germany. The largest number of Sudeten Germans were designated to reside in Bavaria in the American zone, and the Americans first delayed and then slowed down the transfers for months, hoping to guarantee decent rail transportation to Germany and housing and food when the refugees arrived. The problem was that despite Allied protests, the Czechs continued to hound the Germans, removing them from their homes and villages to work and prison camps, where many thousands were brutalized, took sick because of the lack of decent food and hygiene, and died.[68] At the former Nazi camp at Theresienstadt (Teresin), the Germans worried openly about what would happen to them if the local Russian commandant did not protect them against the Czechs. One secret Soviet report back to the Central Committee in Moscow noted that the Germans repeatedly begged the Russians to stay: "'If the Red Army leaves, we are finished!' We now see the manifestations of hatred for the Germans. They [the Czechs] don't kill them, but torment them like livestock. The Czechs look at them like cattle."[69]

By the fall of 1947, almost the entire Sudeten German population was transferred to Germany.[70] Place-names were changed, Germans monuments destroyed, and graveyards plundered. German property was seized and in some cases turned over to Czech settlers from urban areas. As in other cases of ethnic cleansing, the Czechs were determined to erase the memory, as well as the culture, civilization, and history, of the Sudeten Germans. Also as in the other cases, ethnic cleansing was justified by immediate causes; the Germans had been traitors to the interwar Czechoslovak Republic and, in order for the new state to survive, they would have to be expelled. But the deportations, like the others, also represented long-standing rivalries and resentments against German domination of the Czechs, going back to White Mountain and including ill-treatment at the hands of the Habsburgs.[71] Finally, Communists and non-Communists alike approved, indeed urged, the expulsion of the Germans as part of a new stage in the development of the Czechoslovak social and economic order. To be sure, the national enmity that surfaced naturally as a consequence of the war gave the expulsions the character of a spontaneous wave of nationalist revenge for the German occupation. But the Czechs framed this national upheaval in terms of a social revolution to remove German landowners and factory owners from positions of power and seize their properties in the name of a radical democratic, antifascist state.[72]

Poland

The case of the expulsion of the Germans from Poland is both more and less complicated than that of their expulsion from Czechoslovakia. It is less complicated because the nature of the German occupation of Poland, in which the Poles were exploited, brutalized, and subject to mass murder, puts their lust for revenge and their fearsome attacks on the Germans in a more understandable context. The Czechs, after all, did not suffer terribly at the hands of the Germans, certainly not in comparison to the Poles. It is a more complicated problem for several reasons. First of all, Polish demands for the expulsion of the Germans were related to the shifting sands of Polish territorial claims during the war. The Soviet Union was increasingly insistent on incorporating eastern Poland (western Belorussia and western Ukraine) into its territories, much as it had done as a result of the Nazi-Soviet Pact of 1939. As this demand became increasingly likely to become transformed into a reality, the Poles sought compensation in the West from the Germans, though one should be clear that Polish claims on Danzig (Gdansk), east Prussia, and German territories east of the Oder and Neisse were presented to the Allies long before it became apparent they would lose territories in the East. Early internal memorandums (1942) of the London government indicated that the Poles were interested in territory east of the Oder but were ready to settle for the eastern Neisse. They worried about the overwhelming number of Germans living between the two branches of the Neisse, who would be impossible to incorporate into the new Polish Republic and who could not be expelled because—it was thought—Western public opinion would not tolerate it.[73] But as the war progressed, Polish ambitions grew, even to the point of demanding occupation rights along the Baltic as far as Rostock-Warnemünde and Rügen and participating in the occupation of the Kiel Canal.[74]

Although the Polish case is also complicated by the fact that the Soviets broke off relations with the government-in-exile in April 1943, ostensibly over the Katyn affair (involving mass graves of Polish soldiers found in the Katyn Forest), there remained few differences between the Communists and non-Communists on the issue of expelling the Germans. In London the Polish government-in-exile worked out legal procedures that would deprive the Germans of Polish citizenship and of their property.[75] But the end result was to be the same: the total expulsion of the Germans from the Western Territories. When Stanislaw Mikolajczyk returned to Poland in June 1945, to join the new Government of National Unity agreed to at Yalta, his speeches were as militant about ridding the country of Germans as were those of Wladyslaw Gomulka, Communist minister for the "Recovered Territories" (*Ziemia odzyskana*). As deputy prime minister of the new government and head of the Polish Peasant Party, Mikolajczyk saw the expulsion of the Germans as a social as well as national act. German exploiters, the German middle class, and German landowners would be expelled and replaced by Poles. The Polish peasantry would no longer suffer at the hands of the German upper class.[76] Meanwhile, Gomulka sent out orders to Party officials to get rid of the Germans: "We must expel all the Germans because countries are built on national lines and not on multinational ones."[77]

The situation of Germans in the Western Territories was also much more fluid and uncertain than that of the Germans in the Sudetenland. The Red Army reached the Oder already in January and February of 1945, halting for a strategic regrouping before the final assault on Berlin in April. Many hundreds of thousands of Germans fled before the advancing Soviet armies, only to return to their homes after the capitulation in early May. In Wrocław (Breslau) for example, some tens of thousands of Germans returned after the signing of the armistice, assuming that their native city would remain German, as it had been for centuries.[78] Between May and the Potsdam conference in late July, tens of thousands of Germans were moving in both directions, west and east. (One is reminded of the story frequently recounted of the sad plight of the Jews after the Nazi-Soviet Pact. They crossed the river Neman between the Soviet and Nazi zones heading in both directions from the opposite banks, those going to Soviet territory and to German territory gesticulating to the others that they were crazy.) The Germans who returned to their Silesian and Pomeranian homes counted on the fact that these lands, temporarily assigned to Polish occupation by the Yalta Conference, would be returned to Germany by the eventual Peace Conference. Even after Potsdam, where the Allies agreed to the transfer of Germans from territory occupied by the Poles, the Germans continued to hope that either a Peace Conference would return these lands to German control or that Allied cooperation itself would break down and German sovereignty over the territory would be restored.[79]

Those who fled west did so under fierce Polish pressure. No less than the Czechs, Poles attacked, subdued, and humiliated German civilians, seizing their property and goods and sometimes throwing them out of their homes. Germans were murdered and beaten senseless; there were thousands of cases of suicide, more often than not of whole families.[80] The Poles turned the former concentration camps of the Third Reich (Auschwitz, Birkenau, Jaworzno, and others) into labor camps for Nazis and suspected Nazis. Some camps were used simply to house Germans scheduled for transfer. In both cases, Germans suffered disease, malnutrition, and fearsome abuse. Thousands died as a consequence.[81]

In this Polish "Wild West" (*dziki Zachod*), gangs of marauders, usually from Central Poland (the so-called *centralniacy*), stole as much as they could from the Germans before returning to their homes laden with loot (*szaber*, from the German *Schabernack*): furniture, clothes, valuables, and foodstuffs.[82] Rape and pillage were common; it made no difference to the Poles whether the Germans they attacked had been antifascists or not. To make matters worse, the police and civilian Polish authorities were weak and ineffective in the face of these depredations, and they were generally unwilling to interfere on behalf of the Germans. Sometimes the Soviets protected Germans against the Poles but very inconsistently.[83] By the end of 1945, Polish settlers from the eastern lands given over to the Soviet Union arrived in the Western Territories in search of homes and farmsteads. The pressure on the Germans increased even more, and they quickly joined the rail transports to occupied Germany provided by the Allies.

That reasons of state lay behind the expulsion of the Germans is apparent from the important exceptions made to the wholesale expulsion of Germans from the region. Both Communist and non-Communist Polish leaders understood perfectly well that their ability to hold on to the "Reclaimed Lands" depended on contradictory needs: first, to expel Germans from the occupied territories so that German claims to them would be weakened and, second, to make these lands economically useful to Poland and the rest of Europe. One simply could not expel all the Germans and hope to keep industry, mining, transportation, and manufacturing from grinding to a complete halt. The result was that while continuing to insist that all Germans be expelled, they also applied a liberal definition of nationality when confronted with the problem of who was, after all, a German. It was recognized that many Germanized Poles had taken on German citizenship as a way to survive the war in their homes; many of these were allowed to become Polish citizens. The so-called autochthons—Mazurians, Silesians, Kashubians, and others—were designated as Germanized Poles and encouraged to "re-Polonize" and remain.[84] Moreover, many thousands of German workers were kept in place by the Polish authorities. They were given special rations and housing privileges; their work was invaluable to maintaining the economic infrastructure of a badly destroyed Poland.[85] Mikolajczyk encouraged the government to undertake training programs for Polish peasants and workers resettled from the East so that they could move into these jobs occupied by the Germans, but he also was determined to rid Poland of every last German: "for us there can be no doubt that every German is before anything else a German nationalist."[86]

In deporting the Germans wholesale, the Poles were less concerned than the Czechs with the negative role played by the German minority in the interwar Republic, though they too were not unhappy to see minority rights disappear. Like the Czechs, they looked at the new stage of state building after the war as one where a homogeneous Polish population would not be impeded by large "alien" minorities such as the Germans, Ukrainians, and

Jews. Ironically, the Communists insured that Roman Dmowski's ultranationalist dream of "Poland for the Poles" would be accomplished. Yet, even more important to the Poles when thinking about the expulsions was the fact that Allied recognition of the incorporation (versus occupation) of the Recovered Lands could only take place if the territories were thoroughly Polonized and integrated into the new Poland.[87] The Poles also used strategic arguments to defend the expulsion of the Germans. The Baltic coastline of Poland had to be secured from German control and influence from east Prussia to the Oder. Mikolajczyk argued, moreover, that German domination of East Central Europe depended on their control of the Oder and its tributaries to the south. Therefore, the Oder and western Neisse border was critical to depriving the Germans of their expansionist routes.[88]

Conclusions

Stalin used the cover of war to take care of unfinished business with the Chechens, Ingush, and Crimean Tatars. Nationalist sentiment and reasons of state impressed on him and his lieutenant Beria the need to get the Chechens-Ingush (and Balkars and Karachaevtsy—two small Muslim mountaineer nationalities in the Northern Caucasus) out of the mountains of the Northern Caucasus. From the available documentation, one can only speculate about Stalin's motives. He may have been interested, for example, in creating some form of "Christian"—if not purely Slavic—domination of the mountainous borderlands between Russia and the Caucasian region by turning the region over to Georgians, Northern Ossetians, and Russians from the Stavropol region. The Soviets' reasoning in the case of the Crimean Tatars may have been much the same. The Crimea, perceived as vulnerable to Turkish and Western penetration, was to be cleared of the Tatars, as well as Bulgarians, Armenians, and Greeks. (The Germans had already done the job of dealing with the Jews and Karaites.) They would be replaced by Russians and Ukrainians.

From the point of view of the Soviet leadership, Crimean Tatars and Chechens-Ingush were too attached to their cultures, mores, and histories to become effective Soviet nationalities. They were also small enough to be moved en masse and not to be missed as critical members of the labor force or as reliable masters of contiguous territory. For Stalin and Beria, these peoples were to be sentenced to extinction as nationalities. The idea was that their individual cultures—if not the peoples themselves—would perish in the vastness of their new and alien Central Asian special settlements. They would be assimilated into the Kazakh and Uzbek worlds, and their homelands would be absorbed by other, ostensibly more reliable nations, renamed, and given a new history. This was less a racist concept than a nationalist one, though racism was never terribly far from the surface in the treatment of these peoples by the Soviet authorities. The peoples could survive, just not as the claimants to their homelands.

The Czechs and Poles also used the cover of war and the transition from war to peace to settle old scores. The problem of the German minority had plagued both countries in the interwar period. Nationalist sentiments and the understandable desire for revenge permeated the Polish and Czech populations, as they eagerly and brutally turned the tables on their former German persecutors. But a major motivation of the Czechs and Poles for expelling the Germans, like the Soviet cases, derived from the desire of the new postwar governments (and their predecessors in London) to rationalize and control their societies by making them ethnically homogeneous, fully responsive to the needs and goals of the dominant nationality. Throughout Europe and the Soviet Union, this seemed to be the dominant theme of the new stage of state building that accompanied the end of World War II. The era of the recognition of minority rights, which was at least formally accepted as part of the post–World War I settlement, had come to a crashing end.

Politics also played an important role in Poland and Czechoslovakia, as it did in Stalin and Beria's decisions to deport the Chechen-Ingush and Crimean Tatars. No Communist or non-Communist political leader in Prague or Warsaw could hurt his or her chances for success by adopting a virulently anti-German stance. Strategic, historical, and economic arguments played a role; no one wanted the Germans to remain in territory that might be contested in the future by a German government. But the desire of both communists and democrats to build and consolidate power through popular approval buried any arguments that antifascist Germans, or those considered progressive citizens of interwar Poland or interwar Czechoslovakia, should be allowed to stay. Politics in the Soviet Union were more subtle and are much more difficult to discern given the paucity of documents. Still, conflicts between Russians and Tatars in the Crimea obviously influenced the decision of Stalin and Beria to deport the Tatars. The Northern Ossetians, Georgians, and Stavropol Russians had their eyes on Grozny's oil industry and pieces of Chechen-Ingush territory, and that must have made a difference to Stalin and Beria's decision to deport the Chechens and Ingush.

As a brief postscript to the history of ethnic cleansing at the end of the war and beginning of the peace, it is worth noting that none of these stories is finished. The Chechens continue to resist Russian attempts to incorporate them into the new Russian state. Serious evidence was discovered indicating that the Russians advocated deporting the Chechens once again in the mid-1990s if they lost the war.[89] Recent journalistic accounts emphasize that the trauma of 1944 plays a major role in contemporary Chechen thinking about resistance.[90] The Crimean Tatars seek to regain their homes and villages through protracted political lobbying between rival Ukrainian and Russian parties in the Crimea. Progress has been stymied by the impasse between the Ukrainian government and local Crimean (Russian) authorities. The Poles and Germans finally signed a treaty in June 1991 that put an end to decades of uncertainty about the incorporation of the Western Territories into Poland. The Poles apologized to the Germans for the bitter fate they suffered after the war; the Germans begged the Poles forgiveness for the horrible events of the occupation. Relations between the two nations improved markedly as a result.

Given the relatively benign Nazi occupation of the Czech lands under the Protectorate during the war, it is counterintuitive that the Czechs were as brutal in their retribution against the Germans as the Poles, who suffered under the Germans in much more profound ways. For similar reasons, it is hard to understand that it took the Czechs and Germans so long to come to the same kinds of agreements concluded by the Poles and Germans earlier in the 1990s. Finally, in January 1997, a treaty was signed between the Czechs and Germans, by which both sides apologized for the brutalities in the war and both sides agreed to recognize the finality of the expulsion, though in Czech the word *odsun* (transfer) is still used. Politics explains much of the difference between the Polish and Czech cases. The powerful Sudeten German lobby, located in Bavaria and able to influence the Christian Social Union (CSU), made it very difficult for the ruling Christian Democratic Union (CDU) to engage in dialogue with the Czechs. But the Czechs themselves were not entirely blameless. Nationalism in the service of political leaders remains a force to be reckoned with everywhere.

YAEL ZERUBAVEL 11

Female Images in a State of War

The Israeli War Widow in Fiction and Film

EVERY NATION creates myths, symbols, and rituals that embody the essence of its unique history and identity. Invoking figures, sites, and objects associated with past events, these symbolic forms create an awareness of common roots and a continuous tradition. Their emphasis on the nation's historical continuity implies not only a shared past but also a vision of a shared future.[1] By reinforcing the nation's boundaries vis-à-vis other groups, they provide evidence that supports and substantiates the claim for a distinct national identity. As a result, myths, symbols, and rituals become an important tool for rendering the nation a less-elusive reality, turning what Benedict Anderson referred to as an "imagined community" into a more tangible collective experience.[2]

These symbolic forms thus belong to the sacred domain of society's life, binding its members into a historical, political, and moral community.[3] Hence, the construction of these collective symbolic forms is most critical during the nation's formative years. Often, the emphasis on a shared origin is further enhanced by the experience of a struggle to defend the group's identity and heritage against external pressures. The experience of a national struggle intensifies the need for the creation of symbolic forms in support of the national cause. Myths, symbols, and rituals thus play a central role in shaping the nation's patriotic heritage and agenda.[4] When the national struggle is resolved, the changing political situation is likely to modify the status and meaning of these symbolic forms. With the establishment of a nation-state, these forms often assume an official, or semiofficial, status. Paradoxically, although this formalization indicates their success, it is likely to result in a process of distancing. Excessive formalization runs the risk of a loss of popular appeal and political relevance. In less extreme cases, however, the formalization may expose these forms to a more critical scrutiny and thus lead to a significant modification of their meaning.[5]

This chapter examines the transformations of a national symbol in Israeli culture since the late 1940s to date, focusing on the representation of the war widow in fiction and film. Given her affiliation with the Fallen Soldier, a key mythical figure in Israeli national culture, the war widow too has become a symbolic figure of national significance. The war widow's image is therefore tied to the centrality of patriotic death to Zionist ideology and culture.

In its heyday Zionism developed an elaborate patriotic lore that raised sacrifice for the nation as a supreme value. Influenced by traditional Jewish concepts of martyrdom on the one hand and European romantic views of nationalism and sacrifice on the other hand, Hebrew national culture created its own heroic myths and symbols. Zionism's perspective on Jewish history enhanced the importance of national struggle and, with it, the theme of patriotic sacrifice.

This study's point of departure is the 1940s, a critical decade that witnessed the massive murder and persecution of European Jewry in the Holocaust, the escalating conflict with the Arabs in Palestine, and the struggle against the British mandate to establish a Jewish state. The decade culminated with the breakout of the 1948–49 war following the declaration of Israel's Independence. In this context, patriotic sacrifice was no longer an ideological construct or a limited phenomenon; it became part of a grim everyday reality. And yet, as Israeli society developed throughout the following decades, its heroic myths and symbols have gradually been transformed. The examination of the Israeli war widow's changing image thus allows us to explore the process of constructing and deconstructing a national symbol within the context of a changing political culture.

Israel's pantheon of heroes is almost exclusively male. Men fight in wars and receive medals and citations for their heroic acts, and their death in battle is commemorated and glorified. Women, like children, enter the domain of collective national symbols through their relation to men.[6] When a son, husband, or father dies in the war, the woman's social status is transformed into a "bereaved mother," a "war widow," or a "war orphan." Like other female representations, the war widow is relegated to the margins of the landscape of war imagery. Her entry into this domain begins upon her husband's death and is intimately linked to his posthumous career as a national symbol.

In societies where gender roles have been professedly traditional, this situation may be taken for granted. In Israeli society, however, this reality can come as something of a surprise. After all, the socialist founders of this society in the earlier part of this century had prided themselves on their progressive social views regarding gender equality. Women were active members of underground movements for national liberation prior to the foundation of the state and are still recruited for a military service at the age of eighteen. Yet, as historical studies on gender issues have recently shown, there is a marked gap between the rhetoric of equality and historical reality in relation to gender issues. This was the case in socialist communes that advocated an egalitarian social order during the beginning of the century,[7] and during the struggle for national liberation in the 1940s.[8] The ideological rhetoric was nonetheless instrumental to shaping Israelis' self-images and thereby diffuse social awareness of these discrepancies.[9] Following the foundation of the state, women's service in the Israel Defense Forces was further adjusted to more traditional gender prescriptions and restricted to noncombat roles.[10] Ironically, even when women put their lives at a greater risk than men, as was the case of nurses who reported to the hospitals during the Gulf War while their husbands remained at home with the children, these experiences were largely ignored in public memory.[11]

The war of that followed Israel's declaration of independence established the marginal status of war widows in the community of mourners. Known in Israel as "The War of Liberation" or "The Independence War," it was a traumatic experience with a high level of casualties (close to six thousand Jews died, i.e., about 1 percent of the Jewish population).[12] The relatively young age of most casualties emphasized the soldiers' role as sons, who gave their lives for the newly established state.[13] When a bereaved parents' organization, *Yad Labanim* (the Memorial for the Sons) was founded in 1949, the parents were regarded as representing the entire community of mourners; women who lost their spouses or companions received little attention.[14] The social emphasis on the collective sacrifice and loss experienced by Israeli society served to delegitimize public displays of individual pain and veil individuals' difficulties in coping with the private consequences of that loss.[15]

As Lea Shamgar-Handelman notes in her pioneering study of war widows, the term emerged as a social category in public discourse only after the 1967 Six-Day War. The plight of the widow attracted the media's attention as if it were a new and unfamiliar phenomenon, and the government responded to public pressure to establish new procedures to care for the widows and their children. And it was only after the 1973 Yom Kippur War that the widows founded their own organization in affiliation with Yad Labanim.[16] Although this development indicated a new awareness of the widows' distinct needs, it also reflected the continuing perception of their secondary position relative to the bereaved parents.

Jewish tradition emphasizes the significance of remembrance in prayer and ritual, and Israeli culture has continued this tradition, as is evident in the large number of monuments, memorial books, poetry, and fiction devoted to this subject.[17] Like other widows, the war widow functions as a symbolic extension of her dead husband and the carrier of his memory. Her burden, however, exceeds that of any other widow because of her husband's death as a soldier. In this case, the state assumes the moral obligation to cherish the memory of his patriotic sacrifice and the responsibility to support his wife and children. That the Ministry of Defense assumes this task marks the shift in the widow's new status as a member of the "bereaved family."[18]

The husband's death as a soldier thus introduces the state as a third party into the dyadic husband-wife relationship and transforms the symbolic role of each of its components. The dead is no longer merely a husband; he is also a "fallen soldier" whose death is commemorated publicly every year on Israel's Memorial Day, and the state claims ownership over his memory. The widow is not only a wife but assumes a symbolic role vis-à-vis the state as representing her dead husband within the community of the living.

In this new set of relationships the widow becomes a living memorial for the fallen soldier, and in this capacity she too enters the domain of national symbols. In this capacity she is the object of public scrutiny and is under pressure to behave in conformity with the social prescription of this role. Society's expectations from her, however, are often ambiguous and contradictory. She is expected to go through a process of mourning and recovery and reenter social life as a full-fledged member of society. But at the same time she is also expected to maintain her role as a symbolic representation of her dead husband.

The literary and cinematic works examined here provide insights into the changing perception of the war widow in Israeli culture since the foundation of the state of Israel. During the earlier part of this period, the unique situation of the war widow was largely marginalized or ignored. The 1960s offered a transitory phase, in which the war widow emerged as a figure but was objectified as an extension of her dead husband. More recently, however, a number of works of fiction and film have chosen to portray the war widow as a subject in its own right, portraying the vulnerability of her position as a woman subject to ambivalent social attitudes. By highlighting social and psychological tensions that society tends to ignore, these works provide their own commentary to the state of the war widow in contemporary Israeli society. As such they may be seen as agents of change, evoking public awareness of the war widow's unique situation and stimulating public discourse on these issues.

The Mute Widow

Perhaps the most famous novel of the late 1940s, Moshe Shamir's *He Went Through the Fields* (1947) provides our point of departure.[19] The novel was one of the first examples of what is known as the literature of the "1948 generation." These works of literature, written by young Israeli writers who reached adulthood in the 1940s, tend to focus on an adolescent man who, like these writers, grows up in prestate Israeli society and participates in the collective mission of nation building. The women are mostly featured as companions to the male protagonists, objects of their gaze, desire, or frustration.

In line with this predominant trend, *He Went Through the Fields* revolves around the figure of the first son of the kibbutz, Uri, who returns home following his graduation from high school. His girlfriend, Mika, a Holocaust survivor who recently joined the kibbutz, is a minor figure in the novel. When Uri is summoned by the underground, she attempts to dissuade him from going. Uri's education does not allow him to put personal needs before the call for national service, whereas Mika's experiences lead her to regard his departure as desertion and betrayal. The novel ends with Uri's death in an accident. At this point, Mika appears to become the focus of his parents' attention, yet the interest in her lies in her role as the biological link between their dead son and his future child, whom she carries in her womb. For the bereaved parents, the promise of continuity within the family line brings a measure of comfort as a symbolic compensation for the loss of their own son. In the film by the same title, which is based on the novel, this point is further highlighted by the opening and concluding scenes featuring Uri's son, named after his dead father.[20] Returning to the kibbutz as a soldier, young Uri is greeted by his grandfather in the very same way the latter had greeted the father years earlier. This coda reinforces the emphasis on the male line, showing the grandson as taking the place of the dead son. The women are absent from these scenes.

Shamir's novel provides an example of how the experience of widowhood is silenced through the marginalization of the female character.[21] Mika occupies the center stage only briefly in her symbolic role as a womb. Her future as a war widow and her child's experiences as an orphan lie beyond the interest of this work. The narrative's focus on the dead male hero thus silences the widow's story, which would typically begin where her husband's life ends.[22]

Even when the widow plays a greater role in a novel, this does not necessarily imply that the experience of widowhood receives the attention it deserves within the narrative. Two later works of fiction provide examples of how the war widow remains mute about her experience of widowhood even when she is allowed to have a more prominent place within the narrative or assert her voice on other matters of social concern.

Nathan Shaham's novel *Aller Retour* (1972) depicts a young woman whose husband was killed in the 1967 war,[23] whereupon she decides to take a year leave from her kibbutz and go abroad. The novel describes her experiences in London and ends with her return home. Although she serves as the main protagonist in this work, her recent experience of being widowed receives only scant and superficial treatment. The novel provides the impression that her young age shields the heroine from suffering deep psychological injury as a result of her husband's death. The heroine moves from the role of "wife" to that of a "single woman" and a "daughter," and the novel offers little reflection on the impact of this transition. At some point, the widow admits that she used her husband's death as an excuse to fulfill an old wish to see the world beyond her closed kibbutz environment. This statement may reflect Shaham's own approach to the issue of her widowhood in the construction of the novel: *Aller Retour* uses the experience of widowhood in order to address the theme of the young "wandering Israelis" who feel the urge to escape home in order to free themselves from the pressures of their immediate environment and struggle on their own to define their futures.[24] Within this framework, the protagonist's social role as a daughter clearly becomes more significant than her status as a war widow.

In a similar fashion, Batya Gur's *Cohabitation: Murder in the Kibbutz* revolves around the murder of the kibbutz's secretary, who is a war widow. This fact, however, is of minor significance for the plot. To the limited extent that we learn about the heroine's inner and social worlds, her childhood experiences appear to have a far greater impact on her life. Having come to the kibbutz as a refugee girl (her entire family had perished in the Holocaust) and desiring to distance herself from her mother, a loose woman who was unable to take care of her, the secretary strives to gain a position of respectability within the close-knit kibbutz community.[25] Her strong commitment to reforming one of the fundamental principles in the social organization of kibbutz life (i.e., children's sleeping arrangements) is nurtured by her early painful experience as an outside child. For the concerned observer she appeared "as if she were setting a score without being aware of that" (132). In contrast, her husband's death seems to have left no apparent scar or void in her life.

The husband's death in the War of Lebanon may have reinforced the attractive widow's efforts to deny her sexuality in order to discourage advances by male kibbutz members and diffuse possible suspicions by other women. It may also explain her covert affair with a married politician, who, like her, had come to the kibbutz as an "outside child" yet chose to leave. The author's interest appears to lie in the issue of the intergenerational struggle between the veteran ideologues and the young reform-seekers during a critical moment in the life of a kibbutz community. The widow's experiences are hardly explored in the novel.

Ultimately, the woman's position as a daughter—in relation to her own biological mother whom she rejected, and her mother-in-law, the prominent educator whose ideological stance she now challenges—is more critical to the novel than her position as a wife, a widow, or a mother.[26] The centrality of the ideological battle is also evident in the case of the mother-in-law who turns out to be the widow's murderer. *Cohabitation: Murder in the Kibbutz* reveals no internal conflict or ambivalence on the old woman's part in killing her dead son's wife, who is also the mother of her orphaned grandchildren. In Gur's work, like in Shaham's novel, the kibbutz serves as a microcosm for Israeli society in order to demonstrate the priority of collective over individual needs. Although the author clearly wishes to criticize this trend within the kibbutz's society, her work ultimately colludes with it by obscuring the widow's internal struggle in the face of broader social and political concerns.

The image of the mute widow becomes the explicit focus of a more recent short story, "Written in Stone," by Savyon Liebrecht,[27] yet this story presents the war widow from a different perspective through a narrator who is positioned close to her consciousness. The story therefore reveals the widow's own perception of her muteness, as well as her inner struggle to overcome this loss of voice within the context of her relations with her husband's family, to whose house she is drawn every year on the anniversary of his death. The in-laws, North African immigrants who do not subscribe to the national-secular ethos of Israeli culture, express overt hostility toward the widow. They relate to her not only as a stranger invading their private sorrow but also as a representative of Israeli society who took away their son and is responsible for his death. The widow experiences these annual memorials as an annual ritual of humiliation and suffering. Shrinking in the corner under their hostile gaze and unfriendly silence, the subdued widow too withdraws into silence. When she leaves, she promises to herself: "Next year I'll talk" (110).

The conflict between the widow and the mother-in-law can be clearly interpreted as a power struggle over the ownership of memory: "The women watched her in silence through the years. . . . They watched her as she sat among them like one who had come to claim her share, as if telling them without words: he is mine too. You will not shut me out of memories" (100).[28] The husband's family feels entitled to their son's memory and prefers to ignore the widow's claim to it made through her mute presence and the wedding ring she deliberately displays.

The resolution of this impasse is reached only when the mother breaks through the silence, engaging for the first time in a conversation with the widow. The older woman hands over to the widow a letter that her husband had mailed before his death and which she has kept secret for twelve years. This limited gesture of acknowledgment of the widow's entitlement to the son makes it possible for the latter to finally break through her silence and express her anger and pain at the rejecting mother-in-law. Yet the mother-in-law's gesture is soon followed by her request that the widow relinquish her hold on the past and her annual visits to the family's house and that she refrain from naming her future baby after her dead husband. The old woman's insistence on separation liberates the widow from the hold of the past and allows her to move on to the future. Whereas her earlier attempts to rebuild her life were doomed to fail,[29] once she regains her voice she can abandon the past and her husband's memory. This solution does not present the viable possibility of integrating her newly found voice and her experience of widowhood: by gaining the one, she loses her entitlement to that past.[30] This ultimately reinforces the image of the widow as a mute figure.

A Living Memorial

The films *The Hero's Wife* (Eshet ha-Gibor) and *Siege* (Matsor), made in 1963 and 1969 respectively, construct a different representation of the war widow.[31] The two films allow the war widow to move from a marginal position to center stage, demonstrating that her experiences are unique and complex and that this is a topic that deserves attention in its own right. The narratives of these movies describe the war widow's struggle to cope with memories and loneliness as well as with her status as a collective symbol. Both films choose to focus on the widows' social life among their peers.

In spite of their common themes, there is a remarkable difference between the two movies. *The Hero's Wife* portrays a widow who for fifteen years following her husband's death appears to be functioning well in the work sphere but is socially withdrawn and lives in extended mourning. Her groomed public appearance and high social standing in her kibbutz thus stand in sharp contrast to her inner life and private space, which, like a shrine, is full of relics from the past. As the film title suggests, the widow sees herself (and is seen by many) not as an independent person but as "the hero's wife." Although her friends encourage her to become more socially engaged, she appears unable to unlock the hold of this role.

The war widow's unexpected sexual awakening is triggered by a young American volunteer at the kibbutz. Unimpressed with her role as a living memorial for her much admired husband, he pursues her unabashedly. The film focuses on the widow's internal struggle between her sense of moral obligation to the dead, her embracement of the kibbutz's collectivist ethos, and her attraction to the cynical, carefree outsider. The impasse is broken when the kibbutz becomes the target of enemy fire. In spite of his earlier individualist statements, the young volunteer proves his readiness to risk his life to save the kibbutz. Upon discovering that he survived his heroic deed, the widow lets down her defenses and becomes his lover. The brief encounter the night before the volunteer leaves the kibbutz shows how both individuals have been transformed: he has learned to recognize the moral bounds of his professed individualism, and she is released from the moral and social constraints of her role as a living memorial for her husband and rediscovers herself as a woman of flesh and blood. As the lover leaves the kibbutz, the conclusion of the film suggests the budding possibility of a new relationship between her and another loyal friend, whose love for her she had long ignored, thus providing a more socially acceptable resolution.

The Hero's Wife has many faults: the characters are unidimensional, the dialogue is often shallow and unconvincing, the acting is heavily theatrical, and the use of stereotypical images abundant. Marked by its period, the movie is clearly colored by its heavy nationalist thrust. Moreover, unlike later works, *The Hero's Wife* presents an extremely favorable portrayal of the kibbutz as a nurturing environment for widows, allowing the heroine some private space during her withdrawal and encouraging her recovery without making her anxious about the possible criticism of her behavior. In spite of the film's faults, its readiness to address the widow's inability to recover from the mourning process and her withdrawal from social life was an important step in the exploration of war widowhood.

Made in the aftermath of the Six-Day War, the film *Siege* presents a more mature and complex representation of the war widow's process of mourning, withdrawal, and recovery. Influenced by the New Wave films and shot in black and white, the movie follows the widow's shifts between temporal frameworks and levels of consciousness, as memories of the past invade her present interactions. In exploring the state of widowhood, *Siege* is particularly interested in portraying the ambivalence that underlies the relations between the war widow and her dead husband's friends: the friends offer the widow protection, help, and support out of loyalty to the dead, and they care for her as an extension of their bond with him. Although grateful for their support, the widow also experiences their attitude as social control. The tension is heightened when the late husband's best friend finds out that the war widow is pursuing a new relationship without his knowledge or approval. Critical and alarmed at first, he eventually accepts her lover and supports her choice. The widow and the friend thus succeed in averting the danger of creating another rupture in her life, maintaining their friendship while providing her the necessary space for a psychological and social recovery. When the best friend gives her an album for the dead husband's photographs that are displayed throughout her house, the widow is symbolically released from shaping her life and environment as a living memorial for the dead in order to allow for her continued recovery.

The Eternal Widow

Had the movie *Siege* ended at the point described above, its message would have been optimistic; yet the ending is quite different. As the War of Attrition continues to waver on the borders, the lover is called for reserve duty. The widow hears news on the radio about critically wounded soldiers in the area where her lover serves, and not being able to get further information she goes up to that area with her dead husband's best friend to find out the fate of her lover. The movie ends ambiguously as the narrative shifts its focus from the individual's story to the political situation, implying that the recurrent state of war in Israel does not allow the heroine to recover from widowhood. The widow's state of being internally besieged is reinforced by society's analogous state of siege in the continuing conflict. The broader political situation therefore creates a deterministic framework that renders futile the woman's personal struggle for recovery.

In this respect *Siege* was an early exploration of a theme that would preoccupy Israeli literature, theater, and film of the 1970s and the 1980s. During these two intense decades of conflict, including the Yom Kippur War, the War of Lebanon, and the Intifada, there was a growing sense of disillusionment and skepticism about the continuing toll on human life with no hope for a resolution in sight. The feeling of entrapment within a continuous cycle of wars and bloodshed thus emerged as a major theme that served as a critique of the heroic-national lore of earlier periods.

The theme of being besieged within the role of the war widow is also explored in the 1982 film *Repeat Dive* (Tslila Ḥozeret), directed by Shimon Dotan. This film portrays a marine commando unit during the 1969 War of Attrition, and it offers two interlinking subplots: the first focuses on the marines' attempts to cope with a comrade's death in action as they pursue their military practice and risky operations; the second traces the relationship between the widow and her dead husband's childhood and commando friend. Connecting the two subplots is a recorded monologue made by the husband during a party that his best friend brings to the widow. In this tape, the husband jokingly declares that he leaves his wife to that friend, as he goes on to boast about his sexual pursuits with other women.

Though the widow responds with anger to the revelation of her dead husband's infidelity and to being handed down as an object to another man, she behaves as if she is overpowered by her dead husband's will. She soon announces her intention to marry his best friend, and the two get married. This union, however, is undermined by its forced character, the lack of sexual and emotional intimacy between the two partners, and the new husband's decision to extend his military service in the marine commando, in spite of his wife's deep-seated fear that he too will be killed in action. Held together by a sense of moral indebtedness to the dead, this marriage is reduced to a living memorial for him.

More than exploring the widow's inner and social worlds, *Repeat Dive* addresses the gap between the Israeli male soldier's heroic image and his psychological and social immaturity outside of the military sphere. The film narrative is interspersed with the marines' cynical comments on patriotic sacrifice and is imbued with antiwar sentiments and morbid humor. Yet ultimately, despite its attempt to provide a critique of gender stereotypes, the film remains trapped by them. The war widow is depicted as an enigmatic woman who is seen through the male gaze as both erratic and neurotic. She is incomprehensible but controlling, demanding but not giving. She is highly critical of the marines' values and behavior, yet proceeds to throw herself into their midst and imposes her presence on them. Mostly, she appears to have no world of her own, independent of her double role as a wife and a war widow. The film shows that Israeli society is trapped within an endless cycle of war and bloodshed that does not allow its men to mature and that leaves its women lonely and suffering. The woman is locked into a predetermined track that moves her from the position of a wife to that of a war widow, without hope of escaping this fate.

Like *Repeat Dive*, other works of fiction, film, and theater show that given the continuous cycle of bloodshed, Israeli women cannot escape the heritage of widowhood. The film *Atalia* (1984), directed by Akiba Tevet, portrays a woman who became a war widow in the Sinai campaign of 1956 and faces the likelihood of losing her young lover when the Yom Kippur War breaks out in 1973. Although the lover is spared from service for medical reasons, her daughter's boyfriend is killed in action. The role of the war widow is thus passed on from mother to daughter as if part of a family tradition.[32] Similarly, a recent play by David Shrir, entitled *Daria*,[33] features three women of the same family: the mother and her aunt are widows of the 1967 and 1948 wars respectively, whereas the daughter narrowly escapes their fate when her spouse is severely wounded.

The war widow thus assumes a symbolic function that goes well beyond her individual case. Her personal state of siege turns into an allegory for the state of siege in which Israeli society exists, locked into a vicious cycle of conflict, injuries, and death. Rather than being associated with the symbolism of national heroism as an extension of her dead husband, the eternal widow is displayed in these works as a collective metaphor of victimization. This symbolic transformation can also be seen as a new version of the biblical story of the *Akeda*, the binding of Isaac. Given the symbolic significance of the Akeda in Jewish tradition and its deliberate inversion in modern Hebrew literature,[34] the feminist reinterpretation of this story is quite telling. In contrast to the traditional male version (Abraham's readiness to sacrifice his son as evidence of his faith in God and Isaac's compliance) and the transformed contemporary male version (the sons' protest against their sacrifice by the fathers in Israel's wars), this feminist interpretation introduces the woman into this story and presents her as the one who makes the sacrifice and struggles to cope with its long-term consequences. The eternal widow thus emerges as a counterimage to the male hero, replacing him as the young person who is forever tied to the altar in that liminal zone between the communities of the living and the dead.

Ironically, by offering the eternal war-widow image, these works continue an earlier trend of objectifying the widow to support an ideological agenda. In their desire to critique the national lore, they end up relating to the widow not as an individual woman who struggles to cope with her state of widowhood but as a collective symbol.

The Irreverent Widow

Recent works of fiction mark a shift in the representation of the war widow by allowing the reader direct access to her consciousness or positioning the narrator close to her perspective. These works therefore focus on the war widow's experiences as seen by her and provide a voice to the otherwise muted figure who is used as a national symbol. By shifting her position within the narrative and by allowing her voice and perspective to take over, these works reveal a more complex response to widowhood. No longer presenting a two-dimensional portrait that answers society's need to see her as a symbol, they create a figure of flesh and blood who discloses the ambivalence, anger, despair, desires, and frustrations that she experiences.

Having access to the widow's perspective makes it possible to reflect on her response to the expectation that she functions as a symbolic extension of her husband. For the widow, life under the shadow of memory can become an oppressive experience. Atalia addresses her protest against the burden of memory to her dead husband, Matti:

> "Almost twenty years have passed. A third of my life I knew you," she tells him, "and only one-tenth of this time I was with you. I left you when you were twenty-four years old and I am already a bit over forty now. How dare you direct my path, stop me, caution me. I am a grown woman and you are still a boy. Years have passed by and the world is different, Matti."[35]

The widow's role as a living memorial for her husband calls for her participation in official commemorations of fallen soldiers. In a recent film on war widows entitled *Sex, Lies and Dinner*,[36] one of the widows remarks on how they are expected to attend every memorial service and spend every Israel's Memorial Day for the fallen soldiers in the military cemetery. "An awesome entertainment for a twenty-four-year-old woman," she adds dryly. "Once," she tells her friends, "someone even tried to come on to me in the cemetery." "And what?" "What's what? I told him that I am already taken, I already have a tombstone here." Miri, the heroine of Lea Aini's *Sand Tide*, refuses to go to a memorial ceremony for her husband sponsored by the Ministry of Defense. "I refuse to participate in the glorification of memory that is offered to me as an exclusive substitute . . . for my dead husband whom I love," she protests.[37] Helping a tourist who is looking for a match in the matchmaking office where she works, she wants to tell him: "It is easy to come here, to this land of the dead, and catch an Israeli woman. Simply, because they die less [than the men]. But because men die around them all the time, throughout their lives, grandparents and fathers and husbands and sons, they have become hardened."[38] In the play *Daria* the widow of the 1967 war exclaims: "I don't want to fill my life with albums and memorial rooms." To which her aunt, who was widowed in 1948, replies: "You don't know how it is when people forget. Who remembers today my war of 1948? This is what I live for, to remind them." In this respect, she goes on to explain, she functions as a monument to that war, not unlike those burned armored cars left on the side of the road to Jerusalem.

The burden of memory becomes even more acute when one considers the contrast between the short duration of the couple's shared life and the long-term impact of the husband's death on the widow.[39] In the story "Written in Stone," the widow was married less than three months yet feels bound to her husband's family and memory for more than twelve years. The childless heroine of *The Hero's Wife* lives under the shadow of memory for fifteen years following her husband's death. The oppressive nature of memory is further highlighted in *Sand Tide* through the image of the widow whose husband was killed in the Polish army in 1936, immediately after their wedding. Not able to overcome this traumatic experience, she remained mentally disconnected from the present for decades.[40]

The widow's feeling that her husband's memory is fading evokes both guilt and frustration. The pressure worsens when she is faced with the expectation to romanticize their relationship: "Isn't it true that big love remains forever, Atalia? Isn't it true that you cannot forget Dad?" her daughter asks her.[41] The widow attempts to affirm that view while aware that the reality was quite different: their brief marriage was prompted by her pregnancy and was devoid of love or joy.

The widow's awareness of the gap between the official commemoration of the dead and her own experiences is further highlighted in the pervasive theme of accidental death in works about war widows. The husband's death, we learn, is not the product of a heroic stand in the battlefield but rather results from an accident. Thus, Uri was killed during the underground's practice (*He Went Through the Fields*),[42] and the husband in *Siege* was killed by a stray bullet. Though the dead are publicly commemorated as fallen soldiers, the widows' awareness of the real circumstances of their husbands' death raises doubts about the significance of their husbands' sacrifice and makes it more difficult for the widows to accept its glorification. "What a way he found to die. What a time. Later, out of some kind of pity . . . he became a war casualty," Atalia reflects on her husband's death to herself.[43] Miri of *Sand Tide* refers at one point to "that idiotic accident" that caused her husband's death, and in another she reproaches him for being hit by a road mine "like a jerk" (24–25). And in the film *Sex, Lies, and Dinner*, a widow discloses that her husband died on the way to the men's room from an accidental gunshot by a new recruit. The incongruity of the circumstances of this death with the conventional glorification of fallen soldiers as heroes creates a humorous juxtaposition, but it also puts to question the assumption regarding the inevitability of death and the value of sacrifice for both the husband and the surviving widow.

The war widows' black humor and cynical remarks express discomfort at the fact that the state imposes the memory of the dead on them for its own needs and that society does not acknowledge their personal needs under their public masks. *Sand Tide*, *Daria*,[44] and *Sex, Lies, and Dinner* are examples of a recent novel, play, and film, respectively, that depict morbid humor as a response to this pressure. Such expressions of cynicism and black humor contribute to the image of the irreverent widow. This image deliberately challenges sacred patriotic values of Israeli society, such as the importance of heroic sacrifice on the man's part and its full acceptance despite high personal cost on the surviving widow's part. The irreverent widow challenges the national significance attributed to her sacrifice and displays her doubts about its inevitability and worthiness. The emergence of black humor in response to the war and its impact is hardly unique to the case of the war widow. The prevalence of morbid jokes during wars, especially those that were not supported by a national consensus (i.e., the Lebanon War and the Intifada) demonstrates humor's function as an expression of emotions and doubts that cannot be openly articulated and therefore appear in that more diffused form.[45]

Indeed, the humorous framework in these works goes beyond its depiction of irreverent widows. The narrative itself assumes an irreverent position to its subject matter by focusing on the woman's intimate thoughts and bodily needs, as well as social circumstances. The method of acknowledging the widow's sexuality and exposing her inner life and bodily needs is in itself subversive to her sacred mythical image, for it engages the reader in viewing the widow as a woman rather than a public figure who is watched from a disarming distance.

Sex, Lies, and Dinner is a drama about widows that openly addresses the tensions between their social and sexual needs, public face, and private life. The film presents two radically different models of responses to widowhood: the hostess, a seemingly carefree woman who prides herself on being sexually uninhibited and determined to have a good time, and the widow who fears to undermine her social reputation by going out with men and hence avoids any intimate contacts. As the evening proceeds the hostess invites a performance by a male striptease-dancer and later invites to her home several men to join the widows for drinks.[46] The film is interspersed with comic scenes, yet the widows' pain and struggle with loneliness become increasingly evident. The juxtaposition of the widows' attempts to preserve the humorous framework with their later acknowledgment of continuing hardships they suffer in trying to come to terms with the loss makes *Sex, Lies, and Dinner* a powerful drama.

Similarly, *Sand Tide* is imbued with the narrator's humorous descriptions of her own life as a widow following her husband's death. The humor serves to support the widow's denial of the situation as well as to diffuse the acute pain she experiences. The novel opens with a scene that leaves no doubt in the reader's mind that this work presents an unconventional portrayal of widowhood. "Your father called. I was sitting on the toilet, exhausted, though it was already nine o'clock in the morning, and was looking at the wonders of my naked private parts." The opening is deliberately shocking. The widow is not put on the pedestal as a national symbol but described as a woman sitting on the toilet, examining her vagina in order to see the effects that her husband's absence has had on her body. She is not the object of public gaze described in the third person but an agent, a woman of flesh and blood who acts on her own will.

The heroine does not relate to her loss as a sacrifice for the nation but as the inexplicable disappearance of her husband who is no longer there to make love to her. She does not only acknowledge her deprived sexuality but centers on it. In spite of this appearance of openness, it is important to remember that Miri examines herself in the privacy of her own bathroom, protected from others' gaze and knowledge. Her openness about her innermost feelings and thoughts is directed in her mind toward her dead husband. It is the fact that her subversiveness is hidden that allows Miri to be acceptable socially. As we shall see below, when the irreverent widow proceeds too far, she becomes cast as a social misfit who poses a threat to the social order.

The Widow as a Social Misfit

The fictional representations of the war widow reveal the difficulties that she encounters in negotiating her double role as a war widow and a single woman. They portray her own ambivalence about her social position as well as the ambiguous and often contradictory messages from society. The widow's public status as a collective symbol provides license to others to constantly observe her behavior and thereby make her feel—as one widow describes it in *Siege*—as if she were performing on stage. Yet this critical public measures up the widow's performance according to an ambiguous script. If she embraces too heavily the role of the widow, she is bound to be criticized for excessive withdrawal; but if she is suspected of acting upon her needs as a woman, she might be seen as betraying her role as a widow. To avoid this conflict she may try to adhere to her public image as a symbol and deny her personal needs, or else she may run the risk of undermining her privileged social status as a war widow.

But as the literary and cinematic representations of the war widow show, the definition of her position is not necessarily in the woman's control: in a society marked by its strong family orientation, the perception of the widow as young and single also marks her as an available woman. As such she is perceived as a destabilizing presence and a potential threat to the established familial order.

In a few works, the widow feels rejected by her husband's family. A great deal of the tension stems from the contrast between their respective roles in relation to the dead. Whereas parents-son relations have a longer time span, marriage is described in most of these works as relatively short, because often those who die in action are young men. No less significant is the potential transitory status of widowhood that stands in sharp contrast to the role of bereaved parents: whereas the widow may remarry and lose her status and rights as a war widow, the parents' status as bereaved is irreversible.

Social tensions may arise in the widow's relation with her in-laws. In "Written in Stone" the widow's feeling of being rejected by her hostile mother-in-law emerges as a central theme, focusing on the issue of entitlement to the dead man's memory. Similarly, in the film *Repeat Dive* the widow is confronted by her mother-in-law's demand to hand over to her all of her son's photographs. The tension between the mother-in-law and the widow is evident also in *Sand Tide* and *Cohabitation*, although in the latter it appears to be focused on an ideological issue.

A more recurrent theme in the fictional representation of the widow is her fear that as a single woman she risks being labeled a "loose woman." Several works portray how the widow deliberately suppresses her own sexuality and avoids relationships with men in order to prevent such a development.[47] Thus, for example, in *The Hero's Wife* the protagonist protects her status by cutting herself off emotionally, until the moment of sexual awakening fifteen years later liberates her from these constraints. The war widow in *Cohabitation* directs her energy to public service in her kibbutz and attempts to suppress her beauty and sensuality. The uninhibited widow in *Sex, Lies and Dinner*, who boasts about her sexual pursuits, is juxtaposed with the elegant yet repressed widow from the kibbutz. Indeed, that the kibbutz is featured so prominently in these works serves to further dramatize the widow's difficulties in confronting the tensions between collective and individual needs.[48]

The widow exercises such extreme caution because of her vulnerability as a single woman. Even when she does not pursue new relationships with men, she faces the risk of being perceived as open to sexual advances.[49] Although other single women share a similar situation, the widow stands to lose more when suspected of stepping out of her role as a living memorial to her dead husband. This moral dimension puts her in a disadvantaged position relative to other single women, who are given greater license to express their sexuality.

The fictional representations of the war widow show her susceptibility to suspicion, criticism, and moral accusations even when there is no legitimate ground for it. A couple of months following her husband's death, the heroine of *Sand Tide* faces an accusation by her angry mother-in-law, who claims that she secretly desires to sleep with other men and might have already done so.[50] Daria complains that all her friends have stopped coming to see her, and one of the widows in *Sex, Lies and Dinner* cynically remarks that her female friends disappeared because they were afraid she might steal their men. When the heroine of *Siege* goes out to the city and buys some new clothes, she is faced with the neighbors' stares and gossip.[51] And in spite of the war widow's deliberate attempt to curb her attractiveness, in *Cohabitation* a jealous kibbutznik, who suspects her of having an affair with her husband, screams at her in public: "A whore, a family destroyer, like your mother, that's what you are."[52] In a remarkable similarity, Atalia is accused by other members of the kibbutz of being sexually loose when she invites three visitors to her room for a cup of coffee. When she actually becomes involved with a married member of the kibbutz twelve years later, she tells herself that she has nothing to lose: "Anyway they think of me as a whore."[53]

The fictional representations demonstrate the depth of the gap between the widow's overt behavior and internal conflict. Even when the widow remarries, as is the case in "Written in Stone," she is unable to let go of the past. Although the film *Sex, Lies, and Dinner* depicts a wide range of responses to widowhood, it shows that as the evening the widows spend together unfolds, the difference between the widows becomes blurred: they all suffer from a deep longing for warmth and physical contact and from loneliness.[54]

The illusion of appearances is a central theme in *Sand Tide*. The widow's apparent accommodation to her new situation masks her growing anger at the social constraints imposed on her. Although Miri appears to be highly functional—she finds a new job and begins working a month after the death of her husband—she is, in fact, engaged in a complex and private process that in the end reveals her failure to integrate her husband's death into her life. The novel offers a sharp contrast between the widow's rejection of external forms of mourning and the evidence of private signs of mourning: quite symbolically, it is not the hair of her head, but her pubic hair, that turns white, hidden from the public gaze. Whereas to all appearances the heroines of *Sand Tide* and "Atalia" seem to have adjusted to their position as widows, these works are constructed as interior monologues directed at their dead husbands. In both cases, the bond with the husband seems particularly significant in light of the women's weakening ties to their social environment.

The widow's feeling of being marginalized stands in sharp contrast to her official status within society as a collective symbol of patriotic sacrifice. In these works, her marginality is further dramatized by association with other socially marked persons. Thus, *The Hero's Wife* portrays the widow as attracted to an American volunteer who is largely disliked by the kibbutz members. The heroine of *Siege* finds her refuge in a relationship with an Israeli whose occupation as an operator of a bulldozer represents a lower status than the men she otherwise meets. Both these films, however, indicate that the hidden qualities of the chosen men (that later become public) redeem their marginality. The heroine in *Aller Retour* falls for an uprooted, tortured French intellectual whom she meets in London. The heroine of *Sand Tide* finds solace in developing friendships with an older immigrant of dubious standing with the police whose friend is a transvestite, an extremely unattractive single woman who cannot find a spouse, and an abused child. In the film *Atalia* the heroine begins an affair with a young man of her daughter's age who is discharged from the army for medical reasons. The widows of *Sex, Lies and Dinner* invite for drinks foreign workers who can hardly speak any Hebrew and suffer from social discrimination. Last but not least, Daria falls in love with a Palestinian man who belongs to "the enemy camp." With varying degrees of marginality, these characters with whom the war widows associate provide them company, intimacy, or warmth that is otherwise missing in their contacts from their prewidowhood days.

As a couple of works show, the widow's growing sense of marginality and alienation may push her over the edge of accepted social behavior. Under this pressure, the widow makes a desperate attempt to take revenge or rebel against society and is publicly recognized as a social misfit: she loses her place in society and must be removed from it in order to restore the social order. In both *Cohabitation* and *Daria* the widows encounter their death: the widowed secretary is murdered, and Daria commits suicide when her relationship with the Palestinian lover gives way to social pressure.

More complex, perhaps, is the fate of Atalia, the heroine of Yitzḥak Ben-Ner's story. Feeling herself an outcast in the kibbutz where she has lived for thirty-four years, and deserted by the men she loved (first her husband, then her lover), an outraged Atalia sets the kibbutz's barn on fire. The kibbutz, in turn, expels her from its ranks. Within Israeli culture, where setting crops on fire is an act of terrorism or revenge by Palestinians, this subversive act positions the widow as "an enemy" of her community.[55] For a kibbutz member to perform this act can be interpreted only as an act of madness.

In *Sand Tide*, the widow plans an act of personal protest against society, which, she feels, imposes on her the separation from her dead husband. Unwilling to live with elusive memories or settle on a meaningless future, Miri wishes to create a situation that would allow her to be close to her dead husband in a boundless present. Sneaking into the military cemetery she builds a tent on her husband's grave, thereby defying the social norms that require a clear separation between the world of the living and the dead. Unlike the custom of suttee, in which the Hindu widow is burned in order to join her husband in death,[56] Miri chooses to live, not to die, with her dead husband. But her solution is far more original and, admittedly, more deeply subversive than Atalia's. From society's point of view, her act can only be seen as a proof for her failing mental state. When she is put away in a mental clinic, she reflects on the irony of her situation: "It is really funny, isn't it? Strange. Of all times it is now that they think I was getting lost. A few months ago, when I was really lost, nobody raised an eyebrow, inquired; and today, yesterday, when things started to fall into place, they bring me here."[57]

Like Atalia, who is defined as crazy by her fellow kibbutzniks, the widow is considered unfit for normal social life and is therefore hospitalized. The theme of madness, of course, is not a new theme in literature about women. Being trapped in a situation that offers no other way out, women may escape into a world of fantasy and madness that offers them a liberating outlet from the unbearable constraints of their immediate situation.

Conclusion

The war widow's image is closely linked to broader developments that have taken place in Israeli society. The initial emphasis on the war widow's role as a national symbol reflects prevalent social and political attitudes of that period. The idealization of the Israeli-born youth, which reached its height in the 1940s and the 1950s, focused on the Israeli male of European descent, the offspring of Israel's Zionist founders. The Israeli male hero was admired for his courage, resourcefulness, commitment, and readiness to die for his country. The portrayal of the war widow in earlier works indicated an attitude of flattening and distancing that went hand in hand with her elevation as a national symbol. The widow became a two-dimensional figure who served as a symbolic extension of the fallen soldier, a living monument of the dead. She was further marginalized in relation to the fallen soldier's parents, who were seen as the primary mourners for their son and in some cases considered her an outsider with competing claims over the dead.

In the following decades, the romantic idealization of the Israeli-born youth gradually gave way to a more complex, ambivalent, and even critical attitude. Furthermore, a wider range of literary and cinematic works replaced the Israeli-born hero, whose parents came from Europe as Zionist pioneers in the prestate era, reflecting a growing awareness of the multicultural character of Israeli society and a growing interest in the pre-Israeli, Jewish past. More recent expressive and artistic forms thus provide voice and center stage to immigrants, women, and minorities, as well as explore the impact of exilic history and the Holocaust on contemporary Israeli society.[58] The continuing Israeli-Palestinian conflict and the frequent wars and military confrontations have raised increasingly poignant questions about the cost of the repeated call to arms and heroic action. The national heroic myths constructed in earlier periods have been subject to heated debates and generated alternative interpretations of their meaning.[59]

The gradual transformation of the national heroic lore liberated the war widow and allowed her to assume a more central role and a voice of her own. Recent literary and cinematic works refuse to romanticize the widow's experience in order to protect her symbolic image. They focus on the widow's everyday and emotional life, including her fantasies, fears, dreams, and desires. In a number of works humor, anger, and pain are portrayed as inseparable strategies of coping with widowhood. These recent depictions of the war widow thus defy the stereotype of the glorified widow who willingly and heroically accepts her fate.

Moving away from the national rhetoric that define her as a passive participant in the events that shape the course of her life, the more recent works empower her as an actor, representing her experiences from her own perspective. These fictional images of the war widow challenge the representation of the Israeli war widow as a collective symbol and focus on her as an individual. Their interest lies in the social and psychological dimensions of her life, illuminating the issues and struggles that she confronts and the ambiguity of her social position.

The recurrence of certain themes in these works emphasizes society's ambivalence toward the widow and the painful discrepancy between official and popular attitudes. Her dual position as a sacred symbol and a potential social misfit puts her in an impossible situation in which she might repress her own needs or risk becoming a subversive figure for society. The recurrent association of the war widow as a child survivor of the Holocaust or as an orphan further accentuates the theme of suffering and loss. The husband's death thus triggers the destabilizing experience of retraumatization. The literary and cinematic portrayals thus reveal a world torn apart by a sudden death and describe the war widow's struggle to reshape her life and identity following this crisis.

This transformed focus presents a profound challenge to the earlier representations of the war widow and a different approach to the national discourse on war and nationalism. The interest in the female character and her private life, body, fears, needs, frustrations, and hopes presents an individualistic discourse that serves as an alternative to the earlier emphasis on the collectivist, male-centered, national discourse. In so doing, these literary and cinematic works offer the war widow the stage and the voice that she was denied in earlier works and become subversive texts that express and contribute to the very process of change.

The changing image of the war widow provides an interesting example of the process in which national myths, symbols, and rituals can be transformed and their meaning redefined in the face of major social and political changes. As part of the nation's sacred tradition, these symbolic forms are subject to a continuing reexamination and reinterpretation. A widening gap between their symbolic meaning and the reality they are meant to represent is therefore likely to lead to changes in their interpretation in order to preserve their political relevance. In this case, the myth would be gradually transformed in the public discourse, and these modifications could eventually lead to further changes in the state's official and educational discourse. In other cases, the national tradition may continue to be maintained by the state agencies yet lose its popular appeal. Recent works of fiction and film that focus on the Israeli war widow disclose the tensions between her official status and popular attitudes toward her, between her symbolic role and the social reality that she encounters. These works also reflect the conflicting attitudes toward heroism and patriotic sacrifice in contemporary Israeli society, suggesting the multivocality of Israeli national tradition.

Reference Material

Notes

Translations of quotations throughout the Notes section are those of the individual chapter authors unless otherwise indicated.

INTRODUCTION, *Weiner*

1. Plutarch on Sparta, circa A.D. 50–124, cited in Michael Burleigh, "Eugenic Utopias and the Genetic Present," *Totalitarian Movements and Political Religions* 1, no. 1 (Summer 2000): 56.

2. On the evolution of the all-embracing nature of the secular state, see Benjamin Kedar, "Expulsion as an Issue of World History," *Journal of World History* 7, no. 2 (1996): 165–80; and James C. Scott, *Seeing Like a State: How Certain Schemes to Improve the Human Condition Have Failed* (New Haven, Conn.: Yale University Press, 1998), 11–102.

3. For powerful arguments for the Puritan Revolution as the launching pad of the above-mentioned transition, especially mass self-introspection, impersonal, ideological loyalties, and a Manichaean, warlike view of politics unleashed against the old order, see Michael Walzer, *The Revolution of the Saints: A Study in the Origins of Radical Politics* (Cambridge, Mass.: Harvard University Press, 1965); and John Rogers, *The Matter of Revolution: Science, Poetry and Politics in the Age of Milton* (Ithaca, N.Y.: Cornell University Press, 1996). For the lessons drawn from the limited scope of the French Revolution, see Bernard Yack, *The Longing for Total Revolution: Philosophic Sources of Social Discontent from Rousseau to Marx and Nietzsche* (Princeton, N.J.: Princeton University Press, 1986).

4. On the origins of the belief in "statistical thinking" and the constant efforts to overcome unpredictability and standardize the populace via multiple bureaucratic agencies, see David Landes, "Statistics as a Source for the History of Economic Development in Western Europe: The Protostatistical Era," in Val Lorwin and Jacob Price, eds., *The Dimensions of the Past: Materials, Problems, and Opportunities for Quantitative Work in History* (New Haven, Conn.: Yale University Press, 1972): 53–91, here, 54; Stephen Stigler, *The History of Statistics: The Measurement of Uncertainty Before 1900* (Cambridge, Mass.: Harvard University Press, 1986); Theodore Porter, *The Rise of Statistical Thinking, 1820–1900* (Princeton: Princeton University Press, 1986); Theodore Porter, *Trust in Numbers: The Pursuit of Objectivity in Science and Public Life* (Princeton, N.J.: Princeton University Press, 1995). Scott, *Seeing Like a State.*

5. Scott, *Seeing Like a State*, 1–8, 87–102. Scott's otherwise impressive study does not engage the impact of the state's transformative schemes on the ideological makeup of the citizenry and the latter's often eager participation in such projects. This aspect has been the focus of several recent studies of the Soviet and Nazi polities, notably Jan Gross, *Revolution from Abroad: The Soviet Conquest of Poland's Western Ukraine and Western Belorussia* (Princeton, N.J.: Princeton University Press, 1988); Stephen Kotkin, *Magnetic Mountain: Stalinism as a Civilization* (Berkeley: University of California Press, 1995); Jochen Hellbeck, "Fashioning the Stalinist Soul: The Diary of Stepan Podlubnyi," *Jahrbucher fur Geschichte Osteuropas* 44 (1996): 344–73; Jochen Hellbeck, "Laboratories of the Self: Diaries from the Stalin Era," Ph.D. dissertation, Columbia University, 1998; and Robert Gellately, *Backing Hitler: Consent and Coercion in Nazi Germany* (Oxford: Oxford University Press, 2001). Surprising, too, is the glossing over of transformative schemes by the radical Right, especially with respect to race. The same applies to Maria Sophia Quine's penetrating overview, *Population Politics in Twentieth Century Europe: Fascist Dictatorships and Liberal Democracies* (New York: Routledge, 1996), which ignores communist countries and the role of professional associations in advocating and orchestrating eugenic policies.

6. Hannah Arendt, *The Origins of Totalitarianism* (New York: Harcourt, Brace, 1951); George Mosse, *The Nationalization of the Masses: Political Symbolism and Mass Movements in Germany from the Napoleonic Wars Through the Third Reich* (New York: H. Fertig, 1975); Jacob Talmon, *The Origins of Totalitarian Democracy* (London: Secker and Warburg, 1952); Talmon, *Political Messianism: The Romantic Phase* (London: Secker and Warburg, 1960); and Talmon, *The Myth of the Nation and the Vision of the Revolution* (London: Secker and Warburg, 1981).

On corporatism, see also Charles Maier, *Recasting Bourgeois Europe: Stabilization in France, Germany, and Italy in the Decade After World War I* (Princeton, N.J.: Princeton University Press, 1975); and Neil Harding, "Socialism, Society, and the Organic Labor State," in Neil Harding, ed., *The State in Socialist Society* (Albany, N.Y.: SUNY Press, 1984), 1–50; Stephen Kotkin, "Modern Times: The Soviet Union and the Interwar Conjuncture," *Kritika* 2, no. 1 (Winter 2001): 111–64.

7. For an eloquent discussion of the self-imposed restraints of the liberal state, see Scott, *Seeing Like a State*, 101–2.

8. Andrew Jenks, "A Metro on the Mount: The Underground as a Church of Soviet Civilization," *Technology & Culture* 41, no. 4 (October 2000): 697–724, here, 697.

9. Pitirim Sorokin, *Man and Society in Calamity: The Effects of War, Revolution, Famine, Pestilence upon Human Mind, Behavior, Social Organizations and Cultural Life* (New York: E.P. Dutton, 1942), 122–24. See, also, Sigmund Freud, "Thoughts for the Times on War and Death," in James Strachey, ed., *The Standard Edition of the Complete Psychological Works of Sigmund Freud*, vol. 14 (London: Hogarth Press, 1957), 275–300.

10. For the pan-European discourse of degeneration, see Daniel Pick, *Faces of Degeneration: A European Disorder, c.1848–1948* (Cambridge: Cambridge University Press, 1989).

11. Nikolai Kol'tsov, quoted in Mark B. Adams, "Eugenics in Russia, 1900–1940," in Mark B. Adams, ed., *The Wellborn Science: Eugenics in Germany, France, Brazil, and Russia* (New York: Oxford University Press, 1990), 162.

12. Burleigh, "Eugenic Utopias," 62.

13. Frank Dikotter, "Race Culture: Recent Perspectives on the History of Eugenics," *American Historical Review* 103, no. 2 (April 1998): 467–68.

14. Burleigh, "Eugenic Utopias," 62.

15. See Nancy Leys Stepan's study of Argentina, Brazil, and Mexico, *"The Hour of Eugenics": Race, Gender, and Nation in Latin America* (Ithaca, N.Y.: Cornell University Press, 1991).

16. Burleigh, "Eugenic Utopias," 63–64.

17. Gunnar Broberg and Mattias Tyden, "Eugenics in Sweden: Efficient Care," in Broberg and Nils Roll-Hansen, eds., *Eugenics and the Welfare State: Sterilization Policy in Denmark, Sweden, Norway, and Finland* (East Lansing: Michigan State University Press, 1996), 109–110, here, 107; "A Survey of the Nordic Countries," *Economist*, January 23, 1999; "Sweden Plans to Pay Sterilization Victims," *New York Times*, January 27, 1999.

18. Paul Weindling, *Health, Race, and German Politics Between National Unification and Nazism, 1870–1945* (Cambridge, Mass.: Cambridge University Press, 1989), 482–83.

19. See the lucid commentary by Mark Mazower, *Dark Continent: Europe's Twentieth Century* (London: Alfred Knopf, 1997), 86–87.

20. Katerina Clark, *Petersburg: The Crucible of Cultural Revolution* (Cambridge, Mass.: Harvard University Press, 1995).

21. On the combination of scientific, rational reordering of society and revolutionary politics during the Enlightenment era, see Bronislaw Baczko, *Utopian Lights: The Evolution of the Idea of Social Progress*, trans. Judith L. Greenberg (New York: Paragon House, 1989), 144–57; and Keith Baker, *Condorcet: From Natural Philosophy to Social Mathematics* (Chicago: University of Chicago Press, 1975).

22. Georg Simmel, "Soziologische Aesthetik," *Die Zukunft* 17 (1896): 208, 209–10.

23. Simmel, "Soziologische Aesthetik," 210–11.

24. See, for example, the Nazis' use of the meticulous Dutch registering and mapping of the population for the implementation of their anti-Jewish policies in Bob Moore, *Victims and Survivors: The Nazi Persecution of the Jews in the Netherlands 1940–1945* (London: Arnold, 1997), 194–99; Scott, *Seeing Like a State*, 78–79. For the Soviet use of passportization in executing deportations in the annexed territories in 1939, see Gross, *Revolution from Abroad*, 188–89; and for the defining and persecuting of internal enemies throughout the prewar era, see Peter Holquist's contribution to this volume.

25. Among the voluminous literature on the lethal combination of legality and biological-medical science in the service of modern extermination campaigns, see especially Omer Bartov, *Murder in Our Midst: The Holocaust, Industrial Killing, and Representation* (New York: Oxford University Press, 1996), esp. 67–70; Ingo Muller, *Hitler's Justice: The Courts of the Third Reich* (Cambridge: Cambridge University Press, 1987); Michael Stolleis, *The Law Under the Swastika: Studies on Legal History in Nazi Germany* (Chicago: University of Chicago Press, 1998); Michael Burleigh, *Death and Deliverance: "Euthanasia" in Germany 1900–1945* (Cambridge: Cambridge University Press, 1994); Henry Friedlander, *The Origins of Nazi Genocide: From Euthanasia to the Final Solution* (Chapel Hill: University of North Carolina Press, 1995); Detlev Peukert, "The Genesis of the 'Final Solution' from the Spirit of Science," in Thomas Childers and Jane Caplan, eds., *Reevaluating the Third Reich* (New York: Holmes & Meier, 1993), 234–52. See also Richard Weisberg, *Vichy Law and the Holocaust in France* (New York: New York University Press, 1996), for the culpability of the legal ethos and profession in

the persecution of French Jewry; and David Horn, *Social Bodies: Science, Reproduction, and Italian Modernity* (Princeton, N.J.: Princeton University Press, 1994), on the employment of reproductive policies and technologies in the service of social engineering in interwar Italy.

26. For the prominent role played by intellectuals and professionals in a variety of social-engineering enterprises in the twentieth century, from ethnic cleansing to eugenics and welfare policies, see Norman Naimark, *Fires of Hatred: Ethnic Cleansing in Twentieth-Century Europe* (Cambridge, Mass.: Harvard University Press, 2001); Burleigh, "Eugenic Utopias," 60; Ian Robert Dowbiggin, *Keeping America Sane: Psychiatry and Eugenics in the United States and Canada, 1880–1940* (Ithaca, N.Y.: Cornell University Press, 1997); Mazower, *Dark Continent*, 87–88.

27. For an insightful analysis of this phenomenon, see Michael Geyer, "The Militarization of Europe, 1914–1945," in John Gillis, ed., *The Militarization of the Western World* (New Brunswick, N.J.: Rutgers University Press, 1989), 65–102.

28. The systematic uprooting of Muslims patterned after the conscious urge to reorder society and the increasing desire for ethnoreligious homogeneity in the course of imperial Russian consolidation of rule over Crimea and the Caucasus, along with the disintegration of the Ottoman Empire and the rise of Balkan nationalism, is considered a turning point in modern population policies. Willis Brooks, "Russia's Conquest and Pacification of the Caucasus: Relocation Becomes a Pogrom in the Post-Crimean War Period," *Nationalities Papers* 23 (1995): 675–86; Rogers Brubaker, *Nationalism Reframed: Nationhood and the National Question in the New Europe* (Cambridge: Cambridge University Press, 1996), 152–56; Peter Holquist, "To Count, to Extract, to Exterminate: Population Statistics and Population Politics in Late Imperial and Soviet Russia," in Ronald Suny and Terry Martin, eds., *State of Nations: Empire and Nation-Making in the Age of Lenin and Stalin* (New York: Oxford University Press, 2001): 111–44; Kemal Karpat, *Ottoman Population, 1830–1914* (Madison: University of Wisconsin Press, 1985), 65–75. Whereas the origins and frequent use of mass population transfers were unmistakably European, they were soon adopted by postcolonial non-European regimes as well. Despite the passage of time and the new research on individual cases, Joseph Schechtman's work is still a good starting point. See *European Population Transfers, 1939–1945* (New York: Oxford University Press, 1946); *Postwar Population Transfers in Europe, 1945–1955* (Philadelphia: University of Pennsylvania Press, 1962); and *Population Transfers in Asia* (New York: Hallsby Press, 1949).

29. Michael Marrus, *The Unwanted: European Refugees in the Twentieth Century* (Oxford: Oxford University Press, 1985), 3–121.

30. Joseph Conrad, *Heart of Darkness* (London: Penguin Books, 1995), 20.

31. Mazower, *Dark Continent*, 100. For the use of *Askari*, see *The Stroop Report*, trans. Cybil Milton (New York: Pantheon Books, 1979), unpaginated photo section under document no. 33/202z, no. 4527. In this light, Hannah Arendt's suggestive treatise on the relations between imperialism and continental policies is still indispensable and substantiated by recent research of German military practices in East Africa and later doctrine and conduct in Europe.

32. On the conscious removal of restraints on violence in colonial wars—mainly the erasure of the distinction between combatants, noncombatants, and prisoners of

war—ideologically based dehumanization of the enemy and its culture, and a concerted effort to destroy the socioeconomic structure of the foe, see Sabine Dabringhaus, "An Army on Vacation? The German War in China, 1900–1901"; Trutz von Trotha, "'The Fellows Can Just Starve': On Wars of 'Pacification' in the African Colonies of Imperial Germany and the Concept of 'Total War'"; and Robert Utley, "Total War on the American Indian Frontier," both in Manfred Boemeke et al., eds., *Anticipating Total War: The German and American Experiences, 1871–1914* (Cambridge: Cambridge University Press, 1999). See also Adam Hochschild, *King Leopold's Ghost: A Story of Greed, Terror, and Heroism in Colonial Africa* (New York: Mariner Books, 1998) on the greatest colonial massacre in Belgian Congo, which cost some ten million lives.

33. Georgii Glezerman, *Likvidatsiia ekspluatators kikh klassov i preodelenie klassovykh razlichii v SSSR* (Moscow: Gos. Izd-vo polit. lit-ry, 1949), 229.

34. M. D. Kammari, *Marksizm-Leninizm o roli lichnosti v istorii* (Moscow: Gos. izd-vo. polit. lit-ry, 1953), 235. Looking back at the fate of the revolution, Viacheslav Molotov, Stalin's most loyal lieutenant, observed with unconcealed disdain the pretense of the post-Stalin leadership to reach Communism via an evolutionary, peaceful path. "The task of elimination of social classes is arduous and revolutionary. But 'we are building communism' is only a lame excuse for avoiding this question and an effort to escape revolutionary tasks. Communism, they say there [at the top], springs on its own as classes are eliminated. This is a typical rightist position. There is no need to eliminate the kulak, he will do it himself. Here we have the morality of the rightists: 'let us find an explanation for needless cruelty; we must be humanists, and laws must be obeyed.' But this morality is not revolutionary. . . . The whole point is that you cannot arrive at communism without having resolved this question." *Sto sorok besed s Molotovym: iz dnevnika F. Chueva* (Moscow: Terra, 1991), 483, 490.

35. Cited in Saul Friedländer, *Nazi Germany and the Jews*, vol. 1, *The Years of Persecution, 1933–1939* (New York: Harper Collins, 1997), 102.

36. In his speech at the meeting of SS major-generals at Posen on October 4, 1943, when the extermination process was reaching its maximum intensity, Heinrich Himmler stated that no danger was expected at that point from Communists in the Reich, because "their leading elements, like most criminals, are in our concentration camps." Office of United States Chief of Counsel for Prosecution of Axis Criminality, *Nazi Conspiracy and Aggression*, vol. 4 (Washington, D.C.: U.S. GPO, 1946), 560.

37. Arendt, *Origins of Totalitarianism*, 464.

38. On the number of employees and informants of the political police as an indicator of a lower level of self-policing and the regime's popularity, see Sheila Fitzpatrick, "Introduction to the Practices of Denunciation in Modern European History," *Journal of Modern History*, 68, no. 4 (December 1996): 755, 758; Jeffrey Brooks, *Thank You, Comrade Stalin! Soviet Public Culture from Revolution to Cold War* (Princeton, N.J.: Princeton University Press, 2000), 10. The selectivity of the Nazis in the choice of their targets is effectively argued by Eric Johnson in *Nazi Terror: The Gestapo, Jews, and Ordinary Germans* (New York: Basic Books, 1999). On communal policing in the postwar Soviet Union, see Amir Weiner, *Making Sense of War: The Second World War and the Fate of the Bolshevik Revolution* (Princeton, N.J.: Princeton University Press, 2000), 317–22; Theodore Friedgut, *Political Participation in the USSR* (Princeton, N.J.: Princeton University Press, 1979), 235–88; Oleg Kharkhordin, *The Collective and the Individ-*

ual in Russia: A Study of Practices (Berkeley: University of California Press, 1999), 75–117, 279–303.

39. Counsel for Prosecution of Axis Criminality, *Nazi Conspiracy and Aggression*, vol. 4:563–64.

40. Ernst Klee, Willie Dressen, and Volker Riess, eds., *"The Good Old Days": The Holocaust as Seen by Its Perpetrators and Bystanders* (New York: Free Press, 1991), 150. In a similar manner, the Catholic and Protestant divisional chaplains who inspected the place where the children were locked prior to their execution expressed indignation over the horrifying conditions in which the children were held and, tellingly, over the visibility of the situation but not over the executions themselves. Klee, Dressen, and Riess, *"Good Old Days,"* 143–44.

41. See the complaint of an SS officer against the beating of Jewish deportees in Berlin, dated March 4, 1943, in John Steiner, *Power, Politics, and Social Change in National Socialist Germany: A Process of Escalation into Mass Destruction* (Atlantic Highlands, N.J.: Humanities Press, 1976), 418–21.

42. In the above-mentioned massacre of Jewish children in Bila Tserkva, the Waffen-SS officer ordered to carry out the execution bluntly refused and the task was handed over to the Ukrainian militia. Klee, Dressen, and Riess, "Good Old Days," 153–54. See also Omer Bartov, *Hitler's Army: Soldiers, Nazis, and War in the Third Reich* (Oxford: Oxford University Press, 1991), 164–65; Christopher Browning, *Ordinary Men: Reserve Police Battalion 101 and the Final Solution in Poland* (New York: HarperCollins, 1992), 55–77; Mark Mazower, "Military Violence and National Socialist Values: The Wehrmacht in Greece, 1941–1944," *Past and Present* 134 (February 1992): 129–58.

43. See Robert Ian Moore, "Heresy as Disease,' in W. Lourdaux and D. Verhelst, eds., *The Concept of Heresy in the Middle Ages (11th–13th C.)* (Leuven, Belgium: University Press, 1976), preface and 1–11, here, 11.

44. Reference here is to Stalin's famous speech on March 5, 1937, and editorials before and during the 'uncovering' of the "Doctors Plot" in early 1953. See *Komsomol'skaia pravda*, February 12, 1953; January 15, 1953; *Izvestiia*, January 15, 1953.

45. Stephane Courtois et al., *The Black Book of Communism: Crimes, Terror, Repression*, trans. Jonathan Murphy and Mark Kramer (Cambridge, Mass.: Harvard University Press, 1999).

46. Although, as several recent studies have pointed out, Italian Fascism was far more violent than is conventionally assumed, it still remained largely a concentrated drive to stylize social life that more often than not refrained from cutting into the flesh of its own subjects. Without downplaying the domestic brutality of Italian Fascism, the fact remains that the most systematic violence was applied against external foes in the colonies and not against internal opponents of the regime. The latter were often subjected to segregation and rehabilitation, rather than physical extermination. See the excellent studies by Ruth Ben-Ghiat, *Fascist Modernities: Italy, 1922–1945* (Berkeley: University of California Press, 2001), 5, 123–30, 148–57; and Simonetta Falasca-Zamponi, *The Fascist Spectacle: The Aesthetics of Power in Mussolini's Italy* (Berkeley: University of California Press, 1997), 28–38.

47. Margarete Buber, *Under Two Dictators*, trans. Edward Fitzgerald (New York: Dodd, Mead & Co., 1949), 215.

48. On the prevalence of this dilemma in Stalinist Russia and the struggles of individuals to cope with it, see the works cited in Note 5. On the tension between "class as political behavior" and "natural redness" in Communist China, see Lynn T. White III, *Policies of Chaos: The Organizational Causes of Violence in China's Cultural Revolution* (Princeton, N.J.: Princeton University Press, 1989), 222–25, 267; Richard Curt Kraus, *Class Conflict in Chinese Socialism* (New York: Columbia University Press, 1981), 89–141; and the contributions of Stuart Schram, Susan Shirk, Jonathan Unger, and Lynn White III, in James L. Watson, ed., *Class and Social Stratification in Post-Revolution China* (Cambridge: Cambridge University Press, 1984).

49. M. Loginov, "Vozvrashchenie k zhizni," in Gosudarstvennyi Arkhiv Rossiiskoi Federatsii (GARF), f. 9414, op. 4, d. 145, l. 3. Notably, a decade earlier, it was the Western penal system that was the favorite point of reference. Maxim Gorky et al., *Belomor: An Account of the Construction of the New Canal Between the White Sea and the Baltic Sea* (New York: H. Smith and R. Haas, 1935), 328.

50. Mark Mazower, *Dark Continent.*

51. Asher Arian, Ilan Talmud, and Tamar Hermann, *National Security and Public Opinion in Israel* (Boulder, Colo.: Westview Press, 1988), 56–67.

CHAPTER 1, *Holquist*

I am indebted to Omer Bartov, Jochen Hellbeck, David Hoffmann, Eric Naiman, Jan Plamper, Amir Weiner, and Eric Weitz for stimulating comments on this essay.

1. N. I. Bukharin, *Problemy teorii i praktiki sotsializma* (Moscow, 1989; original, 1920), epigraph: 168, information about Lenin's underlining: 454 n. 34. See also Maxim Gorky's similar but more critical formulation of this project: *Untimely Thoughts* (New Haven, Conn., 1995; original, 1917–1918), 88–89; discussion of Lenin's underlining: 149.

2. Maxim Gorky et al., *Belomor: An Account of the Construction of the New Canal Between the White Sea and the Baltic Sea* (New York: H. Smith and R. Haas, 1935), 301, 308.

3. The best recent treatment is Oleg Khlevniuk, "The Objectives of the Great Terror," in Julian Cooper, Maureen Perrie, and E. A. Rees, eds., *Soviet History, 1917–1953: Essays in Honor of R. W. Davies* (New York, 1995); Alexander Solzhenitsyn, *The Gulag Archipelago*, 3 vols. (New York, 1974) is still valuable.

4. J. Arch Getty, *Origins of the Great Purges: The Soviet Communist Party Reconsidered, 1933–1938* (New York, 1985); Gábor Tamás Rittersporn, *Stalinist Simplifications and Soviet Complications: Social Tensions and Political Conflicts in the USSR* (Philadelphia, 1991); J. Arch Getty and Roberta Manning, eds., *Stalinist Terror: New Perspectives* (New York, 1993). For a critique of this approach, see Oleg Khlevniuk, "Les mécanismes de la 'Grand Terreur' des années 1937–1938 au Turkménistan," *Cahiers du Monde russe* 39, nos. 1–2 (1998): 197–208, here, 197–98.

5. Robert Thurston, *Life and Terror in Stalin's Russia, 1934–1941* (New Haven, Conn., 1995), esp. 58, 227.

6. Many years ago, Hannah Arendt concluded that totalitarian terror "has ceased to be a mere means for the suppression of opposition, though it is also used for such purposes." *The Origins of Totalitarianism* (New York, 1973), 464.

7. "Nationalsozialisimus und Stalinismus: über Gedächtnis, Willkür und Tod," in Dan Diner, *Kreisläufe: über Nationalsozialismus und Gedächtnis* (Frankfurt am Main, 1995).

8. Ian Kershaw, "Totalitarianism Revisited: Nazism and Stalinism in Comparative Perspective," *Tel-Aviver Jahrbuch für deutsche Geschichte* 23 (1994): 23–40; Ian Kershaw and Moshe Lewin, "Afterthoughts," in Ian Kershaw and Moshe Lewin, eds., *Stalinism and Nazism* (Cambridge, England, 1997); Michael Burleigh and Wolfgang Wipperman, *The Racial State: Germany, 1933–1945* (New York, 1994), 15–16, 306.

9. Along somewhat different lines, see Stefan Plaggenborg, "Gewalt und Militanz in Sowjetrussland, 1917–1930, *Jahrbücher für Geschichte Osteuropas* 44, no. 3 (1996): 409–30; for the Soviet postwar use of violence, see Amir Weiner's contribution to this volume.

10. V. Shklovsky, "Iskusstvo kak priëm," in *Sbornik po teorii poeticheskogo iazyka* (Saint Petersburg, 1917). See the excellent treatment in Katerina Clark, *Petersburg: Crucible of Cultural Revolution* (Cambridge, Mass., 1995), 32–34.

11. Modris Eksteins, *Rites of Spring* (New York, 1989), 70.

12. "The Logic of Totalitarianism" and "The Image of the Body in Totalitarianism," both in Claude Lefort, *The Political Forms of Modern Society*, ed. John Thompson (Cambridge, Mass., 1986). For a somewhat similar formulation, see the compelling argument by Michael Mann, "The Contradictions of Continuous Revolution," in Kershaw and Lewin, *Stalinism and Nazism.*

13. Stephen Kotkin, "1991 and the Russian Revolution," *Journal of Modern History* 70, no. 2 (1998): 384–425, here, 421. Kotkin, however, focuses mostly upon the Sovietological practitioners of totalitarianism; his argument for viewing the Soviet experience as 'modernity' can be made consonant, I believe, with the more historical, non-Sovietological variant of totalitarianism.

14. See Abbot Gleason, *Totalitarianism: The Inner History of the Cold War* (New York, 1995), for the career of the concept.

15. Carl Friedrich and Zbigniew Brzezinski, *Totalitarian Dictatorship and Autocracy* (New York, 1966; original, 1956); Arendt, *Origins of Totalitarianism*; Jacob Talmon, *The Origins of Totalitarian Democracy* (London, 1952). See the treatment of these two schools by Gleason, *Totalitarianism*, chapters 6–7.

16. For the prophylactic argument in the specifically German context, see Zygmunt Bauman, *Modernity and the Holocaust* (Ithaca, N.Y., 1991); Detlev Peukert, "The Genesis of the 'Final Solution' from the Spirit of Science," in Thomas Childers and Jane Caplan, eds., *Reevaluating the Third Reich* (New York, 1993). For this argument in other contexts, see Mary Poovey, *Making a Social Body* (Chicago, 1995), esp. 90–94; Robert Nye, *Crime, Madness and Politics: The Medical Concept of National Decline* (Princeton, N.J., 1984); and David Horn, *Social Bodies: Science, Reproduction and Italian Modernity* (Princeton, N.J., 1994).

17. Solzhenitsyn, *Gulag Archipelago*, vol. 1:42, 77; F. Chuev, *Sto sorok besed s Molotovym* (Moscow, 1991), 390–91. The most suggestive treatments along this line have been Stephen Kotkin's analysis of the Terror as a drive for purity, a secular Inquisition (*Magnetic Mountain* [Berkeley, Calif., 1994]) and Eric Naiman's discussion of fears of contamination during NEP (*Sex in Public: the Incarnation of Soviet Ideology* [Princeton, N.J., 1997]).

18. Sander Gilman, *Disease and Representation* (Ithaca, N.Y., 1988), xiii–xiv, 2, 5; also George Mosse, *Towards the Final Solution*, chapter 2.

19. Gorky, *Untimely Thoughts*, 231 (1918).

20. N. Dmitrieva, "Esteticheskaia kategoriia prekrasnogo," *Iskusstvo*, no. 1 (1952): 79. Among examples of socialist aesthetics, Dmitrieva counts canals and industrial installations.

21. Jochen Hellbeck, "Laboratories of the Soviet Self: Diaries from the Stalin Era," Ph.D. dissertation, Columbia University, 1998, demonstrates this point; see also Clark, *Petersburg*; Naiman, *Sex in Public*; Boris Groys, *The Total Art of Stalinism* (Princeton, N.J., 1992); and Vladislav Todorov, *Red Square, Black Square* (Albany, N.Y., 1995). For treatments of the simultaneity of the aesthetic and technical in the German context, see Modris Ekstein's *Rites of Spring* (Boston, 1989), esp. 315–31; Klaus Theweleit, *Male Fantasies*, 2 vols., trans. Erica Carter, Stephen Conway, and Chris Turner (Minneapolis, 1987–89), esp. vol. 2: 197–206; Horn, *Social Bodies*.

22. Peter Fritzsche, "Nazi Modern," *MODERNISM/Modernity* 3, no. 1 (1996): 1–21, here, 8–10. For other expressions of the fantastic and aesthetic as part of the National Socialist program, see Eksteins, *Rites of Spring*, 303–4; and Saul Friedländer, *Nazi Germany and the Jews, 1933–1939* (New York, 1997), 86–87.

23. Alexis de Tocqueville, *The Old Regime and the French Revolution* (New York, 1983), 192. See also Keith Michael Baker, "Representation," in Keith Baker, ed., *The Political Culture of the Old Regime* (New York, 1986); and Roger Chartier, "The Chimera of Origins," in Jan Goldstein, ed., *Foucault and the Writing of History* (Cambridge, Mass., 1994).

24. Keith Baker, *Condorcet: From Natural Philosophy to Social Mathematics* (Chicago, 1975), x. On the rise of the social, see also Poovey, *Making a Social Body*; Jacques Donzelot, *The Policing of Families* (New York, 1979); and, on a later period, Horn, *Social Bodies*.

25. Catherine Gallagher, "The Body Versus the Social Body in the Works of Thomas Malthus and Henry Mayhew," *Representations* 14 (1986): 83–106. See also Ian Hacking, "Biopower and the Avalanche of Printed Numbers," *Humanities in Society* 5, nos. 3–4 (1982): 279–95, and Joan Scott, "Statistical Representations of Work," in Steven Kaplan and Cynthia Koepp, eds., *Work in France* (Ithaca, N.Y., 1986).

26. Alf Lüdtke, "The Permanence of Internal War," in Stig Förster and Jörg Nagler, eds., *On the Road to Total War* (Washington D.C., 1997), here, 388–89; see also Nye, *Crime, Madness and Politics*.

27. Alain Blum, "Oublier l'état pour comprendre la Russie (XIXe–XXe siècles)," *Revue des Etudes slaves* 66, no. 1 (1994): 135–45; on the significance of military statistics, see Peter Holquist, "'To Count, To Extract, To Exterminate': Population Statistics and Population Politics in Late Imperial and Soviet Russia," in Terry Martin and Ron Suny, eds., *A State of Nations: Empire and Nation-Making in the Age of Lenin and Stalin* (Oxford, England, 2001).

28. On the deportations, see Eric Lohr, "Enemy Alien Politics in the Russian Empire During World War One," Ph.D. dissertation, Harvard University, 1999; S. Nelipovich, "V poiskakh 'vnutrennego vraga': deportatsionnaia politika Rossii (1914–1917)," in *Pervaia mirovaia voina i uchastie v nei Rossii (1914–1918)*, 2 vols. (Moscow, 1994); Daniel Graf, "Military Rule Behind the Russian Front," *Jahrbücher für Geschichte*

Osteuropas 22, no. 3 (1974): 390–411; Mark von Hagen, "The Great War and the Mobilization of Ethnicity," in Barnett Rubin and Jack Snyder, eds., *Post-Soviet Political Order* (New York, 1998). For documents, see "Dokumenty o presledovanii evreev," *Arkhiv russkoi revoliutsii* 19 (1928): 245–84.

29. On measures during the course of the First World War to protect imperial forces from "harmful actions by the Jewish population," including the taking of hostages and mass deportations, see "Dokumenty o presledovanii evreev," 248, 250–51, 256–58, here, 275 (Jews described as a "pernicious element"). See also *The Jews of the Eastern War Zone* (New York, 1916); and *Evakuatsiia i rekvizitsiia: spravochnik deistvuiushchikh uzakonenii i rasporiazhenii* (Petrograd, 1916), 99–102, for the August 3, 1914, instruction sanctioning hostage taking in order to facilitate requisitioning in the war zone.

30. Nikolai Kharlamov, "Izbienie v pervoprestolnoi: nemetskii pogrom v Moskve v mae 1915," *Rodina* 1993, no. 8/9: 127–32; also Iu. Kir'ianov, "'Maiskie bezporiadki' 1915 g. v Moskve," *Voprosy istorii* 1994, no. 12:137–50.

31. Peter Holquist, "'Information is the Alpha and Omega of Our Work,'" *Journal of Modern History* 69, no. 3 (1997): 415–50 and "To Count."

32. See Elisabeth Domansky's contribution to this volume. On the First World War as creating a culture of violence in Russia, see Gorky, *Untimely Thoughts*, 9–12, 76–77, 128–30, 185, 195–99 (1917–18); Leon Trotsky, *Terrorism and Communism* (Ann Arbor, Mich., 1961; original, 1920), 65–68; Plaggenborg, "Gewalt"; and Roger Pethybridge, *The Social Prelude to Stalinism* (New York, 1974), chapter 3.

33. Peter Holquist, "Research Note: Anti-Soviet *Svodki* from the Civil War," *Russian Review* 56, no. 3 (1997): 445–50.

34. Peter Kenez, "Pogroms and White Ideology in the Russian Civil War," in John Klier and Shlomo Lambroza, eds., *Pogroms and Anti-Jewish Violence in Modern Russian History* (New York, 1992); A. L. Litvin, "Krasnyi i belyi terror v Rossii, 1917–1922," *Otechestvennaia istoriia* no. 6 (1993): 46–62; E. I. Dostovalov, "O belykh i belom terrore," *Rossiiskii arkhiv* 6 (1995): 637–97, "filtering," 678.

35. David Hoffmann, "European Modernity and Soviet Socialism," in David Hoffmann and Yanni Kotsonis, eds., *Russian Modernity: Politics, Knowledge, Practices* (New York, 2000); Kotkin, *Magnetic Mountain*.

36. Peter Holquist, "'Conduct Merciless, Mass Terror': Decossackization on the Don, 1919," *Cahiers du Monde russe* 38, nos. 1–2 (1997): 127–62.

37. I. I. Reingol'd to the CC, "Dokladnaia zapiska," in *Bol'shevistskoe rukovodstvo: perepiska, 1912–1927* (Moscow, 1997), 107–10, here, 108.

38. Peukert, "Genesis." Nye (*Crime, Madness, and Politics*, xi, 67–73) makes a similar observation about ideas of degeneracy in France.

39. The Soviets were quite explicit about this: for a postwar recapitulation of this point, see G. Glezerman, "Likvidatsiia ekspluatatorskikh klassov v SSSR," in F. Konstantinov, M. Kammari, G. Glezerman, eds., *O sovetskom sotsialisticheskom obshchestve* (Moscow, 1948).

40. This point is treated in greater detail in Holquist "To Count." Such campaigns share some features of later Nazi "cleansing operations" (*Säuberungsunternehmen*) in the Second World War: see Omer Bartov, *The Eastern Front: German Troops and the Barbarization of Warfare* (New York, 1986); and Mark Mazower, *Inside Hitler's Greece* (New Haven, Conn., 1993).

41. For the Don in 1921, see Rossiiskii gosudarstvennyi voennyi arkhiv (RGVA), f. 25896, op. 1, d. 8, ll. 2–12, 15 (yearly report of Don Military assembly to combat banditry and report of local plenipotentiary); for the Soviet anti-insurgency campaign against Antonov, see Viktor Danilov, ed., *Antonovshchina: dokumenty i materialy* (Tambov, Russia, 1994).

42. Danilov, *Antonovshchina*, 182.

43. Quotation "we must strive . . ." from RGVA, f. 25896, op. 1, d. 8, l. 15; for analogous orders, see Danilov, *Antonovshchina*, 165–66, 172, 182, 187.

44. Holquist, "To Count."

45. *Bol'shevistskoe rukovodstvo*, 150; commendation as cited in Litvin, "Krasnyi i belyi terror," 55–56.

46. Solzhenitsyn, *Gulag Archipelago*, vol. 1:39, 77.

47. Naiman, *Sex in Public*, 263; similarly, Clark, *Petersburg*, 211.

48. On the emergence of the system of concentration camps, see Michael Jakobson, *Origins of the Gulag: The Soviet Prison Camp System, 1917–1934* (Lexington, Ky., 1993); and the documents in Diane Koenker and Ronald Bachman, eds., *Revelations from the Russian Archives* (Washington, D.C., 1997), 132–40.

49. "Lageria prinuditel'nykh rabot na Orlovshchine v nachale 1920-kh godov," *Rekviem*, vol. 2 (Orel, Russia, 1995), 20–27.

50. Dzerzhinsky to Lenin in Richard Pipes, ed., *The Unknown Lenin* (New Haven, Conn., 1996), 119–21; on the Moscow camps, see also Koenker and Bachman, *Revelations from the Russian Archives*, 134–38.

51. This account is based on A. P. Belobrov, "Kak bol'sheviki 'fil'trovali' flotskikh ofitserov," *Istochnik* no. 3 (1996): 64–81. On the place of autobiographies in Bolshevik hermeneutics, see Igal Halfin's "From Darkness to Light: Student Communist Autobiographies in the 1920s," *Jahrbücher für Geschichte Osteuropas* 45, no. 2 (1997): 210–36; and Igal Halfin, *Class, Consciousness, and Salvation in Revolutionary Russia* (Pittsburgh, Pa., 1999).

52. "Kazach'ia sem'ia Khripunovykh: vospominaniia E.V. Kalabinoi," *Voprosy istorii*, nos. 11–12 (1996): 73–86. For orders that captured officers are to be processed first by "special departments" and then dispatched to concentration camps, see *Rezoliutsii i postanovleniia vtorogo donskogo s"ezda sovetov* (Rostov, Russia, 1920), 19–20; *Prikazy sovetskim voiskam 9-oi armii* (n.p., 1920), 340; Gosudarstvennyi arkhiv Rostovskoi oblasti (GARO), f. R-97, op. 1, d. 516, l. 36 (Don Cheka directive ordering all officers to be held in concentration camps in the far rear).

53. "'Sfotografirovannye rechi': govoriat uchastniki 'likvidatsii antonovshchiny,'" *Otechestvennye arkhivy*, no. 2 (1996): 34–66.

54. Iu.V. Doinykh, "Predshestvenniki Solovkov: novye arkhivnye svidetel'stva," *Otechestvennye arkhivy*, no. 1 (1994): 76–80.

55. This figure is in Doinykh, "Predshestvenniki Solovkov," 80.

56. For the underlying logic of the terror of 1937–38, but with an analysis of the geopolitical conjuncture that made its particular unfolding possible, see Kotkin, *Magnetic Mountain*, chapter 7.

57. Solzhenitsyn, *Gulag Archipelago*, vol. 1, chapter 2; Nicolas Werth, "De la trêve au 'grand tournant,'" in Stéphane Courtois et al., eds., *Le livre noir du communism* (Paris, 1997), esp. 150–55; S. A. Krasil'nikov, "Ssylka v 1920-e gody," *Minuvshee*, vol. 21 (Moscow–Saint Petersburg, 1997): 175–239.

58. See V. N. Zemskov, "Zakliuchennye v 30-e gody: demograficheskii aspekt," *Sotsiologicheskie issledovaniia*, no. 7 (1996): 3–14.

59. Solzhenitsyn, *Gulag Archipelago*, vol. 1, chapter 2; Oleg Khlevniuk, *Politbiuro: mekhanizmy politicheskoi vlasti v 1930-e gody* (Moscow, 1996), 196.

60. These examples are from the Smolensk Archive, WKP 166, ll. 3–5, 30–38; for similar documents on the Poles'e and the Khar'kov regions, see Koenker and Bachman, *Revelations from the Russian Archives*, 402, 416. On the dekulakization campaign, see Lynne Viola, *Peasant Rebels Under Stalin* (Oxford, England, 1997).

61. N. Ia. Gushchin, *'Raskulachivanie' v Sibiri (1928–1934)* (Novosibirsk, 1996), 111–12 (emphasis in original).

62. Holquist, "To Count"; Viola, *Peasant Rebels*, 175–79; and the language employed in the OGPU directive no. 4421 (see following note).

63. OGPU directive no. 4421 in *Neizvestnaia Rossiia*, vol. 1 (Moscow, 1992), 237–45; quotations from Viola, *Peasant Rebels*, 37; figure on sentences, Khlevniuk, *Politbiuro*, 19.

64. Kotkin, *Magnetic Mountain*, 217; on the kulak "special settlers," see the documentary publication *Spetspereselentsy v Zapadnoi Sibiri*, 3 vols. (Novosibirsk, 1992–93).

65. For the reports at this plenum, see *Voprosy istorii*, nos. 5–6 (1993). On how the geopolitical situation played into the Terror, see Kotkin, *Magnetic Mountain*, 303, 310, 319–20, 334, 337; on how Bolshevik eschatology contributed to the dynamic, see Halfin, "From Darkness to Light" and *Class, Consciousness and Salvation*, as well as Stephen Hanson, *Time and Revolution* (Chapel Hill, N.C., 1997), 166–70.

66. For the Central Committee resolution and NKVD order no. 00447, see *Trud*, June 4, 1992; for increases in the arrest and execution target figures, see *Izvestiia*, April 3, 1996, 5. For the conduct of this operation in two regions, see Khlevniuk, "Les mécanismes," 197–208; and D. I. Bogomolov et al. eds., *Leningradskii martirolog*, vol. 1 (Saint Petersburg, 1995), 38–48.

67. *Moskovskie novosti*, June 21, 1992; also *Izvestiia*, April 3, 1996. The number of victims of this operation certainly exceeded its official "limits" (Khlevniuk, "Les mécanismes," 202–4).

68. For example, J. Arch Getty, *Origins of the Great Purges*; contra this, see Solzhenitsyn, *Gulag Archipelago*, vol. 1:70.

69. For instance, 96 percent of the victims in the Tomsk region did not belong to the Party (V. N. Uimanov, *Repressii: kak eto bylo* [Tomsk, Russia, 1995], 50–51). However, Zemskov ("Zakliuchennye," 8) notes that such figures did not include those who had earlier been expelled from the Party. Undoubtedly, Party members suffered disproportionately in the Terror. The point, however, is that violence was not circumscribed to the Party.

70. On German and Russian Marxists' fascination with eugenics, see Loren Graham, "Science and Values: The Eugenics Movement in Germany and Russia in the 1920s," *American Historical Review* 82, no. 5 (1977): 1133–64. Both Eric Naiman (*Sex in Public*) and Halfin (*Class, Consciousness and Salvation*) deal extensively with Soviet notions of degeneracy.

71. Arendt, *Origins of Totalitarianism*, 185.

72. Among a vast literature, see Pradeep Barua, "Inventing Race: the British and India's Martial Races," *Historian* 58, no. 1 (1995): 107–16; David Ludden, "Orientalist

Empiricism: Transformations of Colonial Knowledge," in Carol Breckenridge and Peter van der Veer, eds., *Orientalism and the Postcolonial Predicament* (Philadelphia, 1993); Benedict Anderson, *Imagined Communities*, expanded ed. (New York, 1991); Bernard Cohn, "The Census, Social Stratification and Objectification in South Asia," in *An Anthropologist Among the Historians* (New Delhi, 1987).

73. Sven Lindqvist, *"'Exterminate All the Brutes!'"* (New York, 1996); Isabel Hull, "German Final Solutions in the Wilhelmine Period" (unpublished manuscript); Fran Hirsch, "An Empire of Nations," Ph.D. dissertation, Princeton University, 1998); Holquist, "To Count."

74. Hirsch ("An Empire of Nations") presents Soviet measures as a self-conscious attempt to implement "colonial models" of rule.

75. *Programmy statisticheskikh kursov raionnykh i guberskikh* (Moscow, 1920), 10–11; Kotkin, *Magnetic Mountain*, 94–105.

76. Michel Foucault, "The Political Technology of Individuals," in Luther Martin, Huch Gutman, and Partick Hutton, eds., *Technologies of the Self* (Amherst, Mass., 1988) and Keith Baker, "A Foucauldian French Revolution," in Jan Goldstein, *Foucault and the Writing of History.* For how Nazi Germany and Fascist Italy situated the individuals within a politicosocial matrix, see Götz Aly and Karl Heinz Roth, *Die restlose Erfassung: Volkzählen, Identifizieren und Aussondern im Nationalsozialisimus* (Berlin, 1984); Horn, *Social Bodies*; and Carl Ipsen, *Dictating Demography: The Problem of Population in Fascist Italy* (New York, 1996).

77. Sheila Fitzpatrick, "Ascribing Class: the Construction of Social Identity in Soviet Russia," *Journal of Modern History* 65, no. 4 (1993): 745–70.

78. Fitzpatrick, "Ascribing Class," and Elise Kimerling, "Civil Rights and Social Policy in Soviet Russia, 1918–1936," *Russian Review* 41, no. 1 (1982): 24–46.

79. V. B. Zhiromskaia, "Vsesoiuznye perepisi naseleniia 1926, 1937, 1939 godov," *Istoriia SSSR* no. 3 (1990): 84–104; Catherine Merridale, "The 1937 Census and the Limits of Stalinist Rule," *The Historical Journal* 39, no. 1 (1996): 225–40; and Francine Hirsch, "The Soviet Union as a Work-in-Progress: Ethnographers and the Category of *Nationality* in the 1926, 1937, and 1939 Censuses," *Slavic Review* 56, no. 2 (1997): 251–78. National Socialist censuses likewise had a constructivist agenda; Nazi statisticians described their task as *deutsche Aufbauwerk* (Aly and Roth, *Die restlose Erfassung*, 8).

80. Cited in Naiman, *Sex in Public*, 76.

81. Paul Weindling, *Health, Race and German Politics Between Unification and Nazism, 1870–1945* (Cambridge, England, 1993), 384–85.

82. Naiman, *Sex in Public*, 77, for Bukharin's critique of Enchmen; Lars Lih, "The Mystery of the *ABC*," *Slavic Review* 56, no. 1 (1997): 50–72, Bukharin's enthusiasm for statistical bureaus, 53–54.

83. Mervyn Matthews, *The Passport Society* (Boulder, Colo., 1993), 16–19.

84. Sheila Fitzpatrick, *Stalin's Peasants* (New York, 1994), 92–95.

85. *Pravda*, December 28, 1932. See also Kotkin, *Magnetic Mountain*, 99–101, and V. P. Popov, "Pasportnaia sistema v SSSR (1932–1976)," *Sotsiologicheskie issledovaniia* nos. 8–9 (1995), who argues that the Soviet passport system differed fundamentally from its prerevolutionary predecessor (no. 9: 5).

86. Stepan Podlubnyi, *Tagebuch aus Moskau*, ed. Jochen Hellbeck (Munich, 1996),

109, 115, 122, 127 (original Russian text from personal communication, Jochen Hellbeck, October 14, 1997); see also Jochen Hellbeck, "Fashioning the Stalinist Soul," *Jahrbücher für Geschichte Osteuropas* 44, no. 3 (1996): 351–55.

87. Popov, "Pasportnaia sistema," no. 8:11–13; also "Pasportnaia sistema Sovetskogo soiuza," Nicolaevsky collection, series 227, box 296, folder 18 (I thank Amir Weiner for help in obtaining this document).

88. Popov, "Pasportnaia sistema," no. 8:14, n. 4.

89. Nicolas Werth and Gaël Moullec, ed., *Rapports secrets soviétiques, 1921–1991* (Paris, 1994), 45–47.

90. Rogers Brubaker, "Nationhood and the National Question in the Soviet Union and Post-Soviet Eurasia," *Theory and Society* 23 (1994): 47–78; Hirsch, "Soviet Union as a Work-in-Progress."

91. On photography and the emergence of the human archive, see Allen Sekula, "The Body and the Archive," *October* 39 (1986): 3–64. See also Susanne Regener, "Ausgegrenzt: die optische Inventarisierung des Menschen im Polizeiwesen und in der Psychiatrie," *Fotogeschichte* 10, no. 38 (1990): 23–38; David Green, "Veins of Resemblance: Photography and Eugenics," *Photography/Politics: Two* (1986): 9–21; and Daniel Arasse, *The Guillotine and the Terror*, 140–41. The Nazis later relied on passport photographs to amass an inventory of Jewish faces (Freidländer, *Nazi Germany and the Jews*, 245).

92. For samples of Soviet criminal dossiers with their photographs, see "'Troika postanovila: rasstreliat,'" *Volia* no. 2-3 (1994): 21–79; for other examples, see *Rekviem* (Orel, Russia, 1995), 55–60 and Vitaly Shentalinsky, *Arrested Voices* (New York, 1996).

93. Bogomolov, *Leningradskii martirolog*, photograph 23; for the use of photographs among Gulag inmates, see Peter Maggs, *The Mandelstam and "Der Nister" Files* (Armonk, N.Y., 1996), 20, M-6, K-25.

94. Maggs, *Mandelstam and "Der Nister" Files*, 38–40, M-10, M-16.

95. These questionnaires invariably inquired after one's social and political standing at specific moments in Soviet history. For Red Army questionnaires for defectors (1919), see RGVA, f. 100, op. 2, d. 78, ll. 159–60; also RGVA, f. 1389, op. 1, d. 124, l. 160; for questionnaires for captured Antonov insurgents (1921), see Danilov, *Antonovshchina*, 283–92; for the forms of the Bureaus on Cooperation with the GPU on "suspicious and counterrevolutionary elements" (1922), see "Khoroshii kommunist v to zhe vremia khoroshii chekist," *Vestnik staroi ploshchadi* no. 1 (1996): 115–19; for questionnaires for arrestees from Moscow in 1937–38, see *Volia*, nos. 2–3 (1994): 23; for forms required of Party members in the Red Army in 1939–40, see V. Zenzinov, *Vstrecha s Rossiei* (New York, 1944), 570–71. For how such "mythic" events came to structure frameworks of meaning for Soviet citizens, see Amir Weiner, "The Making of a Dominant Myth," *Russian Review* 55, no. 4 (1996): 638–60.

96. Popov, "Pasportnaia sistema," no. 8:13.

97. Examples are legion. For the extensive documentation on a former Antonov leader, sentenced to exile in 1930 and executed in 1937, see Danilov, *Antonovshchina*, 283–92; the two Cossack brothers mentioned above, whose father was executed while they successfully passed through the civil war's filtration, were rearrested and executed in 1937, in part for their participation in the White Army ("Kazach'ia sem'ia Khripunovykh," 74–75).

98. Sekula, "Body and the Archive"; Michel Foucault, *Discipline and Punish: The Birth of the Prison* (New York, 1979), 281; and Note 91 above. For how the compilation of a human archive facilitated the Nazi applications of violence against Jews, Gypsies, "the asocial," and the hereditarily and mentally ill, see Aly and Roth, *Die restlose Erfassung*; Burleigh and Wipperman, *Racial State*; Friedländer, *Nazi Germany and the Jews*, vol. 1, chapter 6; and Weindling, *Health, Race and German Politics*, 384–85, 526–30. Weindling notes that "these surveys were a precondition for extermination" (528).

99. V. E. Korneev and O. N. Kopylova, "Arkhivist v totalitarnom obshchestve: bor'ba za 'chistotu' arkhivnykh kadrov," *Otechestvennye arkhivy* no. 5 (1993): 29–43, here, 29.

100. T. I. Khorkhordina, *Istoriia otechestva i arkhivy: 1917–1980-e gody* (Moscow, 1994), 176–79. I thank Jan Plamper for bringing this work to my attention.

101. V. E. Korneev and O. N. Kopylova, "Arkhivy na sluzhbe totalitarnogo gosudarstva," *Otechestvennye arkhivy* 1992, no. 3:13–24.

102. Khorkhordina, *Istoriia otechestva i arkhivy*, 177–78.

103. Korneev and Kopyleva, "Arkhivy na sluzhbe," 19–20.

104. Korneev and Kopylova, "Arkhivy na sluzhbe," 20–22.

105. Patritsiia Kennedi Grimsted [Patricia Kennedy Grimstead], "Zarubezhnaia arkhivnaia Rossika i Sovetika," *Otechestvennye arkhivy* 1993, no. 1:20–53, here, 42–43.

106. Zemskov, "Zakliuchennye," 7; also Uimanov, *Repressii*, 25, 27, 47; Solzhenitsyn, *Gulag Archipelago*, vol. 1:34–35; Khlevniuk, *Politbiuro*, 196.

107. Bogomolov, *Leningradskii martirolog*, 38–48, esp. 39.

108. Khlevniuk, "Les mécanismes," 203.

109. For Nazi Germany, see Burleigh and Wipperman, *Racial State*, 167–82. One of the targeted groups during the operation against anti-Soviet elements was the entire recidivist criminal population: see V. N. Uimanov and Iu. A. Petrukhin, eds., *Bol' liudskaia: kniga pamiati tomichei, repressirovannykh v 30–40-e i nachale 50-kh godov*, 4 vols. (Tomsk, Russia, 1994), vol. 3:64, and Bogomolov, *Leningradskii martirolog*, 47–48.

110. I am indebted to Omer Bartov for pressing me on this point. Stephen Wheatcroft, "German and Soviet Repression and Mass Death," *Europe-Asia Studies* 48, no. 8 (1996): 1319–53, esp. 1323, is a helpful first step in this tortuous comparison.

111. Friedländer, *Nazi Germany and the Jews*.

112. Tony Judt, "The Longest Road to Hell," *New York Times*, December 22, 1997.

113. Lefort, *Political Forms of Modern Society*, 282, 299.

114. Rossiiskii gosudarstvennyi arkhiv sotsial'no-politicheskoi istorii (RGASPI), f. 17, op. 65, d. 34, l. 115 (Frenkel' to Central Committee), ll. 85–89 (Trifonov's report).

115. Nikolai Bukharin, *Teoriia istoricheskogo materializma: populiarnyi uchebnik marksistskoi sotsiologii* (Moscow-Petrograd, 1923), 11–13 (all emphases in original).

116. Gorky et al., *Belomor*, 71, 127, 325.

117. On Marr, see Yuri Slezkine, "N. Ia. Marr and the Origins of Soviet Ethnogenetics," *Slavic Review* 55, no. 4 (1996): 826–62, and Clark, *Petersburg*, chapter 9; on Lysenko within the broader context of Soviet politics and culture, see Boris Gasparov, "Development or Rebuilding? Views of Academician Lysenko in the Context of the Late Avant-Garde," in John Bowlt and Olga Matich, eds., *Laboratory of Dreams* (Stanford, Calif., 1996).

118. Laura Engelstein, *The Keys to Happiness: Sex and the Search for Modernity in Fin-de-Siècle Russia* (Ithaca, N.Y., 1992), 129, 137; similarly, 132.

119. For this provocative argument, see Eli Weinerman, "Racism, Racial Prejudice and Jews in Late Imperial Russia," *Ethnic and Racial Studies* 17, no. 3 (1994): 442–95.

120. Yuri Slezkine, "The Fall of Soviet Ethnography, 1928–1938," *Current Anthropology* 32, no. 4 (1991): 476–84, here, 480; Slezkine, "Marr," 847.

121. Hirsch, "Soviet Union as Work-in-Progress," 268, likewise 260; also Slezkine, "Marr," 853.

122. Fitzpatrick, "Ascribing," 758.

123. Nikolai Bukharin, *Tiuremnye rukopisi*, 2 vols. (Moscow, 1996), vol. 1:145, vol. 2:195, 201 (emphasis in original).

124. Iurii Murin, ed., "'Nevol'niki v rukakh germanskogo reikhsvera': rech' I.V. Stalina v Narkomate oborony," *Istochnik* 1994, no. 3:72–88.

125. On the significance of trajectories toward consciousness in Party autobiographies and purge trials, see Halfin, "From Darkness to Life."

126. For Hess's quote, see Robert Lifton, *The Nazi Doctors* (New York, 1986), 31. The Cambodian experience seems to corroborate that this sociological method is a product of a Marxist worldview. On the role of photographs and archives in the Cambodian genocide, strikingly analogous to that of the Soviet experience, see Chris Riley, ed., *The Killing Fields* (Santa Fe, N. Mex., 1997); Seth Mydans, "Cambodia's Bureaucracy of Death: Reams of Evidence in Search of a Trial," *New York Times*, July 20, 1997; Michael Kimmelman, "Poignant Faces of the Soon to be Dead," Art Review, *New York Times*, June 20, 1997; Seth Mydans, "Faces from Beyond the Grave," *New York Times Book Review*, May 25, 1997, 21; Seth Mydans, "Cambodian Killers' Careful Records Used Against Them," *New York Times* June 7, 1996.

127. On the significance of the biological paradigm for Nazi politics and the role of medical specialists in "biologically" determining such categories, see (among many others) Weindling, *Health, Race and German Politics*, esp. 321–22, 327, 331; Burleigh and Wipperman, *Racial State*; Götz Aly, Peter Chroust, and Christian Pross, eds., *Cleansing the Fatherland: Nazi Medicine and Racial Hygiene* (Baltimore, 1994); Michael Burleigh, *Death and Deliverance: "Euthanasia" in German, c. 1900–1945* (Cambridge, England, 1994).

128. On the emergence in the 1920s of Soviet political culture's highly ritualized methodology of unmasking, see Michael David-Fox, *Revolution of the Mind* (Ithaca, N.Y., 1997), chapter 3; and Naiman, *Sex in Public*, esp. 105. For how this political culture contributed to the violence of 1937–38, see Kotkin, *Magnetic Mountain*, chapter 7.

129. Gorky et al., *Belomor*, 325; the authors explicitly contrast this approach to Lombroso's biological determinism (127).

130. Kotkin, *Magnetic Mountain*, 217.

131. For a sense of the breadth and depth of the Soviet inquest into souls, see Shentalinsky, *Arrested Voices* and Halfin, *Class, Consciousness and Salvation*; see also any of the "memory books" cited in Note 141 for excerpts from the voluminous case records and extensive correspondence on individual rehabilitations from the 1950s on.

132. Podlubnyi, *Tagebuch aus Moskau*, may be read as one Soviet citizen's tortured attempt to negotiate his past status with his desire to be a Soviet man in the present, a desire constantly undermined by Podlubnyi's awareness that he had been insincere about his past.

133. Bogomolov, *Leningradskii martirolog*, 48–51; on the Selifontovo mass grave in the Iaroslavl' region, see *Ne predat' zabveniiu* (Iaroslavl', Russia, 1993), 90–102, 203–5, 294. On the uncovering of these mass graves, see Kathleen Smith, *Remembering Stalin's Victims* (Ithaca, N.Y., 1996), 163–65; and Adam Hochschild, *The Unquiet Ghost* (New York, 1995), chapters 14–16.

134. On industrial killing as a defining feature of the Holocaust, see Omer Bartov, *Murder in Our Midst: The Holocaust, Industrial Killing and Representation* (New York, 1996).

135. On the more general emergence of this modern form of penal theory, see Foucault, *Discipline and Punish*, esp. 126, 252.

136. On the fundamentally ideological and exterminatory nature of Nazi labor camps, see Ulrich Herbert, "Labour and Extermination: Economic Interest and the Primacy of *Weltanschauung* in National Socialism," *Past and Present* 138 (1993): 144–95. On "enlightenment" efforts in Soviet camps, see earlier discussion in this chapter for Rychkov's comments on the Tambov concentration camp in 1921; Kotkin, *Magnetic Mountain*, 133–35, 230–35; John Scott, *Behind the Urals* (Bloomington, Ind., 1989); and Gorky et al., *Belomor*. For reports on the "political mood" of the Gulag, see *Spetspereselentsy v Zapadnoi Sibiri, 1930–31* (Novosibirsk, 1992), 114–23, 149–51, 195–96, 233–35 and Werth and Moullec, *Rapports secrets sovietiques*, 355–430.

137. David Dallin and Boris Nicolaevsky, *Forced Labor in Soviet Russia* (New Haven, Conn., 1947) and James Harris, "The Growth of the Gulag: Forced Labor in the Urals Region," *Russian Review* 56, no. 2 (1997): 265–80.

138. Maksim Gorky et al., *Belomorsko-baltiiskii kanal imeni Stalina* (Moscow, 1934), 11–20 (Gorky quotation); V. G. Makurov, ed., *Gulag v Karelii, 1930–1941: sbornik dokumentov i materialov* (Petrozavodsk, Russia, 1992), 9–11, 28–31 59–60, 142–43, 148–50 (on the library holdings); T. I. Slavko, *Kulatskaia ssylka na Urale, 1930–1936* (Moscow, 1995), 11–12, 78–79, 87–88, 102–14; for the reduction of sentence for detainees after the completion of Belomor, see Gorky et al., *Belomor*, chapter 31; *Revelations from the Russian Archives*, 153–54; *Gulag v Karelii*, 72.

139. For NKVD operational order no. 00486 on the arrest of wives of traitors (but not their execution), see *Bol' liudskaia*, vol. 4:148; the film *Europa, Europa* portrays one such NKVD "orphanage." In 1936, the NKVD administration at Belomor ordered that all children under the age of eight living in the Belomor camp alongside their parents were to be transferred to orphanages (*Gulag v Karelii*, 117).

140. On the rehabilitations, see Smith, *Remembering Stalin's Victims*, 133–38; for documents generated on individual cases in the process of such individual appeals, see any of the "memory books" cited in the following note. Wheatcroft ("German and Soviet Repression") finds it significant that Stalin documented his victims, while Hitler made no pretense to.

141. Iu. I. Kalinichenko, V. Iu. Lisianskii, N. P. Monikovskaia, eds., *Iz bezdny nebytiia: kniga pamiati repressirovannykh kaluzhan*, 2 vols. (Kaluga, Russia, 1993); V. P. Golikov and V. A. Vinogradov, eds., *Ne predat' zabveniiu: kniga pamiati repressirovannykh v 30–40-e i nachale 50-kh godov, sviazannykh sud'bami s Iaroslavskoi oblast'iu* (Iaroslavl', Russia 1993); L. P. Rychkova, ed., *Kniga pamiati zhertv politicheskoi repressii Novgorodskoi oblasti*, vol. 1 of several (Novgorod, Russia, 1993); Iu. N. Balakin, ed., *Rekviem: kniga pamiati zhertv politicheskikh repressii na Orlovshchine*, 2 vols. (Orel, Russia, 1994); Uimanov and Petrukhin, *Bol' liudskaia*; Bogomolov, *Leningradskii martirolog*.

142. Shentalinsky, *Arrested Voices* and esp. Il'mira Stepanov's praise of Bogomolov, *Leningradskii Martirolog* ("Sorok tysiach imen," *Russkaia mysl'*, no. 4092 [September 14–20, 1995]) and the indignant protest of the Veniamin Iofe on behalf of Memorial ("Kto sostavlial 'Leningradskii martirolog,'" *Russkaia mysl'*, no. 4095). I am grateful to Jan Plamper for alerting me to this latter exchange and reminding me of Akhmatova's lines.

143. Smith, *Remembering Stalin's Victims*, 165–66. Again, the parallel with Cambodia is striking.

CHAPTER 2, *Domansky*

1. Exceptions were the wars of the French Revolution, the American Civil War, and the Franco-Prussian War during its second phase. See James McPherson, *Battle Cry of Freedom: The Civil War Era* (New York, 1988); Michael Howard, *The Franco-Prussian War: The German Invasion of France, 1870–1871*, 4th ed. (London, 1997), 224–431; Stig Förster and Jörg Nadler, eds., *On the Road to Total War: The American Civil War and the German Wars of Unification, 1861–1871* (Washington, D.C., Cambridge and New York, 1997).

2. This means that one out of eight soldiers who served was killed. This death toll was not distributed evenly among the combatants. The war cost by far more lives on the Eastern Front than on the Western Front. France and Germany lost 1 out of 6 and Great Britain 1 out of 8 men who served. Two million Russian soldiers were killed, a number that constituted 10 percent of the men who were mobilized. Bulgaria, Romania, and Turkey each lost 25 percent of all the soldiers who served and Serbia 37 percent. Jay Winter and Blaine Baggett, *The Great War and the Shaping of the Twentieth Century* (New York, 1996), 108, 266, 362. On the Western Front see also Alistair Horne, *The Price of Glory: Verdun 1916* (London, 1962); Robin Prior and Trevor Wilson, *Passchendaele: The Untold Story* (New Haven, Conn., 1996). A very high number of casualties on the Eastern Front resulted from war-related epidemics and diseases. See Paul Weindling, *Epidemics and Genocide in Eastern Europe, 1890–1945* (Oxford, England, and New York).

3. During the battle of Verdun (1916) 300,000 soldiers were killed and close to 800,000 wounded within ten months. The battles of the Somme (1916) and of Passchendaele (1917) produced similar results within just about four months. Winter and Baggett, *Great War*, 157, 179, 195.

4. See, for example, Michael Walzer's discussion of the famous "Melian Dialogue," in Thucydides, *The History of the Peloponnesian War* (mid-fifth-century B.C.), in Michael Walzer, *Just and Unjust Wars: A Moral Argument with Historical Illustrations*, 2d ed. (New York, 1991), 4–13. For insights into individual and spontaneous violence, see John Keegan, *The Face of Battle* (London, 1976); Richard Holmes, *Acts of War: The Behavior of Men in Battle* (New York, 1989); and especially Jonathan Shay, *Achilles in Vietnam: Combat Trauma and the Undoing of Character* (New York and Toronto, 1994). On German atrocities, see Alan Kramer, "'Greueltaten': Zum Problem der deutschen Kriegsverbrechen in Belgien und Frankreich 1914," in Gerhard Hirschfeld and Gerd Krumeich, eds., "*Keiner fühlt sich hier mehr als Mensch . . .": Erlebnis und Wirkung des Ersten Weltkriegs* (Essen, Germany, 1993), 85–114; and John Horne and Alan Kramer,

"German 'Atrocities' and Franco-German Opinion, 1914: The Evidence of German Soldiers' Diaries," *Journal of Modern History* 66, no. 1 (1994): 1–33. On the German general staff's strategy to destroy French morale by inflicting heavy losses on the French army, see Michael Geyer, "German Strategy in the Age of Machine Warfare," in Peter Paret, ed., *Makers of Modern Strategy from Machiavelli to the Nuclear Age* (Princeton, N.J., 1986), 527–97, esp. 534–35. On the ethical problems of the British blockade of Germany, see Walzer, *Just and Unjust Wars*, 170–75.

5. "Population Management" (the subject and the title of the conference at Stanford in 1997 out of which this volume developed) is, in my opinion, a term that is very well suited to differentiate between previous forms of "population politics" as *means to an end* and new visions of states and societies of such politics as *goals*. See Amir Weiner's Introduction to this volume as well as Peter Holquist's chapter.

6. See Richard G. Hovannisian, ed., *The Armenian Genocide: History, Politics, Ethics* (Basingstoke, England, and London, 1992). See also Krikor Beledian, "Die Erfahrung der Katastrophe in der Literatur der Armenier," in Kristin Platt and Mihran Dabag, eds., *Generation und Gedächtnis: Erinnerungen und kollektive Identitäten* (Opladen, Germany, 1995), 186–254.

7. The only exceptions were, for different reasons, the United States and the Soviet Union. On war and postwar attempts at coming to terms with World War I, see Paul Fussell, *The Great War and Modern Memory* (Oxford, England, 1975); Jay M. Winter, *Sites of Memory, Sites of Mourning: The Great War in European Cultural History* (Cambridge, England, 1995). For comparisons between the remembrance of World Wars I and II, see George L. Mosse, *Fallen Soldiers: Reshaping the Memories of the Two World Wars* (New York, 1990); Gottfried Niedhart and Dieter Riesenberger, eds., *Lernen aus dem Krieg? Deutsche Nachkriegszeiten 1918 and 1945* (Munich, 1992); Elisabeth Domansky, "A Lost War: World War II in Postwar German Memory," in Alvin Rosenfeld, ed., *Thinking About the Holocaust: After Half a Century* (Bloomington, Ind., 1997), 233–72, esp. 239–44.

8. This reconstruction process has been described as the "militarization of the Western world." See the contributions to John Gillis, ed., *The Militarization of the Western World, 1870 to the Present* (New Brunswick, N.J., 1989). The result was, as military historians have argued conclusively, a fundamentally new relationship between "the military and civil society, between war and peace, production and destruction." Michael Geyer, "The Militarization of Europe, 1914–1945," in Gillis, *Militarization*, 72. There was also, as I have shown elsewhere, a fundamentally new relationship between military destruction, industrial production and the organization of the social and biological reproduction of society. Elisabeth Domansky, "Militarization and Reproduction in World War I Germany," in Geoff Eley, ed., *Society, Culture, and the State in Germany, 1870–1930* (Ann Arbor, Mich., 1996), 427–63.

9. For Germany see Ulrich Heinemann, *Die verdrängte Niederlage: Politische Öffentlichkeit und Kriegsschuldfrage in der Weimarer Republik* (Göttingen, West Germany, 1983); Michael Geyer, "Nation, Klasse und Macht: Zur Organisation von Herrschaft in der Weimarer Republik," *Archiv für Sozialgeschichte* 26 (1986): 27–48.

10. In addition to the literature quoted in Note 7, see also Eric J. Leed, *No Man's Land: Combat & Identity in World War I* (New York, 1979); Modris Eksteins, *Rites of Spring: The Great War and the Birth of the Modern Age*, 2d ed. (New York, 1990).

Hirschfeld and Krumeich, "*Keiner fühlt sich hier mehr als Mensch . . .*"; Gerhard Hirschfeld et al., eds., *Kriegserfahrungen: Studien zur Sozial- und Mentalitätsgeschichte des Ersten Weltkriegs* (Essen, Germany, 1997); Wolfgang Mommsen, "German Artiststs, Writers and Intellectuals and the Meaning of War, 1914–1918," in John Horne, *State, Society and Mobilization in Europe During the First World War* (Cambridge, England, 1997), 21–38. See also Elvio Fachinelli's little-known but extremely interesting psychoanalytical interpretation of fascism as an attempt to "undo" the death of the fatherland. Elvio Fachinelli, *La freccia ferma: Tre tentativi di annulare il tempo* (Milan, 1979).

11. See, for example, Pat Barker, *The Regeneration Trilogy* (London, 1996; orig. *Regeneration*, 1991; *The Eye in the Door*, 1994; *The Ghost Road*, 1995); Sébastien Japrisot, *A Very Long Engagement* (New York, 1993); David Malouf, *Fly Away Peter* (London, 1982). See also Peter Weir's film *Gallipoli* (1981) and Bertrand Tavernier's film version of Japrisot's novel, entitled *Life and Nothing But* (1989). Japrisot was born in 1931, Malouf in 1934, Tavernier in 1941, Barker in 1943, and Weir in 1944. There is no comparable new phase of addressing the legacies of World War I in the United States, the former Soviet Union, or Germany, because of these countries' focus on World War II.

12. On the "industrialization of war" see Geyer, "Militarization of Europe"; see also Michael Geyer, *Deutsche Rüstungspolitik, 1860–1980* (Frankfurt am Main, 1984).

13. In the case of Germany, this refers particularly to Erich von Falkenhayn's strategic and tactical concepts. Haig and Joffre, however, do not seem to have understood the conditions of modern warfare any better. See Geyer, "German Strategy," 534–37; Winter and Baggett, *Great War*, 68–70, 165–71, 178–207.

14. Georges Clemenceau, for example, is quoted to have said: "I make war, war and nothing else." Quoted from Winter and Baggett, *Great War*, 209. See also David S. Newhall, *Clemenceau: A Life at War* (Lewiston, N.Y., 1991). On Lloyd George see David French, *The Strategy of the Lloyd George Coalition, 1916–1918* (Oxford, England, and New York, 1995). On Falkenhayn see Holger Afflerbach, *Falkenhayn: Politisches Denken und Handeln im Kaiserreich* (Munich, 1994); on Bethmann Hollweg: Konrad Jarausch, *The Enigmatic Chancellor* (New Haven, Conn., and London, 1973); on Ludendorff: Martin Kitchen, *The Silent Dictatorship: The Politics of the German High Command Under Hindenburg and Ludendorff, 1916–1918* (London and New York, 1976).

15. See Walzer, *Just and Unjust Wars*, 240.

16. On the readiness to accept war among the elites and the population in general, see Edward R. Tannenbaum, *1900: The Generation Before the Great War* (Garden City, N.Y., 1976); Roland N. Stromberg, *The Intellectuals and 1914* (Lawrence, Kans., 1982); Robert Wohl, *The Generation of 1914* (Cambridge, Mass., 1979); Eksteins, *Rites of Spring*; Geoffrey Best, "The Militarization of European Society, 1870–1914," in Gillis, *Militarization*, 13–29. See also Klaus Vondung, ed., *Kriegserlebnis: Der Erste Weltkrieg in der literarischen Gestaltung und symbolischen Deutung der Nationen* (Göttingen, West Germany, 1980), and his *Die Apokalypse in Deutschland* (Munich, 1988); Bernd Hüppauf, ed., *Ansichten vom Krieg: Vergleichende Studien zum Ersten Weltkrieg in Literatur und Gesellschaft* (Königstein, West Germany, 1984); J. Dülffer and K. Holl, eds., *Bereit zum Krieg. Kriegsmentalität im wilhelminischen Deutschland 1890–1914* (Göttingen, West Germany, 1987); Klaus Schwabe, *Wissenschaft und Kriegsmoral: Die deutschen Hochschullehrer und die politischen Grundfragen des Ersten Weltkriegs* (Göttingen, West Germany, 1969); Richard Cork, "'A Murderous Carnival': German Artists

in the First World War," in Bernd Hüppauf, ed., *War, Violence and the Modern Condition* (Berlin and New York, 1997), 241–76.

17. On the parallel and intertwined history of film and war technology see Paul Virilio, *War and Cinema: The Logistics of Perception* (London, 1989). In Germany, the development of the modern film industry is inextricably linked to World War I and the military's interest in using films for propaganda purposes. See Hans Barkhausen, *Filmpropaganda für Deutschland im Ersten und Zweiten Weltkrieg* (Hildesheim, West Germany; Zurich; and New York, 1982); Klaus Kreimeier, *Die Ufa-Story: Geschichte eines Filmkonzerns* (Munich and Vienna, 1992). On war and photography see Jorge Lewinski, *The Camera at War: A History of War Photography from 1848 to the Present Day* (London, 1978), and Caroline Brothers, *War and Photography: A Cultural History* (London and New York, 1997). See also Brigitte Werneburg, "Ernst Jünger and the Transformed World," *October* 62 (Fall 1992): 43–64.

18. On German opposition movements (strikes, demonstrations, food riots, and the military strike at the end of the war), see *Deutschland im Ersten Weltkrieg*, 3 vols. (Berlin [East], 1968–69); F. L. Carsten, *War Against War: British and German Radical Movements in the First World War* (London, 1982); Friedhelm Boll, *Massenbewegungen in Niedersachsen, 1906–1920: Eine sozialgeschichtliche Untersuchung zu den unterschiedlichen Entwicklungstypen Branschweig und Hannover* (Bonn, 1981); Ute Daniel, *Arbeiterfrauen in der Kriegsgesellschaft: Beruf, Familie und Politik im Ersten Weltkrieg* (Göttingen, Germany, 1989); Wolfram Wette, ed., *Der Krieg des Kleinen Mannes: Eine Militärgeschichte von unten* (Munich, 1992); Daniel Horn, *German Naval Mutinies of World War I* (New Brunswick, N.J., 1969). On the German prowar movement see Reinhard Rürup, "Der 'Geist von 1914' in Deutschland: Kriegsbegeisterung und Ideologisierung des Krieges im Ersten Weltkrieg," in Hüppauf, *Ansichten vom Krieg*, 1–30; Roger Chickering, *We Men Who Feel Most German: A Cultural Study of the Pan-German League* (London, 1984). The German prowar movement founded its own party, the "Deutsche Vaterlandspartei," in 1917. See Heinz Hagenlücke, *Die Deutsche Vaterlandspartei: Die nationale Rechte am Ende des Kaiserreichs* (Düsseldorf, 1997).

19. This is the title of one of the subchapters in Winter and Baggett, *Great War*, 138. On this issue see also the literature quoted in Note 16.

20. See the literature quoted in Note 16. On women's (self-)mobilization for war see Ute Frevert, *Women in German History: From Bourgeois Emancipation to Sexual Liberation* (Oxford, England, and New York, 1989); Richard J. Evans, *The Feminist Movement in Germany, 1894–1933* (London, 1976); Sabine Hering, *Die Kriegsgewinnlerinnen: Praxis und Ideologie der deutschen Frauenbewegung im Ersten Weltkrieg* (Pfaffenweiler, Germany, 1990); Doris Kaufmann, *Frauen zwischen Aufbruch und Reaktion: Protestantische Frauen in der ersten Hälfte des 20. Jahrhunderts* (Münster, West Germany, 1988); Daniel, *Arbeiterfrauen*; Margaret Randolph Higonnet et al., eds., *Behind the Lines: Gender and the Two World Wars* (New Haven, Conn., 1987).

21. The term *project* denotes the blending of imagination and reality that is characteristic of modernism. See Vladislav Todorov's fascinating exploration of the modernist project: *Red Square, Black Square: Organon for Revolutionary Imagination* (New York, 1995).

22. Alain Touraine, *The Self-Production of Society* (Chicago, 1977).

23. Mary Poovey has theorized this development most convincingly. Mary

Poovey, *Making a Social Body: British Cultural Formation 1830–1864* (Chicago and London, 1995). See esp. 1–19. See also Gilles Deleuze's foreword "The Rise of the Social," in Jacques Donzelot, *The Policing of Families* (London, 1979), ix–xvii. James Sheehan's study is, in my eyes, the best survey of these developments. James J. Sheehan, *German History, 1770–1866* (Oxford, England, 1989). On Italy see David Horn, *Social Bodies: Science, Reproduction, and Italian Modernity* (Princeton, N.J., 1994); on Russia see Eric Naiman, *Sex in Public: The Incarnation of Early Soviet Ideology* (Princeton, N.J., 1997).

24. On the development of German science, its professionalization, and German society's fascination with science see Sheehan, *German History*, 802–20, whose bibliographical references are very useful. See also the literature quoted in Notes 36 and 38.

25. Such efforts included, to give but two examples, attempts to combine science and religion and class struggle and science. On the former see Sheehan, *German History*, esp. 816–17. The latter did not simply consist of concepts of "scientific management," such as Taylorism, but also of attempts to "rationalize" labor conflicts. See Elisabeth Domansky, "The Rationalization of Class Struggle: Strikes and Strike Strategy of the German Metalworkers' Union, 1891–1922," in Leopold Haimson and Charles Tilly, eds., *Strikes, Wars, and Revolutions in an International Perspective: Strike Waves in the Late Nineteenth and Early Twentieth Centuries* (Cambridge, England, and Paris, 1989), 321–55.

26. See Paul Weindling, *Health, Race and German Politics Between National Unification and Nazism, 1870–1945* (Cambridge, England, and New York, 1989); Michael S. Teitelbaum and Jay M. Winter, *A Question of Numbers: High Migration, Low Fertility, and the Politics of National Identity* (New York, 1998). See also the older study by the same authors: *The Fear of Population Decline* (Orlando, Fla., 1985), and Michael S. Teitelbaum and Jay M. Winter, eds., *Population and Resources in Western Intellectual Tradition* (New York, 1989).

27. See the literature quoted in Note 26 and also John E. Knodel, *The Decline of Fertility in Germany, 1871–1939* (Princeton, N.J., 1974).

28. See the literature quoted in Notes 26 and 27.

29. To avoid misunderstandings: By this, I do not mean to say that all interpretations of class conflict as economic and social interest conflicts were given up. I want to stress, however, that the end of the nineteenth century saw a gradual biologization of politics. This development was by no means limited to the middle class. Notions of a "birthstrike" in order to further women's emancipation or ideas that proletarian women should bear children for their class also existed. See, for example, Anne E. Freier, *"Dem Reich der Freiheit sollst Du Kinder gebären": Der Antifeminismus der proletarischen Frauenbewegung im Spiegel der "Gleichheit," 1891–1917* (Frankfurt am Main, 1981).

30. Again, as in the case of class (see the previous note), I am not saying that existing boundaries between the domain of the social and the family were dissolved immediately. There can be no doubt, however, that a process of redrawing these boundaries was on its way.

31. To give an English example from World War I that shows the materiality of that fusion: Great Britain decided not to bring its fallen soldiers home after the war. Rather, the soil where a British soldier had shed his blood was considered to have turned into British soil. See Winter, *Sites of Memory*.

32. Michael Howard also links the willingness to sacrifice millions of lives to social Darwinism. Michael Howard, "Men Against Fire: The Doctrine of the Offensive in 1914," in Paret, *Makers of Modern Strategy*, 510–26.

33. On liberalism and its concepts of political participation, see James J. Sheehan, *German Liberalism in the Nineteenth Century* (Chicago, 1978) and his "Some Reflections on Liberalism in Comparative Perspective," in H. Köhler, *Deutschland und der Westen* (Berlin [West], 1984), 44–58. On liberal feminism see Frevert, *Women in German History*, and Evans, *Feminist Movement*.

34. These views were articulated into the theory of "Organized Motherliness." See especially Ann Taylor Allen, "Spiritual Motherhood: German Feminists and the Kindergarten Movement, 1848–1911," *History of Education Quarterly*, 22, no. 3 (Fall 1982): 319–39; Ann Taylor Allen, "Mothers of the New Generation: Adele Schreiber, Helene Stöcker, and the Evolution of a German Idea of Motherhood, 1900–1914," *Signs*, 10, no. 3 (1985): 418–38; Ann Taylor Allen, *Feminism and Motherhood in Germany, 1800–1914* (New Brunswick, N.J., 1991). It is important to note, however, that such ideas were by no means limited to Germany. See, for example, Sheldon Garon, "Rethinking Modernization and Modernity in Japanese History: A Focus on State-Society Relations," *Journal of Asian Studies* 53, no. 2 (May 1994): 346–66, 353, 358–60; Sheldon Garon, *Molding Japanese Minds: The State in Everyday Life* (Princeton, N.J., 1997), esp. 131–44; Elizabeth Waters, "The Modernization of Russian Motherhood, 1917–1937," *Soviet Studies* 44, no. 1 (1992): 123–35.

35. The inherent racism of these concepts is as evident as it is in those of male racial hygienists. This racism is, however, not a specifically German phenomenon. See, for example, Anna Davin, "Imperialism and Motherhood," *History Workshop* 5 (Spring 1978): 9–65. In general see George L. Mosse, *Towards the Final Solution: A History of European Racism* (New York, 1978).

36. On the influence of Darwinism and social Darwinism in Germany, see Hans-Günter Zmarzlik, *Der Sozialdarwinismus in Deutschland: Ein Beitrag zur Vorgeschichte des Dritten Reiches* (Freiburg im Breisgau, West Germany, 1961); Alfred Kelly, *Descent of Darwin: The Popularization of Darwinism in Germany, 1860–1914* (Chapel Hill, N.C., 1981); Weindling, *Health, Race and German Politics*; Paul Weindling, *Darwinism and Social Darwinism in Imperial Germany: The Contribution of the Cell Biologist Oscar Hertwig, 1849–1922* (Stuttgart, Germany; New York; and Mainz, Germany, 1991); Eric H. Vieler, *The Ideological Roots of German National Socialism* (New York, 1999). See also the unusual book by Sven Lindquist, *"Exterminate all the Brutes"* (London, 1997), esp. part 4.

37. Contemporary observers such as Heinrich von Treitschke and Max Weber were well aware of the fact that the advantages of civil society were unevenly distributed. They also knew that the resulting economic inequality was one of the cornerstones of modern bourgeois society and secured by law. It was Walther Rathenau who coined the famous phrase of the "glass walls" that divided bourgeois society into those who had access to its advantages and those who did not. Sheehan, *German History*, 786–91.

38. On (social) Darwinism in the working class see esp. Richard Weckert, *Socialist Darwinism Evolution in German Socialist Thought from Marx to Bernstein* (San Francisco, 1998). See also Freier, *"Dem Reich der Freiheit."*

39. Hannah Arendt firmly rooted totalitarianism in nineteenth-century European culture while, however, emphasizing World War I's function as a catalyst. Han-

nah Arendt, *The Origins of Totalitarianism* (New York, 1951). Jacob Talmon, in *The Origins of Totalitarian Democracy* (London, 1952), rooted totalitarianism of the Left in Enlightenment thinking. One of the most interesting recent attempts to theorize totalitarianism and to reflect on its link with democracy is Claude Lefort's, *The Political Forms of Modern Society* (Cambridge, Mass., 1986), to which I owe my concept of a totalitarian society. See also Peter Holquist's contribution to this volume. As a survey see Abbott Gleason, *Totalitarianism: The Inner History of the Cold War* (New York and Oxford, England, 1995).

40. See Note 32.

41. See the literature quoted in Notes 14, 16, 18, 20, and 36. On the lack of popular enthusiasm in August 1914 see Gerd Krumeich, "L'Entrée en guerre en Allemagne," in Jean-Jacques Becker and Stéphane Audoin-Rouzeau, eds., *Les Sociétes européennes et la guerre de 1914–1918* (Paris, 1990), 65–74.

42. The concept of the short-war-illusion dominated historiographical debates on World War I for decades and even became the title of a book: Lancelot L. Farrar, *The Short War Illusion: German Policy, Strategy, and Domestic Affairs August–December 1914* (Oxford, England, 1973). Recent research, however, demonstrates conclusively that this concept needs to be thoroughly revised. See Stig Förster's essay "Der deutsche Generalstab und die Illusion des kurzen Krieges, 1871–1914: Metakritik eines Mythos," in Johannes Burkhardt et al., *Lange und kurze Wege in den Ersten Weltkrieg: Vier Augsburger Beiträge zur Kriegsursachenforschung* (Munich, 1996), 115–58. See also Michael Geyer, "German Strategy," 530–31.

43. These were the words that Helmuth von Moltke used in his last speech before the German Reichstag on May 14, 1890. Quoted from Förster, "Der deutsche Generalstab," 121. See also 144–51.

44. Förster, "Der deutsche Generalstab," 138, 148–51, 157–58.

45. Förster, "Der deutsche Generalstab," 142–55. See also Lothar Burchardt, *Friedenswirtschaft und Kriegsvorsorge: Deutschlands wirtschaftliche Rüstungsbestrebungen vor 1914* (Boppard, West Germany, 1968).

46. Förster, "Der deutsche Generalstab," 127, 134–51; Geyer, "German Strategy," 530–31. See also essays in contemporary military and medical journals, such as P. M. Awtokratow, "Die Geisteskranken im russischen Heere während des japanischen Krieges," *Allgemeine Zeitschrift für Psychiatrie*, no. 2/3 (1907): 286–319; V. Kurnatowski, "Die moralischen Lehren des Russisch-Japanischen Krieges," *Jahrbücher für die deutsche Armee und Marine, 1913* (January–June): 396–409. See also Wilhelm Lamszus, *Das Menschenschlachthaus: Bilder vom kommenden Krieg* (Munich, 1980; orig. 1912). Such views of future wars were also widespread among the military and the public in other countries. See for example T. H. E. Travers, "Technology, Tactics, and Morale: Jean de Bloch, the Boer War, and British Military Theory, 1900–1914," *Journal of Modern History* 51 (June 1979): 264–86; Keith Neilson, "'That Dangerous and Difficult Enterprise': British Military Thinking and the Russo-Japanese War," *War & Society*, 9, no. 2 (October 1991): 17–37; Howard, "Men Against Fire"; Manfred F. Boemeke, Roger Chickering, and Stig Förster, eds., *Anticipating Total War: The German and American Experiences, 1871–1914* (Washington, D.C.; Cambridge, England; and New York, 1999).

47. See, for example, Volker R. Berghahn, *Germany and the Approach of War in 1914* (London, 1973); Samuel Williamson and P. Pastor, eds., *Essays on World War I: Origins*

and Prisoners of War (New York, 1983); George Kennan, *The Fateful Alliance: France, Russia and the Coming of the First World War* (New York, 1984); H. W. Koch, ed., *The Origins of the First World War: Great Power Rivalry and German War Aims* (London, 1984); Paul Kennedy, *The Rise and Fall of the Great Powers: Economic Change and Military Conflict from 1500 to 2000* (New York, 1987); Richard J. W. Evans and Hartmut Pogge von Strandmann, eds., *The Coming of the First World War* (Oxford, England, and New York, 1988); James Joll, *The Origins of the First World War*, 2d ed. (London and New York, 1992.

48. This argument has been put forward most forcefully by Michael Geyer. See Geyer, "German Strategy," esp. 527–37.

49. "Wenn wir auch darüber zugrunde gehen, schön war's doch." Quoted from Förster, "Der deutsche Generalstab," 158.

50. Fritz Stern, *The Politics of Cultural Despair: A Study in the Rise of German Ideology* (Berkeley, Calif., 1974).

51. On social Darwinist thought in the European military, see Dieter Storz, *Kriegsbild und Rüstung vor 1914: Europäische Landstreitkräfte vor dem Ersten Weltkrieg* (Herford, Germany, 1992), 79–91; see also Förster, "Der deutsche Generalstab," 157–58; Antulio J. Echevarria II, "On the Brink of the Abyss: The Warrior Identity and German Military Thought Before the Great War," *War & Society* 13, no. 2 (October 1995): 23–40. Social Darwinist ideas among the military corresponded to its anti-Semitism. See Werner T. Angress, "Prussia's Army and the Jewish Reserve Officer Controversy Before World War I," in James J. Sheehan, ed., *Imperial Germany* (New York, 1976), 93–128. On the attempted transformation of society see also Werneburg, "Ernst Jünger," esp. 54–64.

52. See Geyer, "German Strategy," 537–54; the quotation is from page 537. On the Third Supreme Command see also Martin Kitchen, *Silent Dictatorship*, and the Introduction to Wilhelm Deist, ed., *Militär und Innenpolitik im Weltkrieg 1914–1918*, 2 vols. (Düsseldorf, 1970), vol. 1:xv–lxxv, esp. xl–lxvi; Wilhelm Deist, "The German Army, the Authoritarian Nation-State and Total War," in John Horne, *State, Society and Mobilization*, 160–72.

53. I am following Michael Geyer's arguments. Geyer, "German Strategy," 537–54; the quotation is from page 546.

54. This was a gradual process that did not develop evenly, but from 1916 this process was definitely organized consciously. Geyer, "German Strategy," 537–54.

55. On the military-industrial complex see esp. the literature quoted in Note 12. See also Gerald D. Feldman, *Army, Industry and Labor in Germany*, 1914–1918 (Princeton, N.J., 1966).

56. This is the title that Martin Kitchen chose for his book on the Third Supreme Command. See Note 14.

57. On the continued rule of the "war machines" see Geyer, "German Strategy" and *Deutsche Rüstungspolitik*. I first argued that the war's new social organization also lasted beyond the war's end in my essay on "Militarization and Reproduction." See esp. 428–34 and 459–63. See also my references to the literature from which I depart with my assessment, "Militarization and Reproduction," n. 5. In addition to the works quoted there, see Richard Bessel, *Germany After the First World War* (Oxford, England, 1993).

58. I have decided to use capital letters in "National Body" mainly because I want to make clear that this is a formation that is fundamentally different from a "social body" (see Note 23) and that it is, by definition, a body at war.

59. On the German family see Dieter Schwab, *Grundlagen und Gestalt der staatlichen Ehegesetzgebung in der Neuzeit bis zum Beginn des 1., Jahrhunderts* (Bielefeld, West Germany, 1967); Ingeborg Weber-Kellermann, *Die deutsche Familie: Versuch einer Sozialgeschichte* (Frankfurt am Main, 1974); Werner Conze, ed., *Sozialgeschichte der Familie in der Neuzeit Europas* (Stuttgart, West Germany, 1976); Michael Mitterauer and Reinhard Sieder, *The European Family: Patriarchy to Partnership from the Middle Ages to the Present* (Oxford, England, 1982).

60. This is one of my main arguments in "Militarization." See also Young-Sun Hong, "The Contradictions of Modernization in the German Welfare State: Gender and the Politics of Welfare Reform in First World War Germany," *Social History* 17, no. 2 (May 1992): 251–70.

61. See the literature quoted in Note 59 and, in addition, Sheehan's brief, but very perceptive discussion. Sheehan, *German History*, 784–86.

62. This is particularly, although not exclusively, true for the German working class. Demonstrations, food riots, and strikes, though officially often dealing with specified issues, were from early on also protests against the war system. On those protests see the literature quoted in Note 18. See also Domansky, "Militarization," 457–59.

63. Early on, there had also been a female public sphere that women who were active in charity and patriotic organizations had carved out for themselves. See Jean Quataert, "German Patriotic Women's Work in War and Peace Time," in Förster and Nadler, *Road to Total War*. On children's mobilization see Domansky, "Militarization," 445–46, 458; Hong, "Contradictions."

64. Winter and Baggett, *Great War*, 362. See also Karin Hausen, "The German Nation's Obligations to the Heroes' Widows of World War I," in Higonnet et al., *Behind the Lines*, 126–40, 128. The mobilization proportions for other countries were France: 80 percent; Austria-Hungary: 75 percent; Great Britain, Serbia, and Turkey: 50 percent–60 percent; Russia: 40 percent; and the United States (in eighteen months): 16 percent. Winter and Baggett, *Great War*, 362. On wounded and disabled soldiers, see Robert Weldon Whalen, *Bitter Wounds: German Victims of the Great War, 1914–1939* (Ithaca, N.Y., 1984); Stephan Garton, *The Cost of War* (Oxford, England, 1996). See also Joanna Bourke's study on England: Joanna Bourke, *Dismembering the Male: Men's Bodies, Britain and the War* (Chicago, 1996).

65. On organizations representing German war victims in the Weimar Republic, see Whalen, *Bitter Wounds*.

66. Whalen, *Bitter Wounds*; Hausen, "Nation's Obligations." A study that reflects the privatization of the social costs of war in an interesting and illuminating way regarding World War II is Vera Neumann, *Nicht der Rede wert: Die Privatisierung der Kriegsfolgen in der frühen Bundesrepublik* (Münster, Germany, 1999).

67. The contemporary terms that were used most often were *shell shock* and *war neurosis*. The concept of post-traumatic stress disorder (PTSD) was developed in clinical work with and studies on Vietnam veterans. The results of those studies also shed light on soldiers' traumatic experiences in World War I. See Jonathan Shay, *Achilles in Vietnam: Combat Trauma and the Undoing of Character* (New York, 1994).

68. Reinhard Sieder, "Behind the Lines: Working-Class Family Life in Wartime Vienna," in Richard Wall and Jay Winter, eds., *The Upheaval of War; Family, Work and Welfare in Europe, 1914–1918* (Cambridge, England, 1988), 109–38, esp. 115–16, 128–38; Whalen, *Bitter Wounds*, esp. 78–81.

69. On the economic consequences of the gendered organization of war for families see Domansky, "Militarization," 443–52; Daniel, *Arbeiterfrauen*; Birthe Kundrus, *Kriegerfrauen: Familienpolitik und Geschlechterverhältnisse im Ersten und Zweiten Weltkrieg* (Hamburg, 1995), esp. 124–41.

70. State compensations were based on men's military rank, not on their prewar incomes. Because most working-class and lower middle-class men were common soldiers, their families received the lowest compensation rates. Daniel, *Arbeiterfrauen*, esp. 29–34, 169–83; Whalen, *Bitter Wounds*, esp. chapters 5–8; Kundrus, *Kriegerfrauen*, 45–97. Women's and young adults' incomes could not replace men's; the wage system remained gendered. Women's average daily wages did not reach even 50 percent of men's average daily wages. Daniel, *Arbeiterfrauen*, 111 ff; Kocka, *Facing Total War: German Society, 1914–1918* (Leamington Spa, England, 1984), 21 ff. See also Richard Wall, "English and German Families and the First World War, 1914–1918," in Wall and Winter, *Upheaval of War*, 106–43.

71. This was a result of the war's long duration, the Allied blockade of Germany, and bureaucratic mismanagement. On Germany's decentralized and chaotic organization for war, see Feldman, *Army, Industry and Labor*. See also Jay M. Winter, "Some Paradoxes of the First World War," in Wall and Winter, *Upheaval of War*, 9–49.

72. According to estimates, there were 300,000 civilian deaths in Germany that were directly war related. Winter, "Some Paradoxes," 30. These estimates are probably too low. A study that has recently questioned assumptions about war-related starvation in Germany is Avner Offer, *The First World War: An Agrarian Interpretation* (Oxford, England, 1989). But compare Jay Winter and Jean-Louis Robert, *Capital Cities at War: Paris, London, Berlin, 1914–1919* (Cambridge, England, and New York, 1997).

73. Domansky, "Militarization," 450–51.

74. On the effects of malnutrition and exposure to chemical substances, see Domansky, "Militarization," 440–41, 450–51; Volker Ullrich, *Kriegsalltag: Hamburg im Ersten Weltkrieg* (Cologne, 1982). On the collections of women's hair, see the title page to Ernst Johann, ed., *Innenansicht eines Krieges: Deutsche Dokumente, 1914–1918* (Munich, 1973). To my knowledge, there is no study of the consumption of women's bodies in World War I.

75. On welfare in World War I Germany, see Ludwig Preller, *Sozialpolitik in der Weimarer Republik* (Düsseldorf, 1971); Daniel, *Arbeiterfrauen*; Hong, "Contradictions"; Kundrus, *Kriegerfrauen*, 71–123. On the connections between the emergence of the Western welfare state and military interests and on the gendered nature of the welfare state, see Seth Koven and Sonya Michel, eds., *Maternalist Politics and the Origins of the Welfare State* (New York, 1993).

76. Daniel, *Arbeiterfrauen*, 29–34, 169–83; Whalen, *Bitter Wounds*, chapters 5–8; Kundrus, *Kriegerfrauen*, 142–56.

77. On the connection between welfare and patriotism, see Quataert, "German Patriotic Women's Work"; Kundrus, *Kriegerfrauen*, 157–82.

78. Domansky, "Militarization," 435–36, 447.

79. On family consumption see Armin Triebel, "Variations in Patterns of Consumption in Germany in the Period of the First World War," in Wall and Winter, *Upheaval of War*, 159–95; see also Belinda Davis, *Home Fires Burning: Food, Politics and Everyday Life in World War I Berlin* (Chapel Hill, N.C., 2000).

80. On the erosion of the family's reproductive and sexual autonomy, see in greater detail Domansky, "Militarization," 448–51.

81. Howard, "Doctrine of the Offensive," in Paret, *Makers of Modern Strategy*, esp. 521–26.

82. I have developed this argument first in Domansky, "Militarization." See esp. 436–39. On wartime sexual and reproductive politics, see in greater detail "Militarization," 448–51. See also Daniel, *Arbeiterfrauen*, 139–47; Weindling, *Health, Race and German Politics*, esp. 282–85.

83. Pregnancy was definitely more important than legitimacy. See Cornelie Usborne, "'Pregnancy is the Womans's Active Service,'" in Wall and Winter, *Upheaval of War*, 389–416.

84. A wealth of sources regarding this aspect can be found in Magnus Hirschfeld, Andreas Gaspar et al., *Sittengeschichte des Ersten Weltkriegs*, 2d ed. (Hanau am Main, West Germany, 1966). See also Kundrus, *Kriegerfrauen*, 212–19.

85. It is important to note once again that this was not only true for Germany. See, in Note 31, mention of the belief that fallen British soldiers' blood would turn the soil into British soil. In France, there were great fears that children of French women who had been raped by German soldiers could be a kind of "second invasion." See Ruth Harris, "The 'Child of the Barbarian': Rape, Race and Nationalism in France During the First World War," *Past and Present*, no. 141 (November 1993): 170–206.

86. Domansky, "Militarization," esp. 428 and 437–38.

87. On the uneven distribution of resources see especially Winter and Robert, *Capital Cities at War*.

88. Winter and Robert, *Capital Cities at War*. See also Jay Winter and Joshua Cole, "Fluctuations in Infant Mortality Rates in Berlin During and After the First World War," *European Journal of Population* 9 (1993): 235–63.

89. See Kundrus, *Kriegerfrauen*, 157–82; Boll, *Massenbewegungen*.

90. See the first part of this chapter.

91. Erich Ludendorff, *Der totale Krieg* (Munich, 1935), 10.

92. See the literature quoted in Notes 18, 36, and 51.

93. On Germany's war aims, see Fritz Fischer's classic study *Griff nach der Weltmacht: Die Kriegszielpolitik des kaiserlichen Deutschland, 1914/18* (Düsseldorf, 1961). See also Chickering, *We Men Who Feel Most German*; Rüdiger vom Bruch, *Wissenschaft, Politik und öffentliche Meinung: Gelehrtenpolitik im wilhelminischen Deutschland 1890–1914* (Husum, West Germany, 1980); Rürup, "Der 'Geist von 1914' in Deutschland," in Hüppauf, *Ansichten vom Krieg*, 1–30; Klaus Vondung, "Geschichte als Weltgericht: Genesis und Degradation einer Symbolik," in Vondung, *Kriegserlebnis*, 62–84.

94. See Egmont Zechlin (under Mitarbeit von Hans Joachim Bieber), *Die deutsche Politik und die Juden im Ersten Weltkrieg* (Göttingen, West Germany, 1969); on the Third Supreme Command's fantasies about a "Jewish Conspiracy," see Abraham J. Peck, *Radicals and Reactionaries: The Crisis of Conservatism in Wilhelmine Germany* (Washington, D.C., 1978), esp. 215.

95. See the works quoted in Notes 18 and 93.

96. Domansky, "Militarization," esp. 457–59.

97. Winter, *Sites of Memory*.

98. Winter, *Sites of Memory*. See also Uwe-K. Ketelsen, "Die Jugend von Langemarck: Ein poetisch-politisches Motiv der Zwischenkriegszeit," in Thomas Koebner, Rolf-Peter Janz, and Frank Trommler, *Mit uns zieht die neue Zeit: Der Mythos Jugend* (Frankfurt am Main, 1985), 68–96.

99. On the concept of "militarized peace" see Cynthia Enloe, "Beyond Steve Canyon and Rambo: Feminist Histories of Militarized Masculinity," in Gillis, ed. *Militarization*, 121.

100. Locating the National Socialist project within the broader project of modernity has become quite accepted by now. See especially Zygmunt Bauman, *Modernity and the Holocaust* (Ithaca, N.Y., 1989) and *Modernity and Ambivalence* (Ithaca, N.Y., 1991); Omer Bartov, *Murder in our Midst: The Holocaust, Industrial Killing, and Representation* (Oxford, England, and New York, 1996); Peter Fritzsche, "Nazi Modern," *Modernism/Modernity* 3, no. 1 (1996): 1–21.

101. Max Horkheimer and Theodor W. Adorno, *Dialektik der Aufklärung*, in Max Horkheimer, *Gesammelte Schriften*, vol. 5 (Frankfurt am Main, 1987).

102. Joseph Conrad, *Heart of Darkness* (London, 1998); see also Adam Hochschild's intriguing essay in which he argues that the character of Kurtz was based on a historical figure, Léon Rom. Adam Hochschild, "Mr. Kurtz, I Presume," *New Yorker*, April 14, 1997: 40–47.

CHAPTER 3, *Orlovsky*

1. The master narrative of 1917 refuses to die—even after several decades of so-called revisionist scholarship. The most recent full-scale history of the Russian Revolution, for example, provides a very standard and traditional and indeed truncated treatment of the Provisional Government embedded in the standard 1917 narrative. Orlando Figes labels the Provisional Government as a "distant liberal state." He ascribes to it the usual characteristics of faith in the people, self-government, noncoercion, and the like. Iconoclasm, or violent rejection of the old, the flaw in the Russian *narod* (people), becomes the master trope rather than any sustained analysis of the workings of power behind popular discourse. Orlando Figes, *A People's Tragedy: The Russian Revolution 1891–1924* (London, 1996).

2. William G. Rosenberg, "Sozdanie novogo gosudarstva v 1917g.:predstavleniia i deistvitel'nost'," in Rossiiskaia Akademiia Nauk (RAN), Otdelenie istorii, Institut russkoi istorii, Sankt-Petersburgskii filial, *Anatomiia revoliutsii: 1917 god v Rossii: massy, partii, vlast'* (Saint Petersburg, 1994), 76–97; and D. Orlovsky, "K voprosu o formakh demokratii nakanune oktiabria 1917 goda," in Moskovskii gosudarstvennyi universitet im. M.V. Lomonosova, Istoricheskii fakul'tet, *P.A. Zaionchkovskii 1904–1983 gg.: stat'i, publikatsii i vospominaniia o nem* (Moscow, 1998), 407–29. For a pioneering work on the "ecology" of revolution and revolutionary politics in 1917, see Peter Holquist, "A Russian Vendee: The Practice of Revolutionary Politics in the Don Countryside, 1917–1921," Ph.D. dissertation, Columbia University, 1995. Also see Michael C. Hickey, "Discourses of Public Identity and Liberalism in the February Revolution:

Smolensk, Spring 1917," *Russian Review* 55, no. 4 (1996): 615–37; "Local Government and State Authority in the Provinces: Smolensk, February–June 1917," *Slavic Review* 55, no. 4 (1996): 863–81; and F. A. Gaida, "Fevral' 1917 goda: revoliutsiia, vlast', burzhuaziia," *Voprosy istorii*, no. 3 (1996): 31–45.

3. A. B. Nikolaev and O. L. Polivanov, "K voprosu ob organizatsii vlasti v fevrale–marte 1917 g.," RAN, *Fevral'skaia revoliutsiia: ot novykh istochnikov k novomu osmysleniiu* (Moscow, 1997), 131–44.

4. Charles S. Maier, *Recasting Bourgeois Europe: Stabilization in France, Germany and Italy in the Decade After World War I* (Princeton, N.J., 1975), 9–10.

5. Maier, *Recasting Bourgeois Europe*, 9.

6. From the outset of the February Revolution, Duma members and staff played major roles in administration and governance—very often behind the scenes, as commissars, investigators, troubleshooters, and the like. After a point, these individuals no longer acted in the name of the Duma as parliamentary institution. A. B. Nikolaev, "Komissary Vremennogo Komiteta Gosudarstvennoi Dumy (February–March 1917 g.), personal'nyi sostav," *Iz glubiny vremen* (Saint Petersburg, 1995), 46–74, here, 47–48. See also A. B. Nikolaev, "Dumskie komissary v russkoi armii (February–March 1917 goda)," *Novyi chasovoi*, no. 4 (1996).

7. Gosudarstvennyi Arkhiv Rossiiskoi Federatsii (GARF), F. 1778, op. 1, d. 372, l. 62.

8. GARF, F. 1778, op. 1, d. 247, l. 1.

9. Fascism as a form of corporatism stressed the idea of occupations and functions of individuals and groups as opposed to individual citizenship with the goal of organizing society for national goals. Thomas Childers has shown that in Weimar Germany, for example, the social vocabulary of political discourse contained appeals aimed at highly defined social and occupational groups (*Berufständ*). And all parties made special appeals to the Civil Service. The goal was a society knit tightly by occupational estate, an arrangement that would favor the intellectually and politically productive *Mittelstand*. The goal was a *berufstandige* representation with specific competencies alongside Parliament.

The National Socialists adopted this kind of corporatist rhetoric. In 1929 they proclaimed a social platform oriented toward the Berufständ. They said that the idea of occupation will be one of the strongest pillars of the coming National Socialist state. "We know that our national resurgence is bound up with a revitalization of occupational life (*Berufsleben*)." Thomas Childers, "The Social Language of Politics in Germany: The Sociology of Political Discourse in the Weimar Republic," *American Historical Review* 95 (1990): 331–58.

10. This and the following quotations and summaries are taken from *Volia naroda*, June 29, 1917.

11. GARF, F. 1778, op. 1, d. 49, l. 1.

12. *Volia naroda*, June 23, 1917.

13. *Volia naroda*, June 23, 1917.

14. *Volia naroda*, June 21, 1917.

15. See I. L. Afanas'ev's very suggestive essay "Problema dvoevlastiia i natsional'noe dvizhenie na Ukraine i v Zakavkaz'e," in RAN, *Anatomiia revoliutsii*, 324–33; and also V. Iu. Cherniaev, "Rossiiskoe dvoevlastie i protsess samoopredeleniia Finliandii," in RAN, *Anatomiia revoliutsii*, 308–23.

16. Z. Galili, A. Nenarokov, and L. Haimson, eds., *Mensheviki v 1917 godu*, vols. 2 and 3 (Moscow, 1995, 1996).

17. The tragic failure of the moderate Left and center to create such a government was played out at the Democratic Conference in mid-September 1917.

18. A. Bogolepov, *Pravo*, nos. 27–28, July 11, 1917, cols. 1068–70.

19. B. I. Kolonitskii, "Antiburzhuaznaia propaganda i 'antiburzhuiskoe' soznanie," in RAN, *Anatomiia revoliutisii*, 188–202.

20. *Niva*, no. 10, March 18, 1917.

21. *Niva*, March 25, 1917.

22. *Zemlia i Volia*, June 15, 1917.

23. *Niva*, May 13, 1917.

24. A. B. Nikolaev offers a cogent analysis in his article "Istoricheskii opyt russkogo parlamentarizma: gosudarstvennoe soveshchanie 1917 goda," in RAN, IRI SPb filial, *Istorik i revoliutsiia: sbornik statei k 70-letiiu so dnia rozhdeniia Olega Nikolaevicha Znamenskogo* (Saint Petersburg, 1999), 161–75.

25. This is in line with the observations of B. Kolonitskii, who in examining the language used in public debate during 1917 notes both a religious dimension and a tendency even among Provisional Government leaders to view the revolution as a "Russian experience," whose features and outcome would be guided by a "Russian way." Such views of the Russian Revolution as a "national" experience are in direct opposition to the master narrative view of February as a bourgeois revolution to be understood according to the transnational categories of class. B. Kolonitskii, "Antiburzhuaznaia propaganda." See also B. I. Kolonitskii, "'Demokratiia' kak identifikatsiia: k izucheniiu politicheskogo soznaniia fevral'skoi revoliutsii," RAN, *Fevral'skaia revoliutsiia*, 109–18.

26. Daniel Orlovsky, "The Lower Middle Strata in Revolutionary Russia," in E. Clowes, S. Kassow, J. West, eds., *Civil Society in Late Imperial Russia* (Princeton, N.J., 1991); "The Lower Middle Strata in the Russian Revolution," in E. Acton and W. Rosenberg, eds., *Critical Dictionary of the Russian Revolution* (London, 1997).

27. Jonathan Sanders, "The Union of Unions in the 1905 Revolution," Ph.D. dissertation, Columbia University, 1983.

28. Daniel T. Orlovsky, "Professionalism in the Ministerial Bureaucracy on the Eve of the February Revolution of 1917," in Harley Balzer, ed., *The Professions in Tsarist and Soviet Russia* (New York, 1996).

29. Similar phenomena could be observed even in such institutions as the Orthodox Church. T. G. Furmenkova, "Vysshee pravoslavnoe dukhovenstvo v Rossii v 1917 g.," *Iz glubiny vremen* (Saint Petersburg, 1995), 74–94.

30. S. D. Kirpichnikov, *Vestnik inzhenerov*, March 29, 1917.

31. *Vestnik inzhenerov*, July 2, 1917.

32. John F. Hutchinson, *Politics and Public Health in Revolutionary Russia 1890–1918* (Baltimore, 1990).

33. For the most recent work on teaching as a profession in the revolutionary years and on educational policy in general, see N. N. Smirnov, *Na perelome: Rossiiskoe uchitel'stvo nakanune i v dni revoliutsii 1917 goda* (Saint Petersburg, 1994); "Rossiiskaia intelligentsiia v gody pervoi mirovoi voiny i revoliutsii 1917g. (nekotorye voprosy istoriografii problemy)," in RAN, *Intelligentsiia i Rossiiskoe obshchestvo v nachale XX veka* (Saint Petersburg, 1996), 139–60; "Uchitel'stvo i obshchestvenno-politicheskoe dvizhe-

nie Rossii v 1917 g.," in RAN, *Rabochie i Rossiiskoe obshchestvo vtoraia polovina XIX–nachalo XX veka: Sbornik statei i materialov posviashchennyi pamiati O. N. Znamenskogo* (Saint Petersburg, 1994), 138–50.

34. *Russkaia shkola*, no. 1 (1917), 35.

35. Smirnov, *Na perelome*, 113–15.

36. GARF, F. 1778, op. 1, d. 367, ll. 4ff.

37. GARF, F. 1778, op. 1, d. 367, ll. 6–7.

38. GARF, F. 1778, op. 1, d. 56, ll. 2–4 ob.

39. GARF, F. 1783, op. 1, d. 82, l. 1.

40. As, for example, in GARF, F. 1796, op. 1, d. 45.

41. GARF, F. 1796, op. 1, d. 72, l. 1.

42. GARF, F. 1796, op. 1, d. 45, ll. 16–16 ob.

43. Moscow officials of the public organizations and city soviet had created with Provisional Government sanction a Committee for the Security of the New Order. A commission and court made up of members from the various parties met for several months and decided the worthiness of certain individuals to remain fully entitled citizens of the "new order." See D. Orlovsky, "Defining a New Civil Order in 1917: The Commission to Secure the New Order and the Inter-Party Court of Conscience," paper read at the AAASS Annual Meeting, Boca Raton, Fla., September 1998.

44. For a recent Russian analysis of the Kerensky "phenomenon" and its relationship to the social psychology of the masses in the revolution, see A. G. Golikov, "Fenomen Kerenskogo," *Otechestvennaia istoriia*, no. 5 (1992): 60–63. Golikov argues that just as Kerensky was created as a hero by the media, so he was dropped and deflated by the end, portrayed as powerless, an image that only served to increase his powerlessness. See also M. I. Basmanov, G. A. Gerasimenko, and K. V. Gusev, *Aleksandr Fedorovich Kerenskii* (Saratov, Russia, 1996).

45. GARF, F. 1778, op. 1, d. 247, l. 177.

46. GARF, F. 1778, op. 1, d. 372, ll. 8–15 ob.

47. GARF, F. 1778, op. 1, d. 247, ll. 380–84.

48. GARF, F. 1778, op. 1, d. 78, l. 1.

49. The best recent analysis is L. G. Protasov, *Vserossiiskoe uchreditel'noe sobranie: istoriia, rozhdeniia i gibeli* (Moscow, 1997).

CHAPTER 4, *Roberts*

The argument of this essay is elaborated more fully in Chapter 4 of my book *Civilization Without Sexes: Reconstructing Gender in Postwar France* (Chicago: University of Chicago Press, 1994). The title of the essay was inspired by Joshua Cole, with whom I sat on a panel at the French Historical Studies Conference in Vancouver in March 1991.

1. The penalties for propaganda on abortion were six months to three years in prison and a fine of between one hundred and three thousand francs. As for propaganda on contraception, the penalty was six months in prison and a fine of between one hundred and five thousand francs. See Robert Talmy, *Histoire du mouvement familial en France, 1896–1939*, vol. 2 (Paris: Union nationale des caisses d'allocations familiales, 1962), 11. For a written text of the law, see *La Femme et l'Enfant*, September 1, 1920.

2. André Berthon was a deputé of Paris from 1919 to 1932. He was a lawyer and although he had no official party affiliation, he was known as a Socialist. He was elected for the first time in November 1919 and was therefore at the beginning of his career when the July 1920 debates took place. He became a Communist at the Congrès du Tours in 1920 and then ran as a Communist in 1924. Paul Morucci was deputé of Bouches-du-Rhône from 1919 to 1924. He was a doctor and also a Socialist; he, too, was a newcomer in July 1920. His legislative interests were the merchant marine, medical assistance, and questions of hygiene. This and all other information concerning legislators in the Parliament is taken from J. Jolly, *Dictionnaire des parliamentaires françaises, 1899–1940*, 8 vols. (Paris: Documentation française, 1960–1977).

3. *Journal Officiel, Débats Parlementaires, Chambre*, July 24, 1920, 3069.

4. *Journal Officiel, Débats Parlementaires, Chambre*, July 24, 1920, 3072. He was speaking specifically of the letters to her daughter, Madame de Grignan.

5. *Journal Officiel, Débats Parlementaires, Chambre*, July 24, 1920, 3069.

6. *Journal Officiel, Débats Parlementaires, Chambre*, July 24, 1920, 3072.

7. *Journal Officiel, Débats Parlementaires, Chambre*, July 24, 1920. See 3073 for the argument about "des récidivistes du crime."

8. According to Paul Cocquemard, "Vote de la loi réprimant la propagande malthusienne," *La Femme et l'Enfant*, September 1, 1920, Morucci "s'est écroulé sous les bâillements et les sourires de l'Assemblée" (has broken down under the indifference and smirks of the assembly). The article accuses Socialists such as Berthon and Morucci of naive stupidity concerning the fact that contraceptive propaganda has been designed as a German plot against the French.

9. Angus Mclaren, *Sexuality and the Social Order: The Debate over the Fertility of Women and Workers in France, 1770–1920* (New York: Holmes and Meier, 1983), 1; Françoise Thébaud, *Donner la vie: Histoire de la mère en France entre les deux guerres* (Paris: Thèse du Troisième cycle, 1982), 59.

10. Francis Ronsin, *La Grève des ventres: Propagande néo-malthusienne et baisse de la natalité française* (Poitiers, France: Aubier Montaigne, 1980), 140–41. He argues that the bill "a, en effet, subi une gestation extraordinaire longue et mouvementée." In *Sexuality and Social Order*, 169, McLaren refers to the law as "the culmination of the long struggle of populationists launched in the 1870s against the forces of depopulation."

11. As one prominent French doctor put it, "La depopulation est devenue actuellement, en France, la grande préoccupation des penseurs, des savants et des législateurs." See Dr. J.-A. Doleris and Jean Bouscatel, *Néo-malthusianisme, maternité et féminisme, education sexuelle* (Paris: Maison et Cie, 1918), 2; Philip Ogden and Marie-Monique Huss describe the interwar period as "the apogee of pronatalism." See their "Demography and Pronatalism in France in the Nineteenth and Twentieth Centuries," *Journal of Historical Geography* 8 (1982): 292.

12. For the term *counter-discourse*, see Richard Terdiman, *Discourse/Counterdiscourse: The Theory and Practice of Symbolic Resistance in Nineteenth-Century France* (Ithaca, N.Y.: Cornell University Press, 1985).

13. The 1923 law "correctionalized" abortion, that is, put it under the legal jurisdiction of the *Cour d'Assises*, where cases were heard by a judge, not a jury. Because juries in the past had pitied and acquitted women who had in some way participated in an abortion, it was believed that the change in jurisdiction would increase the

prosecution rate. For a full explanation of the law, see Vérone, "La Répression de l'avortement," *L'Œuvre*, April 26, 1923.

14. Maurice Agulhon and A. Nouschi, *La France de 1914 à 1940* (Paris: Nathan, 1971), 22. Thébaud, *Donner la vie*, 60; and McLaren, *Sexuality and Social Order*, 169.

15. See Richard Tomlinson, Marie-Monique Huss, and Philip Ogden, "France in Peril: The French Fear of Denatalité," *History Today* 35 (April 1985), 26. The antinatalist Socialist position represented a change from before the war. For example, in 1887 Guesde argued that depopulation would decimate the working class. After the founding of the Communist Party (PCF) in 1920, the Socialist attitude became more ambivalent because abortion had just been legalized in the USSR. In the thirties, Socialists (including Léon Blum, who was known earlier for his liberal views on marriage) once more became pronatalist. For the Socialist view on pronatalism in the thirties, see Françoise Thébaud, "Maternité et famille entre les deux guerres: Idéologie et politique familiale," in Rita Thalman, *Femmes et fascismes* (Paris: Editions Tierce, 1987), 94.

16. In *Grève des ventres*, 146, Ronsin argues that the law's passage stemmed from the defection of certain groups usually allied to neo-Malthusianism. Among them were the working class and those who argued on the basis of freedom of speech.

17. Ronsin, *Grève des ventres*, 144–45. Proportionally, France's casualty rate was the highest in Europe: 16.5 percent of those mobilized, in comparison to 14.7 percent for Germany. See Colin Dyer, *Population and Society in Twentieth Century France* (New York: Holmes and Meier, 1978), 39–40. Theodore Zeldin quotes completely different figures: 17.6 percent for France and 15.1 percent for Germany. See his *France, 1848–1945*, vol. 2 (New York: Oxford University Press, 1977), 950.

18. An earlier form of the bill focused more on the problem of child mortality by providing *maisons d'accouchement*, state-funded obstetrical institutions for the unwed or poor mother. Significantly, although they were approved by the Senate on November 21, 1918, they were struck from the Chamber version of the bill, presented by Edouard Ignace on July 23, 1920, for the purpose of streamlining and forcing progress of the proposal. For earlier social legislation aimed at the problem of infant mortality, such as the 1874 Roussel law regulating the wet-nursing industry, see George D. Sussman, *Selling Mother's Milk: The Wet-Nursing Business in France, 1715–1914* (Urbana: University of Illinois, 1982); Josh Cole, "'A Sudden and Terrible Revelation': Infant Mortality, Maternal Responsibility, and the Roussel Law of 1874," in "The Power of Large Numbers: Population and Politics in Nineteenth-Century France," Ph.D. dissertation, University of California, Berkeley, 1991; Sylvia Schafer, *Children in Moral Danger and the Problem of Government in Third Republic France* (Princeton, N.J.: Princeton University Press, 1997), chapter 2. For the problem of infant mortality, see also Mary Lynn Stewart, *Women, Work and the French State: Labour Protection and Social Patriarchy, 1879–1919* (Kingston, Canada: McGill's Queen's University Press, 1989), 178–85; Rachel G. Fuchs, "The Right to Life: Paul Strauss and the Politics of Motherhood," in Elinor Accampo, Rachel Fuchs, and Mary Lynn Stewart, eds., *Gender and the Politics of Social Reform in France, 1870–1914* (Baltimore: Johns Hopkins University Press, 1995), 82–105.

19. See Joseph Spengler, *France Faces Depopulation: Postlude Edition, 1936–1976* (Durham, N.C.: Duke University Press, 1979), 240, where he refers to "the exception" of the laws passed in 1920 and 1923 against neo-Malthusianism and abortion and de-

scribes most other pronatalist legislation as assuming the form of "positive pecuniary aids to parents and of reductions in certain burdens incident on parents." See also Jack Ellis, *The Physician-Legislators of France: Medicine and Politics in the Early Third Republic, 1870–1914* (Cambridge: Cambridge University Press, 1990), 221–22, where he discusses the more positive tenor of legislation passed to encourage natality in the prewar period.

20. See McLaren, *Sexuality and Social Order*, 182. For the way in which gender had figured into republican social policy throughout the nineteenth century, see Elinor Accampo's excellent introductory essay "Gender, Social Policy and the Third Republic," in Elinor Accampo, Rachel Fuchs, and Mary Lynn Stewart, eds., *Gender and the Politics of Social Reform*, as well as other chapters in this volume. For an important look at the regulation of abortion and birth control before the war, see Jean Elisabeth Pedersen, "Regulating Abortion and Birth Control: Gender, Medicine and Republican Politics in France, 1870–1920," *French Historical Studies* 19, no. 3 (Spring 1996): 673–98.

21. In *Grève des ventres*, 193, Ronsin makes this comment on the effect of the law: "largement inefficace pour lutter contre la limitation volontaire des naissances." Paul Paillat and Jacques Houdaille argue that despite 1920 law, two out of every three births were prevented in the 1920s. See their "Legislation Directly or Indirectly Influencing Fertility in France," in M. Kirk, A. Livi-Bacci, and E. Szabady, eds., *Law and Fertility in Europe* (Dolhain, Belgium: Ordina Editions, 1975), 24.

22. *J.O. Débats Parlementaires, Chambre*, July 24, 1920, 3070. Pinard's reputation as a doctor and scientist was extremely high. He was a member of the Académie de Médecine and published many works on obstetrics and gynecology. He entered the Chamber in 1919 and stayed until 1929 as a member of the Radical Party. At the time of the debates, Pinard had been a prominent Parisian doctor for almost forty years. His work in the Chamber reflected his interests, where he strove for the defense and protection of the family, women, and children. He is described by Jolly as "le défenseur acharné et clairvoyant du relèvement de la natalité" (the relentless and visionary champion of increased natalism). After Pinard made the statement quoted above, both Berthon and Morucci referred to it several times; they were obviously aware of Pinard's influence in these matters and wanted to use it to their full advantage.

23. See Cole, "Power of Large Numbers," chapter 4, and Spengler, *France Faces Depopulation*, for a full accounting of pronatalist arguments at the turn of the century. See also Joshua H. Cole, "'There Are Only Good Mothers': The Ideological Work of Women's Fertility in France Before World War I," *French Historical Studies* 19, no. 3 (Spring 1996): 639–72; Karen Offen, "Depopulation, Nationalism, and Feminism in Fin-de-siècle France," *American Historical Review* 89 (June 1984): 648–76. The division of property under the Napoleonic inheritance laws became a common explanation of the crisis of depopulation even in the 1920s. See, for example, Fernand Auburtin, *La Natalité: La Patrie en danger!* 4th ed. (Paris: G. Crès et Cie, 1921).

24. For more on "persuasion," see Ellen Rooney, *Seductive Reasoning: Pluralism as the Problematic of Contemporary Literary Theory* (Ithaca, N.Y.: Cornell University Press, 1989), chapter 2.

25. See, for example, John Hunter, "The Problem of the French Birth Rate on the Eve of World War I," *French Historical Studies* 2 (1962): 492; Eugen Weber, *France, Fin-*

de-siècle (Cambridge, Mass.: Harvard University Press, 1986), 12. In *France 1848–1945*, vol. 2:950, Zeldin makes the argument that historians look at the problem in this way, then tries to move beyond it in his own analysis.

26. According to Mclaren, *Sexuality and Social Order*, 15, the most commonly accepted theory is that in a modernizing, industrial society, children are no longer seen by their parents as instruments of cheap labor but rather expensive investments in terms of clothing, feeding, and education. Based on this change in the "utility value" of children, the theory goes, parents make a rational decision to limit the number of their progeny.

27. *J. O., Débats Parlementaires, Sénat*, November 22, 1918, 776. Delahaye was senator of Maine-et-Loire from 1903 to 1932. He had a reputation as a royalist, who sat on the far Right, and as a volatile and temperamental senator, taken to intervening at the podium often and dramatically.

28. *J. O., Débats Parlementaires, Sénat*, January 29, 1919, 49. Similarly, a comment, 50, made by Felix Martin (Saône-et-Loire) that "la race est menacée; la patrie est en danger" evoked a torrent of "très biens" and applause from the other senators.

29. *J. O., Débats Parlementaires, Sénat*, November 22, 1918, 776. Many illegitimate and orphaned children, Cazeneuve went on to argue, using statistics from the Rhône, "have made courageous soldiers" who have been decorated with the Croix de Guerre and have died "bravely doing their duty."

30. *J. O., Débats Parlementaires, Sénat*, January 25, 1919, 32.

31. Cazeneuve claimed that there were approximately one hundred doctors in the Chamber and the Senate in 1919. See *J. O., Débats parlementaires, Sénat*, January 29, 1919, 40. Historian Jack Ellis's numbers are more conservative: forty-four doctors and five pharmacists. However, Ellis argues that doctors were second only to lawyers in terms of their relative representation in the national politics of the Third Republic, a phenomenon that "had few counterparts in other societies." See his *Physician-Legislators of France*, 3–5. Ellis argues that the postwar period was a political turning point for the physician-legislator, marked by "a conservative drift among the older republican groups on the left, especially as they became outflanked by socialists and communists." For other uses of medical science as a way to address depopulation, see Robert Nye, *Crime, Madness, and Politics in Modern France: The Medical Concept of National Decline* (Princeton, N.J.: Princeton University Press, 1984), 132–70.

32. *J. O., Débats parlementaires, Sénat*, January 29, 1919, 51–52. Reveillaud was senator of the Charente-Inférieure from 1912 to 1921. He was a lawyer and, according to Jolly, spoke out openly against neo-Malthusian propaganda and abortion as early as 1910.

33. *J. O., Débats parlementaires, Sénat*, January 25, 1919, 30. Emile Goy was the senator of Haute-Savoie from 1910 to 1925. He was a doctor and a member of senatorial commissions on teaching, hygiene, and social assistance.

34. *J. O., Débats parlementaires, Sénat*, January 25, 1919, 30.

35. See Sylvia Schafer, "'Si les parents ne remplissent pas leurs devoirs . . .': Parental Obligation, Paternal Authority and State 'Intervention,'" unpublished manuscript. According to Schafer, the metaphor of the state as a "metaparent" can be traced back to Napoleon's organization of the Service des Enfants Assistés at the beginning of the century. See also Schafer's excellent monograph, *Children in Moral Danger*, where these issues are fully elaborated, particularly in the introduction, 15.

36. *J.O. Débats parlementaires, Sénat,* January 29, 1920, 49. Such an equation of the child with the future of France characterized pronatalist discourse from its conception. See Cole, "Power of Large Numbers," 193; and Schafer, *Children in Moral Danger.*

37. *J.O. Débats parlementaires, Sénat,* January 25, 1919, 32.

38. Daniel Sherman, "Monuments, Mourning and Masculinity in France After World War I," *Gender and History* 8 (1996): 82–107; Jay Winter, *Sites of Memory, Sites of Mourning: The Great War in European Cultural History* (Cambridge: Cambridge University Press, 1995); Modrus Eksteins, *Rites of Spring: The Great War and the Birth of the Modern Age* (New York: Doubleday, 1989).

39. *J.O. Débats parlementaires, Sénat,* January 25, 1919, 37.

40. *J.O. Débats parlementaires, Sénat,* November 22, 1918, 777.

41. See also Paul Bureau, "L'Avortement," *Pour la vie,* June 1919.

42. Given the sparsity of actual discussion of the law in the Chamber on July 23, 1920, I have tried to piece together related documents in order to determine whether it was conceived in the same way as in the Senate.

43. *J.O., Documents parlementaires, Chambre,* Annexe no. 201, Session January 22, 1920, F713955, Malthusianisme, 1919–20, Archives Nationales.

44. Here and elsewhere in my analysis of the sexualized nature of this language, I am indebted to the observations of Ann-Lou Shapiro in her comment of my paper "How Can We Ever Heal Such a Wound?: Pronatalism, Cultural Crisis and the Abortion Law of 1920," *French Historical Studies,* March 23, 1991.

45. *J.O., Documents parlementaires, Chambre,* Annexe no. 1357, Session July 23, 1920, 2065, Exposé de motifs, presentée par M. Edouard Ignace.

46. *J.O., Débats parlementaires, Sénat,* November 22, 1918, 780.

47. For a European-wide survey of the postwar reconstruction, see Charles Maier, *Recasting Bourgeois Europe: Stabilization in France, Germany and Italy in the Decade After World War I* (Princeton, N.J.: Princeton University Press, 1975). For the specific case of the French bourgeoisie, see Adeleine Daumard, *Les Bourgeois et la Bourgeoisie en France depuis 1815* (Paris: Aubier-Montaigne, 1987), 278. In *L'Histoire politique de la Troisième Republique,* vol. 3, *L'Après-guerre* (Paris: Presses Universitaires de France, 1968), 26, E. Bonnefous quotes this "Témoignage de Louis Marcellin," from *Politique et Politiciens après la guerre:* "Le charbon est rare, le beurre introuvable, il est difficile de se procurer des oeufs; le sucre est un object de haut luxe, la viande renchérit sans cesse et tout est hors de prix. On ne trouve rien ou presque rien aux Halles." (Coal is scarce, butter is nowhere to be found, it is difficult to find eggs, sugar is a luxury, the price of meat is endlessly getting more expensive and all is exorbitant. There's nothing or almost nothing at Les Halls [the famous Parisian market].) For other contemporary views on inflation and the high postwar cost of living, see also "Les Vainquers sous le joug," *L'Œuvre,* February 2, 1919, and "La Bourgeoisie française dans la lutte pour la vie," *La Renaissance Politique,* July 24, 31, 1920.

48. Between 1919 and 1920 the franc fell by 50 percent and by 1924 was down to less that one-tenth of its prewar value. For a full description of the crises in the franc that plagued France throughout the decade see P. Bernard and H. Dubief, *The Decline of the Third Republic, 1914–1918* (Cambridge: Cambridge University Press, 1985), particularly 94–107. Dubief argues that the effect of the instability of the franc throughout the 1920s added up to a set of "serious blows . . . dealt to public morality in general and respect for institutions in particular," 107. For inflation and the ef-

fects of it on the bourgeoisie, see Daumard, *La Bourgeoisie*. See Gordon Wright, *France in Modern Times*, 4th ed. (New York: W.W. Norton, 1987), 348–49, for the economic illiteracy of the politicians.

49. See James McMillan, *From Dreyfus to DeGaulle* (London: E. Arnold, 1985), 95. Recent diplomatic historiography emphasizes the war and postwar periods as a period of decline in international power and prestige for France. For a summary and evaluation of this material, see Michael Carley, "Le Declin d'une grande puissance: La Politique étrangère de la France en Europe," *Canadian Journal of History*, 21 (1986). In this review essay, 397, Carley stresses "l'affaiblissement de la France comme grande puissance à cause de la guerre" (the decline of France as a great power because of the war).

50. Bernard and Dubief, *Decline*, 125. See also Maier, *Recasting Bourgeois Europe*, 144; he also argues that utopian, nostaglic efforts mark the decade. In *La France de l'entre-deux-guerres*, C. Fohlen also calls the postwar period "Les Temps des Illusions" (Paris: Casterman, 1972).

51. Nelly Roussel, "Posons nos conditions," originally written in December 1919 and posthumously reprinted in *Derniers Combats* (Paris: L'Emancipatrice, 1932), 86.

52. See the following for an example of the pronatalist views of Madeleine Vernet and Maria Vérone, two prominent postwar feminists: Madeleine Vernet, "Le Mensonge social et la maternité," *Le Mère Educatrice*, December 1919; "La Science qui tue," and "A Toutes les Femmes," *La Mère Educatrice*, n.d., Dossier Vernet, Bibliothèque Marguerite Durand. Maria Vérone, "45.000 francs pour les parlementaires, 180 francs pour les mères," *L'Œuvre*, August 10, 1926; "La Répression de l'avortement," *L'Œuvre*, April 26, 1923, and "Le Plus Beau Sport: La Maternité," *L'Œuvre*, November 29, 1923, both in Articles de Journaux, box no. 6, Fonds Marie Louise Bouglé, Bibliothèque Historique de la ville de Paris.

53. See, in particular, Schafer, *Children in Moral Danger*, 9.

54. Cheryl Koos, "Gender, Anti-individualism, and Nationalism: The Alliance Nationale and the Pronatalist Backlash Against the *Femme moderne*, 1933–1940," *French Historical Studies* 19, no. 3 (Spring, 1996): 699–724. For more on Vichy family policy, including its declaration of the death penalty for abortionists, see Miranda Pollard, *Regime of Virtue: Mobilizing Gender in Vichy France* (Chicago: University of Chicago Press, 1998).

CHAPTER 5, *Koonz*

1. Eugenia Semyonovna Ginzburg, *Journey into the Whirlwind*, trans. Paul Stevenson and Max Hayward (San Diego, New York, and London: Harcourt, 1995), 182.

2. Lev Kopelev, *The Education of a True Believer*, trans. Gary Kern (New York: Harper and Row, 1980). Craig R. Whitney, "Lev Kopelev, Soviet Writer in Prison 10 Years, Dies at 85," *New York Times*, June 20, 1997.

3. Dave Grossman, *On Killing: The Psychological Cost of Learning to Kill in War and Society* (Boston: Back Bay Books, 1995). The author examines desensitization techniques applied by U.S. military instructors and compares them to the violence of televised and filmed popular culture. For an excellent review of this question in German history, compare Stephen G. Fritz, "'We Are Trying . . . to Change the Face of the World,' Ideology and Motivation in the *Wehrmacht* on the Eastern Front: The View from Below," *Journal of Military History* 60, no. 4 (1996): 683–710.

4. Robert Gellately, "Denunciations in Twentieth-Century Germany: Aspects of Self-Policing in the Third Reich and the German Democratic Republic," *Journal of Modern History* 68, no. 4 (December 1996), 931–67.

5. Paul Rose, *German Question / Jewish Question: Revolutionary Antisemitism from Kant to Wagner* (Princeton, N.J.: Princeton University Press, 1990), 385.

6. John Weiss, *Ideology of Death: Why the Holocaust Happened in Germany* (Chicago: Ivan R. Dee, 1996), ix, viii. "The murder of millions in five years needed the voluntary complicity of tens of thousands" (342), but by collapsing prewar Nazi assault against Jews into a single chapter (306–16) and examining the wartime mass murders as a series of actions and high-level decisions (Chapter 21, 317–42), Weiss overlooks the role of sophisticated hate propaganda—leaving the impression that prior beliefs provided a sufficient motivation for average Germans' collaboration.

7. Daniel Jonah Goldhagen, *Hitler's Willing Executioners: Ordinary Germans and the Holocaust* (New York: Knopf, 1996), 440–41. Compare Bettine Birn, "Historiographical Review: Revising the Holocaust," *Historical Journal* 40, no. 1 (1997), 193–213. Not surprisingly, as these historians stake out claims about a uniquely German anti-Semitism, others insist on the uniqueness of the Holocaust. Avishai Margalit and Gabriel Motzkin, "The Uniqueness of the Holocaust," *Philosophy and Public Affairs* (Winter 1996), 65–83; and Alan S. Rosenbaum, *Is the Holocaust Unique? Perspectives on Comparative Genoncide* (Boulder, Colo.: Westview/HarperCollins, 1996).

8. Theodor W. Adorno, *The Authoritarian Personality* (New York: Harper and Row, 1969); Robert Jay Lifton, *The Nazi Doctors: Medical Killing and the Psychology of Genocide* (New York: Basic Books, 1986).

Raphaël Lemkin, who coined the term *genocide*, believed the scale of slaughter justified a special word, although he carefully surveyed precedents from Carthage through the Thirty Years' War and the Turkish extermination of the Armenians. *Axis Rule in Occupied Europe* (Washington, D.C.: Carnegie, 1944).

9. Richard Rubenstein, *The Cunning of History* (New York: Harpers, 1978), 91, 195.

10. Zygmunt Bauman, *Modernity and the Holocaust* (Ithaca, N.Y.: Cornell University Press, 1989), 93.

11. Bauman, *Modernity*, 57. Interestingly, Hitler used the garden metaphor in a very different sense when he railed against the notion ("as truly Jewish in its effrontery as it is stupid!") that human agency could "conquer" Nature rather learn her secrets and collaborate with her. Adolf Hitler, *Mein Kampf*, trans. Ralph Manheim (Boston: Sentry, 1962), 286–87.

12. Nira Yuval-Davis and Floya Anthias, in their anthology *Women-Nation-State* (London: Macmillan, 1989) suggest that a gendered analysis can account for women as biological reproducers of future generations, as markers of community and kin systems through marriage customs, as socializers of their children, and as fighters in battles for independence. Symbolically, gendered images form the core of narratives about the nation. Ann Stoler made a major contribution to this literature by linking gender to the racialized discourse of "civility" in imperial settings: *Race and the Education of Desire* (Durham, N.C.: Duke, 1996), 96–99.

13. Sven Lundquist, *"Exterminate All the Brutes,"* trans. (from the Swedish) Joan Tate (New York: New Press, 1996), 142–75.

14. As noted in Domasky's contribution, "Mobilization of Imagination" is the ti-

tle of one of the subchapters in Jay Winter and Blaine Baggett, *The Great War and the Shaping of the Twentieth Century* (New York, 1996).

15. Other cases, such as Cambodia, more closely resemble the Stalinist precedent because of a relatively backward communications network and the reliance primarily on military troops rather than civilians. Ben Kiernan, *The Pol Pot Regime: Race, Power, and Genocide in Cambodia* (New Haven, Conn.: Yale University Press, 1996).

16. Robert M. Hayden, "Imagined Communities and Real Victims: Self-determination and Ethnic Cleansing in Yugoslavia," *American Ethnologist* 23, no. 4 (November 1996): 783–800. Benedict Anderson asks and does not answer, "why people are ready to die for these inventions." *Imagined Communities* (London: Verso, 1990), 141. Other cases of ethnic cleansing in the 1990s that have received recent scholarly attention include attacks against Nepalese in Bhutan; Gypsies in Central Europe; Kosovo Albanians; Palestinians; and Hutus and Tutsi in Rwanda, Burundi, and Congo. Compare also Aleksandr Kislov, "Ethnic Conflict," *Current Digest of the Post-Soviet Press* 47, no. 28 (August 9, 1995), 15–17.

17. Claude Lefort, *Political Forms of Modern Society, Bureaucracy, Democracy, Totalitarianism*, ed. and introduced John B. Thompson (Cambridge: M.I.T. Press, 1986), 212–14, 218–19.

18. Gerd Albrecht, *Nationalsozialistische Filmpolitik: Eine soziologische Untersuchung über die Spielfilme des Dritten Reiches* (Stuttgart, West Germany: Ferdinand Enke, 1969), 468f. David Welch, *Propaganda and German Cinema: 1933–1945* (Oxford, England: Clarendon, 1983).

19. For an excellent review of the literature plus a new interpretation, compare Thomas Mathieu, *Kunstauffassungen und Kulturpolitik in Nationalsozialismus: Studien zu Adolf Hitler, Joseph Goebbels, Alfred Rosenberg, Baldur von Schirach, Heinrich Himmler, Albert Speer, Wilhelm Frick* (Sarbrücken, Germany: Pfau, 1997).

20. Gerhard Paul, *Aufstand der Bilder: Die NS-Propaganda vor 1933* (Berlin: J.H.W. Dietz Nachf., 1990), 11–16, 23–79.

21. "DissemiNation," in Homi K. Bhabha, ed., *Nation and Narration* (New York: Routledge, 1990), 292. Bhabha speaks here of national identity formation, and we may want to discuss to what extent a specifically racist/racialist identity is radically different or fundamentally the same. Hannah Arendt insisted on the utter incommensurability of the two in "Race Thinking Before Racism," in *The Origins of Totalitarianism* (Cleveland and New York: Meridian Books, World Publishing Company, 1958) and linked Nazi racial thinking to nineteenth-century imperialism.

22. Alice Yaeger Kaplan, "Fascism and Banality," *Reproductions of Banality: Fascism, Literature, and French Intellectual Life* (Minneapolis: University of Minnesota Press, 1986), 49–54, quotation from 43.

23. Linda Schulte-Sasse, *Entertaining the Third Reich: Illusions of Wholeness in Nazi Cinema* (Durham, N.C.: Duke University Press, 1996), 36–43. For an excellent comparative perspective, compare Boris Groys, *The Total Art of Stalinism*, trans. Charles Rougle (Princeton, N.J.: Princeton University Press, 1992), 33–74.

24. Greenberg, *Art and Culture. Critical Essays* (Boston: Beacon, 1961), 19. His classic definition of Kitsch appeared in the same essay: "Where there is an avant-garde, generally we find also a rear-guard. . . . Kitsch is vicarious experience and faked sensations. Kitsch changes according to style, but remains always the same. Kitsch is the epitome of all that is spurious in the life of our times." Kitsch appropriates the con-

ventions of earlier great art and makes them available to the general public. Matei Calinescu, *Five Faces of Modernity: Modernism, Avant-Garde, Decadence, Kitsch, Postmodernism* (Durham, N.C.: Duke University Press, 1986), 247.

25. For a lucid examination of how this process functions, compare William A. Connolly, *Identity/Difference: Democratic Negotiations of Political Paradox* (Ithaca, N.Y., and London: Cornell University Press, 1991), 67–68. "Madness [or] . . . severe abnormality is doubly entangled with the identity of the rational agent and the normal individual: it helps to constitute practical reason and normality by providing a set of abnormal conducts and 'vehement passions' against which each is defined, but it also threatens them by embodying characteristics that would destabilize the normal if they were to proliferate." Thus, the targets of racial hygiene policies both constituted and threatened the normalized racial community.

26. See Carl Schorske's study of mass politics as a modernist project, *Fin-de-siècle Vienna: Politics and Culture* (New York: Knopf, 1980), 116–79.

27. Marina Warner, *Monuments and Maidens: The Allegory of the Female Form* (New York: Atheneum, 1985). "Generally, however, the revelation of the lower body of a woman . . . marks the figure as a prime and exclusive object of desire," 294–327, here, 315.

28. Ludmilla Jordanova, *Sexual Visions: Images of Gender in Science and Medicine Between the Eighteenth and Twentieth Centuries* (Madison: University of Wisconsin Press, 1989), 89–91. Compare also her analysis of female nudity in the film *Metropolis*, in *Sexual Visions*, 111–33.

29. Goebbels's ministry underwrote only two predominantly anti-Semitic films after the invasion of Poland—*Die Rotschilds, Jud Suß* (1940) and *Der ewige Jude* (1940) and approved of two comedies (in 1939) that included negative images of Jewish characters Robert und Bertram and Leinen aus Irland. David Welch, *The Third Reich Politics and Propaganda* (London: Routledge, 1993), 76–78.

30. Karl Ludwig Rost, *Sterilisation und Euthanasie im Film des "Dritten Reiches": Nationalsozialistische Propaganda in ihrer Beziehung zu rassenhygienischen Maßnahmen des NS-Staates* (Husum, West Germany: Matthiesen, 1987).

31. Linda Schulte-Sasse, *Entertaining*, 9.

32. Slavoj Zizek, *The Sublime Object of Ideology* (London: Verso, 1989), 87–130.

33. Paul Weindling, *Health, Race and German Politics Between National Unification and Nazism, 1870–1945* (Cambridge: Cambridge University Press, 1989).

34. Raul Hilberg, *The Destruction of the European Jews*, student ed. (New York: Homes and Meier, 1985).

35. Walter Groß, *Nationalsozialistische Rassenpolitik: Eine Rede an die deutschen Frauen*, delivered in Cologne, October 13, 1934 (Dessau, Germany: C. Dünnhaupt. 1934), 8.

36. Karl A. Schleunes, *The Twisted Road to Auschwitz: Nazi Policy Toward German Jews 1933–1939* (Urbana, Ill.: University of Illinois Press, 1990), 48. For an example of the pairing of these two July 14s, compare the unsigned article, "Der 14. Juli 1789, deutsch gesehen," *Ziel und Weg* 9, no. 14 (1939): 431.

37. For an excellent summary of this legislation and the scholarly literature about it, see Gabrielle Czarnowski, "Hereditary and Racial Welfare," *Social Politics* 4, no. 1 (Spring 1997): 114–35.

38. In Germany, as in all other industrializing nations, eugenicists and racial hy-

giene advocates had lobbied intensively for legislation, but by 1933 they had not achieved any success. Paul Weindling, *Health, Race*; and Frank Dikötter, "Race Culture: Recent Perspectives on the History of Eugenics," *American Historical Review* 103, no. 2 (April 1998): 467–78.

39. Garland E. Allen, "Science Misapplied: The Eugenics Age Revisited," *Technology Review*, August–September 1996, 23–31.

40. Joseph Wulf, *Presse und Funk im Dritten Reich: Eine Dokumentation* (Gütersloh, West Germany: Sigbert Mohn, 1964), 252–55. Wulf notes also instructions about what kinds of images party officials' instructions said to publish.

41. "Der richtige Geschaftsmann," *Fliegende Blätter* 90 (1889): 2279.

42. In using this expression, follow Tom Childers's description of the Nazi Party before 1933 as a "catchall" party that drew disaffected from a variety of splinter parties into the well-organized Nazi Party. *The Nazi Voter: The Social Foundations of Fascism in Germany, 1919–1933* (Chapel Hill: University of North Carolina Press, 1983), 13–14, 262–69.

43. G. Paul, *Aufstand*, 238. In Weimar Nazi cartoons, the Jew was the "wire puller" (*Drahtzieher*) behind the scenes, 236. See Sasse-Schulte's insightful analysis of Jüd Suss in her *Entertaining*, 47–91.

44. Schulte-Sasse, *Entertaining*, 71.

45. Ian Kershaw, "How Successful Was Nazi Propaganda?" in David Welch, ed., *Nazi Propaganda* (London and New York: Croom-Helms, 1993), 198.

46. Quoted in Welch, *The Third Reich: Politics and Propaganda* (London and New York: Routledge, 1993), 78.

CHAPTER 6, *Bartov*

1. For some examples, see Benedict Anderson, *Imagined Communities: Reflections on the Origin and Spread of Nationalism*, rev. ed. (London, 1991); Rogers Brubaker, *Citizenship and Nationhood in France and Germany* (Cambridge, Mass., 1992); Liah Greenfeld, *Nationalism: Five Roads to Modernity* (Cambridge, Mass., 1992); E. J. Hobsbawm, *Nations and Nationalism Since 1780: Programme, Myth, Reality*, 2d ed. (Cambridge, England, 1992); Peter Sahlins, *Boundaries: The Making of France and Spain in the Pyrenees* (Berkeley, Calif., 1989); Eugen Weber, *Peasants into Frenchmen: The Modernization of Rural France, 1870–1914* (Stanford, Calif., 1976).

2. In the context of this chapter, I refer especially to Germany. See, for example, George L. Mosse, *The Nationalization of the Masses: Political Symbolism and Mass Movements in Germany from the Napoleonic Wars Through the Third Reich*, 2d ed. (Ithaca, N.Y., 1991). There are, of course, many other examples, each of which differs according to the different national circumstances. In France, for instance, the status of Jews was questioned at times of crisis, such as the Dreyfus Affair or the 1930s, let alone Vichy. Some of the recent literature on the latter is reviewed in my article "The Proof of Ignominy: Vichy France's Past and Present," *Contemporary European History* 7 (1998). In Poland, anti-Jewish policies and an urge to expel Jews from the country increased throughout the interwar period. On the similarities and differences between Polish and German anti-Semitism, see, most recently: William W. Hagen, "Before the 'Final Solution': Toward a Comparative Analysis of Political Anti-Semitism in Interwar Germany and Poland," *Journal of Modern History* 68 (June 1996), and the literature

cited therein. The Polish example has many similarities to other East European countries. See also D. D. Moore, ed., *East European Jews in Two Worlds: Studies from the YIVO Annual* (Evanston, Ill., 1990). Italy, by contrast, had a very small and well-integrated Jewish community, on the one hand, and developed a sense of national identity very late, on the other, which may explain the relative absence of anti-Semitism there. The Gypsies, or Sinti and Roma, are another case in point, which cannot be discussed in this chapter for reasons of space and conceptual clarity. The most important study on the genocide of the Sinti and Roma is Michael Zimmermann, *Rassenutopie und Genozid: Die nationalsozialistische "Lösung der Zigeunerfrage"* (Hamburg, 1996). For an interesting discussion of postwar German attitudes toward this group, see Gilad Margalit, "Die deutsche Zigeunerpolitik nach 1945," *Vierteljahrshefte für Zeitgeschichte* 45 (1997).

3. For documentation on early French discussions about Jewish citizenship, see Lynn Hunt, ed., *The French Revolution and Human rights: A Brief Documentary History* (Boston, 1996); Scott Glotzer, "Napoleon, the Jews and the Construction of Modern Citizenship in Early Nineteenth Century France," Ph.D. dissertation, Rutgers University, 1997. See further, for instance, in Arthur Hertzberg, *The French Enlightenment and the Jews: The Origins of Modern Anti-Semitism* (New York, 1968); Jacob Katz, *Out of the Ghetto: The Social Background of the Emancipation of the Jews, 1770–1870* (New York, 1978); George L. Mosse, *Confronting the Nation: Jewish and Western Nationalism* (Hanover, N.H., 1993); Magdalena Opalski and Israel Bartal, *Poles and Jews: A Failed Brotherhood* (Hanover, N.H., 1992); Jehuda Reinharz and Walter Schatzberg, eds., *The Jewish Response to German Culture: From the Enlightenment to the Second World War* (Hanover, N.H., 1985); Gershom Scholem, *On Jews and Judaism in Crisis: Selected Essays*, ed. Werner J. Dannhauser (New York, 1976); David Sorkin, *The Transformation of German Jewry, 1780–1840* (New York, 1987).

4. See, for example, Michael Adas, *Machines as the Measure of Men: Science, Technology, and Ideologies of Western Dominance* (Ithaca, N.Y., 1989); Modris Eksteins, *Rites of Spring: The Great War and the Birth of the Modern Age* (New York, 1989); Stephen Kern, *The Culture of Time and Space, 1880–1918* (Cambridge, Mass., 1983); Daniel Pick, *War Machine: The Rationalisation of Slaughter in the Modern Age* (New Haven, Conn., 1993), and his *Faces of Degeneration: A European Disorder, c. 1848–c. 1918* (Cambridge, England, 1989); Anson Rabinbach, *The Human Motor: Energy, Fatigue, and the Origins of Modernity* (Berkeley, Calif., 1992). A key and pioneering text for understanding the relationship between anti-Semitism, imperialism, and totalitarianism is still Hannah Arendt's *The Origins of Totalitarianism* (New York, 1951).

5. See, among others, Stéphane Audoin-Rouzeau, *Men at War, 1914–1918: National Sentiment and Trench Journalism in France During the First World War*, trans. Helen McPhail (Providence, R.I., 1992); Jean-Jacques Becker, *The Great War and the French People*, trans. Arnold Pomerans (Leamington Spa, England, 1985); Frans Coetzee and Marilyn Shevin-Coetzee, eds., *Authority, Identity, and the Social History of the Great War* (Providence, R.I., 1995); Paul Fussell, *The Great War and Modern Memory* (New York, 1975); Gerhard Hirschfeld, Gerd Krumeich, and Irina Renz, eds., *Keiner fühlt sich hier mehr als mensch . . . Erlebnis und Wirkung des Ersten Weltkriegs* (Essen, Germany, 1993); Leonard V. Smith, *Between Mutiny and Obedience: The Case of the French Fifth Infantry Division During World War I* (Princeton, N.J., 1994); Jack Snyder, *The Ideology of the Offensive: Military Decision Making and the Disasters of 1914* (Ithaca, N.Y., 1984).

6. On instances of frustration, rage, mutiny, and violence during and after the war, see, for example, Gloden Dallas and Douglas Gill, *The Unknown Army: Mutinies in the British Army in World War I* (London, 1985); Guy Pedrocini, *Les mutineries de 1917* (Paris, 1967); Antoine Prost, *In the Wake of War: "Les Anciens Combattants" and French Society, 1914–1939*, trans. Helen McPhail (Providence, R.I., 1992); Dennis E. Showalter, *Little Man, What Now? Der Stürmer in the Weimar Republic* (Hamden, Conn., 1982); Klaus Theweleit, *Male Fantasies*, trans. Stephen Conway, 2 vols. (Minneapolis, 1987–89); Robert Weldon Whalen, *Bitter Wounds: German Victims of the Great War, 1914–1939* (Ithaca, N.Y., 1984). Further on the veterans and the *Freikorps* of 1920s Germany in James M. Diehl, *Paramilitary Politics in Weimar Germany* (Bloomington, Ind., 1977); R. G. L. Waite, *Vanguard of Nazism: The Free Corps Movement in Postwar Germany, 1918–1923*, 2d ed. (Cambridge, Mass., 1970); Volker R. Berghahn, *Der Stahlhelm* (Düsseldorf, 1966).

7. Twelve thousand German Jews were killed in the war. On the "Jew count" and its repercussions, see Michael Brenner, *The Renaissance of Jewish Culture in Weimar Germany* (New Haven, Conn., 1996), 31–35; Werner T. Angress, "Das deutsche Militär und die Juden im Ersten Weltkrieg," *Militärgeschichtliche Mitteilungen* 1 (1976). Colonel-General von Fritsch wrote in a private letter in 1939, that is, *after* he was dismissed by Hitler as commander in chief of the army on the fabricated accusation of homosexual relations, that soon after the Great War he had concluded that for Germany to be powerful again, it would have to win the battle against the Jews. See John Wheeler-Bennett, *The Nemesis of Power*, 2d ed. (London, 1980), 380. Ludwig Beck, who was later the architect of Hitler's army as its chief of staff, only to become a major figure in the resistance after 1938, wrote in a private letter on November 28, 1918, as a young staff officer: "At the most difficult moment in the war we were attacked in the back by the revolution, which I now do not doubt for an instant had been prepared long before." Cited in Klaus-Jürgen Müller, *General Ludwig Beck* (Boppard, West Germany, 1980), 323. See further in Wilhelm Deist, *Militär, Staat, und Gesellschaft* (Munich, 1991), 83–233. For a remarkable account by a Jewish officer in the Austro-Hungarian army that illustrates the extent of anti-Semitism in its ranks, see Avigdor Hameiri, *The Great Madness* (New York, 1929).

8. Apart from works cited above, see also V. R. Berghahn, *Germany and the Approach of War in 1914*, 2d ed. (New York, 1993), for background to the war; Richard Bessel, *Germany After the First World War* (Oxford, England, 1993), for its aftermath. See also suggestive essays in Wolfgang J. Mommsen, *Imperial Germany, 1867–1918: Politics, Culture, and Society in an Authoritarian State*, trans. Richard Deveson (London, 1995); Geoff Eley, *From Unification to Nazism: Reinterpreting the German Past* (London, 1986). On popular pre-1914 nationalism see also Marilyn Shevin Coetzee, *The German Army League: Popular Nationalism in Wilhelmine Germany* (New York, 1990); Geoff Eley, *Reshaping the German Right: Radical Nationalism and Political Change After Bismarck*, 2d ed. (Ann Arbor, Mich., 1991).

9. One of the best recent studies of the growth of an anti-Semitic ideology among the young academic elites of the period is Ulrich Herbert, *Best: Biographische Studien über Radikalismus, Weltanschauung und Venunft, 1903–1989* (Bonn, 1996), part 1, and the literature cited therein; see also his 1996 unpublished paper, "Den Gegner vernichten, ohne ihn zu hassen: Loathing the Jews in the World View of the Intellectual Leader-

ship of the SS in the 1920s and 1930s." Older studies on Weimar culture and the role of the Jews in it include Walter Laqueur, *Weimar: A Cultural History, 1918–1933* (New York, 1974), and Peter Gay, *Weimar Culture: The Outsider as Insider* (New York, 1968). A recent study on the revival of tradition in Weimar Jewry, is Brenner, *Renaissance of Jewish Culture.* A recent work on Jewish immigration in Weimar and the Third Reich is Doron Niederland, *German Jewry—Immigrants or Refugees? A Study of Immigration Patterns Between the World Wars* (Jerusalem, 1996 [in Hebrew]). See also the works cited in the notes above, especially Mosse, *Confronting the Nation*; Reinharz and Schatzberg, *Jewish Response*; and Scholem, *Jews and Judaism.* Interpretations of Weimar as the site of a crisis of modernity or of a new type of reactionary modernism, whatever their merits and problems, do not undermine the point made here, although I think that especially the former underestimates its importance. See Detlev J. K. Peukert, *The Weimar Republic: The Crisis of Classical Modernity*, trans. Richard Deveson (New York, 1992); Jeffrey Herf, *Reactionary Modernism: Technology, Culture, and Politics in Weimar and the Third Reich*, 2d ed. (Cambridge, England, 1984).

10. See further suggestive comments in Michael Hughes, *Nationalism and Society: Germany 1800–1945* (London, 1988); Woodruff D. Smith, *The Ideological Origins of Nazi Imperialism* (New York, 1986); and Steven E. Aschheim, *Culture and Catastrophe: German and Jewish Confrontations with National Socialism and Other Crises* (New York, 1996).

11. For conflicting views on this issue, see Ian Kershaw, *Popular Opinion and Political Dissent in the Third Reich: Bavaria, 1933–1945* (Oxford, England, 1983); David Bankier, *The Germans and the Final Solution: Public Opinion Under Nazism* (Oxford, England, 1992).

12. On the manner in which this was reflected in German attitudes toward foreign enemies, see Jürgen Förster, "The German Army and the Ideological War Against the Soviet Union," in Gerhard Hirschfeld, ed., *The Policies of Genocide: Jews and Soviet Prisoners of War in Nazi Germany* (London, 1986); Omer Bartov, *Hitler's Army: Soldiers, Nazis, and War in the Third Reich* (New York, 1991).

13. For an account of the origins of anti-Semitic thinking within German liberalism and its links to the politics of gender, see Dagmar Herzog, *Intimacy and Exclusion: Religious Politics in Pre-revolutionary Baden* (Princeton, N.J., 1996).

14. See esp. Reinhard Rürup, *Emanzipation und Antisemitismus* (Göttingen, West Germany, 1975); Jacob Katz, *From Prejudice to Destruction: Anti-Semitism, 1700–1933* (Cambridge, Mass., 1980); Peter Pulzer, *The Rise of Political Anti-Semitism in Germany and Austria*, 2d rev. ed. (Cambridge, Mass., 1988); Shulamit Volkov, *Jüdisches Leben und Antisemitismus im 19. und 20. Jahrhundert* (Munich, 1990). See also Norman Cohn, *Warrant for Genocide: The Myth of the Jewish World-Conspiracy and the Protocols of the Elders of Zion* (Harmondsworth, England, 1970); Binjamin W. Segel, *A Lie and a Libel: The History of the Protocols of the Elders of Zion*, trans. and ed. Richard S. Levy (Lincoln, Nebr., 1995).

15. See esp., Robert N. Proctor, *Racial Hygiene: Medicine Under the Nazis* (Cambridge, Mass., 1988); Paul P. Weindling, *Health, Race and German Politics Between National Unification and Nazism 1870–1945* (Cambridge, England, 1989); Michael Burleigh, *Death and Deliverance: "Euthanasia" in Germany 1900–1945* (Cambridge, England, 1994); Henry Friedlander, *The Origins of Nazi Genocide: From Euthanasia to the*

Final Solution (Chapel Hill, N.C., 1995). See, also, George L. Mosse, *The Image of Man: The Creation of Modern Masculinity* (New York, 1996).

16. See the important article by Peter Holquist, "'Information Is the Alpha and Omega of Our Work': Bolshevik Surveillance in Its Pan-European Context," *Journal of Modern History* 69 (September 1997), and the literature cited therein. See also Michael B. Miller, *Shanghai on the Métro: Spies, Intrigue, and the French Between the Wars* (Berkeley, Calif., 1994). Some of Alfred Hitchcock's 1930s films reflected (and at the time also enhanced) the period's obsession with espionage, intrigue, and conspiracy. See, for example, *The Man Who Knew Too Much* (1934), *The Secret Agent* (1936), *Sabotage* (1937; title in the United States: *The Woman Alone*), *The Lady Vanishes* (1939). For a discussion of French interwar apocalyptic films and novels, see also Philippe Burrin, *France Under the Germans: Collaboration and Compromise*, trans. Janet Lloyd (New York, 1996), 43–46; and for views about foreigners and about fear of war, see Eugen Weber, *The Hollow Years: France in the 1930s* (New York, 1994), 87–110, 237–56, respectively.

17. Another twist in this history is the play by Yehoshua Sobol, *Otto Weininger's Last Night* (Tel Aviv, 1982 [in Hebrew]), first performed in Israel on October 2 that year under the name *Nefesh yehudi* (The Soul of a Jew), which created a stir on the intellectual scene. Weininger, who committed suicide in Vienna in 1903 at the age of twenty-four, was the author of the book *Geschlecht und Charakter* (Vienna, 1903), translated as *Sex and Character* (New York, 1908, 1975), which presented Judaism as an extreme manifestation of the feminine principle, about to clash with Aryanism, the manifestation of the masculine principle. According to Weininger, Zionism embodied all that was good and noble in the Jewish soul, but it would be defeated from within by Judaism, which would return the Jews to their natural place: Destruction and the Diaspora. Rejected by Freud, obsessed by the "Jewish principle" within himself (which led him to convert to Protestantism in 1902), and devastated by the cool reception of his book (based on his Ph.D. dissertation in philosophy, and subsequently a sensational best-seller), he shot himself in the same room where Beethoven had died. On Jewish, and especially Zionist, preoccupation with degeneration around the turn of the century, see, for example, John M. Effron, *Defenders of the Race: Jewish Doctors and Race Science in Fin-de-Siècle Europe* (New Haven, Conn., 1994); Delphine Bechtel et al., eds., *Max Nordau, 1849–1923: Critique de la dégénérescence, médiateur franco-allemand, père fondateur du sionisme* (Paris, 1996); Sander Gilman, *Jewish Self-Hatred: Anti-Semitism and the Hidden Language of the Jews* (Baltimore, Md., 1986).

18. Apart from the literature cited in the notes above, see also Uriel Tal, *Christians and Jews in Germany: Religion, Politics, and Ideology in the Second Reich, 1870–1914*, trans. Noah Jonathan Jacobs (Ithaca, N.Y., 1975); George Mosse, *Germans and Jews: The Right, the Left, and the Search for a "Third Force" in Pre-Nazi Germany* (New York, 1970); Jacques Kornberg, *Theodor Herzl: From Assimilation to Zionism* (Bloomington, Ind., 1993); Paul Mendes-Flohr and Jehuda Reinharz, eds., *The Jew in the Modern World: A Documentary History*, 2d ed. (New York, 1995); Pierre Birnbaum and Ira Katznelson, eds., *Paths of Assimilation: Jews, States, and Citizenship* (Princeton, N.J., 1995); Bruce F. Pauley, *From Prejudice to Persecution: A History of Austrian Anti-Semitism* (Chapel Hill, N.C., 1992); Steven Beller, *Vienna and the Jews, 1867–1938: A Cultural History* (Cambridge, England, 1989).

19. For an excellent discussion of the importance of the myth of the Volksge-

meinschaft in prewar Nazi Germany, which revises the previous tendency to dismiss it altogether, see Gisela Diewald-Kerkmann, *Politische Denunziation im NS-Regime, oder Die kleine Macht der "Volksgenossen"* (Bonn, 1995), 33–50. The most extreme position on the role of anti-Semitism was recently taken by Daniel Jonah Goldhagen, *Hitler's Willing Executioners: Ordinary Germans and the Holocaust* (New York, 1996); my own criticism of it, arguing that anti-Semitism is insufficient in explaining the Holocaust, can be found in Omer Bartov, "Ordinary Monsters," *New Republic*, April 29, 1996, 32–38. Another argument for the importance of anti-Semitism in Germany and Austria is presented in John Weiss, *Ideology of Death: Why the Holocaust Happened in Germany* (Chicago, 1996). A more subtle interpretation, which highlights what the author calls "redemptive antisemitism," can be found in Saul Friedländer, *Nazi Germany and the Jews*, vol. 1, *The Years of Persecution* (New York, 1997). The previous position, which asserted the relative unpopularity of anti-Semitism within the German population, is well argued in Sarah Gordon, *Hitler, Germans, and the "Jewish Question"* (Princeton, N.J., 1984); it is criticized in turn by Robert Gellately, *The Gestapo and German Society: Enforcing Racial Policy, 1933–1945* (Oxford, England, 1990). The classic argument for the evolution of Nazi anti-Jewish policies with anti-Semitism largely left out is in Karl A. Schleunes, *The Twisted Road to Auschwitz: Nazi Policy Toward German Jews, 1933–1939*, 2d ed. (Urbana, Ill., 1990). The most important arguments for the resistance of the working class to Nazi ideology are to be found in Tim Mason, *Social Policy in the Third Reich: The Working Class and the "National Community,"* trans. John Broadwin, ed. Jane Caplan (Providence, R.I., 1993), originally published as *Arbeiterklasse und Volksgemeinschaft* (Opladen, West Germany, 1975).

20. Hitler's speech on January 30, 1939, cited in J. Noakes and G. Pridham, eds., *Nazism, 1919–1945: A Documentary Reader*, vol. 3, *Foreign Policy, War and Racial Extermination* (Exeter, England, 1988), 1049. On references to the Jews in his political testament, see Alan Bullock, *Hitler: A Study in Tyranny*, rev. ed. (New York, 1962), 794; Joachim C. Fest, *Hitler*, trans. Richard and Clara Winston, 2d ed. (New York, 1982), 746; Gerald Fleming, *Hitler and the Final Solution* (Berkeley, Calif., 1984), 186–89, and reproduction of the original document between pages 92–93. On his foreign policy "program," see Noakes and Pridham, *Nazism*, 609–23; Eberhard Jäckel, *Hitler's World View: A Blueprint for Power*, trans. Herbert Arnold (Cambridge, Mass., 1981). A recent interpretation gives this speech special prominence as Hitler's commitment to annihilate the Jews in case of a *world* war (*Weltkrieg*). Thus, it is argued, Hitler ordered the "Final Solution" only after the Soviet counteroffensive and the German declaration of war on the United States, both in December 1941, which transformed the war into a prolonged universal confrontation. Hitler's (still elusive) order therefore came just in time to change the original agenda of the postponed Wannsee Conference, ostensibly intended to discuss only the status of the *Mischlinge* ("half-breeds"). See Christian Gerlach, "The Wannsee Conference, the Fate of German Jews, and Hitler's Decision in Principle to Exterminate All European Jews," in Omer Bartov, ed., *The Holocaust: Origins, Implementation, Aftermath* (London, 2000).

21. Omer Bartov, *The Eastern Front, 1941–1945: German Troops and the Barbarisation of Warfare* (London, 1985); Bartov, *Hitler's Army*. See also Ian Kershaw, *The "Hitler Myth": Image and Reality in the Third Reich* (Oxford, England, 1987); Marlis Steinert, *Hitler's War and the Germans: Public Mood and Attitude During the Second World War*,

trans. Thomas E. J. de Witt (Athens, Ohio, 1977). Further on soldiers' attitudes, see Stephen G. Fritz, *Frontsoldaten: The German Soldier in World War II* (Lexington, Kentucky, 1995); Theo Schulte, *The German Army and Nazi Policies in Occupied Russia* (Oxford, England, 1989).

22. Quotation from order of the day issued by the commander of 6 Army, Field Marshal von Reichenau, on October 10, 1941, cited in Bartov, *Hitler's Army*, 129–30. See also speech by Himmler to SS soldiers on October 4, 1943, in Posen, where he speaks of "the extermination of the Jewish people" as an action that "appalled everyone, and yet everyone was certain that he would do it the next time if such orders should be issued and it should be necessary." See also Himmler's speech at a meeting of army generals in Sonthofen on May 5, 1944, where he said:

> You can understand how difficult it was for me to carry out this military (*soldatisch*) order which I was given and which I implemented out of a sense of obedience and absolute conviction. If you say: "We can understand as far as the men are concerned but not about the children," then I must remind you of what I said at the beginning. In this confrontation with Asia we must get used to condemning to oblivion those rules and customs of past wars which we have got used to and prefer. In my view, we as Germans, however deeply we may feel in our hearts, are not entitled to allow a generation of avengers filled with hatred to grow up with whom our children and grandchildren will have to deal because we, too weak and cowardly, left it to them.

Both citations in Noakes and Pridham, *Nazism*, 1199–1200. Further examples in Ernst Klee, Willi Dressen, and Volker Riess, eds., *"The Good Old Days": The Holocaust as Seen by Its Perpetrators and Bystanders*, trans. Deborah Burnstone (New York, 1988).

23. The extraordinary extent to which all representatives of the Reich in occupied areas were involved in the killing of Jews, and the intentional selection of known anti-Semites to positions of power in such territories, has now been thoroughly documented at least for one very important region. See Dieter Pohl, *Nationalsozialistische Judenverfolgung in Ostgalizien, 1941–1944: Organisation und Durchführung eines staatlichen Massenverbrechens* (Munich, 1996). Pohl also argues that it was impossible for Germans not directly involved in the killing, as well as for the population in the rear, to be unaware that mass murders were taking place, although precise details were not always known.

24. Gitta Sereny, *Into That Darkness: An Examination of Conscience* (New York, 1983), 201, 232–33, here, 201. To my mind, this is also the manner in which one should read the evidence presented in Christopher R. Browning, *Ordinary Men: Reserve Police Battalion 101 and the Final Solution in Poland* (New York, 1992).

25. Apart from the works by Burleigh, Friedlander, Proctor, and Weindling cited above, see also Robert J. Lifton, *The Nazi Doctors: Medical Killing and the Psychology of Genocide* (New York, 1986); Michael H. Kater, *Doctors Under Hitler* (Chapel Hill, N.C., 1989); Ernst Klee, *"Euthanasie" im NS Staat: Die "Vernichtung lebensunwerten Lebens"* (Frankfurt am Main, 1983), his *Dokumente zur "Euthanasie"* (Frankfurt am Main, 1985), and his *Was sie taten—was sie wurden. Ärzte, Juristen und andere Beteiligte am Kranken- oder Judenmord* (Frankfurt am Main, 1986).

26. For the best and most balanced assessment of the liberal states' attitudes to-

ward the Holocaust, see Tony Kushner, *The Holocaust and the Liberal Imagination: A Social and Cultural History* (Oxford, England, 1994). The earlier literature on this issue is cited and analyzed in the introduction to that book, esp. pages 1–18.

27. See examples in Steven E. Aschheim, "The German-Jewish Dialogue and Its Limits: The Case of Hermann Broch and Volkmar von Zuehlsdorff," and his "Hannah Arendt and Karl Jaspers: Friendship, Catastrophe and the Possibilities of German-Jewish Dialogue," both in Aschheim, *Culture and Catastrophe*, 85–114; Hannah Arendt, "The Aftermath of Nazi Rule," *Commentary* 10 (October 1950); Dan Diner, "Negative Symbiosis: Germans and Jews After Auschwitz," in Peter Baldwin, ed., *Reworking the Past: Hitler, the Holocaust, and the Historians' Debate* (Boston, 1990), 251–61.

28. For a recent attempt to associate the Holocaust with other war-related atrocities and instances of mass killing of civilian populations, see Eric Markusen and David Kopf, *The Holocaust and Strategic Bombing: Genocide and Total War in the 20th Century* (Boulder, Colo., 1995).

29. For the long prewar history of Auschwitz, once part of the medieval German eastern expansion, its impact on Nazi plans in the area, and subsequent postwar attempts to dissociate it from German history, see Debórah Dwork and Robert Jan van Pelt, *Auschwitz: 1270 to the Present* (New York, 1996).

30. See, especially, Gordon J. Horwitz, *In the Shadow of Death: Living Outside the Gates of Mauthausen* (New York, 1990).

31. As, for example, in Alain Resnais's 1955 film *Night and Fog*, which neither distinguishes between the concentration camps and the killing facilities, nor makes any mention of the fact that the vast majority of the victims in the death camps were Jews.

32. An excellent summary and analysis of Holocaust historiography can be found in Dieter Pohl, "Die Holocaust Forschung und Goldhagens Thesen," *Vierteljahrshefte für Zeitgeschichte* Heft 1 (1997).

33. For a recent important analysis, see Robert G. Moeller, *War Stories: The Search for a Usable Past in the Federal Republic of Germany* (Berkeley, Calif., 2001). More specifically for the 1950s, see Robert G. Moeller, ed., *West Germany Under Construction: Politics, Society, and Culture in the Adenauer Era* (Ann Arbor, Mich., 1997); Klaus Naumann, ed., *Nachkrieg in Deutschland* (Hamburg, 2001); and Robert Frei, *Adenauer's Germany and the Nazi Past: The Politics of Amnesty and Integration*, trans. Joel Golb (New York, 2002). For recent examples, see Klaus Naumann, "Die Mutter, das Pferd und die Juden: Flucht und Vertreibung als Themen deutscher Erinnerungspolitik," *Mittleweg 36*, no. 4 (August/September 1996); and his "Dresdner Pietà: Eine Fallstudie zum 'Gedenkjahr 1995,'" *Mittelweg 36*, no. 4 (August/September 1995). For an argument on the centrality of the politics of collective memory for German postwar politics, see Andrei S. Markovits and Simon Reich, *The German Predicament: Memory and Power in the New Europe* (Ithaca, N.Y., 1997).

34. For an incisive analysis of the role of the Holocaust in German sexual politics, see Dagmar Herzog, "'Pleasure, Sex, and Politics Belong Together': Post-Holocaust Memory and the Sexual Revolution in West Germany," *Critical Inquiry* 24 (Winter 1988).

35. This is evident, for instance, in the last part of Edgar Reitz's 1984 film saga *Heimat*, which presents the final loss of the homeland as occurring after Nazism, with the infiltration of American norms and values. The same could be said about

Rainer Werner Fassbinder's film *The Marriage of Maria Braun* (1979). On another German filmmaker's view of history, see Omer Bartov, "War, Memory, and Repression: Alexander Kluge and the Politics of Representation in Postwar Germany," in Omer Bartov, *Murder in Our Midst: The Holocaust, Industrial Killing, and Representation* (New York, 1996), 139–52. See also Dan Diner, *America in the Eyes of the Germans: An Essay on Anti-Americanism*, trans. Allison Brown (Princeton, N.J., 1996).

36. These themes were of course reflected in the German historians' controversy, or the *Historikerstreit*. See, for example, *Forever in the Shadow of Hitler? Original Documents of the Historikerstreit, the Controversy Concerning the Singularity of the Holocaust* (Atlantic Highlands, N.J., 1993); Charles S. Maier, *The Unmasterable Past: History, Holocaust, and German Nationalism* (Cambridge, Mass., 1988); Richard Evans, *In Hitler's Shadow: West German Historians and the Attempt to Escape from the Nazi Past* (New York, 1989). More recently, this issue has been revived in the controversy surrounding Goldhagen, *Hitler's Willing Executioners*. See, for instance, Julius H. Schoeps, ed., *Ein Volk von Mördern? Die Dokumentation zur Goldhagen-Kontroverse um die Rolle der Deutschen in Holocaust* (Hamburg, 1996). A balanced review of the historiography is Ian Kershaw, *The Nazi Dictatorship: Problems and Perspectives of Interpretation*, 3d ed. (London, 1993).

37. Examples can be found, for instance, in the early works of Siegfried Lenz, Heinrich Böll, and Günter Grass. For a more detailed analysis, see Omer Bartov, "' . . . seit die Juden weg sind': Germany, History, and Representations of Absence," in Scott Denham, Irene Kacandes, and Jonathan Petropoulos, eds., *A User's Guide to German Cultural Studies* (Ann Arbor, Mich., 1987); and Omer Bartov, "Trauma und Leere seit 1914: Teil 2," *Mittelweg 36*, no. 4 (August/September 1996).

38. Frank Stern, *The Whitewashing of the Yellow Badge: Antisemitism and Philosemitism in Postwar Germany*, trans. William Templer (Oxford, England, 1992). On Jewish life in postwar Germany, see Michael Brenner, *After the Holocaust: Rebuilding Jewish Lives in Postwar Germany* (Princeton, N.J., 1997); John Borneman and Jeffrey M. Peck, *Sojourners: The Return of German Jews and the Question of Identity* (Lincoln, Nebr., 1995).

39. The category of *Mischlinge* was the focus of a debate during the Wannsee Conference, where Reinhard Heydrich coordinated the participation of state and party agencies in the "Final Solution" and asserted his overall responsibility for this undertaking. Several other meetings took place in order to decide the question of whether murdering Germans of mixed "Aryan" and Jewish ancestry would ensure the total elimination of the Jewish peril or rather destroy the good "Aryan" blood that might otherwise be saved in such Mischlinge. See Kurt Pätzold and Erika Schwarz, *Tagesordnung: Judenmord. Die Wannsee-Konferenz am 20. Januar 1942. Eine Dokumentation zur Organisation der "Endlösung,"* 3d ed. (Berlin, 1992); Mark Roseman, *The Wansee Conference and the Final Solution: A Reconsideration* (New York, 2002).

40. The cover page of the widely read weekly magazine *Der Spiegel* greeted the screening of Steven Spielberg's film *Schindler's List* with a cover photograph of Liam Neeson, the actor who played Oskar Schindler in the film (rather than the man himself), accompanied by the possibly ironic caption "The good German" (*Der gute Deutsche*). See further, including a reproduction of the magazine's cover, Liliane Weissberg, "The Tale of a Good German: Reflections on the German Reception of *Schindler's List*," in Yosefa Loshitzky, ed., *Spielberg's Holocaust: Critical Perspectives on*

Schindler's List (Bloomington, Ind., 1997). There are several other interesting articles in this collection.

41. It has been argued that the enthusiastic reception by third-generation Germans of Goldhagen, *Hitler's Willing Executioners*, which argued that in the Third Reich Nazis and Germans were synonymous, was related to this sense of the past being "another country" or, rather, the grandparents' Fatherland. See, for example, Evelyn Roll, "Goldhagens Diskussionsreise: Der schwierige Streit um die Deutschen und den Holocaust: Eine These und drei gebrochene Tabus," *Süddeutsche Zeitung*, September 9, 1996; Volker Ullrich, "Daniel J. Goldhagen in Deutschland: Die Buchtournee wurde zum Triumphzug," *Die Zeit* 38, September 13, 1996; Josef Joffe, "Goldhagen in Germany," *New York Review*, November 28, 1996. Conversely, recent outbreaks of neo-Nazism in Germany, especially after reunification, also very much among the young and far more prevalent in the former German Democratic Republic, are attributed both to economic hardship and widespread unemployment and to the Communist rejection of any responsibility for Nazism and hence the lack of anti-Nazi education. See, for instance, Alan Cowell, "Neo-Nazis Carving Out Fiefs in Eastern Germany," *New York Times*, February 8, 1998. More generally, see Hermann Kurthen, Werner Bergmann, and Rainer Erb, eds., *Antisemitism and Xenophobia in Germany After Unification* (New York, 1997).

42. Apart from the literature cited above, see also the excellent analysis in Elisabeth Domansky, "'Kristallnacht,' the Holocaust and German Unity: The Meaning of November 9 as an Anniversary in Germany," *History and Memory* 4 (Spring/Summer 1992).

43. Early histories of the resistance by non-German scholars were critical of the army's involvement in politics and collaboration with Hitler's regime. See Wheeler-Bennett, *Nemesis of Power: The Germany Army in Politics, 1918–1945* (London, 1945); F. L. Carsten, *The Reichswehr and Politics 1918–33*, 2d ed. (Berkeley, Calif., 1973); and Gordon A. Craig, *The Politics of the Prussian Army, 1640–1945*, 3d ed. (London, 1978). Less negative views of the generals are to be found in Harold C. Deutsch, *The Conspiracy Against Hitler in the Twilight War* (Minneapolis, 1968), and his *Hitler and His Generals* (Minneapolis, 1974). Early German scholarship tended to glorify the resisters. See, for instance, Gerhard Ritter, *Carl Goerdeler und die deutsche Widerstands-Bewegung* (Stuttgart, West Germany, 1954); Joachim Kramarz, *Stauffenberg: The Architect of the Famous July 20th Conspiracy to Assassinate Hitler*, trans. R. H. Barry (New York, 1967); Hermann Graml et al., *The German Resistance to Hitler*, trans. Peter and Betty Ross (London, 1970). However, see also the far more critical position taken in Klaus-Jürgen Müller, *The Army, Politics and Society in Germany, 1933–45* (New York, 1987).

44. For more recent works on the resistance, see Peter Hoffmann, *German Resistance to Hitler* (Cambridge, Mass., 1988), which is relatively apologetic; Joachim Fest, *Plotting Hitler's Death: The Story of the German Resistance*, trans. Bruce Little (New York, 1996), which is somewhat less so; and Theodore S. Hamerow, *On the Road to the Wolf's Lair: German Resistance to Hitler* (Cambridge, Mass., 1997), which is most critical. See also Peter Hoffmann, *Stauffenberg: A Family History, 1905–1944* (Cambridge, England, 1995). For a useful survey of the literature, see Martyn Housden, *Resistance and Conformity in the Third Reich* (London, 1997). On the treatment of soldiers tried by the Wehrmacht in postwar Germany, see Wolfram Wette, ed., *Deserteure der Wehrmacht: Fei-*

glinge—Opfer—Hoffnungsträger? Dokumentation eines Meinungswandels (Essen, Germany, 1995); Norbert Haase and Gerhard Paul, eds., *Die anderen Soldaten: Wehrkraftzersetzung, Gehorsamsverweigerung und Fahnenflucht im Zweiten Weltkrieg* (Frankfurt am Main, 1995). See also contributions to "Gehorsam bis zum Mord? Der verschwiegene Krieg der deutschen Wehrmacht—Fakten, Analysen, Debatte," in *Zeit-Punkte*, special issue of *Die Zeit* (n.d.); and Hannes Heer and Klaus Naumann, eds., *War of Extermination: The German Military in World War II, 1941–1944*, multiple translators (New York, 2000).

45. An excellent analysis of this problem is Mary Nolan, "The *Historikerstreit* and Social History," in Baldwin, *Reworking the Past*. For a more general discussion of *Alltagsgeschichte*, see Alf Lüdtke, ed., *The History of Everyday Life: Reconstructing Historical Experience and Ways of Life*, trans. William Templer (Princeton, N.J., 1995).

46. The best recently published example of this attitude is, of course, Victor Klemperer, *I Will Bear Witness: A Diary of the Nazi Years*, trans. Martin Chalmers, 2 vols. (New York, 1998–99). Fischer Verlag has been publishing a series of studies on Jews in Germany under the title *Jüdische Lebensbilder*, which is now being issued in an English translation by Northwestern University Press. See also Avraham Barkai, *From Boycott to Annihilation: The Economic Struggle of German Jews, 1933–1943*, trans. William Templer (Hanover, N.H., 1989). There are, of course, important studies of German Jewry in English. In addition to works cited above, see, for example, Ruth Gay, *The Jews of Germany* (New Haven, Conn., 1992); Marion A. Kaplan, *The Making of the Jewish Middle Class: Women, Family, and Identity in Imperial Germany* (New York, 1991); Jack Wertheimer, *Unwelcome Strangers: East European Jews in Imperial Germany* (New York, 1987); Paula E. Hyman, *Gender and Assimilation in Modern Jewish History: The Roles and Representation of Women* (Seattle, Wash., 1995).

47. See more on this in the last section of Omer Bartov, "German Soldiers and the Holocaust: Historiography, Research and Implications," in Bartov, *Holocaust*. Conversely, for a recent example of confusing the political with the "racial" victims of the regime, see the otherwise excellent study, Wolfgang Sofsky, *The Order of Terror: The Concentration Camp*, trans. William Templer (Princeton, N.J., 1997).

48. Arendt, "Aftermath."

49. Pierre Vidal-Naquet, *Assassins of Memory: Essays on the Denial of the Holocaust*, trans. Jeffrey Mehlman (New York, 1992); Deborah Lipstadt, *Denying the Holocaust: The Growing Assault on Truth and Memory* (New York, 1993); Hayden White, "Historical Emplotment and the Problem of Truth," in Saul Friedländer, ed., *Probing the Limits of Representation: Nazism and the "Final Solution"* (Cambridge, Mass., 1992); Omer Bartov, "Intellectuals on Auschwitz: Memory, History, and Truth," in Bartov, *Murder in Our Midst*. See, most recently, Richard J. Evans, *Lying About Hitler: History, Holocaust, and the David Irving Trial* (New York, 2001); and Lawrence Douglas, *The Memory of Judgment: Making Law and History in the Trials of the Holocaust* (New Haven, Conn., 2001), 185–256.

50. Claude Lanzmann, *Shoah: An Oral History of the Holocaust: The Complete Text of the Film* (New York, 1985), 138, interview with Walter Stier, ex-member of the Nazi Party, former head of the Reich Railways Department 33.

51. In the present context I cannot go into the question of comprehending the Holocaust even while it was happening, whether by the victims, the bystanders, the Allies, or potential victims in countries not yet occupied by the Germans. There is a growing literature, for instance, on reactions by the Jewish community in Palestine

to news about the Holocaust, as well as to the reactions of the Allies. See, for example, Dina Porat, *The Blue and the Yellow Stars of David: The Zionist Leadership in Palestine and the Holocaust, 1939–1945*, trans. David Ben-Nahum (Cambridge, Mass., 1990); William D. Rubinstein, *The Myth of Rescue: Why the Democracies Could Not Have Saved More Jews from the Nazis* (London, 1997). This last book dismisses the argument that the Allies could have done more, but although it presents some interesting evidence, I find its final argument unconvincing.

52. Jean-François Lyotard, *The Differend: Phrases in Dispute*, trans. Georges Van Den Abbeele (Minneapolis, 1988), 56, has a different position: "Suppose that an earthquake destroys not only lives, buildings, and objects but also the instruments used to measure earthquakes directly and indirectly. The impossibility of quantitatively measuring it does not prohibit, but rather inspires in the minds of the survivors the idea of a very great seismic force. The scholar claims to know nothing about it, but the common person has a complex feeling, the one aroused by the negative presentation of the indeterminate." See also Maurice Blanchot, *The Writing of the Disaster*, trans. Ann Smock (Lincoln, Nebr., 1986). For an insightful discussion on the difficulties of representing Auschwitz in academic and intellectual writings, see Sidra DeKoven Ezrahi, "Representing Auschwitz," *History and Memory* 7 (Fall/Winter 1996).

53. Recent works on the links between genocide and modernity have both the potential of distancing us from the horror (by sanitizing it) and of making us all complicit in it (because we belong to an age that perpetrates horror). See, for example, Detlev J. K. Peukert, *Inside Nazi Germany: Conformity, Opposition, and Racism in Everyday Life*, trans. Richard Deveson (New Haven, Conn., 1982); his *Weimar Republic*; and his "The Genesis of the 'Final Solution' from the Spirit of Science," in Thomas Childers and Jane Caplan, eds., *Reevaluating the Third Reich* (New York, 1993). See also Zygmunt Bauman, *Modernity and the Holocaust*, 2d ed. (Ithaca, N.Y., 1991).

54. By this I do not mean to accept the specious distinction between the so-called mythical memory of the Holocaust among the Jews and the scholarly (*wissenschaftliche*) analysis of the event by a less-involved, younger generation of German historians. Such an argument was made by Martin Broszat in his correspondence with Saul Friedländer, now included in Baldwin, *Reworking the Past*, 106. See also Kershaw, *Nazi Dictatorship*, 80–81.

55. See, most recently, Yisrael Gutman, ed., *Major Changes Within the Jewish People in the Wake of the Holocaust* (Jerusalem, 1995 [in Hebrew]); Y. Kashti et al., eds., *A Quest for Identity: Post War Jewish Biographies* (Tel Aviv, 1996); Rafael Moses, ed., *Persistent Shadows of the Holocaust: The Meaning to Those Not Directly Affected* (Madison, Wis., 1993).

56. For some recent literature on the United States, see Henry L. Feingold, *Bearing Witness: How America and Its Jews Responded to the Holocaust* (Syracuse, N.Y., 1995); Gulie Ne'eman Arad, *America, Its Jews, and the Rise of Nazism* (Bloomington, Ind., 2000); Peter Novick, *The Holocaust in American Life* (Boston, 1999). On the Yishuv and Israel, see Tom Segev, *The Seventh Million: The Israelis and the Holocaust*, trans. Haim Watzman (New York, 1993); Porat, *Blue and Yellow Stars*; Dalia Ofer, *Escaping the Holocaust: Illegal Immigration to the Land of Israel, 1939–1944* (New York, 1990); Yehuda Bauer, *Jews for Sale? Nazi-Jewish Negotiations, 1933–1945* (New Haven, Conn., 1994).

57. See, for example, Jeffrey Shandler, *While America Watches: Televising the Holocaust in the United States, 1945–1995* (New York, 1999).

58. In greater detail, see Omer Bartov, *Mirrors of Destruction: War, Genocide, and Modern Identity* (New York, 2000), 206–30 and references cited therein.

59. Hannah Arendt, *Eichmann in Jerusalem: A Report on the Banality of Evil*, rev. ed. (New York, 1977). A typical attack on her book can be found in the introduction to Shmuel Ettinger, *Modern Anti-Semitism: Studies and Essays* (Tel-Aviv, 1978 [in Hebrew]), x–xi. See also Segev, *Seventh Million*, 357–60, 465. This is discussed further in *History and Memory* 8 (Fall/Winter 1996), special issue *Hannah Arendt and Eichmann in Jerusalem*; and Steven E. Aschheim, "Nazism, Culture and the *Origins of Totalitarianism*: Hannah Arendt and the Discourse of Evil," *New German Critique* 70 (Winter 1997).

In this context mention should be made also of the offspring of victims. Whereas the children of war veterans could say proudly that their father had been a soldier, those of Holocaust survivors tended to hide the fact that their parents were victims; there was nothing heroic or satisfying about that status, quite apart from the fact of growing up in a traumatized family environment. On the case of Britain, see, for example, Jeremy Adler, "The One Who Got Away: H. G. Adler and Theodor Adorno: Two Approaches to Culture After Auschwitz," *Times Literary Supplement* 4879 (October 4, 1996): 18–19. He writes: "In my childhood, there were no secrets at home about this period simply called 'the wicked age' ('*die böse Zeit*') or 'the camp years' ('*die Lagerjahre*') . . . ; yet outside the home a taboo occluded discussion of what, later, was debated as avidly as it had been repressed in terms of 'Auschwitz,' 'the *Holocaust*' and 'the *Shoah*.' My friends could boast of how dad had fought with Monty in the desert. My own father's experiences were unmentionable. They had no place, until recently. The public cycle from repression to obsession in Britain took about fifty years." See also Helen Epstein, *Children of the Holocaust: Conversations with Sons and Daughters of Survivors* (New York, 1979). On children of the perpetrators, see Dan Bar-On, *Legacy of Silence: Encounters with Children of the Third Reich* (Cambridge, Mass., 1989). On children in the Holocaust, see Nechama Tec, *Dry Tears: The Story of a Lost Childhood* (New York, 1984); Debórah Dwork, *Children with a Star: Jewish Youth in Nazi Europe* (New Haven, Conn., 1991); Laurel Holliday, *Children in the Holocaust and World War II: Their Secret Diaries* (New York, 1995); Jane Marks, *The Hidden Children: The Secret Survivors of the Holocaust* (New York, 1993).

60. Raul Hilberg, *The Destruction of the European Jews*, 3 vols., rev. ed. (New York, 1985), originally published in 1961. Also see his *The Politics of Memory: The Journey of a Holocaust Historian* (Chicago, 1996), 110–11, where he cites the letter of rejection from Yad Vashem, dated August 24, 1958, which argued that because his "book rests almost entirely on the authority of German sources," and because of "reservations concerning" his "appraisal of the Jewish resistance (active and passive) during the Nazi occupation," Yad Vashem "cannot appear as one of the publishers."

61. Ettinger, *Modern Anti-Semitism*, x–xi, writes that Arendt

> charged the Jews, their conduct, their leadership, and their actions, with much of the responsibility for the crime of anti-Semitism and even with the extermination of the Jews. . . . At the basis of such arguments are concepts prevalent in German society (and to a large extent even the effects of anti-Semitic and even Nazi views). In the past, Jews who have sought the roots of anti-Semitism occasionally came to accept the approaches and modes of thinking of their environ-

> ment . . . and internalized the image of the Jew as seen by their environment. One might have expected that following the Holocaust this approach would change, but this did not happen to Hannah Arendt, and her attachment to the negative Jewish stereotype distinguishes her from other scholars.

See also Shmuel Almog, ed., *Antisemitism Through the Ages: A Collection of Essays* (Jerusalem, 1980 [in Hebrew]), especially the essays by Almog, Ettinger, Gutman, and Bauer. These writers referred also with a great deal of criticism to Arendt's earlier massive study, *Origins of Totalitarianism.*

62. On the Kasztner Affair in Israel, that preceded the Eichmann trial, see Segev, *Seventh Million*, 255–320. Apart from the literature cited above on the reception of survivors in Israel, see Hanna Yablonka, *Survivors of the Holocaust: Israel After the War*, trans. Ora Cummings (New York, 1999). For a recent controversial study, which claims that the political leadership in Palestine pursued policies of illegal immigration not out of sympathy for the survivors in European "displaced persons" camps but merely to increase the population of the future state, see Idith Zertal, *From Catastrophe to Power: Holocaust Survivors and the Emergence of Israel* (Berkeley, Calif. 1998). This book has elicited a public debate in Israel. Among the most interesting reactions is an essay by the poet, writer, and veteran of the 1948 war, Haim Gouri, "On Books and What Is Between Them," *Alpayim* 14 (1997 [in Hebrew]). Gouri makes reference to another relevant collection of essays by the writer, journalist, and veteran of World War II and the 1948 War, Hanoch Bartov, *I Am Not the Mythological Sabra* (Tel Aviv, 1995 [in Hebrew]). Bartov is also the author of the novel *The Brigade*, trans. David S. Segal (New York, 1968), which describes the encounter of young Jews from Palestine, serving in the Jewish Brigade of the British Army, with the remnants of European Jewry at the end of the Holocaust. For striking examples of the contradictory reactions by immigration agents sent from Palestine upon their first encounter with survivors, see Irit Keynan, "Between Hope and Anxiety: The Image of the Survivors Among the Emissaries from Palestine to the DP Camps in Germany, 1945," in Anita Shapira, ed., *Haapala: Studies in the History of Illegal Immigration into Palestine 1934–1948* (Tel Aviv, 1990 [in Hebrew]), 222. One agent wrote: "I believe that those who survived lived because they were selfish, and cared first and foremost for themselves." Another: "They became used to seeing death, they trampled on the living and on the dead and the will to help others was almost extinguished in them." Yet a third agent claimed that "among the survivors there are people, whose souls were cleansed even by the crematorium, and who speak with such Zionist fervor, that I cannot imagine any circumstance, or any individual who could surpass them." See also Irit Keynan, *Holocaust Survivors and the Emissaries from Eretz-Israel: Germany, 1945–1948* (Tel Aviv, 1996 [in Hebrew]).

63. On the so-called Yeckes, or German Jews in Palestine, see Segev, *Seventh Million*, 15–64; and Gideon Greif, Colin McPherson, and Laurence Weinbaum, eds., *Die Jeckes: Deutsche Juden aus Israel erzählen* (Cologne, Germany, 2000).

64. See, for example, Anita Shapira, *Land and Power: The Zionist Resort to Force, 1881–1948*, trans. William Templer (New York, 1992); Yael Zerubavel, *Recovered Roots: Collective Memory and the Making of Israeli National Tradition* (Chicago, 1995); Yosef Gorny, *The Quest for Collective Identity: The Place of Israel in Jewish Public Thinking,*

1945–1987 (Tel Aviv, 1990 [in Hebrew]); Nurith Gertz, *Myths in Israeli Culture: Captive of a Dream* (London, 2000).

65. See Zeev Sternhell, *The Founding Myths of Israel: Nationalism, Socialism, and the Making of the Jewish State*, trans. David Maisel (Princeton, N.J., 1998); Anita Shapira, *New Jews Old Jews* (Tel Aviv, 1997 [in Hebrew]); and her *Visions in Conflict* (Tel Aviv, 1997 [in Hebrew]); Emmanuel Sivan, *The 1948 Generation: Myth, Profile and Memory* (Tel Aviv, 1991 [in Hebrew]); Mark Tessler, *A History of the Israeli-Palestinian Conflict* (Bloomington, Ind., 1994); Baruch Kimmerling and Joel S. Migdal, *Palestinians: The Making of a People* (Cambridge, Mass., 1994); Meir Litvak, "A Palestinian Past: National Construction and Reconstruction," *History and Memory* 6 (Fall/Winter 1994). On the "new historians" and the so-called *Historikerstreit* (historian's controversy) in Israel, see Jonathan Mahler, "Uprooting the Past: Israel's New Historians Take a Hard Look at Their Nation's Origins," *Lingua Franca* 7 (August 1997); Gulie Ne'eman Arad, ed., *Israeli Historiography Revisited*, special issue of *History and Memory* 7 (Spring/Summer 1995); Amos Elon, "Israel and the End of Zionism," *New York Review*, December 19, 1996. For a savage attack on the critics of traditional Zionist historiography, see Efraim Karsh, *Fabricating Israeli History: The "New Historians"* (London, 1997). For an illuminating comparison between the German and Israeli historical controversies, see José Brunner, "Pride and Memory: Nationalism, Narcissism and the Historians' Debates in Germany and Israel," *History and Memory* 9 (Fall 1997).

66. In this context, see also Dan Diner, "Historical Experience and Cognition: Perspectives on National Socialism," *History and Memory* 2 (1990).

67. This is by no means to say that I accept such relativizing arguments as those recently propounded in Alain Brossat, *L'épreuve du désastre: Le XXe siècle et les camps* (Paris, 1996), 20, 23. Brossat writes that "the prevailing contemporary propensity to perceive extremity and catastrophe as strictly a matter of the past [résolument *passéifiés*]" has resulted in preventing those who "only stress the singularity" of the Shoah from recognizing that "the Palestinian camps are inexorably linked to the Jewish disaster" and that "so long as the plunder and oppression of the Palestinians appears as compensation for the crime of Auschwitz; so long as the 'uniqueness' of the Nazi crimes serves *also* as the alibi for the avoidance, indeed the uninhibited negation of the Soviet extermination or the colonial atrocities—the life without end of catastrophe will continue to pierce the flesh of the democratic order as it expands throughout the world." For my rejection of this position and a contextualization of such arguments currently being aired in France, see Bartov, *Mirrors of Destruction*, 45–89.

68. I am referring here of course to Primo Levi, *The Drowned and the Saved*, trans. Raymond Rosenthal (New York, 1988), published posthumously following Levi's death, possibly by suicide. These essays are not only about coming to terms with the memory of the Holocaust but also with life after the event. See also Ferdinando Camon, *Conversations with Primo Levi*, trans. John Shepley (Marlboro, Vt., 1989). The same problem is confronted in a very different manner by Jean Améry, *At the Mind's Limits: Contemplations by a Survivor on Auschwitz and Its Realities*, 2d ed., trans. Sidney Rosenfeld and Stella P. Rosenfeld (New York, 1986) and in much of the poetry of Paul Celan. Both Améry and Celan committed suicide. On the latter, see John Felstiner, *Paul Celan: Poet, Survivor, Jew* (New Haven, Conn., 1995); Israel Chalfen, *Paul Celan: A Biography of His Youth*, trans. Maximilian Bleyleben (New York, 1991). The question of life after death in the camps is addressed in a very different

manner by the Israeli writer Ka-Tzetnik, *Shivitti: A Vision*, trans. Eliyah Nike De-Nur and Lisa Herman (San Francisco, 1989), who came from a religious background and underwent psychiatric treatment many years after Auschwitz. See more on this issue in Bartov, "Intellectuals on Auschwitz"; and Bartov, *Mirrors of Destruction*, 206–30.

69. Ian Buruma, *The Wages of Guilt: Memories of War in Germany and Japan* (New York, 1995); Carol Gluck, "The Rape of Nanking: How 'The Nazi Buddha' Resisted the Japanese," *Times Literary Supplement* (June 27, 1997); Iris Chang, *The Rape of Nanking: The Forgotten Holocaust of World War II* (New York, 1997). In this context see also the discussions of Alain Resnais's film in Nancy Wood, "Memory by Analogy: *Hiroshima, mon amour*," in H. R. Kedward and Nancy Wood, eds., *The Liberation of France: Image and Event* (Oxford, England, 1995); Cathy Caruth, *Unclaimed Experience: Trauma, Narrative, and History* (Baltimore, Md., 1996), 25–56; Michael Roth, "*Hiroshima Mon Amour*: You Must Remember This," in Robert A. Rosenstone, ed., *Revisioning History: Film and the Construction of a New Past* (Princeton, N.J., 1995), 91–101. For an interesting attempt to find links between Chinese and Jewish history and memory, see Vera Schwarcz, *Bridge Across Time: Chinese and Jewish Cultural Memory* (New Haven, Conn., 1998).

70. Vahakn N. Dadrian, *The History of the Armenian Genocide: Ethnic Conflict from the Balkans to Anatolia to the Caucasus* (Providence, R.I., 1995), and his *German Responsibility in the Armenian Genocide: A Review of the Historical Evidence of German Complicity* (Watertown, Mass., 1996); Richard G. Hovannisian, ed., *The Armenian Genocide in Perspective* (New Brunswick, N.J., 1986); Roger W. Smith, Eric Markusen, and Robert Jay Lifton, "Professional Ethics and the Denial of the Armenian Genocide," *Holocaust and Genocide Studies* 9 (Spring 1995); Yair Auron, *The Banality of Indifference: Zionism and the Armenian Genocide* (New Brunswick, N.J., 2000), his "Again Musa Dagh? And Again the World Is Silent?" *Ha'aretz*, April 18, 1997 (in Hebrew), and his "The Writing Is (Still) on the Wall," *Ha'aretz*, February 25, 1997 (in Hebrew). In this context one might also note that while during the *Historikerstreit* "revisionist" historians used the Armenian genocide as an event that negated the "uniqueness" of the Holocaust, until very recently millions of second- and third-generation Turks in Germany were being denied German citizenship.

71. Ben Kiernan, ed., *The Pol Pot Regime: Race, Power, and Genocide in Cambodia Under the Khmer Rouge, 1975–49* (New Haven, Conn., 1996); Eyal Press, "Unforgiven: The Director of the Cambodian Genocide Program Rekindles Cold War Animosities," *Lingua Franca* (April/May 1997).

72. Seth Mydans, "Confined, Pol Pot Tells Of Feeling 'Bit Bored,'" *New York Times*, October 24, 1997.

73. Leo Kuper, *Genocide: Its Political Use in the Twentieth Century* (New Haven, Conn., 1982); Gérard Prunier, *The Rwanda Crisis: History of a Genocide* (New York, 1997); Raymond Verdier, Emmanuel Decaux, and Jean-Pierre Chrétien eds., *Rwanda: Un génocide du xxe siècle* (Paris, 1995); Dominique Franche, *Rwanda: Généalogie d'un génocide* (Paris, 1997); Timothy P. Longman, "Christian Churches and the Genocide in Rwanda" and Charles de Lespinay, "The Churches and the Genocide in the East African Great Lakes Region," both in Omer Bartov and Phyllis Mack, eds., *In God's Name: Genocide and Religion in the Twentieth Century* (New York, 2001); Philip Gourevitch, *We Wish to Inform You That Tomorrow We Will Be Killed with Our Families: Stories from Rwanda* (New York, 1999).

74. Citations from Mark Danner, "Bosnia: The Turning Point," *New York Review*, February 5, 1998. Other articles in this remarkable series by Danner include "Bosnia: The Great Betrayal," *New York Review*, March 26, 1968; "Bosnia: Breaking the Machine," *New York Review*, February 19, 1998; "America and the Bosnia Genocide," *New York Review*, December 4, 1997. Danner reviews a large number of books concerned with events in the former Yugoslavia. See also Michael A. Sells, "Serbian Religious Mythology and the Genocide in Bosnia," in Bartov and Mack, *In God's Name*, and his *The Bridge Betrayed: Religion and Genocide in Bosnia* (Berkeley, Calif., 1996); Sarah A. Kent, "Writing the Yugoslav Wars: English-Language Books on Bosnia (1992–1996) and the Challenges of Analyzing Contemporary History," *American Historical Review* 102 (October 1997). Emir Kusturica's extraordinary recent film *Underground* (1995) provides some insight into the tangled web of Serbian history, myth, and violence.

75. See Peter Holquist's chapter in this volume. For recent attempts to grapple with this century's genocides and tyrannies, see, for instance, Daniel Chirot, *Modern Tyrants: The Power and Prevalence of Evil in Our Age* (New York, 1994); Yves Ternon, *L'état criminel: Les génocides au XXe siècle* (Paris, 1995). A recent study that fails to distinguish between the Soviet Gulags and the Nazi camps, despite its otherwise admirable moral commitment, is Tzvetan Todorov, *Facing the Extreme: Moral Life in the Concentration Camps*, trans. Arthur Denner and Abigail Pollack (New York, 1996).

76. See Holquist's chapter in this volume, also citing Tony Judt, "The Longest Road to Hell," *New York Times*, December 22, 1997. See further in Bartov, *Murder in Our Midst*, 72, 86–88, 142–44, 193–94, n. 6, and the sources cited therein. Harry Wu, *Troublemaker: One Man's Crusade Against China's Cruelty* (London, 1997), makes analogies to the Holocaust in speaking about Chinese camps, without, however, troubling to make such important distinctions as can be found in Holquist. Bizarre links between Chinese oppression and Nazism are also present in the recent Hollywood production *Seven Years in Tibet* (1997).

77. See Amir Weiner's chapter in this volume. See also his *Making Sense of War: The Second World War and the Fate of the Bolshevik Revolution* (Princeton, N.J., 2000), 129–235. See also Norman Naimark, *Fires of Hatred: Ethnic Cleansing in Twentieth-Century Europe* (Cambridge, Mass., 2001), 57–84.

78. On trauma and memory, see Cathy Caruth, ed., *Trauma: Explorations in Memory* (Baltimore, Md., 1995). See also many of the contributions to Gulie Ne'eman Arad, ed., *Passing into History: Nazism and the Holocaust Beyond Memory*, special issue of *History and Memory* 9 (Fall 1997).

79. For the use and abuse of the traumatic memory of bystander groups that fell victim to policies of collective punishment, see, for example, Madelon de Keiser, "The Skeleton in the Closet: The Memory of Putten, 1/2 October 1944," *History and Memory* 7 (Fall/Winter 1996); Sarah Farmer, *Oradour: Arrêt sur mémoire* (Paris, 1994). On the reworking of the memory of the Holocaust in France, see Annette Wieviorka, *Déportation et génocide: Entre la mémoire et l'oublie* (Paris, 1992).

CHAPTER 7, *Weiner*

1. On the impact of the war on Soviet purification campaigns, see Amir Weiner, *Making Sense of War: The Second World War and the Fate of the Bolshevik Revolution* (Princeton, N.J.: Princeton University Press, 2000), 21–39, 129–90.

2. Yehoshua A. Gilboa, *The Black Years of Soviet Jewry, 1939–1953* (Boston: Little, Brown and Company, 1971), 88.

3. *Partiinyi Arkhiv Vinnyts'koi Oblasti* (PAVO), f. 136, op. 13, d. 186, ll. 224, 228–31, 236–39.

4. *Tsentral'nyi Derzhavnyi Arkhiv Hromads'kykh Ob'iednan Ukrainy* (TsDAHOU), f. 1, op. 23, d. 2366, ll. 25, 27–28.

5. Vasilii Grossman, *Zhizn' i sud'ba* (Moscow: Knizhnaia palata, 1988), 542–43. In his letter to Khrushchev on February 23, 1962, pleading for the publication of his novel, Grossman noted that he had started writing it already during Stalin's life. *Istochnik* 3 (1997): 133.

6. Stanislaw Kot, *Conversations with the Kremlin and Dispatches from Russia* (Oxford: Oxford University Press, 1963), 153; Wladyslaw Anders, *Bez ostatniego rozdzialu: wspomnenia z lat 1939–1946* (Newtown, Wales: Montgomeryshire Printing Co., 1950), 118, 124–25.

7. "Do kontsa razgromit kosmopolitov-antipatriotov!" *Pravda Ukrainy*, March 6, 1949; "Bezridni kosmopolity—nailiutishi vorohy radians'koi kul'tury," *Naddnistrians'ka zirka*, March 27, 1949.

8. Vasilii Ardamatskii, "Pinia iz Zhmerinki," *Krokodil* 8 (March 20, 1953): 13.

9. In his memoirs, Aleksandr Nekrich claimed that he knew "for certain" of a brochure written by Dmitrii Chesnokov explaining the need for deporting the Jews. The brochure was ready for distribution when Stalin died. Nekrich, *Otreshis' ot strakha: vospominaniia istorika* (London: Overseas Publications Interchange, 1979), 114. Nekrich's allegation was recently corroborated by Iakov Etinger, a former professor at the Institute of World Economics and International Relations at the Russian Academy of Sciences. According to Etinger, the book by Chesnokov argued that the Jews proved to be "unreceptive" to socialism. Iakov Etinger, "The Doctors' Plot: Stalin's Solution to the Jewish Question," in Yaacov Ro'i, ed., *Jews and Jewish Life in Russia and the Soviet Union* (Portland, Oreg.: F. Cass, 1995), 118. Throughout the Soviet Union, the secret police recorded private conversations of both Jewish and non-Jewish citizens in which the deportation of the Jews was accepted as fait accompli. See the documents assembled by Mordechai Altschuler, "More About Public Reaction to the Doctors' Plot," *Jews in Eastern Europe* (Fall 1996): 34, 45, 52, 55, 56–57.

10. *Komsomol'skaia pravda*, February 12, 1953.

11. Joseph B. Schechtman, *Star in Eclipse* (New York: T. Yoseloff, 1961), 81. According to Benjamin Pinkus, this statement was authenticated by Jewish immigrants to Israel who held important posts in the Polish Communist Party and government. Pinkus, *The Soviet Government and the Jews 1948–1967: A Documented Study* (Cambridge: Cambridge University Press, 1984), 487, n. 38.

12. *Istochnik* 3 (1994): 97–98.

13. Trohym Kychko, *Iudaizm bez prikras* (Kiev: Vyd-vo Akademii nauk URSR, 1963), 160–61, 164–66. The book appeared in mass publication (twelve thousand copies) and was endorsed by the Academy of Sciences of the Soviet Ukrainian Republic. Adding insult to injury was that such accusations came from one whose own wartime record was marred by allegations of collaboration. In his memoirs, the émigré journalist Leonid Vladimirov tells of his shock when he learned about the content of Kychko's book and the fact that a person accused of collaboration with the Germans rose to such academic status. When Vladimirov asked a friend, a prominent

author in Kiev, the latter told him that the "colorful past of the rogue Kychko was well known in Kiev to all the proper people. However, there are services in Russia for which even collaborators are pardoned. Kychko understood this well, and already long ago, immediately after the war, 'devoted himself' to anti-Semitic scientific research." Leonid Vladimirov, *Rossiia bez prikras i umolchanii* (Frankfurt am Main: Posiev, 1973), 279–81.

That the Kychko affair was not accidental was demonstrated by the belated Soviet reaction after the public storm had subsided. In 1968 the Supreme Soviet of Ukraine awarded Kychko with the Diploma of Honor "for his work for atheist propaganda," which followed the earlier reward of the Order of Lenin. Nora Levin, *The Jews in the Soviet Union Since 1917: The Paradox of Survival*, vol. 2 (New York: New York University Press, 1988), 621; Moshe Decter, "Judaism Without Embellishment," in Ronald Rubin, ed., *The Unredeemed: Anti-Semitism in the Soviet Union* (Chicago: Quadrangle Books, 1968), 135.

14. Weiner, *Making Sense of War*, 201–2.

15. "Zakliuchitel'noe slovo tovarishcha Stalina na plenume TsK VKP(b) 5 marta 1937 g.," *Bol'shevik* 7 (1937): 19.

16. "Rech' I.V. Stalina v Narkomate oborony, 2 iiunia 1937 g.," *Istochnik* 3 (1994): 73–74. In this light, and without underestimating Stalin's anti-Semitism, Lenin could be recognized as a scion of the aristocracy but not as the grandson of the Jew Moishe Itskovich Blank. When Lenin's eldest sister, Anna Elizarova, reminded Stalin in 1932–33 of the Jewishness of their grandfather, her reasoning for publicizing this fact ran against the grain of the Marxist ethos. Lenin's Jewish origins "are further confirmation of the exceptional abilities of the Semitic tribe," she wrote Stalin in 1932. In another letter, a year later, Anna wrote Stalin that "in the Lenin Institute, as well as the Institute of the Brain . . . they have long recognized the gifts of this nation and the extremely beneficial effects of its blood on mixed marriages." Stalin's refusal to publish a word about the matter became the rule for years to come. Dmitrii Volkogonov, *Lenin* (New York: Free Press, 1994), 8–9.

17. Alexis Carell, *Man the Unknown* (London: Harper & Brothers Publishers, 1935), 318–19.

On the wide approval of sterilization of the mentally ill in interwar Europe and the United States, see Henry Friedlander, *The Origins of Nazi Genocide: From Euthanasia to the Final Solution* (Chapel Hill, N.C.: University of North Carolina Press, 1995), 7–9, 18.

18. Michael Burleigh, *Death and Deliverance: "Euthanasia" in Germany 1900–1945* (Cambridge: Cambridge University Press, 1994); Friedlander, *The Origins of Nazi Genocide*. There was, however, a single incident that accentuated the rule. In early 1938 about 170 invalid prisoners in the Moscow region, who had already been tried and convicted for petty crimes such as theft and vagrancy, were tried again for the same charges; only this time they were sentenced to death. The operation was run by the special troika of the Moscow NKVD (the body that reviewed cases and passed sentences during the terror). The motive behind the executions was to make room for the arrival of deported Germans, Poles, Latvians, and other ethnic groups. The chairman of the troika, Mikhail Ilich Semenov, was himself tried and executed in the summer of 1939. *Soprotivlenie v Gulage: Vospominaniia. Pis'ma. Dokumenty* (Moscow: Vozvrashchenie, 1992), 114–27.

19. Ironically, Grossman, who insisted on the commonality of the Soviet and Nazi polities, was also the first observer to recognize that the "conveyor belt execution" was the distinguishing feature of the Nazi exterminatory practices. See his description of Treblinka in Vasilii Grossman and Il'ia Ehrenburg, eds., *Hasefer Hashahor* (The Black Book) (Tel Aviv: Am Oved, 1991), 495–515, esp. 507.

20. Mark B. Adams, "Eugenics in Russia, 1900–1940," in Adams, ed., *The Wellborn Science: Eugenics in Germany, France, Brazil, and Russia* (New York: Oxford University Press, 1990), 194–95.

21. Georgio Agamben, *Homo Sacer: Sovereign Power and Bare Life* (Stanford, Calif.: Stanford University Press, 1998), 114, 146–47. In this sense, Saul Friedländer's recent introduction of "redemptive anti-Semitism" as the guiding logic of Nazi attitudes toward the Jews requires some modification. Redemption implies a linear concept of historical time and a certain finality, alien both to the Nazis' nihilistic violence and their cyclical view of history, one filled with nightmares of a possible defeat at the hands of the Jews. Friedländer, *Nazi Germany and the Jews*, vol. 1, *The Years of Persecution, 1933–1939* (New York: HarperCollins, 1997), 73–112. For a lucid analysis of the place of the Jew within the Nazi racial hierarchy in theory and practice, see John Connelly, "Nazis and Slavs: From Racial Theory to Racial Practice," *Central European History* 32, no.1 (1999): 1–33.

22. A rare admission by a Soviet official of a de facto *numerus clausus* for Jews was offered by Ekaterina Furtseva, a Central Committee secretary, during an interview with the *National Guardian*, June 25, 1956. "The government had found in some of its departments a heavy concentration of Jewish people, upwards of 50 percent of the staff," said Furtseva. "Steps were taken to transfer them to other enterprises, giving them equally good positions and without jeopardizing their rights." These steps were misinterpreted as anti-Semitic, Furtseva told the interviewer. Pinkus, *Soviet Government and the Jews*, 58–59.

23. Eventually, the Soviets and their allies succeeded in omitting the category of political groups from the draft, in a deviation from an earlier resolution of the General Assembly. Nehemiah Robinson, *The Genocide Convention: Its Origins and Interpretation* (New York: Institute of Jewish Affairs, 1949), 15.

24. Aron Naumovich Trainin, "Bor'ba s genotsidom kak mezhdunarodnym prestupleniem," *Sovetskoe gosudarstvo i pravo* 5 (May 1948): 4, 6. The official amendment offered by the Soviet delegation called for the extension of the definition of genocide to "national-cultural genocide," which included "a) ban on or limitation of the use of national language in public and private life; ban on instruction in the national language in schools; b) the liquidation or ban on printing and distribution of books and other publications in national languages; c) the liquidation of historical or religious monuments, museums, libraries and other monuments and objects of national culture (or religious) cult." Trainin, "Bor'ba s genotsidom," 14.

25. For a stimulating discussion of this duality in Soviet nationality policy, see Yuri Slezkine, "The USSR as a Communal Apartment, or How a Socialist State Promoted Ethnic Particularism," *Slavic Review* 53 (Summer 1994): 414–52.

26. Gosudarstvennyi Arkhiv Rossiiskoi Federatsii (GARF), f. 9414, op. 4, d. 145, ll. 11–12b.

27. Anatoly Shcharansky, *Fear No Evil* (New York: Random House, 1988), 10–11.

28. *Eynikayt*, March 15, 1943.

29. Mordechai Altshuler, "Antisemitism in Ukraine Toward the End of the Second World War," *Jews in Eastern Europe* 3 (Winter 1993), 49–50, n. 29.

30. "Druzhba narodov SSSR—moguchii faktor pobedy nad vragom," *Bol'shevik* 23–24 (December 1944): 6. Overall, 160,722 Jews won military awards, the fourth largest group to do so after the Russians, Ukrainians, and Belorussians. These figures should be compared with the data from the 1939 population census that placed the Jews as the seventh largest ethnic group in the Soviet Union. Yossef Guri, "Yehudei Brit-Hamoatsot Bamilhama Neged Hanazim," in *Lohamim Yehudim Bamilhama neged Hanazim* (Tel Aviv: Ha-Irgun Ha-Yisraeli shel hayalim meshuhrarim al yede Sifriyat Poalim, 1971), 41.

31. Some cases indicated that this phenomenon was helped by Jews' own internalization of traditional stereotypes of Jewish appearance and characteristics. "True, in my unit they did not know that I was a Jew. I am strong and tall, a worker," wrote Mikhail Shakerman to Ehrenburg and Khrushchev. PAVO, f. 136, op. 13, d. 184, l. 93.

32. Hersh Smolar, *Vu Bistu Haver Sidorov?* (Tel Aviv: Farlag Y.L. Perets, 1975), 257–58.

33. Mordechai Altshuler, "Escape and Evacuation of Soviet Jews at the Time of the Nazi Invasion: Policies and Realities," in Lucjan Dobroszycki and Jeffrey S. Gurock, eds., *The Holocaust in the Soviet Union: Studies and Sources on the Destruction of the Jews in the Nazi-Occupied Territories of the USSR, 1941–1945* (New York: M.E. Sharpe, 1993), 77–104.

34. Yad Vashem Archive (YVA), the testimony of Zalman Teitelman, #03–3446, page 20.

35. Raymond Arthur Davies, *Odyssey Through Hell* (New York: L.B. Fischer, 1946), 206–7.

36. TsDAHOU, f. 1, op. 23, d. 2366, ll. 23–24.

37. Significantly, Kipnis did not include this paragraph in a shorter version of the story that he published in June 1945 in Kiev under the title *Libshaft*.

38. Kipnis was subjected to harsh criticism for the blasphemous idea of placing the Star of David, the Zionist symbol, side by side with the Soviet star, an "idea that is incompatible for a Soviet writer," as the secretary of the Ukrainian Union of Writers concluded. *Literaturna Hazeta*, September 25, 1947; Haim Loytsker, "Far ideyisher reynkeyt fun undzer literatur," *Der Shtern* (Kiev, 1948): 105–12.

Kipnis's writings appeared to embody the dual sin of the Jewish subversion of the Soviet myth of the war, namely, Jewish particularistic heroism and suffering. This could be traced back to his writing in the 1920s. In 1926 Kipnis published a novel, *Khadoshim un teg* (Months and Days), that focused on the recent pogroms in Ukraine, a fact that was not lost upon Loitsker. "Kipnis, so it turns out, has not forgotten his former *Khadoshim un teg*, although many years have passed. And he has learnt nothing in all these years of Soviet rule," exclaimed Loytsker. Here, 112.

39. Notebooks, entry on November 30, 1945, in Marco Carynnyk, ed., *Alexander Dovzhenko: The Poet as Filmmaker* (Cambridge: MIT Press, 1973), 137.

40. Il'ia Ehrenburg, *Sobranie Sochineniia* (*Liudi, Gody, Zhizn'*), vol. 9 (Moscow: Sovetskii pisatel', 1967), 377.

41. TsDAHOU, f. 1, op. 23, d. 3851, ll. 3–5.

42. See, for example, the report by the Vinnytsia region branch of the commit-

tee in Tsentral'nyi Derzhavnyi Arkhiv Vyshchykh Orhaniv Vlady ta Upravlinnia Ukrainy (TsDAVOVU), f. 4620, op. 3, d. 253.

43. TsDAHOU, f. 1, op. 23, d. 2366, l. 26.

44. TsDAHOU, f. 1, op. 23, d. 2366, l. 16.

45. YVA, #03–6401, the testimony of Hanna Schwartzman, pages 15–16.

46. Abraham Sutzkever, "Il'ia Ehrenburg (A Kapital Zikhronot fon di Yaren 1944–1946)," *Di Goldene Keit* 61 (1967): 30.

47. Grossman and Ehrenburg, *Hasefer Hashahor*, 17.

48. Rossiiskii Gosudarstvennyi Arkhiv Sotsial'no-Politicheskoi Istorii (RGASPI), f. 17, op. 125, r. 1442, d. 438, l. 216.

49. Vasilii Grossman, "Ukraina bez evreev," in Shimon Markish, *Vasilii Grossman. Na evreiskie temy*, vol. 2 (Jerusalem: Biblioteka-Aliia, 1985), 333–40. Here, 334–35. This is a translation back to Russian of the Yiddish version that appeared in *Eynikayt*, November 25, and December 2, 1943. The original version in the Russian language was apparently rejected by *Krasnaia zvezda*.

50. PAVO, f. 136, op. 13, d. 208, ll. 1–7. On the migration to Birobidzhan, see GARF, f. 8114, op. 1, d. 8, l. 59; and Pinkus, *Soviet Government and the Jews*, 378. One may recall Khrushchev's alleged retort a few years earlier that "it would be advisable for Ukrainian Jews who have survived Nazi extermination not to return to the Ukraine. They would do better in Birobidzhan." Leon Leneman, *La Tragedie des juifs en URSS* (Paris: Desclee de Brouwer, 1959), 178–79.

51. Vsevolod Kochetov, *Zhurbiny* (Leningrad: Sovetskii pisatel', 1952), 225, 328–29, 335, 347, 349–50. The first edition of *Zhurbiny* alone enjoyed circulation of 45,000 copies and was supplemented by subsequent editions.

52. See Pieter Lagrou, "Victims of Genocide and National Memory: Belgium, France and the Netherlands 1945–1965," *Past & Present* 154 (February 1997): 191–222.

53. Omer Bartov, "Defining Enemies, Making Victims: Germans, Jews, and the Holocaust," *American Historical Review* 103 (June 1998): 771–816; Tom Segev, *The Seventh Million: The Israelis and the Holocaust* (New York: Hill and Wang, 1993); James Young, *The Texture of Memory: Holocaust Memorials and Meaning*, part 3 (New Haven, Conn.: Yale University Press, 1993); Yael Zerubavel, *Recovered Roots: Collective Memory and the Making of Israeli National Tradition* (Chicago: University of Chicago Press, 1995).

54. Leon Leneman, *La tragedie des Juifs en U.R.S.S*, 179.

55. For the shift in the Western European discourse on the Holocaust in the mid-1960s, see Lagrou, "Victims of Genocide," 215–20.

56. For the decree of August 28, 1964, by the Presidium of the Supreme Soviet, see *Tak eto bylo* (1993), vol. 1:246–47.

57. The rehabilitation was enacted in two resolutions of the Presidium of the Supreme Soviet, December 6, 1963, and April 29, 1964. GARF, f. 7523, op. 109, d. 195, ll. 38–39.

58. Porfirii Gavrutto (Porfyrii Havrutto), *Tuchi nad gorodom* (Moscow: Molodaia Gvardiia, 1968), 165–66. For an extensive documentation of the affair, including Khrushchev's speech and the rebuttal by Moisei Kogan, the falsely accused Jew, see Pinkus, *Soviet Government and the Jews*, 76, 127–33, 493, nn. 113–14.

59. Svetlana Allilueva, *Only One Year* (New York: Harper & Row, 1969), 153. Ironically, this was also the view in Berlin in early 1937. "Again a show trial in Moscow,"

Goebbels noted in his diary on January 25, 1937. "This time again exclusively against Jews. Radek, etc. The Fuhrer still in doubt whether there isn't after all a hidden anti-Semitic tendency. Maybe Stalin does want to smoke the Jews out. The military is also supposedly strongly anti-Semitic." Cited in Friedlander, *Nazi Germany and the Jews*, 185–86.

60. Iurii Larin, *Evrei i antisemitizm v SSSR* (Moscow, 1929), 241–44; PAVO, f. 136, op. 1, d. 96, ll. 25–26; op. 3, d. 219, l. 26.

61. TsDAHOU, f. 57, op. 4, d. 356, l. 186.

62. TsDAHOU, f. 1, op. 23, d. 1385, ll. 4–5.

63. Anastas Mikoyan, *Tak bylo: razmyshleniia o minuvshem* (Moscow, 1999), 514.

64. Altshuler, "More About Public Reaction to the Doctors' Plot," *Jews in Eastern Europe* (Fall 1996): 29, 39–40, 45, 56–57.

65. Altshuler, "More About Public Reaction to the Doctors' Plot," 33.

66. Aleksandr Lokshin, "Delo vrachei": "otkliki trudiashchikhsia," *Vestnik evreiskogo universiteta v Moskve* 1, no. 5 (1994): 56–62.

CHAPTER 8, *Chang*

1. Donald O. Johnson, "The War Relocation Authority Schools of Tule Lake, California," unpublished master's thesis, School of Education, Stanford University, June 1947, 93–94 (emphasis added).

2. For example, see Roger Daniels, *Concentration Camps USA: Japanese Americans and World War II* (New York: Holt, Rinehart and Winston, 1972); Richard Drinnon, *Keeper of Concentration Camps: Dillon S. Myer and American Racism* (Berkeley: University of California Press, 1987); Michi Weglyn, *Years of Infamy: The Untold Story of America's Concentration Camps* (New York: William Morrow, 1976). A few respected journals condemned the internment camps as concentration camps at the time of their inception. See, for example, Michael Evans, "Concentration Camp—USA Style," *Coronet* 12 (October 1942): 43–51; Ted Nakashima, "Concentration Camp: U.S. Style," *New Republic* 106 (June 15, 1942): 822–23; "Life in a California Concentration Camp; Excerpts from Letters," *Nation* 154 (June 6, 1942): 666.

3. United States Commission on Wartime Relocation and Internment of Civilians, *Personal Justice Denied: Report of the Commission on Wartime Relocation and Internment of Civilians* (Washington, D.C.: GPO, 1982), 110–12.

4. Commission on Wartime Relocation, *Personal Justice Denied*, 6.

5. The *Los Angeles Times* editor wrote in February 1942 about what he called "our American-born Japanese":

> A viper is nonetheless a viper wherever the egg is hatched. A leopard's spots are the same and its disposition is the same wherever it is whelped.
>
> So a Japanese-American, born of Japanese parents, nurtured upon Japanese traditions, living in a transplanted Japanese atmosphere and thoroughly inoculated with Japanese thoughts, Japanese ideas and Japanese ideals, notwithstanding his nominal brand of accidental citizenship, almost inevitably and with the rarest exceptions grows up to be a Japanese, not an American, in his thoughts, in his ideas and in his ideals, and himself is a potential and menacing, if not an actual, danger and, as it were, hamstrung.

> [Thus I favor their control because] I cannot escape the conclusion that such treatment, as a matter of national and even personal defense, should be accorded to each and all of them while we are at war with their race. *Los Angeles Times*, February 2, 1942, part 2, page 4.

Leading journalists, civic leaders, and politicians throughout the Western states expressed like views through the early months of 1942. Although the top political leaders of the country did not express such virulent racism publicly, many shared the same ideas privately. Discussion of the biologically based racist thinking of men such as John J. McCloy, Henry L. Stimson, and Franklin Roosevelt are in Drinnon, *Keeper of Concentration Camps*, 30, 33–34, 254–56.

6. Stanford University, School of Education, *Education in Wartime and After* (New York: D. Appleton-Century, 1943), 66. On the rise of cultural relativist views of human difference, see Carl Degler, *In Search of Human Nature: The Decline and Revival of Darwinism in American Social Thought* (New York: Oxford University Press, 1991).

7. Commission on Wartime Relocation, *Personal Justice Denied*, 18.

8. Drinnon, *Keeper of Concentration Camps*, 64–65. The extremists included U.S. senators and congressmen and journalists with the Hearst and McClatchy newspaper chains. For more on popular notions about internment and the limited opposition to the internment order, see Gordon H. Chang, "'Superman is about to visit the relocation centers' and the Limits of Wartime Liberalism," *Amerasia Journal* 19, no. 1 (1993): 37–59.

9. Although public support for internment was enthusiastic, some public figures condemned the decision, offering a decidedly different interpretation of the action. The Quakers, the Socialist Norman Thomas, and individual Japanese Americans spoke out vigorously. Some individuals involved in the internment project actually expressed misgivings in private, revealing some understanding of the ignominy of the decision. Secretary of War Henry Stimson, before his energetic endorsement of internment, confided in his diary that the move would "make a tremendous hole in our constitutional system." Top officials in the Department of Justice, including Attorney General Francis Biddle, feared the constitutional implications of the internment decision but acquiesced and then later presented evidence in the Supreme Court they knew was false. Their rationales persuaded the top court to uphold the internment decision. Because of the exposure of the machinations of the Justice Department in the challenge cases, the Court thirty years later vacated its early decisions on internment.

10. McCloy to Meiklejohn, September 30, 1942, Japanese American Evacuation and Resettlement Study, 67/14, E1.020, Bancroft Library, U.C. Berkeley, and Drinnon, *Keeper of Concentration Camps*, 36. Directed by sociologist Dorothy Swaine Thomas, the JERS wartime project involved social scientists in an independent investigation of internment and its immediate aftermath. This project has been discussed elsewhere: see Yuji Ichioka, ed., *Views from Within: The Japanese American Evacuation and Resettlement Study* (Los Angeles: Asian American Studies Center, UCLA, 1989).

11. John J. McCloy to Jane B. Kaihatsu, April 12, 1984, reproduced in Roger Daniels, Sandra C. Taylor, and Harry H. L. Kitano, eds., *Japanese Americans: From Relocation to Redress* (Salt Lake City: University of Utah Press, 1986), 213–14.

12. Carey McWilliams, "California and the Japanese," *New Republic* 106 (March

3, 1942): 295–97, and "Japanese Out of California," *New Republic*, 106 (April 6, 1942): 456–57.

13. Carey McWilliams, "Japanese Evacuation: Policy and Perspectives," *Common Ground* 2 (Summer 1942): 65–72; and "Moving the West-Coast Japanese," *Harper's* 185 (September 1942): 359–69. Months later, McWilliams again changed his views and focused his comments on the sentiments raging against Japanese Americans. He eventually came to be identified as a vocal opponent of their relocation. In his memoir many years later, McWilliams avoids mentioning his 1942 flirtation with the internment project and implies he had always opposed the idea. See his "Racism on the West Coast," *New Republic* 110 (May 29, 1944): 732–33; *Prejudice, Japanese-Americans: Symbol of Racial Intolerance* (Boston: Little, Brown, 1944); and *The Education of Carey McWilliams* (Boston: Simon and Schuster, 1978), 101–7.

14. Edward H. Spicer, "The Use of Social Scientists by the War Relocation Authority," *Applied Anthropology* 5, no. 2 (Spring 1946): 19, 35–36; and Spicer et al., *Impounded People: Japanese-Americans in the Relocation Centers* (Tucson: University of Arizona Press, 1969), 18–21. Also see Peter T. Suzuki, "Anthropologists in the Wartime Camps for Japanese Americans: A Documentary Study," *Dialectical Anthropology* 6, no. 1 (1981): 23–60.

15. Bogardus, 28:218–34; Bureau of Sociological Research, 100:328–33; Robertson, 20, no. 2, 66–71; Kehoe, 3:55–59; Provinse, 11:4, 396–410; and Spicer (New York: Russell Sage Foundation, 1952).

16. John W. Powell, "Education Through Relocation," *Adult Education Journal* 1, no. 4 (October 1942): 154–57 (emphasis added).

17. Thomas James, *Exile Within: The Schooling of Japanese Americans, 1942–1945* (Cambridge, Mass.: Harvard University Press, 1987), 39–40.

18. Quotes from James, *Exile Within*, 137.

19. "Proposed Curriculum Procedures for Japanese Relocation Centers," Summer 1942, box 153, folder 11, pp. II, 4–5, Paul Hanna Papers, Hoover Institution, Stanford.

20. Jerome T. Light, "The Development of a Junior-Senior High School Program in a Relocation Center for People of Japanese Ancestry During the War with Japan," unpublished Ph.D. dissertation, School of Education, Stanford University, April 1947.

21. Light, "Development of a Program," 498–99.

22. Light, "Development of a Program," 496.

23. Light, "Development of a Program," 589.

24. Discussion of internee reaction to internment draws heavily from my book *Morning Glory, Evening Shadow: Yamato Ichihashi and His Internment Writings, 1942–1945* (Stanford, Calif.: Stanford University Press, 1997). Also see Yuji Ichioka, ed., *Views from Within: The Japanese American Evacuation and Resettlement Study* (Los Angeles: Asian American Studies Center, UCLA, 1989); Lane Ryo Hirabayashi, ed., *Inside an American Concentration Camp: Japanese American Resistance at Poston, Arizona* (Tucson: University of Arizona Press, 1995); and Charles Kikuchi, *The Kikuchi Diary: Chronicle from an American Concentration Camp. The Tanforan Journals of Charles Kikuchi*, ed. John Modell (Urbana: University of Illinois Press, 1973).

25. Chang, *Morning Glory*, 111, 124.

26. Chang, *Morning Glory*, 184, 215.

27. Chang, *Morning Glory*, 286.

28. Dillon Myer, *Uprooted Americans: The Japanese Americans and the War Relocation Authority During World War II* (Tucson: University of Arizona Press, 1971), 3.

29. Quotation from Light, *Exile Within*, 93–94. One anthropologist wrote an entire book on the administrative lessons offered by internment: Alexander H. Leighton, *The Governing of Men: General Principles and Recommendations Based on Experience at a Japanese Relocation Camp* (Princeton, N.J.: Princeton University Press, 1945).

30. In this respect, my interpretation is a modification of the view in the fine book by Elazar Barkan, *Retreat of Scientific Racism: Changing Concepts of Race in Britain and the United States Between the World Wars* (New York: Cambridge University Press, 1992).

31. Norman Thomas, "Dark Day for Liberty," *Christian Century* 59 (July 29, 1942): 929–31. Also see his *Democracy and Japanese Americans* (New York: Post War World Council, 1942).

CHAPTER 9, *Deák*

1. One of Edvard Beneš's émigré publications bears the characteristic title *Détruisez l'Austriche—Hongrie! Le martyre des Tchéco-Slovaques à travers l'histoire* (Paris, 1916). On the Czech situation before and during World War I, see Victor J. Mamatey and Radomir Luža, eds., *A History of the Czechoslovak Republic, 1918–1948* (Princeton, N.J., 1973); and Zybnek (Z. A. B.) Zeman, *The Break-up of the Habsburg Empire, 1914–1918: A Study in National and Social Revolution* (Oxford, England, 1961). Also, Z. A. B. Zeman, *The Masaryks: The Making of Czechoslovakia* (London, 1976).

2. Some of the best accounts of the Balkan states before World War I are Barbara Jelavich, *History of the Balkans*, 2 vols. (Cambridge, England, 1983); Charles and Barbara Jelavich, *The Establishment of the Balkan National States, 1804–1920* (Seattle, 1977); Ivo Banać, *The National Question in Yugoslavia* (Ithaca, N.Y., 1984); John Lampe, *Yugoslavia as History: Twice There Was a Country* (Cambridge, Mass., 1996), 1–98; Henry L. Roberts, *Romania* (New Haven, Conn., 1951); and Richard J. Crampton, *Bulgaria 1878–1918: A History*, East European Monographs, 138 (New York and Boulder, Colo., 1983).

3. On the Serbian military junta see, among others, Joachim Remak, *Sarajevo* (London, 1959); Vladimir Dedijer, *The Road to Sarajevo* (London, 1967); Wladimir Aichelburg, *Sarajevo, 28 Juni 1914* (Vienna, 1984); Friedrich Würthle, *Die Spur führt nach Belgrad: Sarajevo 1914* (Vienna-Munich, 1975); and Lavender Cassels, *The Archduke and the Assassin: Sarajevo, June 28th 1914* (New York, 1984).

4. The role of Czech soldiers in World War I is described in Victor S. Mamatey, "The Czech Wartime Dilemma: The Habsburgs or the Entente?" in Béla K. Király and Nandor F. Dreisziger, eds., *East Central European Society in World War I*, East European Monographs, 196 (New York and Boulder, Colo., 1985), 103–11; and Josef Kalvoda, "The Origins of the Czechoslovak Army," in *East Central European Society*, 419–35.

5. The dilemma of Czechs, Germans, and Jews in Bohemia and Moravia is very well explained in Gary Cohen, *The Politics of Ethnic Survival: Germans in Prague, 1861–1914* (Princeton, N.J., 1981).

6. On the reserve officers in the Habsburg Army, see István Deák, *Beyond Nationalism: A Social and Political History of the Habsburg Officer Corps, 1848–1918* (New York: Oxford University Press, 1990), 86–88, 132–34, 171–75, 180–83, 193–95, passim.

7. Some of the best sources on Hungary and its ethnic problems before World War I are Andrew C. Janos, *The Politics of Backwardness in Hungary, 1825–1945* (Princeton, N.J., 1982); Gábor Vermes, *István Tisza: The Liberal Vision and Conservative Statecraft of a Magyar Nationalist*, East European Monographs, 184 (New York and Boulder, Colo., 1985); Peter F. Sugar, ed., *A History of Hungary* (Blomington, Ind., 1990), chapters 14–15.

8. The Polish dilemma in World War I is colorfully described in Norman Davies, *God's Playground: A History of Poland*, 2 vols. (New York, 1982), vol. 2:378–92. See also Hans Roos, *A History of Modern Poland from the Foundation of the State in the First World War to the Present Day* (New York, 1966).

9. The policy of the Austrian High Command toward the different ethnic groups is well explained in Gunther E. Rothenberg, *The Army of Francis Joseph* (West Lafayette, Ind., 1975), chapters 12–14; Robert A. Kann, Béla K. Király, and Paula S. Fichtner, eds., *The Habsburg Empire in World War I: Essays in Intellectual, Military, Political and Economic Aspects of the War Effort*, East European Monographs, 23 (New York and Boulder, Co., 1977); and Richard G. Plaschka, Horst Haselsteiner, and Arnold Suppan, *Innere Front: Militärassistenz, Widerstand und Umsturz in der Donaumonarchie 1918*, 2 vols. (Vienna, 1974). See also István Deák, "The Ethnic Question in the Multinational Habsburg Army, 1848–1918," in N. F. Dreisziger, ed., *Ethnic Armies: Polyethnic Armed Forces from the Time of the Habsburgs to the Age of the Superpowers* (Waterloo, Ontario, Canada, 1990), 21–49.

On the uneven social and ethnic distribution of the war dead, see the pamphlets of the Austrian statistician Wilhelm Winkler: *Die Totenverluste der öst.-ung. Monarchie nach Nationalitäten* (Vienna, 1919); *Berufsstatistik der Kriegstoten der öst.-ung. Monarchie* (Vienna, 1919); and *Das Anteil der nichtdeutschen Volksstämme an der öst.-ung. Wehrmacht* (Vienna, 1919).

10. There exist a number of fine essays on East Central European prisoners in World War I in Samuel R. Williamson Jr., and Peter Pastor, eds., *Essays on World War I: Origin and Prisoners of War*, East European Monographs, 126 (New York and Boulder, Colo., 1983). The best study by far is Alon Rachamimov, *POWs and the Great War: Captivity on the Eastern Front* (Oxford and New York, 2002).

11. The role of returning POWs in the revolutionary movements is discussed in Manfried Rauchensteiner, *Der Tod des Doppeladlers: Österreich-Ungarn und der Erste Weltkrieg* (Graz, Austria, 1993), chapters 24 and 26.

12. On the Hungarian Soviet Republic, see Oscar Jászi, *Revolution and Counter-Revolution in Hungary* (London, 1924); Peter Pastor, *Hungary Between Wilson and Lenin: The Hungarian Revolution of 1918–1919 and the Big Three*, East European Monographs, 20 (New York and Boulder, Colo., 1976); Peter Pastor, ed., *Revolutions and Interventions in Hungary and Its Neighbor States, 1918–1919*, East European Monographs, 260 (New York and Boulder, Colo., 1988); Rudolf Tokes, *Béla Kun and the Hungarian Soviet Republic* (New York, 1967); and Ivan Volgyes, ed., *Hungary in Revolution, 1918–19: Nine Essays* (Lincoln, Nebr., 1971).

13. On the Paris peace treaties regarding the East Central European states, see Francis Deak, *Hungary at the Paris Peace Conference* (New York, 1942); Béla K. Király, Peter Pastor, and Ivan Sanders, eds., *Essays on World War I: Total War and Peacemaking, a Case Study on Trianon* (New York, 1982); Mária Ormos, *From Padua to the Trianon,*

1918–1920 (New York, 1990); and Ivo Lederer, *Yugoslavia at the Paris Peace Conference: A Study in Frontiermaking* (New Haven, Conn., 1963).

14. On the interwar regimes, see primarily Joseph Rothschild, *East Central Europe Between the Two World Wars* (Seattle, 1974).

15. Of the many studies on East European nationalism, see especially Peter F. Sugar and Ivo Lederer, eds., *Nationalism in Eastern Europe* (Seattle, 1969), and Peter F. Sugar, ed., *East European Nationalism in the Twentieth Century* (Lanham, Md., 1995). Very relevant but of a more general nature are Ernest Gellner, *Nation and Nationalism* (Oxford, England, 1983); Miroslav Hroch, *Social Preconditions of National Revival in Europe*, trans. Ben Gourkes (Cambridge, England, and New York, 1985); Jenö Szücs, *Nation und Geschichte: Studien* (Cologne, 1981); and Rogers Brubaker, *Nationalism Reformed: Nationhood and the National Question in New Europe* (Cambridge, England, and New York).

16. On the events of October 15, 1944, in Hungary, see C. A. Macartney, *October Fifteenth: A History of Modern Hungary, 1929–1945*, 2 vols. (Edinburgh, Scotland, 1956–57), vol. 2. Also see Agnes Rozsnyói, *A Szálasi-puccs* (The coup d'état of Szálasi) (Budapest, 1977); Elek Karsai, ed., *Szálasi naplója* (The diary of Szálasi) (Budapest, 1978); Károly Vigh, *Ugrás a sötétbe* (Leap into the dark) (Budapest, 1985); and Géza Lakatos, *Ahogy én lattam* (As I saw it) (Budapest, 1992).

17. On Nazi Germany's auxiliaries at the Eastern Front, see Peter Gosztony, *Deutschlands Waffengefährte an der Ostfront, 1941–1945* (Stuttgart, West Germany, 1981).

CHAPTER 10, *Naimark*

1. *Ethnic cleansing* is a term that came into common parlance in the spring of 1992 to describe Serbian attacks on the Muslim population of Bosnia. The term is problematic; some suggest, for example, that it is little more than a euphemism for genocide. On the other hand, I find it useful to describe a series of purposeful attempts by modern state leaderships in the twentieth century to drive out, deport, or destroy ethnic "others" and national minorities. See Laura Silber and Allan Little, *Yugoslavia: Death of a Nation* (New York: TV Books, 1996), 244; William Safire, "Ethnic Cleansing," *New York Times Magazine*, March 14, 1993, 24; Andrew Bell-Fialkoff, *Ethnic Cleansing* (New York: St. Martin's Press, 1996), 51–57.

2. For a good summary of Soviet nationality policy in the 1920s and 1930s, see Ronald Grigor Suny, *The Revenge of the Pact: Nationalism, Revolution, and the Collapse of the Soviet Union* (Stanford, Calif.: Stanford University Press, 1993), 102–6. See also Yuri Slezkine, "The USSR as a Communal Apartment, or How a Socialist State Promoted Ethnic Particularism," *Slavic Review* 53 (Summer 1994): 414–52.

3. Hoover Institution Archives (HIA), Nicolaevsky, series 227, box 294, V. Pozdniakov, "Pasportnaia sistema Sovetskogo soiuza," 274–91.

4. Berman to Iagoda, December 8, 1933, State Archives of the Russian Federation (GARF), f. 9421, op. 1, d. 300, l. 10.

5. See Hiroaki Kuromiya, *Stalin's Industrial Revolution: Politics and Workers, 1928–1932* (Cambridge: Cambridge University Press, 1988), 27–45.

6. See Amir Weiner, "Nature, Nurture, and Memory in a Socialist Utopia: Delineating the Soviet Socio-ethnic Body in the Age of Socialism," *American Historical Re-*

view, 104, no. 4 (October 1999): 13–14; 90, n. 30. I am grateful to the author for providing me with numerous useful references, including, above all, a series of stimulating discussions.

7. Terry Martin, "The Origins of Soviet Ethnic Cleansing," *Journal of Modern History* 70, no. 4 (December 1998): 857.

8. On the deportations of Poles, Germans, Koreans, Iranians, and others, see N. F. Bugai, *L. Beriia—I. Stalinu: "Soglasno Vashemu ukazaniiu"* (Moscow: "AIRO-XX," 1995), 8–27; Martin, "Origins of Ethnic Cleansing," 852–56. The deportation of the Koreans to Kazakhstan in September 1937 was in some ways the prototype of the operations that followed. See GARF, f. 5446, op. 57, d. 52, l. 29.

9. Yuri Slezkine, *Arctic Mirrors: Russia and the Small Peoples of the North* (Ithaca, N.Y., and London: Cornell University Press, 1994), 304.

10. Shimon Redlich, ed., *War, Holocaust and Stalinism: A Documented History of the Jewish Anti-Fascist Committee in the USSR* (Luxembourg: Harwood, 1995). See especially the report by Beria to Georgii Maksimilianovich Malenkov on the murder of Mikhoels (April 2, 1953), 448–50. See also Arkady Vaksberg, *Stalin protiv evreev* (New York: Liberty Publishing House, 1995), 273–354.

11. Slezkine, *Arctic Mirrors*, 304.

12. Joanna Nichols states that the Chechens and Ingush are "distinct ethnic groups with distinct languages, but so closely related and so similar that it is convenient to describe them together." The history of these peoples goes back almost six thousand years in the Northern Caucasus. Joanna Nichols, "Who Are the Chechens?" *Center for Slavic and East European Studies Newsletter*, U.C. Berkeley (Spring 1995). See also John B. Dunlop, *Russia Confronts Chechnya: Roots of a Separatist Conflict* (Cambridge: Cambridge University Press, 1998), 1–2.

13. Beria to Stalin, February 29, 1944, GARF, f. 9401, op. 2, d. 64, l. 161.

14. Beria to Stalin, February 24, 1944, GARF, f. 9401, op. 2, d. 64, l. 166.

15. William Flemming, "The Deportation of the Chechen and Ingush Peoples: A Critical Examination," in Ben Fowkes, ed., *Russian and Chechnia: Essays on Russo-Chechen Relations* (New York: St. Martin's Press, 1998), 72.

16. Beria to Stalin, February 23, 1944, in GARF, f. 9401, op. 2, d. 64, l. 165.

17. See Nekrich, *The Punished Peoples: The Deportation and Fate of Soviet Minorities at the End of the Second World War*, trans. George Saunders (New York: W.W. Norton, 1978), 58–59.

18. See D. Khozhaev, "Genotsid: ocherk," and "Krovavyi pepel Khaibakha," in *Tak eto bylo: natsional'nye repressii v SSSR 1919–1952 gody*, vol. 2 (Moscow: Rossiiskii mezhdunarodnyi fond kul'tury, 1993), 170, 175–79. See Flemming, "Deportations of 1944," 74.

19. "Bandity stremilis' . . . sokhranit' fashistskii poriadok," *Voenno-istoricheskii zhurnal*, no. 5 (September–October, 1996): 83–89.

20. Different numbers are used in official statistics, all in the range of 450,000 to 500,000. This number comes from Beria to Stalin, July 9, 1944, GARF, f. 9401, op. 2, d. 65, l. 311. The NKVD reports use ridiculously precise statistics to describe the numbers who were deported and who died. This false precision, which also meant that all the columns in population tables had to add up, indicates a mentality of total control that consistently misrepresented reality.

21. Dunlop, *Russia Confronts Chechnya*, 65–66.

22. Khozhaev, "Genotsid: ocherk," 171.

23. Kazakh NKVD reports to Chernyshev in Moscow NKVD, January 21, 1945, GARF, f. 9479, op. 1, d. 177, ll. 2–4.

24. Official data on births and deaths in exile are in the Main Archive of Contemporary Documentation (TsKhSD), f. 2, op. 1, d. 65, ll. 14, 17, 65.

25. The situation of the deportees is well described in local Kazakh and Kirghiz NKVD reports. See GARF, f. 9479, op. 1, d. 153, ll. 14–20, 37, 42–43. See also d. 183, ll. 46–48, which describes attempts by the Chechens to protest against their fate.

26. Order of the Supreme Soviet of the USSR, March 7, 1944, GARF, f. 7523, op. 4, d. 208, l. 51.

27. Nekrich, *Punished Peoples*, 57–58. Flemming, "Deportation of the Chechen and Ingush Peoples," 66.

28. Dunlop, *Russia Confronts Chechnya*, 58–61. See Robert Conquest, *The Nation Killers*, 2d ed. (New York: Macmillan, 1970), 170.

29. Aleksandr N. Iakovlev, *Po moshcham i elei* (Moscow: Izdatel'stvo "Evraziia," 1995), 120–22.

30. See Russian Center for the Preservation and Study of Documents of Contemporary History (RTsKhIDNI), f. 178, op. 43, d. 2437 and 2438, for Chechen-Ingush obkom discussions of problems with the Chechen population.

31. RTsKhIDNI, f. 17, op. 88, d. 376, l. 5.

32. Nekrich, *Punished Peoples*, 42–46.

33. "O likvidatsii Checheno-Ingushinskoi ASSR i ob administrativnom ustroistve ee territorii," March 7, 1944, GARF, f. 7523, op. 4, d. 208, l. 51. See also GARF, f. 9401, op. 2, d. 64, l. 161.

34. For Grozny obkom records, see RTsKhIDNI, f. 17, op. 45, d. 423, d. 424. For similar results from the Crimean obkom records, see, for example, RTsKhIDNI, f. 17, op. 44, d. 758.

35. Ukaz of July 16, 1956, GARF, f. 7523, op. 4, d. 629, l. 201.

36. See TsK KPSS, "O territorii Checheno-Ingushskoi ASSR, December 25, 1956," TsKhSD, f. 5, op. 32, d. 56, ll. 103–4.

37. "O vosstanovlenii Checheno-Ingushkoi SSSR v sostave RSFSR," January 1957, GARF, f. 7523, op. 72, d. 701, l. 72.

38. The sharp conflict in the Tatar obkom, which met at that point in Sochi, is recorded in the protocols of the November 18, 1942, and July 21, 1943, meetings, RTsKhIDNI, op. 43, d. 1045, ll. 74–84, d. 1044, ll. 251–282.

39. Kamenev to Malenkov, May 11, 1944, RTsKhIDNI, f. 17, op. 123, d. 306, l. 7.

40. Beria already prepared an attack on Bulatov in March 1944. See Sergienko to Beria, March 31, 1944, GARF, f. 9401, op. 2, d. 64, l. 258.

41. Sharp denunciations of Crimean Tatar collaboration are contained in the memoirs of partisans of the region held in the Archive of the Institute of History of the Russian Academy of Sciences (RAN). See especially "Predatel'skaia rol' tatarskogo naseleniia v period okkupatsii Kryma," ll. 1–17. For a defense of the Tatars, see Alan Fischer, *The Crimean Tatars* (Stanford, Calif.: Hoover Institution Press, 1978), 159.

42. Beria to Stalin and Molotov, May 19, 1944, GARF, f. 9401, op. 2, d. 65, l. 115. "At the time of the operation," Beria icily writes, "there were no excesses at all."

43. GARF, f. 9479, op. 1, d. 177, ll. 2–3.

44. Slepov to Malenkov, November 30, 1945, RTsKhIDNI, f. 17, op. 122, d. 122, l. 42.

45. GARF, f. 9479, op. 1, d. 183, l. 290; d. 153, l. 20.

46. Vasilii Subbotin, "Bor'ba s istoriei," *Literaturnaia gazeta*, January 30, 1991, in *Tak eto bylo*, vol. 3 (1993), 71.

47. The large number of homeless orphans were a special problem for the NKVD. Many were rounded up and placed in special NKVD orphanages. RTsKhIDNI, f. 17, op. 118, d. 512, l. 24. In August 1946, a full two and a half years after the deportations, only 20 percent of school-aged Chechen and Ingush children attended schools. Flemming, "The Deportation of Chechen and Ingush Peoples," 81.

48. Edige Kirimal, "The Crimean Turks," *Genocide in the USSR* (New York: Scarecrow Press, 1958), 20. Nekrich, *Punished Peoples*, 106.

49. Beria to Stalin, July 9, 1944, GARF, f. 9401, op. 2, d. 65, l. 275.

50. GARF, f. 9479, op. 1, d. 401, l. 8.

51. On the issue of redeporting returned Tatars, see GARF, f. 9479, op. 1, d. 402, ll. 17–29, and A. Kalinin to Kruglov, September 17, 1948, d. 401, ll. 2–6.

52. See the work of the well-known Soviet scholars B. D. Grekov and Iu. V. Bromlei, who rewrote the history of the Tatars, demonstrating their lack of interest in economic development and their tendencies toward banditry and pillage. Subbotin, "Bor'ba s istoriei," 85.

53. "O pereimenovanii raionov, raionnykh tsentrov, MTS i sovkhozov Kryma," RTsKhIDNI, f. 17, op. 122, d. 83, l. 55.

54. Lausanne is relevant to the eventual Potsdam conference, which approved the deportation of the Germans in that it helped to bring to an end (rather than prevented) brutal ethnic cleansing, which saw many tens of thousands die. See Stephen P. Ladas, *The Exchange of Minorities: Bulgaria, Greece and Turkey* (New York: Macmillan, 1932), 3 ff.

55. Detlef Brandes, *Grossbritannien und seine osteuropaeischen Alliierten 1939–1943* (Munich: R. Oldenbourg Verlag, 1988), 230–31.

56. Alexei Filitov, in Francesa Gori and Silvio Pons, eds., *The Soviet Union and Europe in the Cold War, 1943–53* (New York: St. Martin's Press, 1996), 9 (citing from an Ivan Maisky memorandum of January 11, 1944).

57. Edvard Beneš, "Draft of Conversations Between President Beneš and Mr. Compton Mackenzie," interview by Compton Mackenzie, transcript, 1944, 5–6, HIA, Taborsky Collection, box 4.

58. Foreign Relations of the United States, Diplomatic Papers, *The Conference of Berlin (The Potsdam Conference), 1945*, 2 vols. (Washington, D.C.: United States Printing Office, 1960), vol. 2:1495.

59. See Edvard Beneš's speeches in Pilsen and Melnik during the summer 1945, in Bundesministerium fuer Vertriebene, Fluechtlinge und Kriegsgeschaedigte, *Dokumentation der Vertreibung der Deutschen aus Ost-Mitteleuropa IV: Die Vertreibung der Deutschen Bevolkerung aus der Tschechoslowakei*, vol. 1 (reprinted) (Munich: Deusche Taschenbuch Verlag, 1984), 114, n. 1.

60. Cited in Heinz Nawratil, *Vertreibungs-Verbrechen an Deutschen* (Munich: Ullstein, 1987), 96.

61. Brandes, *Grossbritannien und seine osteuropaeischen Alliierten*, 396–97.

62. Gottwald Proclamation of May 11, 1945, in Bundesministerium fuer Ver-

triebene, Fluechtlinge, and Kriegsgeschaedigte, *Die Vertreibung der Deutschen Bevolkerung aus der Tschechoslowakei*, vol. 1:75, n. 4.

63. See Hans Lemberg, "Die Entwicklung der Plaene fuer die Aussiedlung der Deutschen aus der Tschecholslowakei," in Detlef Brandes and Vaclav Kural, eds., *Der Weg in die Katastrophe: Deutsch-tschechoslowakische Beziehungen 1938–1947* (Essen, Germany: Klartext, 1994), 80–82.

64. Nawratil, *Vertreibungs-Verbrechen an Deutschen*, 95.

65. HIA, Taborsky, box 8, Edvard Taborsky, "Minority Regimes and the Transfer of Populations in Central Europe After This War" (prepared for Beneš, 1943–44), 42–49.

66. Cited in G. P. Murashko and A. F. Noskova, "Natsional'no-territorial'nyi vopros v kontekste poslevoennykh real'nostei Vostochnoi Evropy," *Natsionalnyi vopros v Vostochnoi Evrope* (Moscow: RAN, 1995), 231.

67. For Soviet reports on the Czechs' brutality toward the Germans, see "Ob otnoshenii chekhoslovatskogo naseleniia k nemtsam," May 18, 1945, RTsKhIDNI, f. 17, op. 128, d. 320, l. 161, and Serov to Beria, July 4, 1945, GARF, f. 9401, op. 2, d. 97, ll. 143–44. For endless German accounts, which, however, show absolutely no understanding for the reasons the Czechs felt the need for retributive justice, see *Die Vertreibung der Deutschen Bevoelkerung aus der Tschechoslowakei*, vol. 2. One of the worst cases of random and wanton violence against Germans took place in the town of Aussig, July 30, 1944. See *Die Vertreibung*, 123 ff, and *Dokumente zur Sudetenfrage: Veroeffentlichung des Sudetendeutschen Archivs* (Munich: Langen Mueller, 1984), 71–72.

68. According to Sudeten German sources, some 272,000 Germans (about 8 percent of the total German population in Czechoslovakia) died in the process of being driven out of their homes. This includes a very large number in the category of "missing." Nawratil, *Vertreibungs-Verbrechen an Deutschen*, 71. These figures have been challenged by Czech and German historians, who insist that these claims are wildly exaggerated and that only roughly a tenth of this number died as a result of the "Odsun" (transfer). The recent Czech-German historical commission, for example, states that the number is between nineteen thousand and thirty thousand. *Konfliktni Spolecenstvi, Katastrofa, Uvolneni: Nacrt vykladu nemecko-ceskych dejin od 19.stoleti* (Prague: Spolecna nemecko-ceska komise historiku), 71. The number of thirty thousand is used by Hans Lemberg in his description of the commission's work. Hans Lemberg, "Die Arbeit der deutsch-tschechischen Historikerkommission," *Zeitschrift zur politischen Bildung* 35, no. 4 (1998): 94.

69. Murashko and Noskina, "Natsional'no-territorial'nyi vopros," 235.

70. Actually, as in the case of Poland, many German workers and specialists were so valuable they were not yet deported. According to Radomir Luza, there were still 192,000 Germans left in Czechoslovakia in the fall of 1947, forty thousand of whom were industrial workers. Radomir Luza, *The Transfer of the Sudeten Germans* (New York: New York University Press, 1964), 129.

71. Nawratil, *Vertreibungs-Verbrechen an Deutschen*, 69, 96–97.

72. Brandes, *Grossbritannien und seine osteuropaeischen Allierten*, 505. Beneš describes the expulsion here as a "political, economic, and social Five-Year Plan."

73. HIA, Polish Foreign Ministry, "Granice zachodnie," 341. To Vice Minister of Military Affairs from Ministry of Preparatory Work Concerning the Peace Conference, August 21, 1942, pp. 1–2.

See also Sarah Meiklejohn Terry, *Poland's Place in Europe: General Sikorski and the Origin of the Oder-Neisse Line, 1939–1943* (Princeton, N.J.: Princeton University Press, 1983), 100; and Brandes, *Grossbritannien und seine osteuropaeischen Alliierten*, 406.

74. HIA, "Postwar Borders Poland," and Kierownictwo Marynarki Wojennej, "Potrzeba Polityczno-Militarna Szczecina," November 1943, 7–8.

75. See "Projekt dekretu o likwidacji niemczyzny w Polsce," "Dekret o szczegolnych przypadkach straty obywatelstwa," and "Sprawa wysiedlen i wywlaszczen na przyszlych terytoriach," in HIA, Polish Foreign Ministry, box 78, folder 20.

76. HIA, Mikolajczyk, box 72, "Rezolucje Rady Naczelny P.S.L.," October 6–7, 1946, 6. See also HIA, "Postwar Borders" and "Tezy w Sprawie Wysiedlenia Niemcow z Polski," August 1944.

77. Cited in Antony Polonsky and Boleslaw Drukier, eds., *The Beginnings of Communist Rule in Poland* (London: Routledge and Kegan Paul, 1980), 425.

78. Padraic Kenney, *Rebuilding Poland: Workers and Communists, 1945–1950* (Ithaca, N.Y., and London: Cornell University Press, 1997), 152.

79. See the many stories of Germans who could not accept the loss of their homes: Bundesministerium fuer Vertriebene, Fluechtlinge, and Kriegsgeschaedigte, *Der Vertreibung der deutschen Bevoelkerung aus den Gebieten oestlich der Oder-Neisse*, vols. 1 and 2, reprinted (Munich: Weltbild Verlag, 1993).

80. It is very hard to know not only how many Germans died and were murdered in the process of being driven out of Poland but how many were driven out in the first place. The German-Polish Historical Commission reluctantly uses the number of roughly 3.5 million Germans driven out of Polish territory administered by both Poland and the Soviet Union (meaning, primarily, northeast Prussia). Of these, roughly 400,000 died of various causes. Wlodzimierz Borodziej and Artur Hajnicz, "Der Komplex der Vertreibung: Abschlussbericht," Warsaw, December 7, 1996, 34. A recent statistical study uses the figure of 473,013 dead, of whom 58,256 were shot, 14,356 committed suicide, 80,522 died in camps, 93,283 died while in flight, and 63,876 died while being driven from their homes. Gert von Pistohlkors, "Informationen zur Klaerung der Schicksale von Fluchtlingen aus der Vertreibungsgebieten oestlich von Oder und Neisse: Die Arbeit der Heimatortskarteien (HOK)," in Rainer Schulze, Doris von der Brelie-Lewien, and Helga Grebing, eds., *Fluechtlinge und Vertrieben in der westdeutscher Nachkriegsgeschichte: Bilanzierung der Forschung und Perspektiven fuer die kuenftige Forschungsarbeit* (Hildesheim, West Germany: Verlag August Lax, 1987), 5.

81. For the camps, see Helga Hirsch, *Die Rache der Opfer: Deutsche in polnishcen Lagern 1944–1950* (Berlin: Rowohlt, 1998), 93, 197–203.

82. Kenney, *Rebuilding Poland*, 140–41.

83. See Norman M. Naimark, *The Russians in Germany: A History of the Soviet Zone of Occupation, 1945–1949* (Cambridge, Mass.: Harvard University Press, 1995), 75–76.

84. Ministerial Circular of August 9, 1947, 46. Ministerial Circular of June 5, 1947, 387, in *Die Vertreibung der deutschen Bevoelkerung aus den Gebieten oestlich der Oder-Neisse: Polnische Gesetze und Verordnungen 1944–1955*, vol. 3 (Munich: Weltbild Verlag, 1993).

85. Kenney, *Rebuilding Poland*, 153.

86. "Przemowienia Przesa Polskiego Stronnictwa Ludowego Stanislawa MIKOLAJCZYKA wygloszone na posiedzeniu Rady Naczelnej," October 6, 1946, HIA, Mikolajczyk, box 76, 6.

87. HIA, Mikolajczyk, box 40, Protocol of Meeting of PPS and PPR, September 28, 1945, 6.

88. HIA, Mikolajczyk, box 38, nr. 46. Speech in Opole, April 8, 1946.

89. "Pravitel'stvo Rossiiskoi Federatsii: Rasporiazhenie ot 1 dekabria 1994 g., n. 1887-r, r." Also, "Plan meropriiatii po obespecheniiu evaluatsii naseleniia Chechenskoi Respubliki." Thanks to the Davis Center, Harvard University, Cold War Project for sending me copies of these documents.

90. Sebastian Smith, *Allah's Mountains: Politics and War in the Russian Caucasus* (London: I.B. Tauris, 1998), 60.

CHAPTER 11, *Zerubavel*

I would like to thank Eviatar Zerubavel and Tamar El-Or, for their helpful comments on an earlier version of this chapter, and Eyal Zamir and Na'ama Rokem, for their valuable research assistance. Since the article was written in 1997–98, several important works on the topic of bereavement in Israeli society, some with special attention given to gender, have been published. I regret that the gap between writing and publication did not make it possible to fully incorporate the analysis of these works into the present article.

1. Maurice Halbwachs, *The Collective Memory* (New York: Harper & Row, 1980); John R. Gillis, ed., *Commemorations: The Politics of Modern Identity* (Princeton, N.J.: Princeton University Press, 1994); Yael Zerubavel, *Recovered Roots: Collective Memory and the Making of Israeli National Tradition* (Chicago: University of Chicago Press, 1995), 3–12.

2. Anderson Benedict, *Imagined Communities: Reflections on the Origin and Spread of Nationalism* (London: Verso, 1983).

3. Emile Durkheim, *The Elementary Forms of the Religious Life* (New York: Free Press, 1965); Robert N. Bellah, "Civil Religion in America," *Daedalus* (Winter 1967): 1–21; reprinted in *Beyond Belief: Essays on Religion in a Post-traditional World* (New York: Harper & Row, 1970), 168–86.

4. Paul Connerton, *How Societies Remember* (Cambridge: Cambridge University Press, 1989); Pierre Nora, "Between Memory and History: Les Lieux de Memoire" *Representations* 26 (1989): 7–25; Barry Schwartz, "The Social Context of Commemoration: A Study in Collective Memory," *Social Forces* 61 (1982): 374–402.

5. Zerubavel, *Recovered Roots*, 147–213.

6. Two notable exceptions from the prestate period are the heroic female figures of Sarah Aaronsohn, who was executed by the Turks for her pro-British activities in the NILI (Netsah Israel Lo Ieshaker, i.e., "The strength of Israel will not lie") underground in 1917, and Hana Szenes, who was sent by the Israeli Hangana underground to Hungary during World War II and was captured and executed by the pro-Nazi Hungarian authorities in 1944. The stature of the two, however, did not reach

the prominence of male heroes, such as Yosef Trumpeldor, the hero of Tel Ḥai (see Zerubavel, *Recovered Roots*).

7. Deborah S. Bernstein, ed., *Pioneers and Homemakers: Jewish Women in the Prestate* (Albany: State University of New York Press, 1992).

8. The Palmaḥ underground regarded itself as promoting the spirit of daring, resourcefulness, and readiness for patriotic sacrifice among both its male and female members. The memoirs of Netiva Ben-Yehuda, one of the few females who broke gender constraints and actually fought in the front, demythicized the egalitarian attitude toward women in the Palmah. See her *1948—Between Calendars* (1948—Bein ha-Sefirot) (Jerusalem: Keter, 1981).

In his study of the commemoration of the War of Independence, Immanuel Sivan indicates that although women participated in the war, their participation was marginal. The image of the female fighter thus reflects the Palmah's self-image more than social reality. Immanuel Sivan, *The 1948 Generation: Myth, Profile, and Memory* (Dor Tashah: Mitos, Dyukan, Zikaron) (Ministry of Defense, 1991), 35–39. See also Maoz Azaryahu on the subject of women's contribution to the war and its commemoration. *State Rituals: The Celebration of Independence and the Commemoration of the Dead, 1948–1956* (Pulḥanei Medina: Ḥagigot ha-Atsma'ut ve-Hantsaḥat ha-Noflim, 1948: 1956) (Ben-Gurion University Press, 1995), 125.

9. Lesley Hazleton, *Israeli Women: The Reality Behind the Myth* (New York: Simon & Schuster, 1977); Barbara Swirsky & Marilyn Safir, eds., *Calling the Equality Bluff: Women in Israel* (New York: Pergamon Press, 1991).

10. Iris Jerby, *The Double Price: Women Status and Military Service in Israel* (Ha-Meḥir ha-Kaful: Ma'amad ha-Isha ba-Ḥevra ha-Yisra'elit ve-Sherut ha-Nashim be-Tsahal) (Tel Aviv: Tel Aviv University Press, 1996). It should be noted, however, that recently women's demands to be allowed into the air force and the navy have been met with more openness by the military and indicate a readiness to change this situation.

11. Meira Weiss, "A Mother, a Nurse, and a Soldier: Memoirs of the Gulf War" (Em, Aḥot, ve-Ḥayelet: Zikhronot mi-Milḥemet ha-Mifratz), *Teoria u-Vikoret* 7 (1995): 235–46.

12. Sivan, *1948 Generation*, 17–26.

13. Sivan, *1948 Generation*, 17–21; Azaryahu, *State Rituals*, 131–32.

14. Yad Labanim was founded by bereaved parents in 1949. Widows were part of the scope of the organization's concern for bereaved families, but they were granted no special attention to their needs and little representation on the organization's committees. See Lea Shamgar-Handelman, *Israeli War Widows: Beyond the Glory of Heroism*. (South Hadley, Mass.: Bergin and Garvey, 1986), 23–24.

The tendency to focus exclusively on the parents around the commemoration of the fallen soldiers was so pronounced that it caused a protest against the speeches delivered on Israel's Memorial Day in 1953 that did not also mention the widows and the orphans. Azaryahu, *State Rituals*, 131–32.

15. The lack of social allowance to display one's personal pain and the widows' own reluctance to dwell on their status and experiences as such during that early period were discussed in a recent television program consisting of interviews with Israeli war widows (*To Live with a Husband Who Is No Longer There*), broadcast on May 10, 1977, on the eve of Israel's Memorial Day for Fallen Soldiers. The program featured an

unusually revealing and moving discussion among war widows of various wars. A famous Israeli opera singer, who was widowed in the late 1940s, spoke in public for the first time on her experiences as a war widow; another war widow from the 1948–49 war described how she hid the news of her husband's death from her family in order not to spoil the celebration of the Seder and joined the army as a volunteer soon after that, because she did not wish to allow the role of the widow to take over.

16. Shamgar-Handelman, *Israeli War Widows*, 22–32.

17. Hayim Yosef Yerushami, *Zakhor: Jewish History and Jewish Memory* (Seattle: University of Washington Press, 1983); Zerubavel, *Recovered Roots*; Sivan, *1948 Generation*; Azaryahu, *State Rituals*; Dan Miron, *Facing the Silent Brother: Essays on the Poetry of the War of Independence* (Mul Ha'aḥ Ha-shotek: Iyunim be-Shirat Milḥemet ha-Atsma'ut) (Jerusalem: Keter Publishing House, 1992); Esther Levinger, *War Memorials in Israel* (Andarta'ot la-Noflim be-Yisrael) (Tel Aviv: Hakibbutz Hameuchad, 1993); and Ilana Shamir, *Commemoration and Remembrance: Israel's Way of Molding Its Collective Memory Patterns* (Hantsaḥa ve-Zikaron: Darka shel ha-Ḥevra ha-Yisraelit be-Itsuv Nofei ha-Zikaron) (Tel Aviv: Am Oved, 1996).

18. The Ministry of Defense provides the widow with significant economic privileges, and her assignment to this office sets her apart from "welfare cases" supported by the government. Yet, as Shamgar-Handelman demonstrates, the interpersonal dynamics between the widow and the social workers whose responsibility is to evaluate her functioning and approve requests of support often undermine the widow's sense of entitlement and turn her into a "case." Shamgar-Handelman, *Israeli War Widows*, 32–51.

19. Moshe Shamir, *He Went Through the Fields* (*Hu Halakh ba-Sadot*) (1947; reprinted Tel Aviv: Am Oved, 1972).

20. The film, *He Went in the Fields* (Hu Halakh ba-Sadot), directed by Yosef Milo, was made in 1967. For a more extensive comparison between the novel and the film, see Nurith Gertz, *Motion Fiction: Israeli Fiction in Film* (Sipur meha-Seratim: Siporet Yisraelit ve-Ibudeiha la-Kolno'a) (Tel Aviv: Open University Press, 1993), 63–94.

21. Although she is technically unmarried, the issue of the formal status is insignificant within the context of kibbutz norms of that period and given that Mika's position as the future mother of the dead hero's son clearly marks her as an equivalent of a "war widow." As noted above, the novel predates the construction of the term *war widow.*

22. Indeed, the novel ends before Mika learns about Uri's death. Her part ends when she decides on her own not to pursue her earlier plan to abort the pregnancy, thus guaranteeing the birth of Uri's son.

23. Nathan Shaḥam, *Aller Retour* (Halokh va-Shov) (Tel Aviv: Am Oved, 1972).

24. See Yael Zerubavel, "The 'Wandering Israeli' in Contemporary Israeli Literature," *Contemporary Jewry* 7 (1986): 127–40.

25. The heroine's friend believes that her choice to marry the son of an old-timer and prominent educator stemmed from her desire to enhance her standing in the kibbutz and guarantee her social acceptance there. Batya Gur, *Cohabitation: Murder in the Kibbutz* (Jerusalem: Keter, 1992), 43.

26. Her mother-in-law takes over the role of mothering and guiding the children, and the widow, who turns her energies to the public sphere, seems to have ac-

cepted this situation, though not without some bitterness: "I'm always under the impression that she doesn't trust me to pass on to them the correct values," she confesses to her lover (*Cohabitation*, 44).

27. Savyon Liebrecht, "Written in Stone," (katuv be-Even), in *Horses on the Highway* (Susim al Kevish Geha) (Jerusalem: Keter, 1988), 71–86. The English translation by Gilead Morahg is in *Apples from the Desert: Selected Stories by Savyon Liebrecht* (New York: Feminist Press at CUNY, 1998), 99–118. Quotations in the text refer to the English translation.

28. See also Hannah Naveh, *Captives of Mourning: Perspectives of Mourning in Hebrew Literature* (Bi-Shevi ha-Evel: Ha-Evel bi-Re'i ha-Sifrut ha-Ivrit) (Tel Aviv: Hakkibutz Hameuchad, 1993). In her analysis Naveh emphasizes the impact of the different cultural background on the mourning behavior of the widow and her in-laws and the tensions between them. Although these differences clearly come into play, the story reflects broader patterns that are recurrent in the literature about war widows.

29. The reader learns that five years earlier the widow's second marriage fell apart when her daughter, named after the first husband, died from fatal illness. Liebrecht, "Written in Stone," 116.

30. It is important to note that the story addresses the widow's social and psychological entitlement to the past rather than reflects her legal and economic rights. Because the heroine has already remarried twice, she lost the economic support and legal status as a war widow years earlier.

31. Interestingly enough, both films were directed by foreign, and not Israeli-born, directors: Peter Fry directed *The Hero's Wife* and Gilberto Tofano directed *Siege*. The idea of the script for *Siege*, however, is credited to Gila Almagor, an Israeli actress who later wrote an autobiographical book revolving around the image of her own widowed mother. Gila Almagor, *The Summer of Avia* (Ha-Kaits shel Avi'ya) (Tel Aviv: Am Oved, 1985). On the comparison of these two films, see also Regine Mihal Friedman, "Between Silence and Abjection: The Film Medium and the Israeli War Widows," *Filmhistoria* 3, nos. 1–2 (1993): 79–89.

32. It is important to note that the film is based on Ben-Ner's story by the same title. Yitzḥak Ben-Ner, "Atalia," in *After the Rain: Three Stories* (Aḥarei ha-Geshem) (Jerusalem: Keter, 1979). Yet the cinematic version has introduced major changes into the story. For a detailed analysis of the differences between the fiction and the film, see Gertz, *Motion Fiction*, 289–317.

33. The play *Daria* by David Shrir was performed at the Simta Theater in 1977. I would like to thank David Shrir for giving me a copy of the manuscript for his play.

34. On the literary history of the Akeda, the binding of Isaac, see Shalom Spiegel, *The Last Trial* (New York: Behrman House, 1979). Hillel Weiss observes that "the theme of the Akeda is recurrent in almost all literary works of the period. Time and again the sons protest against the fathers who sacrifice them." *Portraits of the Fighter: Reflections on Heroes and Heroism in the Hebrew Prose of the Last Decade* (Deyokan ha-Loḥem: Iyunim al Giborim u-Gevura ba-Siporet ha-Ivrit shel ha-Asor ha-Aḥaron) (Bar Ilan University Press, 1975), 35. See also Ruth Karton-Blum, "Isaac's Fear: The Myth of the *Akeda* as a Test-Case in Modern Hebrew Poetry" (Paḥad Yitzḥak: Mitos ha-Akeda ke-Mikre Boḥan ba-Shira ha-Ivrit ha-Ḥadasha), in David Ohana and Robert S. Wistrich, eds., *Myth and Memory: Transfigurations of Israeli Con-*

sciousness (Mitos ve-Zikaron: Gilguleiha shel ha-Toda'a ha-Yisraelit) (Jerusalem: Van Leer & Hakibbutz Hameuchad, 1996), 231–47. Yael Zerubavel, "Patriotic Sacrifice and the Burden of Memory in Israel." In Ussama Makdisi and Paul Silberstein, eds., *Memory and Violence in the Middle East* (under review, Duke University Press).

35. Ben-Ner, "Atalia," 11.

36. *Sex, Lies, and Dinner* (Sex, Shekarim, va-Aruhat Erev), directed by Dan Wolman, 1996; broadcast on Israeli television, channel 3, on December 20, 1996.

37. Lea Aini, *Sand Tide* (Ge'ut ha-Ḥol) (Tel Aviv: Hakibbutz Hameuchad, 1992), 117.

38. *Sand Tide*, 23.

39. In *He Walks in the Fields* and the film *Atalia*, the young couples do not get the chance to marry because the young man dies.

40. *Sand Tide*, 62.

41. Ben-Ner, "Atalia," 12.

42. On the possibility of regarding Uri's accidental death as a symbolic suicide see Gertz, *Motion Fiction*, 90; Sivan notes that even though Uri died in an accident during the struggle against the British, he became the prototype of the Sabra who died in the War of Independence. Sivan, *1948 Generation*, 56.

43. Ben-Ner, "Atalia," 14. In Natan Shahan's *Aller Retour* the husband did not die in the war but a month after, while clearing a minefield (12).

44. The two widows in *Daria* break out in a song, making a parody of official memorial ceremonies. Michael Handelsaltz, "The Widows' Friendship Song" (Shir ha-Re'ut shel ha-Almanot), *Ha'aretz*, January 24, 1997.

45. Clearly, black humor is not unique to Israeli culture and can be found cross-culturally. For further discussion on other expressions of black humor in Israeli culture and further references of similar phenomena in other cultures, see Zerubavel, *Recovered Roots*, 167–77.

46. It is not surprising, therefore, that the film's broadcasting on Israeli television was met with strong objection on the part of the organization of widows.

47. The fear of being perceived as a loose woman appears in *Atalia* and *Cohabitation*, the films *The Hero's Wife* and *Sex, Lies and Dinner*, and the play *Daria*. Shamgar-Handelman, in *Israeli War Widows*, makes a similar observation regarding the widows' sense that they are perceived as a threat to married couples, 125–30. On the related issue of the portrayal of the widow's body and viewers' gaze in films, see Friedman's discussion in "Between Silence and Abjection."

48. *He Walks in the Fields*, *Aller Retour*, *Atalia, Cohabitation*, and *The Hero's Wife*. In works that feature more than one widow, *Sex, Lies and Dinner* and *Daria*, the one who chooses to suppress her sexuality in order to protect her reputation lives in a kibbutz.

49. In her study *Israeli Women*, Hazleton registers a war widow's complaint: "All the husbands of my friends started appearing at my door . . . alone" (181). The same theme also appears in the film *Atalia*.

50. *Sand Tide*, 43.

51. Shamger-Handelman also notes the criticism by the social worker at the Ministry of Defense when the widow expresses her sexuality by the way she dresses, evaluating it as a sign of a problem in her functioning. *Israeli War Widows*, 38–39.

52. *Cohabitation*, 45.

53. Ben-Ner, "Atalia," 32. It is interesting to note that the film version actually transforms the story by portraying the widow as a provocative woman and thus conforms more closely to the stereotype of the loose woman that the original story criticizes.

54. The third, younger woman, who was widowed only recently, first observes critically the more casual behavior and cynical remarks of the "veteran" widows. Yet as the evening progresses, she gradually comes out of her visible state of emotional numbness and loosens up while they share more of their pain and suffering.

55. See Yael Zerubavel, "The Forest as a National Icon: Literature, Politics, and the Archeology of Memory," *Israel Studies* 1 (Spring 1996): 60–99; see also Gertz, *Motion Fiction*, 315.

56. Rajeswari Sunder Rajan, *Real and Imagined Women: Gender, Culture, and Postcolonialism* (London: Routledge, 1993).

57. *Sand Tide*, 153.

58. On the transformations of the female image, the development of Israeli women's literature, and a gendered approach to nationalism, see in particular Yael S. Feldman, *No Room of Their Own: Israeli Women's Fiction* (New York: Columbia University Press, 1999); Hannah Naveh, "On Loss, Bereavement, and Mourning in the Israeli Experience" (Al ha-Ovdan, al ha-Shekhol ve'al ha-Evel ba-Havaya ha-Yisraelit), *Alpayim* 16 (1998): 85–120; and Gertz, *Motion Fiction*.

59. Zerubavel, *Recovered Roots*, 147–213.

Index